'This invaluable collection provides an insight into the range of contributions that Colin Holmes made to the historical study of immigration and minorities. The essays collected here are written by his many former students and colleagues and are evidence of the depth of his work and its continuing relevance today. A must read for all who want to situate migration within a broader historical frame.'

Professor John Solomos, Sociology,
University of Warwick, UK

'A fitting tribute to a truly pioneering scholar whose individual endeavour, as well as unstinting support for junior academics, has resulted in a much greater understanding of the importance of migration in modern Britain. Its coverage is truly astounding and its list of contributors reads like a veritable "Who's Who" within this now well-developed and well-respected academic field.'

Dr David Dee, Associate Professor in Modern History,
De Montfort University, UK

'Anyone wandering into the field of Britain's migration history soon discovers that the indispensable work has already been done – by Colin Holmes. Many years before it became a fashionable or topical subject, he became its master. There is not much written on the subject, even now, that does not owe a great deal to his original and inspiring spadework.'

Robert Winder, Migration Museum Project Trustee, UK

MIGRANT BRITAIN

Britain has largely been in denial of its migrant past – it is often suggested that the arrivals after 1945 represent a new phenomenon and not the continuation of a much longer and deeper trend. There is also an assumption that Britain is a tolerant country towards minorities that distinguishes itself from the rest of Europe and beyond.

The historian who was the first and most important to challenge this dominant view is Colin Holmes, who, from the early 1970s onwards, provided a framework for a different interpretation based on extensive research. This challenge came not only through his own work but also that of a 'new school' of students who studied under him and the creation of the journal *Immigrants and Minorities* in 1982.

This volume not only celebrates this remarkable achievement, but also explores the state of migrant historiography (including responses to migrants) in the twenty-first century.

Jennifer Craig-Norton is a British Academy Postdoctoral Fellow at the Parkes Institute for the Study of Jewish/non-Jewish Relations at the University of Southampton, UK.

Christhard Hoffmann is a Professor of Modern European History at the University of Bergen, Norway.

Tony Kushner is Professor of History in the Parkes Institute for the Study of Jewish/non-Jewish Relations at the University of Southampton, UK.

ROUTLEDGE STUDIES IN RADICAL HISTORY AND POLITICS

www.routledge.com/Routledge-Studies-in-Radical-History-and-Politics/book-series/RSRHP

Series editors: Thomas Linehan, *Brunel University*, and John Roberts, *Brunel University*

The series *Routledge Studies in Radical History and Politics* has two areas of interest. Firstly, this series aims to publish books which focus on the history of movements of the radical left. 'Movements of the radical left' is here interpreted in its broadest sense as encompassing those past movements for radical change which operated in the mainstream political arena as with political parties, and past movements for change which operated more outside the mainstream as with millenarian movements, anarchist groups, utopian socialist communities, and trade unions. Secondly, this series aims to publish books which focus on more contemporary expressions of radical left-wing politics. Recent years have been witness the emergence of a multitude of new radical movements adept at getting their voices into the public sphere. From those participating in the Arab Spring, the Occupy movement, community unionism, social media forums, independent media outlets, local voluntary organisations campaigning for progressive change, and so on, it seems to be the case that innovative networks of radicalism are being constructed in civil society that operate in different public forms.

The series very much welcomes titles with a British focus, but is not limited to any particular national context or region. The series will encourage scholars who contribute to this series to draw on perspectives and insights from other disciplines.

Titles include:

Contemporary Trotskyism
Parties, Sects and Social Movements in Britain
John Kelly

Scabs and Traitors
Taboo, Violence and Punishment in Labour Disputes in Britain, 1760–1871
Thomas Linehan

Migrant Britain
Histories and Historiographies: Essays in Honour of Colin Holmes
Edited by Jennifer Craig-Norton, Christhard Hoffmann and Tony Kushner

MIGRANT BRITAIN

Histories and Historiographies:
Essays in Honour of Colin Holmes

Edited by Jennifer Craig-Norton,
Christhard Hoffmann and Tony Kushner

Routledge
Taylor & Francis Group
LONDON AND NEW YORK

First published 2018
by Routledge
2 Park Square, Milton Park, Abingdon, Oxon OX14 4RN

and by Routledge
711 Third Avenue, New York, NY 10017

Routledge is an imprint of the Taylor & Francis Group, an informa business

© 2018 selection and editorial matter, Jennifer Craig-Norton, Christhard Hoffmann and Tony Kushner; individual chapters, the contributors

The right of Jennifer Craig-Norton, Christhard Hoffmann and Tony Kushner to be identified as the authors of the editorial material, and of the authors for their individual chapters, has been asserted in accordance with sections 77 and 78 of the Copyright, Designs and Patents Act 1988.

All rights reserved. No part of this book may be reprinted or reproduced or utilised in any form or by any electronic, mechanical, or other means, now known or hereafter invented, including photocopying and recording, or in any information storage or retrieval system, without permission in writing from the publishers.

Trademark notice: Product or corporate names may be trademarks or registered trademarks, and are used only for identification and explanation without intent to infringe.

British Library Cataloguing in Publication Data
A catalogue record for this book is available from the British Library

Library of Congress Cataloging in Publication Data
Names: Holmes, Colin, 1938– honoree. |
Craig-Norton, Jennifer, editor. | Hoffmann, Christhard, 1952– editor. |
Kushner, Tony (Antony Robin Jeremy), editor.
Title: Migrant Britain : histories and historiographies : essays in honour of
Colin Holmes / edited by Jennifer Craig-Norton,
Christhard Hoffmann and Tony Kushner.
Description: Abingdon, Oxon ; New York, NY : Routledge, 2019. |
Series: Routledge studies in radical history and politics |
Includes bibliographical references and index.
Identifiers: LCCN 2018011033| ISBN 9781138065130 (hardback) |
ISBN 9781138065147 (pbk.) | ISBN 9781315159959 (ebook)
Subjects: LCSH: Immigrants–Great Britain–History. |
Immigrants–Cultural assimilation–Great Britain. |
Great Britain–Emigration and immigration–History. |
Great Britain–Emigration and immigration–Social aspects.
Classification: LCC DA125.A1 M528 2019 | DDC 305.9/06912041–dc23
LC record available at https://lccn.loc.gov/2018011033

ISBN: 978-1-138-06513-0 (hbk)
ISBN: 978-1-138-06514-7 (pbk)
ISBN: 978-1-315-15995-9 (ebk)

Typeset in Bembo
by Out of House Publishing

ALL THAT I AM

This Painting tells a story true
Of times gone by and of someone who
Represents a generation
Whose courage, sweat and determination
Made us who we are today
By laying the foundations and paving the way
For a better life on foreign shores.
A life of opportunity and open doors
Previously closed to his Indian race
Which was deemed inferior by the whiter face
Of a Nation still steeped in Empire days
With its cultural supremacy and colonial ways.

This someone was born not so far
From the Golden Temple in Amritsar.
There he lived to the age of eight
Till India's politics changed his fate
And British policy of divide and rule
(Which fanned the fire and added fuel
To a call for freedom based on religious division)
Ended in the bloody Partition
Of historic Punjab, the land of five rivers
And home of the Sikhs whose swords and quivers
Protected all, against invasion and tyranny
Defending justice, equality and the right to be free.

Away from India's strife and turmoil
His father, working on English soil
Called for the family to join him there
Sending them the journey's fare.
So holding tight his Mata ji's hand
He left behind his Motherland.
Setting sail from the port of Bombay
and braving the oceans all the way
To Tilbury Dock near London's heart
Then onwards to another part
Of England, south of the Pennine Hills
And a city famed for its cotton mills.

Manchester was his new home's name
But nothing about it was the same
As the culture and people he'd left behind

Yet continued to cherish in his heart and mind.
Although only nine, he worked, door to door
Selling pure silk stockings, ties and more
Alongside his father, following family tradition
Whilst dreaming all day of a higher ambition
To seek a profession that would, in effect,
Earn him a position of social respect,
That challenged the Englishman's stereotype view
Of all Indians as "coolies"- except for a few.

As a young man he looked for a skilled career
And worked for a while as an engineer.
Through comics and books he learned to read
And write the language he knew he would need
To become an educated man
And pursue his extraordinary plan
To study for a medical degree –
A first, in his own community
And unheard of then, in a time and place
Where class division, colour and race
Kept you where you were born to be
And dictated your position in society.

Defying the sceptics and against all odds
He succeeded by taking on multiple jobs
To support his family and pay his fees
Through London and Liverpool Universities.
Times were hard and it was not with ease
That he graduated (in fact with several Degrees)
As a Bachelor of Medicine and of Surgery
With Honours in Science and a PhD.
Yet still, his achievements did not wane.
After becoming a Doctor he bought a plane
Gained a pilots licence, and then,
A Certificate in Aviation Medicine.
Reaching Forty, he longed to roam
Back to India and his ancestral home.
So, being himself an adventurous man
He built, with his brothers, a caravan.
And drove his family from the port of Dover
Through Europe, the Middle East, Pakistan and over
    The Wagah border into India at last
Where for nine months they travelled, exploring their past.

Visiting palaces, shrines and historic places
And discovering India's many faces.
Then, back to England, with a reviving stay
In romantic Venice along the way.

Hidden within this painting too
Are details relating to just a few
Of the stories which we, the artists concur
Speak volumes about the character
Of someone who, for us, reflects
The qualities and values we respect.
A man of science but also of Art
A mighty lion with a gentle heart
A man of compassion who's not thought twice
About making personal sacrifice
For the sake of family, which he holds dear.
Principled, determined, fair and sincere.

This someone, we are proud to say
Is our father who in every way
Has been a pillar to us all,
Inspired our lives and helped us stand tall
As daughters, who he's enabled to see
That being proud of your heritage and identity
And striving to be the best you can be
Brings, fulfilment, dignity and security
Not only to oneself and family
But, to the rest of ones community.
And that whatever obstacles are put your way
With belief and hard work you can win the day.

As we offer our tribute here
One thing remains undeniably clear.
To 'All That [He Is]', there is so much more
Than our painting alone, can fully explore.

Cover Artwork and poem
All That I Am
Copyright The Singh Twins
www.singhtwins.co.uk

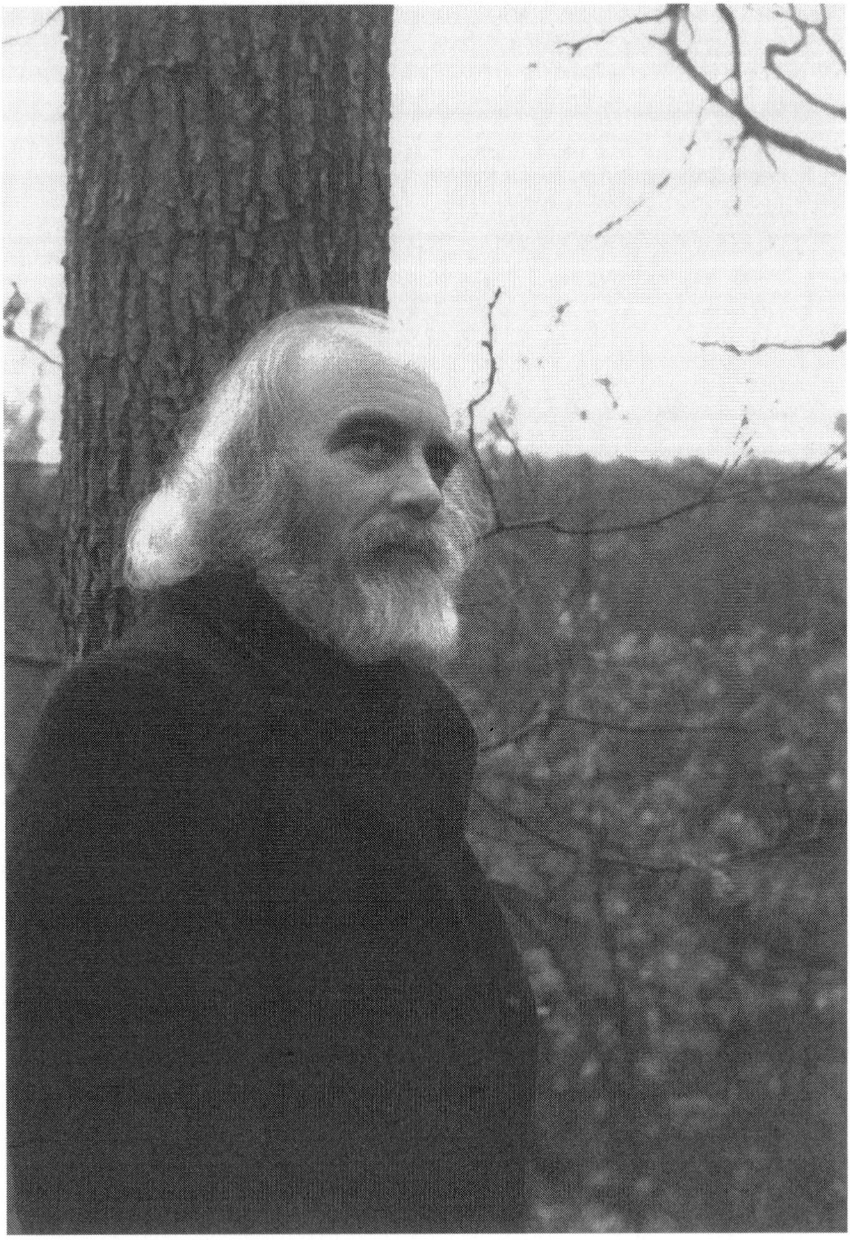

CONTENTS

Acknowledgements   *xv*
Contributors   *xvi*

    Colin Holmes: an introduction   1
    Tony Kushner

SECTION 1
Historiography   **7**

    Introduction
    Jennifer Craig-Norton

1 Uncovering traditions of intolerance: the earlier years of
   Immigrants and Minorities and the 'Sheffield School'   11
   Ken Lunn

2 Colin Holmes and the development of migrant and
   anti-migrant historiography   22
   Tony Kushner

3 Looking beyond the nation state: the history of global
   migrations after 1800   33
   Tobias Brinkmann

4 Class vs. ethnicity: concepts of migrant historiographies in
   Britain and (West) Germany, 1970s–1990s   44
   Christhard Hoffmann

SECTION 2
Places and spaces   **55**

   Introduction
   Tony Kushner

5 From the profitable strangers to the residents of Banglatown:
   an exploration of the historiography of immigrants
   in London's East End   59
   Anne J. Kershen

6 The Chinese connection: an historiography   70
   Anne Witchard

7 The uniqueness of London   80
   Panikos Panayi

8 Spaces of black history   91
   Caroline Bressey

SECTION 3
Community history   **103**

   Introduction
   Christhard Hoffmann

9 Academic duty and communal obligation revisited   107
   Geoffrey Alderman

10 Weaving Italian experience into the British
   immigration narrative   117
   Wendy Ugolini

11 Jewish Refugee historiography: moving beyond
   the celebratory?   128
   Jennifer Craig-Norton

12 *We refugees?* Re-defining Britain's East African Asians 138
   Saima Nasar

SECTION 4
Racisms and anti-migrant politics 149

   Introduction
   Christhard Hoffmann

13 Race and colour revisited: white immigrants in
   post-war Britain 153
   Gavin Schaffer

14 Family misfortunes? Gendered perspectives on West Indian
   migration, welfare policies and cultural racism in post-Second
   World War Britain 162
   Barbara Bush

15 Inside, outside, and in-between: shifting borders in British
   immigration and disease control 173
   Krista Maglen

16 The evolving historiography of the extreme right in Britain 182
   Graham Macklin

SECTION 5
Marginal, neglected and reimagined histories 193

   Introduction
   Jennifer Craig-Norton

17 Gypsy/Romani studies: a few reflections 197
   David Mayall

18 'The poorest, the most intractable, and the most permanent' –
   the invisible nineteenth-century Pole in Britain 206
   Milosz K. Cybowski

19 History of Asians in Britain 1600–1950 213
   Rozina Visram

20 The development of transmigrant historiography in Britain 224
Nicholas J. Evans

SECTION 6
Identities 235

Introduction
Tony Kushner

21 Underground Catholic networks in Ireland and Britain:
the case of Ribbonism before the famine and after 239
Donald M. MacRaild and Kyle Hughes

22 'The most varied, colourful, confusing hubub in the world':
the East End, television and the documentary imagination,
July 1939 251
James Jordan

23 The Equiano effect: representativeness and early black British
migrant testimony 262
Ryan Hanley

24 Framing Polish migration to the UK, from the Second World
War to EU expansion 272
Kathy Burrell

Afterword 282
Tony Kushner

Appendices: Colin Holmes – a Life and Career 283
   1. Colin Holmes: publications 283
   2. The Sheffield School – Colin Holmes postgraduate supervision 290
   3. Colin Holmes interview with Alan Dein 291
Name Index 312
Place Index 319
Subject Index 321

ACKNOWLEDGEMENTS

This volume had its origins in a conference held in September 2016 at the Parkes Institute, University of Southampton. We would like to thank all the speakers, chairs and other participants for their contributions to what was a stimulating event and one that was a fitting tribute to Colin Holmes. Most have now contributed to this volume and the editors are grateful to them, and those who were not able to attend but have subsequently written chapters for this collection, for their excellent work, discipline in keeping to the word length, and good humour as this book was assembled. The Universities of Bergen, Derby, Southampton and Ulster gave support to enable the conference to take place and we would like to record their generosity in so doing. Thanks also to the Parkes Institute administrator, Thomas Emerson, for helping to organise the conference and all at the Highfield House Hotel which hosted the event.

We are extremely grateful to Routledge for their enthusiasm for this project, and especially our editor, Craig Fowlie, who took an interest in it from the start. In helping to prepare it for publication, Lucy Morris and Mag Kushner provided invaluable input. Alan Dein's generosity and enthusiasm when we asked him to interview Colin Holmes is also deeply appreciated and we are delighted to include an edited version of this oral history in the appendix to this volume. We would also like to thank the Singh Twins for permission to reproduce the cover image and its accompanying poem. Finally, to Colin Holmes himself whose presence at the conference was a joy. Many of the contributors were students of Colin. We experienced (always for the good) comments on our drafts with Colin wielding his blue editing pencil, standing for no waffle or unnecessary jargon. The editors thus somewhat nervously hope that the contents of this volume meet with his approval!

Jennifer Craig-Norton, Christhard Hoffmann, Tony Kushner

CONTRIBUTORS

Geoffrey Alderman Michael Gross Professor of Politics & Contemporary History at the University of Buckingham, has written extensively on the history of British Jewry, concentrating especially on its relationship with the British political system and its present-day communal power structure. He has collaborated with Professor Holmes on a number of projects, including the career of the nineteenth-century antisemite Sir Richard Burton. Professor Alderman's *British Jewry Since Emancipation* was published by the University of Buckingham Press in 2014. He is a Fellow of the Royal Historical Society and of the Higher Education Academy, and in 2011 won the Bermant Prize for Journalism.

Caroline Bressey A cultural and historical geographer who researches the black presence in Victorian Britain, particularly focusing on the lives of working people in London. Her first book, *Empire, Race and the Politics of Anti-Caste* (Bloomsbury, 2013), explored the anti-racist community in late nineteenth-century Britain.

Tobias Brinkmann The Malvin and Lea Bank Associate Professor of Jewish Studies and History at Penn State University, University Park, PA. Between 2004 and 2008 he taught at the Department of History and the Parkes Institute for the Study of Jewish/non-Jewish Relations at the University of Southampton, UK. Recent book publications: *Sundays at Sinai: A Jewish Congregation in Chicago* (University of Chicago Press, 2012); *Points of Passage: Jewish Transmigrants from Eastern Europe in Scandinavia, Germany, and Britain 1880–1914* (Berghahn, 2013).

Kathy Burrell Reader in Human Geography at the University of Liverpool. She has published extensively on Polish migration to the UK, in particular from the Second World War through to communist, post-1989 and post-2004 movements, exploring themes such as memory, mobility and material culture. Her most recent article, in

Mobilities, considers how migrants send 'things' home – the infrastructures which are used and created to do this. She is currently working on a comparative project funded by The Research Council of Norway, investigating contemporary Polish migration to Norway, Sweden and the UK.

Barbara Bush Emeritus Professor of History at Sheffield Hallam University, UK. She is the author of *Slave Women in Caribbean Society, 1650–1838* (Indiana University Press, 1990); *Imperialism, Race and Resistance: Africa and Britain, 1919–1945* (Routledge, 1999) and *Imperialism and Postcolonialism* (Pearson Education, 2006). Her current research focuses on the academic social sciences, colonial research and development in the late colonial era, and recent publications include 'Colonial Research and the Social Sciences at the End of Empire: The West Indian Social Survey, 1944–57', *The Journal of Imperial and Commonwealth History* (Volume: 41, Issue: 03, 2013). She has known Colin Holmes as mentor and friend for over 50 years.

Jennifer Craig-Norton British Academy Postdoctoral Fellow, Parkes Institute for the Study of Jewish/non-Jewish Relations at the University of Southampton. Her research focuses on refugees in the interwar period and she has written several articles on the *Kindertransport*. She is currently writing a book on Jewish refugee domestics and nurses in Britain in the 1930s and 1940s. Her monograph on the *Kindertransport* will be published by Indiana University Press in 2019.

Milosz K. Cybowski An independent researcher based in Poznań, Poland. He received his PhD at the University of Southampton and his research interests include nineteenth-century British and Polish relations and British reactions to the widely defined 'Polish Question'. Recently he has been working on a research project devoted to the subject of British public opinion and the issue of Polish independence in the 1830s. He also works as a reviewer and review editor for several websites, including Pol-Int (www.pol-int.org/) and Esensja (www.esensja.pl).

Alan Dein An oral historian and award-winning radio documentary broadcaster. Since the 1980s he has travelled the length and breadth of the nation recording interviews for the BBC, the British Library, English Heritage, the Jewish Museum, the Royal Parks, *The Guardian* and many others. His major oral history projects include 'King's Cross Voices', and 'Lives in Steel'. He is a committee member of the Oral History Society.

Nicholas J. Evans Lecturer in Diaspora History at the Wilberforce Institute for the study of Slavery and Emancipation at the University of Hull. His most recent publication is: 'The Making of a Mosaic: Migration and the Port-City of Kingston upon Hull', in David Starkey, et al. (eds.), *Hull – Culture, History, Place* (Liverpool University Press, 2017).

Ryan Hanley British Academy Postdoctoral Fellow in History at University College London. He is the author of several articles on the African diaspora and black writing in eighteenth- and nineteenth-century Britain. His first monograph, *Black Writing in Britain, 1770–1830*, is forthcoming from Cambridge University Press.

Christhard Hoffmann Professor of Modern European History at the University of Bergen/Norway. He is currently working on a project about Migrant Historiographies in Britain, Germany and Sweden, 1970s–1990s. Recent publications include *The Exclusion of Jews in the Norwegian Constitution of 1814: Origins – Contexts – Consequences* (editor, Metropol Verlag, 2016) and 'Jewish history as a history of immigration: An overview of current historiography in the Scandinavian countries', *Scripta Instituti Donneriani Aboensis* 27 (2016).

Kyle Hughes Lecturer in British History at Ulster University and author of *The Scots in Victorian and Edwardian Belfast* (Edinburgh University Press, 2013). His latest book, *Ribbon Societies in Nineteenth-Century Ireland and its Diaspora: The Persistence of Tradition*, co-written with Don MacRaild, will be published by Liverpool University Press in 2018.

James Jordan Karten Lecturer at the Parkes Institute for the Study of Jewish/non-Jewish Relations, University of Southampton. He is the author of *From Nuremberg to Hollywood* (Vallentine Mitchell, 2015) and co-editor of the journal *Holocaust Studies*. He is currently writing a monograph on the BBC and the Holocaust. He has known Colin Holmes for nearly twenty years and thinks of him as the Brian Clough of migrant history: he may not be the best historian of the subject, but he's in the top one.

Anne J. Kershen Barnet Shine Senior Research Fellow in the Department of Politics at QMUL from 1990 until her retirement in 2010/11. In 1995 she founded the Centre for the Study of Migration at QMUL and was its director until she retired. She serves as series editor for Routledge's series *Studies in Migration and Diaspora*. She is currently an Honorary Senior Research Fellow in the School of Politics and International Relations at QMUL and Honorary Research Associate at the Bartlett School of Architecture at UCL. Anne, together with Colin Holmes, recently edited and contributed to *An East End Legacy: Essays in Memory of William J Fishman* (Routledge, 2018).

Tony Kushner Professor in the Parkes Institute and History Department, University of Southampton and a former student of Colin Holmes. His latest book is *Journeys from the Abyss: The Holocaust and Forced Migration from the 1880s to the Present* (Liverpool University Press, 2017) and he co-edits the journal *Patterns of Prejudice*.

Ken Lunn One of Colin Holmes' first PhD students and co-founder and co-editor of the journal *Immigrants & Minorities*. Based at the University of Portsmouth for many years, Ken has published widely, especially on the relationship between migrant and labour history and more recently, the nature of heritage.

Graham Macklin Assistant Professor/Postdoctoral Fellow at the Center for Research on Extremism (C-REX) at the University of Oslo, Norway. He has published extensively on fascist, extreme right-wing and anti-minority politics in Britain including *Very Deeply Dyed in the Black: Sir Oswald Mosley and the Resurrection of British Fascism after 1945* (I.B. Tauris, 2007) and, as co-editor, *British National Party: Contemporary Perspectives* (Routledge, 2011). A major monograph on the history of white racial nationalism in Britain is forthcoming with Routledge in 2018. He co-edits the Routledge Studies in Fascism and the Far Right book series. He studied with Colin Holmes as an undergraduate and has remained friends ever since.

Donald M. MacRaild Professor of British and Irish History and Head of Humanities at the University of Roehampton. He is author or editor of thirteen books. His latest monograph, *Ribbon Societies in Nineteenth-Century Ireland and its Diaspora: The Persistence of Tradition* (with Kyle Hughes), will be published in 2018 with Liverpool University Press. Don's 1993 Sheffield PhD was supervised by Colin Holmes and David Martin and was published as *Culture, Conflict and Migration: The Irish in Victorian Cumbria* (Liverpool University Press, 1998). Don also has edited *Immigrants and Minorities*, the journal which Colin and Ken Lunn founded in 1982.

Krista Maglen Associate Professor in the history department at Indiana University, Bloomington. She is the author of the book *The English System: Quarantine, Immigration, and the Making of a Port Sanitary Zone* (Manchester University Press, 2014).

David Mayall Professor of History and Head of the School of Humanities and Journalism at the University of Derby. His publications include *The Autobiography of the Working Class: An Annotated Critical Bibliography 1790–1945* (John Burnett and David Vincent (eds.) 3 volumes, Harvester, 1984–1989) and *Gypsy Identities 1500–2000: From Egipcyans and Moon-men to the Ethnic Romany* (Routledge, 2004). Colin acted as David's doctoral supervisor at the University of Sheffield and they co-edited the journal *Immigrants and Minorities* for many years until Colin's retirement. David is now Editor-in-Chief.

Saima Nasar Transnational historian of race, empire and migration. She is Lecturer in the History of Africa and its Diasporas at the University of Bristol.

Panikos Panayi Professor of European History at De Montfort University and a leading expert on the history of immigration. His most important publications in this field include: *An Immigration History of Britain: Multicultural Racism Since c1800* (Longman, 2010; Routledge, 2014; Kindle, 2014; Japanese edition, Jimbun Shoin, 2016); and *The Germans in India: Elite European Migrants in the British Empire* (Manchester University Press, 2017). He is currently writing a book entitled *Real Londoners: Immigration and the Making of London* for Yale Books.

Gavin Schaffer Professor of Modern British History at the University of Birmingham and author of *Racial Science and British Society* (Palgrave MacMillan, 2008) and *The Vision of a Nation: Making Multiculturalism on British Television* (Palgrave MacMillan, 2014). Schaffer's PhD was examined by Colin Holmes in 2003, and he went on to work with him as reviews editor of *Immigrants and Minorities* between 2004–2007.

Wendy Ugolini Senior Lecturer in British History at the University of Edinburgh. Her research interests focus on war and identity formation in twentieth-century Britain. Her first book, *Experiencing War as the 'Enemy Other': Italian Scottish Experience in World War II* (Manchester University Press, 2011), was awarded the Gladstone Prize by the Royal Historical Society. She is currently writing a social, cultural and military history of English Welsh hybridity during the two World Wars.

Rozina Visram Teacher and Head of History in a large London comprehensive school for many years. In 1988 she co-authored a pioneering report for the Geoffrey Museum on presenting histories in a diverse society. She was a consultant researcher for the Museum of London's 'Peopling of London' exhibition and the AHRC-funded research projects, 'Making Britain: South Asian Visions of Home and Abroad, 1870–1950' (2007–2010) and 'Beyond the Frame: Indian British Connections, 1850–1950' (2011–2012). She wrote *Ayahs, Lascars and Princes: Indians in Britain 1700–1947* (1986, Routledge Revivals, Reprint, 2015) and *Asians in Britain: 400 Years of History* (Pluto Press, 2002). She holds an Honorary Doctorate from The Open University.

Anne Witchard Reader in the Department of English, Linguistics and Cultural Studies at the University of Westminster. She is the author of *Thomas Burke's Dark Chinoiserie: Limehouse Nights and the Queer Spell of Chinatown* (Ashgate, 2007), *Lao She in London* (Hong Kong University Press, 2012) and *England's Yellow Peril: Sinophobia and the Great War* (Penguin, 2014). She is co-editor, with Lawrence Phillips, of *London Gothic: Place, Space and the Gothic Imagination* (Continuum, 2010) and editor of *British Modernism and Chinoiserie* (Edinburgh University Press, 2015).

COLIN HOLMES

An Introduction

Tony Kushner

Migration is one of the most pressing issues in the twenty-first century, constantly in the media and at the forefront of political discourse as a 'problem'. Balance is often in short supply and the focus on 'now' has been at the expense of exploring changes and continuities with regard to human movement in both the deep and recent past. And yet it has been pointed out that 'The history of the world includes remarkable stories of migration in every era'. Historians and others have been slow to recognise what Patrick Manning has called the 'human habit' of migration.[1] This is especially true within the historiography of Britain, a nation which is still largely in collective denial of its migrant origins *before* 1945. Those working in the field have thus had their work cut out to work to challenge state and popular mythologies that the British population was rooted and homogenous, at least up to the Second World War. No historian has been more important in querying such assumptions and developing the field of migrant and anti-migrant studies with detailed historical research than Colin Holmes. It would be misleading to state that Colin Holmes created British migrant historiography. Before his *John Bull's Island: Immigration & British Society, 1871–1971* (1988),[2] there were predecessors – some general, some migrant group-specific. They varied in quality from the poorly researched to the detailed and worthy, and from 'ethnic cheerleading'/defensive to anti-alien in purpose. What they had in common, however, was that they remained at the margins of history writing and away from the historiographical 'mainstream' in Britain.[3] It is telling, for example, that the most important and durable of these was Lloyd Gartner's *The Jewish Immigrant in England* (1960), written by a young American historian trained in ethnic and Jewish studies across the Atlantic.[4] Other scholarship which covered the early black presence in Britain were works of sociologists and social anthropologists often paying only lip service to historical background.[5] Without these early studies, Holmes' task would have been much harder. It remains that his work reached another level in terms of its research quality, breadth of vision and inclusivity, wider sense of context (both domestic and international) and overall nuance and balance.

With a subject matter then, and still very much now, distorted by prejudice and polemic, his work was calm and thoughtful. This is not to say there is an absence of a deep moral commitment to fighting intolerance in Colin Holmes' writing (and wider work in communicating it to a broader audience). Moreover, there is an empathy to the migrants and their descendants throughout his opus. Indeed, the ethical underpinnings of his life work are clearly shown in the oral history interview carried out by Alan Dein, an edited version of which is included in this volume.[6]

In the discussion with Alan Dein, Colin Holmes clearly emerges and identifies as an outsider and a challenger of accepted historical and societal truths. Whether within or beyond academia, he is politically and intellectually committed to the less privileged. It reflects his family background in semi-rural Derbyshire where he was born in 1938. Brought up in the village of South Normanton, his father was a miner and his mother had been a domestic coming from a farming family. For someone of his background in the early decades of the post-war era, university (he graduated in Economic and Social History from Nottingham in 1960) was still unusual. That year just over 22,000 students completed their undergraduate degrees in Britain and of these over two-thirds were middle class and beyond. Only one percent, according to the 1963 Robbins Report, came from families whose wage earners were classified as unskilled workers.[7] These statistics reveal both Colin Holmes' ability and determination as well as the encouragement from his mother at home and a sympathetic history teacher at school.

Furthermore, whilst not of migrant origin himself, his sensitive work on so many different groups and individuals who have settled permanently or temporarily in Britain is the answer to essentialist arguments that only those from such backgrounds can understand, and then write about, their own history. For example, as he emphasised to Alan Dein, he felt kinship with his mentor at Sheffield University, Sidney Pollard, a former Jewish refugee from Vienna who had come to Britain aged thirteen on the *Kindertransport*. When told of a possible position at Sheffield and of Pollard's Jewishness and Marxism, Holmes remembers thinking, 'That was enough for me!' It was the beginning of a remarkable career at Sheffield that spanned from 1963 to 1998 and the award of a personal chair in the History Department.

The rich variety of his publications is clear from Colin Holmes' curriculum vitae which accompanies the interview. That alone would (and does) ensure his lasting impact as *the* historian of migrant Britain in the modern era. Colin's almost casual remark in his interview that he wanted to consider 'all sorts of groups in an attempt to be comprehensive' understates the bravery of undertaking such coverage: the historiography for so much of his subject matter had hardly begun as late as the 1970s – a point emphasised in many of the contributions to this volume. He was inspired early on by the innovative work of John Higham on American immigration history which included analysis of nativism in the nineteenth and twentieth centuries (which worryingly now is revived under the Trump presidency with its strong echoes of 1850s 'Know-Nothing' paranoia, then aimed largely at Catholics and now at Muslims). Higham began the research that became *Strangers in the Land* in 1948 and the book was originally published in 1955.[8] It must be emphasised again that there was no British equivalent for Colin Holmes to emulate as he courageously set out to do. But Colin's influence extends much further than his books, articles, chapters and other writings.

This biographically focused section of the Introduction is written by one particular member of the editorial team that has, as the academic cliché of the moment would label it, 'curated' this volume. It is mentioned as I was the only one of the three of us taught (and then supervised as a PhD student) by Colin Holmes. Although Colin mentions teaching and supervision in his interview with Alan Dein, perhaps modesty restrains him from doing himself full justice in a sphere that he rightly saw as a crucial ingredient of academic life (and one before the invention of that ultimate oxymoron, 'quality control'). I was a student in the sadly now defunct Department of Economic and Social History at the University of Sheffield from the late 1970s. Whilst the small group of scholars who made up this academic unit were not united in all ways, there was one collective message – those down the hill (and Sheffield, like Rome, was made up of seven of them) in the Department of History were to be treated with utmost suspicion. If, as L. P. Hartley famously noted, 'The past is a foreign country: they do things differently there', so too the *History* Department at Sheffield. In contrast, in Economic and Social History we studied the lives of ordinary people and history from the 'bottom up'. Colin was very much part of that ethos and he was a remarkable lecturer.

I first experienced Colin in a first-year survey course: 'Marxism versus Liberal Interpretations of History'. The photograph we include of Colin does not do full justice to his magnificent beard and coiffure when I was first taught by him in the autumn of 1978. Had there been an academic equivalent of 'Stars in Their Eyes', both intellectually and in appearance, Colin would have won first prize for his version of 'Karl Marx' ('Tonight, Matthew, I'm going to do dialectical materialism …'). Whether they were convinced or not, the students on this course were utterly engaged with both the content and the delivery of these stunning lectures which often finished with Colin teasingly walking out mid-sentence to maximise the theatric impact of his provocative insights. Some of us needed little convincing, but we were left in no doubt that a particular reading of the past with commitment to the poor and the oppressed (rescuing them, as E. P. Thompson famously argued, from 'the enormous condescension of history'), *mattered*.[9]

Later, in more specific courses in which his specialisms in minorities and racisms featured, there was tough love – no space for lazy sentimentalism in these. New approaches and neglected subject matters did not excuse essays or presentations that were under-researched or poorly presented. The same was true of Colin Holmes as a supervisor, a role in which he excelled. His CV shows the extent and range of the theses he successfully saw to completion. What it does not do is reveal the subtlety of his supervision. In cricketing history terms, his was not a loud captaincy, but a quiet Mike Brearley role (the finest England leader in the post-war period) in which there was a careful interjection when it was needed, alongside an encouragement for the student (including many who were of 'mature' age) to develop their own area and approach. There was firmness but a mischievous smile never far from the surface. We were engaged in serious scholarship but this was also fun and there was joint excitement about the enterprise we had embarked upon.

Quite rightly, Colin has been proud of what these doctoral students achieved and went on to. This volume emerged out of a conference co-organised by the Universities of Southampton, Derby, Ulster and Bergen held in Southampton in September 2016 – a partnership that reflected the diaspora of his academic friends and those taught by him. Moreover, many of those present at the conference and/or in this volume were former PhD students of Colin. Some are the students of these students and, in one case, the student of one of *these* students. That represents four generations in one event and one publication. Alongside these were others, inside and outside academia, who Colin had motivated or encouraged.

The quality of the conference was extremely high. What was also noticeable was the spirit of the event and the affection and respect that was manifest towards Colin Holmes. Academic gatherings are not always the friendliest of spaces but the spirit of being in a joint venture and, again, the *ethical underpinnings* of our collective work was ever present in Southampton – a feature that was made explicit in the final session when Colin was informally interviewed by James Jordan (a precursor to that carried out by Alan Dein and revealing how much potential a full life history would possess, as has shown to be the case).

Colin's legacy is thus not only in the form of his publications but also in the students he inspired. It might be added here and this comes out clearly in the interview, that Colin was not a man for bureaucratic structures. With Ken Lunn, Colin Holmes created the journal *Immigrants & Minorities* and as the former's chapter in this volume shows, its importance in shaping the field and providing an important outlet where new work could be showcased and not dismissed as so much of it was by the 'mainstream' historical profession (remember, they do things differently there!), should not be minimised. The Sheffield School of *historical* studies of migration and prejudice had at its head Colin Holmes. It remains that it does not, and did not, exist as a formal centre as exists elsewhere in related areas (for example, the Parkes Institute for the Study of Jewish/non-Jewish relations at the University of Southampton in which two of the editors are based). But that the Sheffield School was created (curated?!) without any funding or structure is a tribute to the intellectual vision and passion of Colin Holmes. His legacy lives on in the University of Sheffield where the study of migration is now firmly established,[10] but also in many other British higher education institutes where its significance has been belatedly acknowledged (if often without recognising the importance of history in so doing).[11]

This volume is divided into six sections – 'Historiography', 'Places and Spaces', 'Communal History', 'Racism and Anti-Migrant Politics', 'Marginal, Neglected and Reimagined Histories' and 'Identities' – which together allow the subject matter of this collection to be explored from many different perspectives. The three members of the editorial team provide detailed introductions to the overarching themes explored by the chapters under these half a dozen headings. No attempt is thus needed here to cover the twenty-four contributions that are included within them. It should be highlighted at this stage that the authors range in chronology (from the seventeenth century to the present day), geography, disciplinary approach and subject matter which make the collection multi-layered and richly diverse. There is, however, unity of purpose as each provides a brief history and historiographical survey of their field of expertise, informed by case studies from the contributor's own work. That each one, whatever the background of the author, has been directly or indirectly stimulated by the work of Colin Holmes is tribute to his ongoing importance in the field. And that his own work could easily be placed in any or all of these sections is a tribute to its pathbreaking nature and intellectual quality. As Colin reflected to Alan Dein, one historian he owed much to was R. H. Tawney and the need to embrace the 'whole sweep of society', including social, economic, cultural and political aspects of it.

This volume is thus a deeply deserved celebration of the man himself, but one, following the example Colin Holmes himself has provided, that is determined and committed to taking critically the field he pioneered into new territories and to challenge those inside and outside academia to do likewise. I would like to end this introduction with a provocation in the spirit of Colin. 'Migration', as the Paddington Bear inspired T-shirts proclaim, 'is not a crime'. Continuing to ignore their agency and place in history, is, however, a serious dereliction of moral duty for those who in any way would claim that they are true followers of Clio. Colin Holmes noted how, even late in his teaching career, his subject specialism was 'regarded by some as quite peripheral. There was a certain stigma [attached] to it'. When on the job market myself in the late 1980s and early 1990s I faced similar responses, including the very denial of Britain's past diversity. In the second decade of the twenty-first century there is now simply no excuse, with the work of Colin Holmes and all those he has encouraged, for such ignorance and condescension to continue. Instead, and to end on a positive note, let these chapters inspire a new generation to explore the historical depth and variety of 'migrant Britain'.

Notes

1 Patrick Manning, *Migration in World History* (New York: Routledge 2005), xiii, 1.
2 Colin Holmes, *John Bull's Island: Immigration & British Society, 1871–1971* (Basingstoke: Macmillan 1988).
3 For an overview and critique, see Colin Holmes, 'Introduction: immigrants and minorities in Britain', in idem (ed.), *Immigrants and Minorities in British Society* (London: George Allen & Unwin 1978), 13–22.
4 Lloyd Gartner, *The Jewish Immigrant in England* (London: George Allen and Unwin 1960).
5 See, for example, Michael Banton, *The Coloured Quarter* (London: Jonathan Cape 1955).
6 The full interview will be deposited in the British Library, Department of Sound Archives.

7 Figures from Paul Bolton, 'Higher Education and Social Class', (2010), paper from House of Commons Library, SN/SG/620. More generally see Robert Troschitz, *Higher Education and the Student: From Welfare State to Neoliberalism* (Basingstoke: Routledge 2017).
8 John Higham, *Strangers in the Land: Patterns of American Nativism 1860–1925* (New Brunswick: Rutgers University Press 1955).
9 E. P. Thompson, *The Making of the English Working Class* (London: Victor Gollancz 1963), 12.
10 In the 1990s, however, Colin Holmes *was* involved in the Migration and Ethnicity Research Centre at the University of Sheffield. Formed in 1994, it built around his historical work in conjunction with those in Geography and Sociology. One product of this Centre was a collection of oral history interviews carried out between 1995 and 1998 with post-1945 East European migrants to Bradford which are now deposited in the University archives. The Sheffield Migration Research Group in the Department of Sociological Studies is now focused, as are almost all such networks, centres and institutes, on *contemporary* issues with little attention given to historical perspectives.
11 The area of 'refugee studies' is one that is fast-growing but generally present-centred.

SECTION 1
Historiography

Jennifer Craig-Norton

Introduction

The conference from which the present volume is derived was fundamentally historiographic in nature, having as its purpose the honouring of Colin Holmes' pioneering and profound contributions to migration and minority studies. This essentiality is itself a testament to Holmes' novel contributions: orienting the field firmly within the discipline of history, and championing the use of new sources and theoretical approaches. Although all the scholars whose essays appear in this volume have sited their work within historiographical contexts, it is also vital to include a separate section dedicated to an historiographical overview – a survey of the field when Holmes embarked upon the scholarship that would define his career, his own contributions to that body of work, and a sampling of the new contexts and widening ripples inspired by Holmes' work. That there was a negligible historiography in place when Holmes embarked upon his studies of immigrants and minorities is attested to by the fact that a decade prior to his pioneering work *John Bull's Island*, Holmes edited what Tony Kushner describes as a 'pathbreaking' collection, *Immigrants and Minorities in British Society*, whose comprehensive literature review took up fewer than two pages. Forty years on, as outlined by the contributors to this section, the historiography has been transformed and broadened, both in British contexts and internationally – developments which are the focus of the chapters in this section.

No one is better positioned to provide commentary on Colin Holmes' pioneering efforts than his colleague Ken Lunn, the co-founder of the journal *Immigrants and Minorities*. Ken provides an invaluable autobiographical perspective on the emergence of the Sheffield School and the development of the historiography of intolerance, migration, and race narratives in the British context. A contemporary rush to proclaim new and forgotten histories often ignores the foundations of the study of race, immigration, fascism, and the radical right that were laid in the 1960s with the scholarship emanating from the University of Sheffield. Colin Holmes, 'the right leader and the right time', brought historical rigour to the overlapping dimensions of the Sheffield School and blazed the trail for generations of scholars seeking to uncover the traditions of intolerance in British history.

One of Holmes' students, and a contributor to the development of the Sheffield School, Tony Kushner, is also uniquely placed to reflect upon the importance and impact of Colin Holmes' work. A deep and critical assessment of Holmes' seminal work *John Bull's Island* is at the core of this exploration, and Kushner provocatively frames the discussion as an attempt to answer the counterfactual question: What if there hadn't been a Colin Holmes? Continuing the theme of 'right man, right time', it is demonstrated that Holmes realised an original and multidisciplinary scholarship grounded in history that masterfully brought forth the narratives of around fifty national and ethno-religious migrant groups to British shores. This work pointed the way for further in-depth scholarship, which has been impeded by powerful and persistent mythologies about Britishness, tolerance and historical homogeneity, notions about history as the 'poor relation' in migration studies and a reluctance to abandon the imperial/colonial lens when examining migration to the UK. *John Bull's Island* was the springboard encouraging interrogation of the gaps in migration and minority narratives – women, gender, sexuality, space and place and transmigration to name a few – and demanded new historical sources and approaches capable of chipping away at the lingering roadblocks to a more inclusive and comprehensive historiography.

Introducing a comparative perspective, Christhard Hoffmann examines West German, American and British historiographical approaches to narratives about immigrant workers of the late nineteenth and early twentieth centuries. In examining the historiography on Polish workers in the Ruhr, Hoffmann shows that for specific historical and cultural reasons, West German social historians in the 1970s and 80s interpreted their experiences through a class lens while American historians leaned towards concepts of ethnicity to understand the same group. By comparison, British migrant and immigrant historiography was, to quote Hoffmann, 'more comprehensive, manifold and advanced than in Germany' and scholars examining the history of Jewish migration to Great Britain employed a variety of interpretations that resulted in a synthesis that defied simple class vs ethnicity constructs and placed Jewish migrant experiences within British labour and class contexts. Hoffmann concludes with a powerful endorsement of Colin Holmes' approaches to migrant historiography, which eschew the employment of global concepts such as race, class and ethnicity in reductive ways in favour of a complex, nuanced and precise methodology that more accurately reflects the manifold experiences of diverse historical actors.

Widening the focus even further, Tobias Brinkmann examines the emerging historiography of global and transmigration after 1800. The work of Colin Holmes and the Sheffield School legitimised migration studies and made possible the forging of new paradigms in the field which for too long had been constrained by the concentration on single state and regional actors, specific ethno-national groups and rigid concepts of immigration/emigration. A global/transnational approach, on the other hand, is informed by a desire to interrogate 'the process of migration', which includes studying patterns of migration, considering both in and out-migration, as well as internal migration and migrant networks. Brinkmann draws his examples from around the globe, considering Jewish diasporic movements, migration to, from and within the Americas, Russian, Austrian and British Imperial migration among others to discover the interconnectedness of nations-states' immigration laws and the impact on migration of non-state actors such as humanitarian groups and transportation services that operate in transnational space. This historiography has emerged partly in response to contemporary migration debates, much like the rise of the Sheffield School before it, and renews the argument, made over a half-century earlier by Colin Holmes and his colleagues, that migration is not a novel phenomenon and it works to dismantle narratives of refugees and migrants as 'permanent strangers'. Both Brinkmann and Hoffmann also demonstrate the impact that work on global and other national populations has had on British scholarship in the field of migration studies, closing a circle begun nearly half a century earlier by historians of the Sheffield School.

1

UNCOVERING TRADITIONS OF INTOLERANCE

The earlier years of *Immigrants and Minorities* and the 'Sheffield School'

Ken Lunn

The year 2016 saw a considerable emphasis on the history of black and Asian settlers in Britain and on the processes of immigration in British history. The appearance of work such as David Olusoga's *Black and British: A Forgotten History*, with its accompanying BBC television series, has undoubtedly opened up the general area to wider audiences.[1] Exactly what has spurred this renewed interest in such a history can be speculated on endlessly. Twenty-first-century British political and cultural concerns about identity, nationality and ethnicity all play into the agenda and permeate many aspects of the debates. The referendum vote of June 2016 to leave the European Union could be said to be a culmination of many of these concerns and the continuing arguments about the exit processes, often centred around immigration controls and an end to the 'free' movement of people within the borders of the European Union, serves to highlight the continuing divisions and tensions over these issues.

In the academic literature and its more popular spin-offs, an emphasis has been placed upon the continuing 'uncovering' of immigration narratives and the apparent absence of these stories from the broad brushstrokes of this island's story. It is sometimes possible to detect an academic sleight of hand, an ignoring of historiography, in this discovery of the new. In an interview with Olusoga, Arifa Akbar stressed the presence of blacks living in Britain from Roman times, something rarely acknowledged in mainstream textbooks. Thus, he argues, '… there was never a "year zero" or a lost idyll of ethnic purity to which modern-day nativists can hark back'.[2] Olusoga claimed in the interview: '"Black history is a series of missing chapters from British history … I'm trying to put those bits back in"'.[3] It may be valid to identify the absence of black presences from general historical surveys of British society. It is also possible that a generation or two's distance can sometimes obscure the work of predecessors and suggest an originality that is perhaps undeserved. After all, an interest in ethnic and immigration history in Britain was not born purely from the turmoil of Brexit, ultra-nationalism and anti-globalist sentiments. Earlier periods of British history have equally produced serious interrogation of race and ethnicity within its culture and explored its historical formation and significance. Indeed, in a thoughtful review of Olusoga's book, Colin Grant drew attention to one of the key figures in the historiography: 'Three decades ago Peter Fryer offered a corrective, stripping off of the historical bandage. Fryer's *Staying Power: The History of Black People in Britain* was an excoriating book by a tireless Marxist historian skewering British imperial mendacity …'[4] What this essay here seeks to do, sometimes in an autobiographical fashion, is to highlight some of that earlier literature and to assess its overall contribution to themes of race and immigration in British history.

My own engagement in the field began in the autumn of 1971, after a burgeoning interest was aroused during my undergraduate studies at Glasgow University and some absorption of the spirit of 1960s politics and culture. I was accepted at the University of Sheffield to study for a PhD in what was then the Department of Economic History, supervised by Colin Holmes, and settling on a topic around early twentieth-century antisemitism in Britain.[5] During the 1970s, the concept of a Sheffield School became increasingly apparent, although it ought to be said that the coining of the term was rather later, probably from a 1990 review of *John Bull's Island* by Neil Evans.[6] Making reference to Holmes' work alongside that of Richard Thurlow and myself, Evans outlined what he perceived to be the key features of this work.

> This book defines the characteristics of the Sheffield School. First of all Dr. Holmes insists on the need for an historical approach to the subject. He rejects the idea that immigration is a recent feature of British society … he eschews a polemical approach and stresses the complexity of responses and experiences … His insistence on full evidence, that racism needs to be explained, and his suspicion of monocausal simplicity are salutary.[7]

In those earlier years, when perhaps the Sheffield School was in a more embryonic state, its identity centred on research published by Colin Holmes and Richard Thurlow. A growing number of postgraduate students, with a regular Wednesday afternoon postgraduate and staff seminar, focused on a variety of topics around themes of race and of the radical right, mainly within a British context. There was certainly a sense in which a commonality of interests and a sharing of ideas began to emerge.

The 1960s had seen an upsurge in race awareness and the creation of legislation to control immigration but also to outlaw forms of discrimination and racial abuse. Debates within the labour movement and populist campaigns sparked by Enoch Powell's infamous 1968 'Rivers of Blood' speech ensured that the following decade was riven with political and cultural strife over questions of race and immigration.[8] The publicity surrounding Powell's utterances had a significant political impact. One commentator has argued firmly that it helped to 'detach part of Labour's support, especially in the working class … A decline in class allegiance can be explained by many factors, for example "embourgeoiseification". Nevertheless, anti-immigrant views seem to have been a major short-term catalyst'.[9] This was the context which prepared the way for the Conservative election victory in 1979, with what one historian has called the 'sharp popular disillusionment' with successive Labour governments.[10] There can be no doubt that Conservatives played the 'race card' in the 1970s. Margaret Thatcher highlighted this trend in a 1978 *World in Action* interview in which she said, 'People are rather afraid that their country might be rather swamped by people with a different culture', thus mirroring the sentiments of Enoch Powell's pronouncements in the previous decade.[11]

Part of this heightening of race tension and the increasing electoral significance of anxiety over immigration was due to the growth of the National Front. Emerging as a more or less coherent movement by the late 1960s, the Front began standing candidates in the 1970 general election and, by 1979, had over 300 contesting the election of that year.[12] Whilst the percentage of the vote obtained never moved beyond single figures, the presence and impact on the political terrain was much greater.[13] The rise of this racist organisation did not occur without organised and informal opposition. The formation of the Anti-Nazi League in 1977 was also an indication of the challenges to far right politics in this era.[14]

Certain members of the academic community were drawn into these debates. For some, it was the publication of Robert Skidelsky's biography of Oswald Mosley which seemed to offer some connections between contemporary political actions and discourse and the history of what was beginning to be seen as a distinctive pattern of fascism within British culture.[15] Skidelsky's study generated a good deal of controversy. There were those who felt that he had been overly sympathetic towards the man and his politics. Others focused on his lack of critical analysis of the ideology of Mosley's beliefs, particularly his antisemitism. The undervaluing of the existence of a consistent tradition of fascism within British politics was also noted.[16] After a series of conversations within the Sheffield School, Richard Thurlow and I decided to contact a number of academics working in this field with the aim of highlighting interpretations which engaged in a more nuanced evaluation of traditions of British radical right politics and, eventually, in 1980, the collection of essays, *British Fascism*, was published.[17]

This volume diverged significantly from the conventional political science emphasis on the electoral insignificance of Mosley's party in the 1930s and thus its ultimate failure. The perceived irrelevance of British fascism was thus sharply contrasted to the impact of German Nazism and Italian fascism in the same period. Whilst there had been earlier studies on the British Union of Fascists (BUF) by Cross, Benewick and Mandle that operated outside this more conventional approach, they were somewhat neglected by mainstream political commentary.[18] The essays in *British Fascism* paid much closer attention to what were identified as precursors and parallel movements involving analysis of political antisemitism before the First World War, research on the Britons, a 1920s group led by Henry Hamilton Beamish with the sole aim of promoting the arguments of antisemitism, and a study of the Imperial Fascist League, a parallel organisation to, and a rival of, the BUF. A second block of material focused on the BUF itself, on aspects of its ideology, including its antisemitism, on public order issues and on its membership. Finally, there were essays on the wider context, looking at the changing interpretations within the literature and discussions about the perpetuation of a fascist politics in post-1945 Britain. Collectively, the volume flagged up the Sheffield School as offering a significant intervention in this developing debate and was certainly the platform for Thurlow's subsequent corpus of work on this topic.[19]

Another key element of the Sheffield School was orienting itself around the work of Colin Holmes on the history of immigration and racism in Britain, following the publication of *Antisemitism in British Society 1876–1939*.[20] Holmes was seeking to explore not simply the dynamics of that period in terms of its impact on antisemitism, but also to understand the powerful legacy of the previous century in shaping this race-hatred. As Holmes argued, 'It is clear, in fact, that the conflicts after 1876 were influenced by these prior images of Jews which were present in British society.'[21] Kushner's chapter in this section will deal in greater depth with Holmes' writing, so what follows is a more particular account of the growing output of race and immigration history at Sheffield and the diffusion of its influence.

Perhaps the most significant intervention was another edited volume, *Hosts, Immigrants and Minorities*, published in the same year as *British Fascism*.[22] Covering the forty or so years before the First World War, it provided ample evidence of the complex nature of immigration into Britain in this period and the variety of responses sparked within the 'host' society. This allowed for a much more nuanced and detailed identification of that history. There was an impressive range of case studies, analysing, for example, Jewish trade unionism in Manchester and Leeds, Lithuanians in the Lanarkshire coalfields and German clerks in Victorian England, which raised greater awareness of pre-1914 migration.[23]

For me, one of the most significant features of the volume's origins was in the themed conference, held in Sheffield in 1978 and organised by the Society for the Study of Labour History. This meant that many of the contributors were engaging with a labour history perspective, placing both the immigrant and the 'host' society experiences in this wider setting. One of the driving ambitions of some of us within the Sheffield School was to bring ethnic and race history into a more mainstream focus and this 1978 conference and the subsequent publication was an early example of this desire. It was continued in another set of essays, *Race and Labour in Twentieth-Century Britain*, published in 1985. This provided an opportunity to set out a critical framework for this kind of work and gave a platform to authors such as Jacqueline Jenkinson, Neil Evans and Marika Sherwood who would go on to make significant contributions within the discipline. The aims of the collective work were made very clear.[24]

> The new techniques of social history should push us beyond the institutionalized forms of evidence. Local studies will be crucial in the reconstruction of immigrant history and of host responses to those minority groups. Only by dealing with those attitudes within the broader setting of work, community, politics and historical background can we begin to make sense of the detailed picture which is to be uncovered.[25]

Given these objectives, the willingness of the Society for the Study of Labour History to offer its auspices in 1978 for this pioneering conference and the opening-up of this terrain needs to be commended.[26]

These overlapping dimensions of the Sheffield School, the study of fascism and the radical right, and the history of race and immigration, of course continued in their Yorkshire birthplace during the 1980s and 90s but also developed a significant outpost on the south coast of England. I took up a teaching post at the then Portsmouth Polytechnic in 1979 and, a few years later, Tony Kushner, a Sheffield graduate and postgraduate, was appointed to the University of Southampton. The conferences and publications that followed on from our collaboration clearly developed the approaches originating in Sheffield. In particular, there were two volumes of essays which further challenged conventional wisdoms. The first, *Traditions of Intolerance*, appeared in 1989.[27] In this, the emphasis was on the increasing recognition of the importance of an historical dimension in the study of contemporary political racism and fascism.

> This recognition has moved consideration a good deal further than the lip-service paid to historical traditions; 'the legacy of Empire' is a phrase much used in many studies produced in the 1960s, 1970s, and early 1980s, but represents little concrete research. More recent work has opened up the analysis of the traditions of racism and fascism, has begun to look at the context of racism in those years, and assessed the processes of the racialisation of politics, the popularisation of racist views, and methods of cultural transmission and assimilation.[28]

By including further new material on the impact of fascism by writers such as David Cesarani, Richard Thurlow, Colin Holmes and Roger Eatwell, the re-evaluation of that political history was continued. In addition, studies on Jewish stereotyping in English literature and on the revival of English national identity foregrounded themes that were to be more fully articulated in later years.[29] Jointly, the essays drew together a body of work that was ever-conscious of its contemporary relevance.

> Before we can confront the evils of racism and fascism successfully in Britain, it is vital to examine the deep-seated nature of these dehumanising agents. *Traditions of Intolerance* is intended as a small contribution to this process, a process that has to start with the necessary, but painful, task of quashing the myths of Britain's essential 'fairness'.[30]

The Politics of Marginality, which was published in the following year, appeared at a time when there was an often-bitter debate about the role of history in education generally but, by implication, within the political culture of contemporary Britain.[31] The Conservative election victory of 1979 and the ideological forces unleashed by this success clearly made their mark upon the editors' ambitions, as the preface made abundantly clear. Indeed, it was a Conservative government's persistent attempts at intervention in the school history curriculum that provoked a defence of the discipline, not necessarily always successfully. I remember long consultation processes and revisions to proposals to retain a more social history emphasis being frequently ignored or overturned. The preface to the book began with a provocative quote from Sir Geoffrey Elton at an Historical Association lobby in the House of Lords in early 1986: 'Schools need more English history, more kings and bishops ... The non-existent history of ethnic entities and women leads to incoherent syllabuses'.[32] The editors could hardly have asked for more incentive to confront such an attitude and this helped to shape the content and format of *The Politics of Marginality*.

> The aim of this collection of essays is, above all, to try to produce work which will help challenge the oft-stated need for more British history, 'British' (or 'English') being defined as 'Anglo-Saxon' and unwilling to acknowledge racism, conflict, intolerance and ethnicity as part of mainstream society.[33]

There were three sections to the collection: 'Women and Fascism', 'War and Minorities' and 'Racism and Revisionism'. The first group opened up the study of women within the confines of British fascism. Up until these studies, most work in this general field had concentrated upon experiences in Germany and Italy, with an emphasis on the kind of support and involvement which women gave to fascist movements and regimes. There was also a concern with fascist ideology's notions of gender division and the nature of policies directed at women. What the chapters here began to do was to offer a British strand which could stand alongside the narratives of continental Europe. For example, Martin Durham's overview provided a coherent and agenda-setting framework, whilst David Mayall's analysis of Nellie Driver's unpublished memoirs offered a unique insight into the life and beliefs of a BUF woman activist in Lancashire.[34]

In 'War and Minorities', the common theme was the way in which conflict exposes the marginality of ethnic and racial groups so sharply. Most of the work concentrated on the First World War, with studies on Jews and Germans, as well as an analysis of the British Empire Union, an organisation which sat within the spectrum of radical right politics in Britain.[35] The final section opened up the period of twentieth-century history, with, amongst others, an exploration of British reaction to Nazi antisemitism in the period before the Second World War and a survey of British responses to immediate post-Second World War immigration, as centred on the arrival of the *Empire Windrush* from the West Indies in 1948.[36]

Together, these chapters deliberately opened up new directions – gender and fascism, war and minorities and marginality within British culture – the antithesis of Elton's history. It is also worth noting that this volume first appeared as a special issue of the journal *Immigrants and Minorities* and it seems fitting now to turn to the beginnings of this journal and its role in promulgating the directions of the Sheffield School.[37]

Perhaps the first point should be to acknowledge the foresight of the original publishers, Frank Cass and Co., in taking on the publication of this project. It was relatively early in the academic publishing era of Cass' output and they were advertising for new journals as part of this strategy. Colin and I discussed the possibilities of putting forward the notion of a specific historical journal to offer the kind of coverage which we deemed to be so important. We put together a proposal, had a meeting with Frank Cass and one of his editors and received an instant agreement to publish.[38] The editorial in the first issue set out the case for the journal, noting that there appeared to be a gap in the possible outlets for our kind of research. As we saw it, there were two main groups of journals; those such as *Phylon* and *Jewish Social Studies*, which focused on particular ethnic groups, and volumes such as *Race and Class* and *Ethnic and Racial Studies*, more concerned with contemporary situations and only incidentally dealing with historical evidence. 'As for mainstream historical journals, first-class work on racial and ethnic groups stands in isolation.'[39] Colin and I felt that the dominant academic discourses on history rarely offered substantial analysis of the kind of history we were seeking to encourage and to develop. This was, therefore, the gap which we hoped our new proposal could fill. With book reviews, we hoped to move away to some extent from the conventional approach, with longer reviews where appropriate, possibly using two reviewers for the same item and using reviews as a way of looking again at key sources. '[I]t would be our intention to rescue certain books from the historical underground.'[40]

The contents of the first issue reflect the diversity of coverage we had intended. Barbara Bush's piece on slave women in the British Caribbean, Christopher McGimpsey's study of Irish friction in nineteenth-century New York and Murdoch Rodgers' work on Lithuanians in Scotland around the time of the First World War, together with Vic Gilbert's first bibliographical survey, reflected the aims of deep historical analysis and a comparative approach aimed at exploring similarities and differences.[41]

Ultimately, the success and relevance of the journal are for others to judge. However, the conjuncture of circumstances which prompted its appearance cannot be doubted. Indeed, the issues which concerned those early volumes still seem pressing. In a 2014 editorial evaluating the journal's progress and possible new directions, the current editors, Donald MacRaild and David Mayall (both products of the Sheffield School), highlighted those founding principles and context.

> Thirty years later, the issues seem hardly less important. Indeed, despite obvious geo-political changes, the issues remain as starkly revealed in the current national and international discourses around the desirability and impact of immigration and migration.[42]

It seems that there are a number of points which can be made about the contribution of *Immigrants and Minorities* to the discipline. First and foremost, it operated in those early years in a rather freer academic framework, at least in terms of its British origins and contributors. In the main, pressure to research and to publish was more internalised and self-motivated, not answerable to any mechanical evaluation system. This is not to say that the quality of submissions in the first years was necessarily of a higher quality than those in later years but that the ethos of contributors may have been rather different. From a personal point of view, it was also important that one of the editors was employed at a then-polytechnic, indicating that valid academic work could be produced across that somewhat insidious binary division of higher education existing at that time.

Second, there were advantages to being a new journal. Contributors could be said to be taking a calculated risk in publishing with us but it demonstrated their recognition of the aims of the journal. In addition, it took some time for *Immigrants and Minorities* to be acknowledged as a first-off reviewing journal. Publishers were perhaps slow to offer books for review and, consequently, we had a variety of volumes that were not necessarily covered in other journals, and reviewers who might not have been offered the opportunity by more established outlets. This brought freshness and alternative perspectives to the journal's approach, indeed part of its mission.

Third, as indicated by the contents of the first issue, the range of articles in those early years was impressive, both chronologically and geographically, which was always our intention. If we were to encourage comparative approaches within this field of study, then the obligation was on us as editors to promote such a diversity and to highlight the value of comparative work in race and immigration studies.

Fourth, it was rewarding to see the current editors note in their 2014 evaluation the appreciation of Vic Gilbert's bibliographical contributions in those early years. In this largely pre-electronic era, we felt that these bibliographies justified the space taken in the journal. This material was of considerable use to scholars in the field and, again, was a key element in the journal's strategy.

Fifth, virtually from the start of the journal, we gave guest editors the opportunity to put together special issues, giving greater depth to a particular area of study. These special issues were subsequently produced and marketed by Cass as standalone books. As early as 1983, in volume 2, we offered *From the Other Shore: Russian Political Emigrants in Britain, 1880–1917* and 1988 saw the excellent collection *After the Crossing: Immigrants and Minorities in Caribbean Creole Society*.[43] These issues became a hallmark of the journal's approach and, I believe, brought new readers to its pages.

Finally, I think *Immigrants and Minorities* became synonymous with the output of the Sheffield School. Within the first few years, there were appearances from, for example, Barbara Bush, Tony Kushner, David Mayall, Richard Thurlow and Panikos Panayi.[44] As a framework within which these and subsequent 'Schoolers' could operate, developing and enlarging historical approaches to the study of race and immigration, this was perhaps its most important contribution. Its continued existence reflects its contemporary relevance within the discipline.

Notes

1 David Olusoga, *Black and British: A Forgotten History* (Basingstoke: Macmillan 2016).
2 Arifa Akbar, 'The books interview', *The Guardian Review*, 5 November 2016, 13.
3 Ibid.
4 *The Guardian Review*, 19 November 2016, 10. The reference is to Peter Fryer, *Staying Power: The History of Black People in Britain* (London: Pluto 1984).
5 Kenneth Lunn, 'The Marconi Scandal and Related Aspects of British Antisemitism, 1911–1914', PhD thesis, Sheffield University, 1978.
6 Neil Evans, 'Review', *Welsh History Review*, vol. 15, no. 1, 1990, 138. Colin Holmes, *John Bull's Island: Immigration and British Society, 1871–1971* (Basingstoke: Macmillan 1988).
7 Evans, 'Review', 138.
8 For details, see Kenneth Lunn, 'Complex encounters: trade unions, immigration and racism', in John McIlroy, Nina Fishman and Alan Campbell (eds), *British Trade Unions and Industrial Politics: Volume Two: The High Tide of Trade Unionism, 1964–79* (Aldershot: Ashgate 1999), 82–86.
9 Roger Eatwell, 'Fascism and political racism in post-war Britain', in Tony Kushner and Kenneth Lunn (eds), *Traditions of Intolerance: Historical Perspectives on Fascism and Race Discourse in Britain* (Manchester: Manchester University Press 1989), 218–238 (231).
10 Dave Renton, *When We Touched the Sky: The Anti-Nazi League 1977–1981* (Cheltenham: New Clarion Press 2006), 10.
11 Thatcher is quoted in Renton, *When We Touched the Sky*, xv. See Eatwell, 'Fascism and Political Racism in Post-war Britain', 230–231 for comments on Powell.
12 David Butler and Gareth Butler (eds), *Twentieth-Century British Political Facts 1900–2000* (Basingstoke: Macmillan 2000), 177–178.
13 For early studies of the National Front, see Martin Walker, *The National Front* (Glasgow: Fontana 1977) and Michael Billig, *Fascists* (London: Harcourt Brace Jovanovich 1978).
14 See Renton, *When We Touched the Sky*, and Dave Hann, *Physical Resistance Or, A Hundred Years of Anti-Fascism* (Winchester: Zero Books 2013).
15 Robert Skidelsky, *Oswald Mosley* (Basingstoke: Macmillan 1975).
16 For Skidelsky's response to such criticisms, see Robert Skidelsky, 'Reflections on Mosley and British Fascism', in Kenneth Lunn and Richard Thurlow (eds) *British Fascism: Essays on the Radical Right in Inter-war Britain* (London: Croom Helm 1980), 78–99.
17 It is worth noting that this volume was reprinted by Routledge in 2016, albeit with no additional text and without the knowledge of the two editors!
18 Colin Cross, *The Fascists in Britain* (London: Barrie and Rockcliff 1961), R. J. Benewick, *The Fascist Movement in Britain* (London: Allen Lane 1972), and W. F. Mandle, *Antisemitism and the British Union of Fascists* (London: Longman 1968).
19 John Brewer, *Mosley's Men: The British Union of Fascists in the West Midlands* (London: Gower 1984); D. S. Lewis, *Illusions of Grandeur: Mosley, Fascism and British Society, 1931–81* (Manchester: Manchester University Press 1987) are two key examples here. For Thurlow see for example, *Fascism in Britain: A History 1918–1985* (Oxford: Basil Blackwell 1987).
20 Colin Holmes, *Antisemitism in British Society 1876–1939* (London: Edward Arnold 1979).
21 Holmes, *Antisemitism in British Society 1876–1939*, 9.
22 Kenneth Lunn (ed.), *Hosts, Immigrants and Minorities: Historical Responses to Newcomers in British Society 1870–1914* (Folkestone: Dawson 1980).
23 Bill Williams, 'The beginnings of Jewish trade unionism in Manchester, 1889–1891', 263–307; Joe Buckman, 'Alien working-class response: the Leeds Jewish tailors, 1880–1914', 222–262; Kenneth Lunn, 'Reactions to Lithuanian and Polish immigrants in

the Lanarkshire coalfield, 1880–1914', 308–342; Gregory Anderson, 'German clerks in England, 1870–1914: another aspect of the Great Depression debate', 201–221, all in Lunn (ed.), *Hosts, Immigrants and Minorities*. Other historians with either established careers in the field or who went on to make their mark included Holmes, Thurlow and Neville Kirk.
24 See Kenneth Lunn, 'Race Relations or Industrial Relations?: Race and Labour in Britain, 1880–1950', in Kenneth Lunn (ed.), *Race and Labour in Twentieth-Century Britain* (London: Frank Cass 1985), 1–29.
25 Kenneth Lunn, 'Editor's note', in Lunn (ed.), *Race and Labour in Twentieth-Century Britain*, vi.
26 Even labour history, however, did not always follow through with such an approach: see John McIlroy, Alan Campbell and Nina Fishman, 'Approaching post-war trade unionism', in John McIlroy, Alan Campbell and Nina Fishman (eds), *British Trade Unions and Industrial Politics: Vol Two: The High Tide of Trade Unionism, 1964–79* (Aldershot: Ashgate 1999), 4, a volume commissioned by the Society for the Study of Labour History.
27 See note 6.
28 Tony Kushner and Kenneth Lunn, 'Introduction', in Kushner and Lunn (eds) *Traditions of Intolerance*, 1.
29 Bryan Cheyette, 'Jewish stereotyping and English literature, 1875–1920; Towards a political analysis', in Kushner and Lunn, *Traditions of Intolerance*, 12–32 and Paul Rich, 'Imperial decline and the resurgence of English national identity, 1918–1979', in Kushner and Lunn (eds), *Traditions of Intolerance*, 33–52.
30 Kushner and Lunn, 'Introduction', 8.
31 Tony Kushner and Kenneth Lunn (eds), *The Politics of Marginality: Race, the Radical Right and Minorities in Twentieth Century Britain* (London: Frank Cass 1990).
32 *Times Educational Supplement*, 17 January 1986, cited in Kushner and Lunn (eds), *The Politics of Marginality*, vi.
33 Kushner and Lunn, 'Preface', in Kushner and Lunn (eds), *The Politics of Marginality*, vi.
34 Martin Durham, 'Women and the British Union of Fascists, 1932–1940', 3–18 and David Mayall, 'Rescued from the shadows of exile: Nellie Driver, autobiography and the British Union of Fascists', 19–39 both in Kushner and Lunn (eds), *The Politics of Marginality*.
35 David Ceserani, 'An Embattled Minority: The Jews in Britain During the First World War', 61–81; Stella Yarrow, 'The Impact of hostility on Germans in Britain, 1914–1918', 97–112; Panikos Panayi, 'The British Empire Union in the First World War', 113–130; all in Kushner and Lunn (eds), *The Politics of Marginality*.
36 Tony Kushner, 'Beyond the pale? British reactions to Nazi antisemitism', 143–160 and Kenneth Lunn, 'The British State and Immigration, 1945–51: New light on *the Empire Windrush*', 161–174 both in Kushner and Lunn (eds), *The Politics of Marginality*.
37 *Immigrants and Minorities*, vol. 8, no. 1, 1989.
38 For a wry account of the meeting and an appraisal of Frank Cass and his contributions, see Colin Holmes, 'Frank Cass (1930–2007)', *Immigrants and Minorities*, vol. 27, no. 1, 2009, 118–122.
39 Colin Holmes and Kenneth Lunn, 'Introductory Editorial', *Immigrants and Minorities*, vol. 1, no. 1, 1982, 5.
40 Colin Holmes and Kenneth Lunn, 'Book reviews policy', *Immigrants and Minorities*, vol. 1, no. 1, 1982, 142.
41 Barbara Bush, 'Defiance or submission? The role of the slave woman in slave resistance in the British Caribbean', 16–38; Christopher McGimpsey, 'Internal ethnic friction: Orange and Green in nineteenth-century New York, 1868–1872', 39–59; Murdoch Rodgers, 'The Anglo-Russian military convention and the Lithuanian immigrant community

in Lanarkshire, Scotland, 1914–20', 60–88; Victor Gilbert, 'Current bibliography of immigrants and minorities: Monographs, periodical articles and theses, 1979–1980. Part 1', 89–141; all in *Immigrants and Minorities*, vol. 1, no. 1, 1982.

42 Donald M. MacRaild and David Mayall, 'Editorial: Historical studies in ethnicity, migration and diaspora: Some new directions', *Immigrants and Minorities*, vol. 32, no. 1, 2014, 1.

43 John Slatter (ed.), 'From the other shore: Russian political emigrants in Britain, 1880–1917', *Immigrants and Minorities*, vol. 2, no. 3, 1983 and Howard Johnson (ed.), 'After the crossing: Immigrants and minorities in Caribbean creole society', *Immigrants and Minorities*, vol. 7, no. 1, 1988.

44 Bush, 'Defiance or submission?', 16–38; Tony Kushner, 'Looking back with nostalgia? The Jewish museums of England', *Immigrants and Minorities*, vol. 6, no. 2, 1987, 200–211; David Mayall, 'Lorist, reformist and romanticist: the nineteenth-century response to Gypsy travellers', *Immigrants and Minorities*, vol. 4, no. 3, 1985, 53–67; Richard Thurlow, 'The "Jew Wise": Dimensions of British political antisemitism, 1918–1939', *Immigrants and Minorities*, vol. 6, no 1, 1987, 44–65 and Panikos Panayi, 'The Imperial War Museum as a source of information for historians of immigrant minorities: the example of Germans in Britain during the First World War', *Immigrants and Minorities*, vol. 6, no. 3, 1987, 348–361.

2

COLIN HOLMES AND THE DEVELOPMENT OF MIGRANT AND ANTI-MIGRANT HISTORIOGRAPHY

Tony Kushner

Richard Evans has warned of counter-history and the dangers it represents, often reflecting the work of reactionaries who nostalgically long for a lost England.[1] It is perhaps no coincidence that some of the authors he has in mind, such as Niall Ferguson, have been prominent in their anti-migrant views, writing against the invasion of Britain and/or Europe by undesirables since the Second World War.[2] Here, I will start by posing a different type of counterfactualism: that in the field of historiography, what if – academically speaking – Colin Holmes had not existed? In the study of migration to Britain, and responses to it, would it have been necessary, to paraphrase Voltaire, to invent him?

No man is an island – even a *John Bull's Island* – and of course there were many influences – intellectual, political and cultural, within which Colin Holmes' work must be situated. I was lucky to study in the Department of Economic and Social History during the late 1970s and first half of the 1980s where Colin was a key figure.[3] That Department, which was formed in the early 1960s by the radical economic historian and refugee from Nazism, Sidney Pollard,[4] had by my time become one largely of social and labour history. It reflected new approaches, typified elsewhere by the History Workshop movement, within which the study of migration, the study of the far right and intolerance could emerge and flourish with Holmes and Richard Thurlow at the forefront. In different places and with more of a grassroots approach, it is no accident that from the late 1960s, the work of Colin Holmes coincided with that of Bill Williams in Manchester and Bill Fishman in the East End of London.[5]

The work of Fishman and Williams focused largely on the Jewish, especially East European, immigrant experience and whilst that of Colin Holmes also had a strong interest in this field, focusing on the responses to that influx from state, public and society as a whole, it was more inclusive, incorporating *all* groups that had settled or passed through Britain. Holmes' work, culminating in the monumental

John Bull's Island: Immigration & British Society, 1871–1971 (1988), owed much to scholars past and present who had studied particular migratory movements and settlement in Britain.[6] As late as 1984, James Walvin could note the paradox that although 'the English are profoundly interested in, and extremely knowledgeable about, their own history … it is important to remind ourselves of the *lacunae* in [such] awareness'.[7] Walvin had immigration especially in mind. Walvin's *Passage to Britain* was the first post-war attempt to create a book-length study of the subject but one that produced no more than a sketch-map based on the existing secondary literature. Indeed, its limitations highlight the achievement of *John Bull's Island* just four years later. Moreover, as a work of original research and synthesis, significantly in terms of the marginality of the field, Holmes' magnum opus still has no rivals three decades on.

If the national and ethno-religious origins of the migrants covered in *John Bull's Island* are added together, the total is around fifty. To do justice to them all was a remarkable achievement and reflected Holmes' unique knowledge and vision. But underlying this remarkable archaeology is a scholarly expertise alongside a passion to correct a glaring lacuna in the historiography itself, motivated by an ethical imperative. It was noted of Colin Holmes' friend, Bill Fishman, that he was 'a committed historian in two senses of the word … committed to his profession, but much more than that … committed to a people and a place … The place is the East End of London and the peoples are the successive waves of immigrants that have inhabited it for the last hundred year or so.'[8] Holmes' canvas covers the whole of Britain, but the description is equally apt.

Whilst much of what follows relates to *John Bull's Island* specifically, it is, of course, part of Holmes' much larger published work, most recently the study of British fascist and pro-Nazi, William Joyce.[9] Here I want to explore the deeper ideological and cultural reasons why, since its publication, there is still resistance to scholarship which brings together these many migrant stories.

After 1988, the number of detailed historical studies of specific migrant groups, local and regional projects and the study of different racisms in Britain, has grown exponentially. In 1978, in what was a pathbreaking edited collection, *Immigrants and Minorities in British Society*, Colin Holmes provided a succinct historiographical overview and critique of the publications from the late nineteenth century onwards, starting with William Cunningham's *Alien Immigrants to England* (1897) and running through to James Walvin's *Black and White: The Negro in English Society, 1555–1945* (1973). Tellingly, the literature review in terms of footnotes was less than two pages long.[10] A similar exercise today could easily become a book in itself as this volume testifies. This collection reflects the best of older and younger generations involved in British migrant studies. It could, however, for all of its extensive nature, be expanded readily in an area which is growing exponentially in the twenty-first century. Yet, whilst taking different directions, much of this new work would not have been possible without the foundation provided by Colin Holmes. Indeed, some of the gaps highlighted in *John Bull's Island* have now been addressed. This includes, for example, the experiences of women in many migrant movements – even if this is still an area requiring far more attention as is the intersection with gender studies more generally.[11]

In the preface to *John Bull's Island*, Colin Holmes explains that he 'concluded my collection of material in February 1986'.[12] Creating such a research-informed overview bringing together all the secondary literature today would be an even greater monumental task. And yet it is not just the prospect of such a Herculean undertaking that has stopped it happening. I will suggest that it needs to be placed alongside three interrelated factors that, whilst under challenge, are still largely resilient to change.

First and most significant are the powerful and linked mythologies that Britain has not been, until recently, a country of immigration and that it is a country that is uniquely tolerant.[13] For politicians and commentators, mainly on the right but also of the left, the two are intimately connected – the absence of serious racism has depended, and continues to depend, on limited migration and the absence of cultural diversity. What Colin Holmes dubbed more generally as 'The myth of fairness' has especially highlighted the absence of antisemitism in British society.[14] It was one that his first monograph in 1979 carefully demolished but not at the expense in any way of overstating its case. In its conclusion, whilst acknowledging that antisemitism was less severe in the modern period than elsewhere in Europe, Holmes was anxious to dispel the idea of British exceptionalism or, indeed, that it 'was insignificant'.[15]

The other side of the same coin is what I have labelled 'the myth of the *Windrush*' – that British multiculturalism can be dated precisely but only as far back as June 1948 and the arrival of the *Empire Windrush* in Tilbury Docks.[16] It was promoted by Mike and Trevor Phillips to mark the fiftieth anniversary of the ship's arrival but has a much wider societal currency.[17] David Goodhart, for example, for many years editor of the progressive *Prospect Magazine* with its close links to New Labour, sees the period after 1945 as a turning point. Before then, Britain was homogenous, but that was followed by 'two big waves of immigration' – those from the Commonwealth during the 1950s and 1960s and the second 'by asylum-driven migrants from Europe, Africa and the greater Middle East in the late 1990s'. The result, argued Goodhart, was a loss of values and assumptions. He warned that 'as Britain becomes more diverse that common culture is being eroded'. Memories of the Second World War have faded, he adds, leading to 'less and less loyalty'.[18]

Against this, local archives, heritage projects and museums have become much more sensitive to recognising and documenting past migration, led by the Museum of London's *Peopling of London* exhibition (1993) for which Colin Holmes was historical advisor.[19] Indeed, at a national level the creation of a new syllabus on migration to Britain within the History GCSE, coordinated by the Runnymede Trust alongside the Universities of Cambridge and Manchester, is a welcome development.[20] It remains that this is unlikely to be a mainstream option in school history teaching. Similarly, the Migration Museum project, led by former Labour minister Barbara Roche, has developed a series of exciting temporary and touring exhibitions. In 2017 it moved to a year-long home in Lambeth, but only as 'the prelude to establishing a high-profile permanent presence in London'. The current absence of such a settled and properly funded institution is revealing – Britain is way behind France, Germany and other European countries, or former settler societies such as Australia, Brazil, Argentina, Canada and the USA in possessing a prestige national migration museum. The organisers of the Migration Museum argue that 'it is high time that this essential part of the national story is properly addressed in the UK too'.[21]

The Migration Museum's objectives are explicitly to connect past and present and to inform the increasingly polemical debates about immigration and belonging, the power of which was shown with the EU Referendum in June 2016:

> We are creating a migration museum … that puts Britain's important migration story at the forefront of our national consciousness … Migration is a pressing contemporary issue that people discuss … day in, day out – a discussion that highlights public concern about numbers of immigrants, Britishness and belonging, identity and inclusion.[22]

Migration, it adds, 'lies at the centre of the European Union, and it is at the heart of a national anxiety about the current global migrant and refugee "crisis"'.[23] Similarly, the work of writer Robert Winder, one of the leading supporters of the Migration Museum, has the aim of linking 'then' and 'now'. His *Bloody Foreigners: The Story of Immigration to Britain*,[24] first published in 2004 and then revised and updated in 2013, was first a response to the vicious attacks on asylum seekers in political, media and popular discourse, and then the growing debate about national identity in relation to diversity, immigration and migrant presence after the July 2005 London terrorist bombings.

In the preface to the second edition, Winder acknowledged criticism that 'in seeking to highlight the role played by immigration in Britain's history, I overstated its importance'. He still stood by what he saw as a fundamental underpinning of *Bloody Foreigners*: 'that we were all immigrants really – it just depend[s] how far back you go'.[25] And if his book followed the path of the Monty Python scene in *Life of Brian* – 'what have the Romans [in this case, read migrants to the UK] done for us?' – Winder was doing so 'merely [to draw] attention to a common oversight, which was that the role played by immigrants in the story of Britain has been understated and overlooked'.[26] I would agree with Winder's assessment in 2013, which is still applicable, that 'This may be less true today than it was ten years ago, but it remains an easy fact to forget'.[27]

Winder's book is a brilliant intervention and a much-needed positive angle at a time when migrants – forced and voluntary – were and continue to be vilified, especially in right-wing print media and its trinity of hate – the *Daily Mail*, *The Sun* and the *Daily Express*.[28] *Bloody Foreigners* is a work that openly borrows from the detailed research of Colin Holmes, the Sheffield School and many others. In the conclusion to *John Bull's Island*, there is also an acknowledgement of the importance of history in informing contemporary debate: 'Those individuals and organisations concerned with current issues relating to immigration need information [on the past]. It is only through such knowledge in fact, that a serious public discussion on immigration becomes possible, and polemic is put in its proper place.'[29]

But in contrast to *Bloody Foreigners*, there is a striving for balance in *John Bull's Island* where the scale and impact of immigration is neither neglected nor exaggerated. Likewise, Colin Holmes has demolished the idea that racism is somehow 'unEnglish', a theme he developed further in the shorter and punchier *A Tolerant Country?* from 1991. Whilst this title has a forceful question mark added, there is again caution to avoid any simplistic conclusions. Hence, it summarises,

> Throughout the years from 1871 there is abundant evidence of the hostile attitudes and treatment which immigrants, refugees and related minorities have endured in Britain, but it would be an error, nevertheless, to portray Britain as a country in which these groups faced universal and unremitting hostility.[30]

There still remains a lack of maturity and nuance at a popular level when confronting Britain's past, whether distant or recent. Too often debate is bifurcated in relation to the presence or otherwise of migration and intolerance. Increasingly tense discussions about national identity, of Britishness and more explicitly Englishness, desperately need greater subtlety. In this respect, it does not help that those academics who work in this field tend to ignore migration and ethnic diversity. Two members of the Sheffield School – Panikos Panayi in *An Immigration History of Britain: Multicultural Racism since 1800* (2010) and my own *The Battle of Britishness: Migrant Journeys, 1685 to the Present* (2012), have tried to address this lacuna.[31]

But Robert Colls, perhaps the leading figure in Englishness studies and guilty of this omission, has responded angrily to these interventions. For him, it is only *now* that the issue of migration and migrant presence has any importance. Parodying *The Battle of Britishness* he states: 'Fifteen families languishing in Southampton docks in 1879 ... or 20,000 French Protestants settling in early Georgian London in 1720 does not compare to the current situation, where one in every four children in England is born to a foreign mother.' He describes the idea that the British are not homogeneous and are all of migrant origin as simply 'nonsense'. Moreover, Colls deliberately distorts recent work as highlighting only a 'British taste for intolerance, abuse, neglect, discrimination, condescension, and violence'.[32]

What Colls and others, especially politicians and civil servants struggling to deal with the complexity of identities, fail to recognise is that Englishness or Britishness is imaginary and that it has often been defined, often ambivalently, against the 'other'. The 'self' has been constantly constructed and reconstructed in the form of external national rivals as illustrated by Linda Colley in relation to the French, through internal minorities (as argued by a growing body of literature though mainly outside the domain of historical studies) or a combination of both.[33] But the denial of the very possibility of past diversity and past intolerance is deeply rooted inside and outside academia. With all the progress made in the detailed research on migrants coming to and settling in the UK, such work remains on the historiography fringes in the study of Britishness. Both immigration and intolerance are thus regarded as things that happen elsewhere. It is noticeable that in literary and cultural studies such marginalisation does not occur and, indeed, is at the forefront of scholarship.[34] Textual representations are perhaps easier to research, but there has also been a willingness to explore questions of identity in relation to the migrant 'other' which has largely bypassed historians of Britain.

The second overarching factor is closely related – that of history being the 'poor relation' of migrant studies which instead focuses on the 'now'. Whilst the Huguenot Society of London and the Jewish Historical Society of England were formed in the late nineteenth century,[35] the academic study of migrants to Britain can be dated much later and to the immediate post-1945 period. In the study of Britain's black populations, anthropology and sociology dominated. These early scholars were fieldworkers concentrating on specific spaces and places, ones which were perceived by contemporaries as being problematic.[36] Some of this literature challenged the pathological approach to the black presence, but others did not quite break free of it, albeit dismissing the certainties of race science that dominated the treatment of such groups in the interwar period.[37]

If flawed, this work was important, especially in including some material going back further than the twentieth century. It provided the foundation for others, first James Walvin, and then more crucially Peter Fryer and Rozina Visram, to build their classic works.[38] But a tendency was established which continues to this day – at best 'history' in the sociological literature on race relations and migration to Britain is mentioned in passing. The focus is on 'now' and not 'then' and as if the former could be understood without the latter. For those responsible for designing the ten-year census, data is divided into two categories – essential and 'nice to know'.[39] For most sociologists and others studying migration and race relations, it must be suggested that history is relegated to the 'nice to know' domain. One important example of this is provided in relation to the growing field of refugee studies.

Peter Gatrell, the leading scholar in the field, has noted that 'Refugees have been allowed only a walk-on part in most histories of the twentieth century, and even then as subjects of external intervention rather than as actors in their own right.'[40] In *A Tolerant Country?*, Colin Holmes had already identified that absence, pointing out the particular neglect of refugees in British historiography – even within the specific study of migration to Britain.[41] It is a gap that I attempted to fill in *Refugees in an Age of Genocide* with Katharine Knox (1999).[42] This was a start, but it remains that there are still many forced migration movements to be recovered from the medieval period onwards. Surprisingly, however, there is no encouragement within refugee studies itself for this to happen.

When the *Journal of Refugee Studies* was formed in 1988, the list of potential interests included anthropology, economics, health, education, international relations, law, politics, psychology and sociology and *not* history. It is thus not surprising that only four percent of its submitted and published articles are historical.[43] There are those such as B. S. Chimni who argue that the refusal to compare past refugee flows in Europe and more recent ones from the developing world is misleading and creates a 'myth of difference'.[44] There are also historical sociologists such as John Solomos who accept the importance of past attitudes and praxis in understanding more recent developments.[45] These, however, are exceptional individuals working against the dominant forces of their disciplines.

This brings the discussion to its third and final factor in explaining the liminal status of British migration studies and one which is ideological. Multi- and inter-disciplinarity is encouraged in academia, although significantly it remains that funding rarely follows. In reality, it is hard enough to master one discipline, let alone several. But in terms of the study of race and migration, it is not the practical challenges that stop dialogue, but more active resistance. I will use only one example, but it is typical of many. Harry Goulbourne was a leading sociologist of modern British society. His *Race Relations in Britain Since 1945* was published ten years after *John Bull's Island*. In it, Goulbourne insists that the movements of migrants such as Jews and Irish cannot be compared to the 'catalytic role black and brown people played in the process of Britain redefining her identity and place as a post-imperial nation-state'. He continues: 'whilst relations between different European groups or between different groups of white people gave rise to patterns of discrimination, the emergence of the notion of racial differentiation and the subsequent race relations arose out of the dramatic contact and integration of Africans and Asians'. In short, what Goulbourne calls 'white' migrants are not part of the key dynamic: the 'colonial/imperial past'.[46]

There are counter tendencies – concepts of racialisation developed by Goldberg, Small and Solomos amongst others – which are more inclusive and can help explain responses to recent asylum seekers and European Union migrant workers, as does the work on 'whiteness' coming out of American studies.[47] I would argue, however, that the Goulbourne imperial/colonial model is still dominant. Attempts, for example, to bring together Jewish studies and postcolonial studies by scholars including Bryan Cheyette (revealingly, another PhD student of Colin Holmes), Michael Rothberg and Paul Gilroy, are still at an early stage.[48] Even within literary and cultural studies, it remains at the sidelines. Connections and comparisons between groups of migrant origin and responses to them are objected to by many with, in the case of attitudes towards Jewish studies, the politics of the Middle East becoming a particular barrier to engagement.

Thus, there is still much to be confronted and obstacles to be surmounted. Yet rather than conclude pessimistically, I want to return to *John Bull's Island* not in hagiographic mode, but critically as a guide to what was to come, and remains to be done. The book is remarkable not just in itself, but for hinting at or encouraging the coverage of experiences and movements remaining to be explored. And it is approaches, including to sources, with which I want to finish this overview of Colin Holmes' lasting contribution.

John Bull's Island utilises many different types of materials, including those from the cultural sphere – literature, art, memorials, museums, film and television. In this respect, the work of cultural studies has shown the potential of using these sources even further through close reading of texts – a fine example is provided David Glover's cultural analysis of the 1905 Aliens Act published in 2012.[49] Here, through detailed research, the potential of interdisciplinary work is realised (if sometimes hindered by the lack of clarity in such writing – a failure that Colin Holmes' prose never suffers from).

John Bull's Island also utilises the memory of migration in the landscape and through the use of life story testimony. The work of Paul Thompson and Raphael Samuel on memory and the 'myths we live by' is important here and is now part of a more critical migrant historiography.[50] Holmes' work recognises the importance of places such as the East End of London, Liverpool 1 (the multi-national dock area of this port city) and Tiger Bay and particular buildings within them. The work of Doreen Massey and other historical geographers has shown how this can be taken further.[51] I would suggest that this needs to be expanded to cover not just the urban but also the rural landscape with regard to the migrant. In respect of the latter, for example, Caroline Bressey argues how 'white imaginaries of the English rural have ignored historical geographies of the black presence'.[52] Through such processes, places become spaces, enabling insights into how identities are made and re-made.

This contribution has touched upon the neglect of women's migratory histories and to this *John Bull's Island* also mentions in passing sexual tensions within racist violence, especially the riots of 1919. More recent work has developed further issues of gender, including concepts of masculinity, and as Gemma Romain has highlighted, questions of sexuality and the contribution of queer studies need also be taken on board. It further complicates and challenges the overall narrative, but such considerations ultimately enable a more inclusive understanding of the past and how it informs the present.[53]

Finally, in many national migrant historiographies and museum displays, there has been a tendency to focus on the place of settlement as final destination. Through diasporic and transnational studies and more specifically the importance of transmigration, which Nick Evans has pioneered in the study of the British sphere of influence,[54] there is greater awareness of the fluidity and complexity of migratory patterns. These are rarely in the form of a single journey from place of departure to place of arrival and settlement. Saima Nasar's contribution to this volume on the East African Asians is a vivid illustration of migration across four continents, but this observation has a wider if less spectacular validity for most migrations. From this, concepts of 'home' become complicated and always in flux. It confirms that the human experience is one of permanent movement. In turn, responses to migrants from the late nineteenth century onwards whilst locally generated were influenced by international developments as Krista Maglen's work on quarantine neatly illustrates.[55] The local, as Doreen Massey insists, is always in part a product of 'global forces'.[56] This includes the field of historiography itself which Christhard Hoffmann's and Tobias Brinkmann's contribution to this section further emphasise.

All of these add to the richness and multi-layered nature of the field today. But the very best of this cutting-edge work has required the foundation that Colin

Holmes provided from the 1960s onwards. And rather than basic building blocks, his work, as typified by *John Bull's Island*, had, like its author, a twinkle in its eye to encourage and demand not only gaps to be covered, but for new approaches and sources to be employed – all of course, to close with Colin's words, to be 'firmly based on historical evidence'.[57] To return lastly to my original hypothetical question: what would the historiography of migrant Britain look like without the input of Colin Holmes? At both an academic and popular level, it would be decades behind and far less varied and nuanced. In 1978 Colin Holmes noted that 'much still remains to be done' and, with new perspectives and insights, that remains an equal challenge four decades on.[58] It remains that without his work as the 'father' of the historic study of migration to and settlement in Britain, we would not be so aware of the vital scholarly importance and moral necessity of the task ahead.

Notes

1 Richard Evans, '"What if" is a waste of time', *Guardian*, 13 March 2014.
2 In his early journalism, Ferguson, a follower of the 'New Right' and devotee of Margaret Thatcher, had exposed views against asylum seekers (though ironically is now married to one), and has since progressed to Islamophobia, warning against the Muslim takeover of Europe. For his more recent warnings against migrants in Europe, see his 'I was wrong on Brexit', *Boston Globe*, 12 December 2016.
3 See the interview with Alan Dein in this volume.
4 See the obituary of Pollard by Colin Holmes in *The Times*, 18 December 1998.
5 Bill Williams, 'Heritage and community: the rescue of Manchester's Jewish past' in Tony Kushner (ed.), *The Jewish Heritage in British History: Englishness & Jewishness* (London: Frank Cass 1992), 128–146; Trevor Smith, 'William Jack Fishman', in Geoffrey Alderman and Colin Holmes (eds.), *Outsiders & Outcasts* (London: Duckworth 1993), 7–11.
6 Colin Holmes, *John Bull's Island: Immigration & British Society, 1871–1971* (Basingstoke: Macmillan 1988).
7 James Walvin, *Passage to Britain: Immigration in British History and Politics* (Harmondsworth: Penguin 1984), 17–18.
8 Smith, 'William Jack Fishman', 7.
9 Colin Holmes, *Searching for Lord Haw-Haw: The Political Lives of William Joyce* (London: Routledge 2016).
10 Colin Holmes, 'Introduction: immigrants and minorities in Britain', in idem (ed.), *Immigrants and Minorities in British Society* (London: George Allen & Unwin 1978), 13–22. The first work of academic synthesis, albeit at a popular level, came six years later – Walvin's, *Passage to Britain*. This accompanied a Channel 4 series on the same theme and in which Colin Holmes featured.
11 Joan Grant (ed.), *Women, Migration and Empire* (Stoke: Trentham 1996); Linda McDowell, *Migrant Women's Voices: Talking About Life and Work in the UK Since 1945* (London: Bloomsbury 2016).
12 Holmes, *John Bull's Island*, ix.
13 Kathy Burrell and Panikos Panayi (eds), *Histories and Memories: Migrants and their History in Britain* (London: I.B. Tauris 2006) – a fine collection of essays which demolish both these assumptions.
14 Colin Holmes, 'The myth off fairness. Racial violence in Britain 1911–19', *History Today* vol. 35, 1985, 41–45.

15 Colin Holmes, *Anti-Semitism in British Society 1876–1939* (London: Edward Arnold 1979), 233.
16 Tony Kushner, *The Battle of Britishness: Migrant Journeys, 1685 to the Present* (Manchester: Manchester University Press 2012), chapter 7. See also Matthew Mead, 'Empire Windrush: The cultural memory of an imaginary arrival', *Journal of Postcolonial Writing* vol. 45 no. 2, 2009, 137–149.
17 Mike and Trevor Philips, *Windrush: The Irresistible Rise of Multi-Racial Britain* (London: HarperCollins 1999).
18 David Goodhart, 'Too diverse?', *Prospect* no. 95, 2004, 30.
19 Nick Merriman (ed.), *The Peopling of London: Fifteen Thousand Years of Settlement from Overseas* (London: Museum of London 1993).
20 See www.ourmigrationstory.org.uk/about.htlml (accessed 17 June 2017).
21 Migration Museum, 'We are creating a Migration Museum for Britain', leaflet, 2017. See also Mary Stevens, *Stories Old and New: Migration and Identity in the UK Heritage Sector* (London: Institute for Public Policy Research 2009).
22 Migration Museum, *A Migration Museum for Britain* (London: Migration Museum Project 2016), 3.
23 Ibid.
24 Robert Winder, *Bloody Foreigners: The Story of Immigration to Britain* (London: Little, Brown 2004).
25 Robert Winder, *Bloody Foreigners: The Story of Immigration to Britain* 2nd edn (London: Abacus 2013), ix.
26 Ibid.
27 Ibid.
28 Greg Philo, Emma Briant and Pauline Donald, *Bad News for Refugees* (London: Pluto Press 2013).
29 Holmes, *John Bull's Island*, 317.
30 Colin Holmes, *A Tolerant Country? Immigrants, Refugees and Minorities in Britain* (London: Faber and Faber 1991), 110.
31 Panikos Panayi, *An Immigration History of Britain: Multicultural Racism since 1800* (Harlow: Longman 2010); Kushner, *The Battle of Britishness*.
32 Review of *The Battle of Britishness* in *American Historical Review* vol. 119 no. 3, 2014, 979–980. More generally for his approach see Robert Colls, *Identity of England* (Oxford: Oxford University Press 2002).
33 Linda Colley, 'Britishness and Otherness: An Argument', *Journal of British Studies* vol. 31, 1992, 309–329.
34 The influence of Stuart Hall was crucial in this respect. Paul Gilroy, *'There Ain't No Black in the Union Jack': The Cultural Politics of Race and Nation* (London: Hutchinson 1987) is a key publication in new approaches to the subject matter.
35 Founded in 1887 and 1893 respectively.
36 See, for example, Kenneth Little, *Negroes in Britain* (London 1948) and Michael Banton, *The Coloured Quarter* (London: Jonathan Cape 1955).
37 Chris Waters, '"Dark Strangers" in their Midst: Discourses of Race and Nation in Britain, 1947–1963', *Journal of British Studies* vol. 36 no. 2 (1997), 207–238. On the earlier period see Paul Rich, *Race and Empire in British Politics* (Cambridge: Cambridge University Press 1986), chapter 6.
38 James Walvin, *Black and White: The Negro in English Society, 1555–1945* (London: Allen Lane 1973); Peter Fryer, *Staying Power: The History of Black People in Britain* (London: Pluto 1984) and Rozina Visram, *Ayahs, Lascars and Princes: The story of Indians in Britain 1700–1947* (London: Pluto Press 1987) and her contribution to this volume.

39 See the discussion on the census, religion and ethnicity in the special issue of *Patterns of Prejudice* vol. 32 no. 2, 1998, 96.
40 Peter Gatrell, *The Making of the Modern Refugee* (Oxford: Oxford University Press 2013), 283.
41 Holmes, *A Tolerant Country?*, 1.
42 Tony Kushner and Katharine Knox, *Refugees in an Age of Genocide: Global, National and Local Perspectives during the Twentieth Century* (London: Frank Cass 1999).
43 For further comment and analysis, see Tony Kushner, *Remembering Refugees: Then and Now* (Manchester: Manchester University Press 2006), 40.
44 B. S. Chimni, 'The geopolitics of refugee studies: a view from the south', *Journal of Refugee Studies* vol. 11 no. 4, 1998, 350–374.
45 John Solomos, *Race and Racism in Britain* (Basingstoke: Macmillan 1989), chapter 2.
46 Harry Goulbourne, *Race Relations in Britain Since 1945* (Basingstoke: Macmillan 1998), ix–x.
47 Karim Murji and John Solomos (eds), *Racialization: Studies in Theory and Practice* (Oxford: Oxford University Press 2005); Mike Hill, *After Whiteness: Unmaking an American Majority* (New York: New York University Press 2004).
48 Bryan Cheyette, *Diasporas of the Mind: Jewish and Postcolonial Writing and the Nightmare of History* (New Haven: Yale University Press 2013); Michael Rothberg, *Multidirectional Memory: Remembering the Holocaust in the Age of Decolonization* (Stanford: Stanford University Press 2009); Paul Gilroy, *Between Camps: Nations, Cultures and the Allure of Race* (London: Allen Lane 2000).
49 David Glover, *Literature, Immigration, and Diaspora in Fin-de-Siecle England. A Cultural History of the 1905 Aliens Act* (Cambridge: Cambridge University Press 2012).
50 Paul Thompson and Raphael Samuel (eds), *The Myths We Live By* (London: Routledge 1990).
51 Doreen Massey, 'Places and their pasts', *History Workshop* no. 39, 1995, 182–192.
52 Caroline Bressey, 'Cultural archaeology and historical geographies of the black presence in rural England', *Journal of Rural Studies* vol. 25, 2009, 386–395 (386).
53 Gemma Romain, *Race, Sexuality and Identity in Britain and Jamaica: The Biography of Patrick Nelson, 1916–1963* (London: Bloomsbury 2017).
54 Nick Evans, 'Aliens *en route*: European transmigration through Britain, 1836–1914', PhD thesis, University of Hull, 2006.
55 Krista Maglen, *The English System: Quarantine, Immigration and the Making of a Port Sanitary Zone* (Manchester: Manchester University Press 2014).
56 Massey, 'Places and their pasts', 183.
57 Holmes, 'Introduction: immigrants and minorities in Britain', 20.
58 Ibid.

3
LOOKING BEYOND THE NATION STATE

The history of global migrations after 1800[1]

Tobias Brinkmann

Looking beyond the borders of emerging and established nation states and empires helps to better understand developments that are usually studied within the framework of the respective state. This key premise of transnational history applies in particular to the history of migrations after 1800. Following migrants on their journeys to, within, through and back from a specific state shines new light on the redefinition of political borders and the emergence of an internationally recognised system of cross-border movement. Although most authors who endorse the transnational approach identify migration as a key field of study, surprisingly few migration historians have risen to the challenge. Most studies in the field of migration history after 1800 focus on migrations to or from a specific state.

An interesting parallel case illustrates why migration historians have shown limited interest in transnational approaches. In the field of Jewish history after 1800, the nation state paradigm remains of great importance. The Jewish Diaspora can look back on a long and vibrant tradition of exchange and cooperation across cultural and political borders in different parts of the world, before and after 1800. Yet, surprisingly few studies in the field of modern Jewish history take a transnational approach. Important exceptions are studies that treat the Jewish experience in the large multi-ethnic empires during the long nineteenth century. In recent years, the history of Sephardic communities in different parts of the Ottoman Empire has emerged as a major field of study. But many authors covering the history of Jewish communities in the Russian or Ottoman Empires limit themselves to specific places and regions, and tend to neglect the wider context of empire and cross-border migrations.[2] Another example is the Catholic Church. Its transformation after 1800 is largely studied along national lines, although the complex Catholic network of organisations and even some dioceses transcended political boundaries.[3]

Linguistic constraints, distinct historiographies and dispersed archival records only partly explain why few authors have ventured across and beyond national borders. In modern Jewish history the crucial impact of emancipation policies partly explains the division of the field into national subfields. During the first half of the nineteenth century, state bureaucrats across Central and Western Europe designed Jewish emancipation policies and regulated hitherto partly autonomous Jewish communities. As Jews became citizens, their commitment to the state and other citizens outweighed their relationships to foreign Jews, most visibly on the battlefields of nineteenth-century Europe. Jews, however, were not passive objects of state policies but exercised agency. Many pursued their own 'paths of emancipation', for instance, by moving to countries where Jews already enjoyed full civil equality, notably the United States. The last Jews in the German states were formally emancipated in the wake of German unification in 1871. Between 1820 and the 1870s a significant number (between 100,000 and 150,000) moved to the United States. In the Russian Empire and Romania, Jews were not emancipated (with a few individual exceptions) before the First World War. Jewish emigration rates from both states were high. About two million Jews moved from the Russian and Austro-Hungarian Empires and Romania to the United States between 1880 and 1914. It is hardly surprising that immigration has been a major theme in American Jewish history. Thanks to strong immigration from Europe the American Jewish community expanded from a few thousand around 1800 to c. 250,000 by 1880, and over two million by 1910. Yet the scholarship concentrates primarily on the period after arrival. Little has been written about the background, travel routes and transnational ties of Jewish immigrants who moved to the United States and Canada between 1800 and 1914. Scholars in German-Jewish history and Russian Jewish history have largely ignored Jews who left. Looking at modern Jewish history as a field, it is somewhat ironic that even the history of Zionism, a transnationally organised national movement before 1948, is often studied within a specific national framework. This background explains why, until recently, the question of how Jews redefined their links within the Diaspora as they became citizens of nation states (and empires) was sidelined.[4]

Similar constraints and research foci as in modern Jewish history apply to migration history.[5] The very terms 'immigration' and 'emigration' as Annemarie Steidl emphasised recently reflected 'the administrative needs of the nation states'.[6] A prominent theme in migration history was – and is – state policies toward (im-)migrants. The formal terms of inclusion, access, and exclusion were and are, of course, defined, determined, and implemented by the modern state. In most states, the tighter regulation of immigration during the second half of the nineteenth century went hand in hand with a more liberal policy towards emigration. Different states, however, create(d) different categories for their own citizens and non-citizens living within their respective borders. And administrative officials in different states produce(d) their own sets of data that can be hard to link, making it difficult to reconstruct the paths of migrants and the development of migration networks across borders. In the United States, state officials have not registered the religious affiliation of citizens and immigrants. Large numbers of migrants who left the Russian Empire between the 1870s and 1914 did so illegally because it was difficult and expensive to obtain the paperwork required for legal emigration. The Austrian government severely penalised young men escaping the draft. Not surprisingly, young men who emigrated avoided officials as they crossed the border,[7] and few transit countries registered migrants travelling to another country before 1914. Migrants who left without informing the authorities in their home countries only became visible when officials in transit countries stopped them or when they (were) formally registered as immigrants. Archived records by transatlantic steamship lines make it possible to identify the nationality of migrants but usually do not indicate on which paths migrants reached (or departed from) a port. The introduction of the standardized international passport in the years after the First World War highlights increasing state control over migration, but also the rise of an internationally regulated system of cross-border movement.[8]

The impact of the expanding modern state alone does not explain the reluctance of migration historians to look beyond borders. Migration history emerged as a field of study with the rise of social history and ethnic studies during the 1960s. Not surprisingly, migration historians in the United States – a major destination country – examined primarily immigration and immigrant groups, and internal migrations. The openness of many migration historians to work across disciplinary boundaries, notably with social scientists, political scientists, and to a lesser extent with anthropologists, demographers and economists also imposed limitations, notably a preference for quantitative over qualitative analysis, and for micro rather than macro studies.[9] In the wake of the 'ethnic revival' of the 1960s, American and Canadian scholars researched especially members of their respective 'own' ethnic group. Until the late 1980s, relatively few American migration historians studied the context of out-migration for people bound for the United States from another part of the world. The process of migration (i.e. the actual journey), the links of migrants to their place of origin, and their membership in diasporic migrant networks, which stretched beyond a specific place, were also neglected.[10] Admittedly, scholars working on internal migration, for instance, of African Americans to northern cities during the first half of the twentieth century, did trace the migration routes and places of origin.[11] To this day little attention is devoted to inter-ethnic ties and migrant networks that encompassed members of different ethnic and religious groups.[12] Many West German, Scandinavian, Irish, British, and Polish scholars provided the missing link for American (and Canadian) immigration scholars by researching the context of out-migration from their respective states to North America during the nineteenth century, thus linking a nation state-centered analysis in Europe with the ethnic paradigm in American immigration history.[13]

During the 1980s and 1990s American and European migration historians began to pay greater respect to migration networks, especially on a regional level.[14] American immigration historians gradually shifted the focus from European immigrants (and African slaves) to immigrants from Latin America, the Caribbean, East and South Asia. This interest can be traced partly to the strongly rising immigration of non-Europeans after the liberalisation of American immigration policy in 1965. Roger Daniels and several other scholars helped to launch Asian American immigration history with pioneering studies. Daniels covered one of the most difficult chapters of the American involvement in the Second World War, the forced resettlement and detention of more than 70,000 American citizens of Japanese descent after the Japanese attack on Pearl Harbor in 1941. The U.S. government issued a formal apology for violating the constitutional rights of the interned citizens only in 1988. In recent years transpacific migration has emerged as a new subfield. In the twenty-first century, Asian and Latin American immigrant history (and social studies) are vibrant fields. Nevertheless, just as the nation state continues to define migration history in Europe, many American migration historians remain beholden to the 'ethnic paradigm'.[15]

History played an important role in a controversial debate about the immigration from Latin America to the United States, although the main participants were not historians. In his study *Who are We?* the influential political scientist Samuel Huntington alleged Mexican immigrants were undermining the core principles defining American society. Mexican immigrants and their American-born descendants, Huntington asserted, were creating a separate Spanish-speaking culture in the United States. Most reviewers rejected the very basis of Huntington's thesis – his data. He had simply ignored that second- and third generation immigrants from Mexico were overwhelmingly fluent in English. Shortly before Huntington's alarming scenario two sociologists, Victor Nee and Richard Alba, made a rather different case. They argued that the strong post-1965 immigration from Latin America and East and South Asia closely resembled the mass immigration to the United States from Eastern and Southern Europe between 1880 and 1914. Already in the 1890s a well-organised anti-immigration movement had depicted Eastern and Southern Europeans as inassimilable. The basic argument was surprisingly similar to the case Huntington presented in *Who are We?*. The earlier migrants were supposedly un-American because they were not Protestants but Catholics and Orthodox Christians, and Jews. Moreover, in the eyes of many, 'olive-skinned' Italians and Greeks were not 'white' enough to 'pass' as 'Americans'. An Australian immigration opponent characterised Italian immigrants in 1891 as the 'Chinese of Europe', echoing similar sentiments in the United States at the time. Immigrants from Latin America and Asia after 1965 faced similar accusations and little-disguised racist discrimination. Alba and Nee provided copious data to show that the post-1965 immigrants actually were (and are) joining the mainstream just like their much-despised predecessors from Europe.[16]

In the 1980s, European migration historians began researching nineteenth- and twentieth-century immigration to their respective own (but very rarely other) countries – at a time when leading political representatives denounced immigration and migrants encountered much discrimination, even violence. Historians like Gérard Noiriel in France or Colin Holmes in Britain participated in public debates and argued against widely held views describing immigration as a grave threat. Although the citizens of all European states share rather diverse backgrounds, this was and is rarely acknowledged. In his influential study, *John Bull's Island* about migration to Britain between 1871 and 1971, Holmes emphasised that migration to the British Isles has not been a modern, let alone recent phenomenon. As he put it in the introduction, counter to widespread views about English history, 'it would be difficult to locate an epoch when some immigration did not take place'. He went on to show how immigrants but also temporary migrants had shaped British society, economy and culture in important ways.[17] The comparative study *Immigrant Threat* by Leo Lucassen is a more recent and timely contribution to the controversy whether certain immigrants are supposedly inassimilable. Adapting the comparative approach of Alba and Nee, he shows that in Europe, too, unwanted immigrants who had arrived in the decades before the First World War had integrated successfully, in contrast to widely held views. Lucassen compared Poles in Germany, Irish in Britain, and Italians in France before 1914 with Turks in Germany, Algerians in France, and immigrants from the Caribbean in Britain after 1945, groups that are often accused of refusing to assimilate.[18]

Only quite recently have scholars on both sides of the Atlantic taken a closer look at migration as an extended and open process that cannot be reduced to 'emigration' and 'immigration'. For example, return rates for migrants who moved to the United States between 1820 and 1914 averaged at around 30 percent. In some cases, especially among migrants from Sicily and Southern Italy, up to 60 percent of 'immigrants' were sojourners who returned to their place of origin after a few years, sometimes repeating the journey across the Atlantic more than once or moving to urbanising regions in northern Italy. At the same time, more seasonal construction workers and peddlers from rural parts of northern Italy went to Imperial Germany and the Habsburg Monarchy than across the Atlantic. Return migration, correlations between local, regional and intercontinental migrations, and the nature of complex migration systems that straddled political and physical boundaries and sometimes oceans, remain understudied. Several innovative approaches can be traced to the early 1980s. The Labour Migration Project at the University of Bremen between 1980 and 1993 analysed class, gender, ethnicity, and extended migration processes in the Atlantic economy, without limiting the analysis to a single country of origin. And in a 1987 study Dutch historian Jan Lucassen traced the rise and gradual decline of the so-called North Sea System. This extensive pre-industrial migration system extended from Scandinavia to the British Isles, the Netherlands, and parts of Northwest Central Europe and included millions of people, mostly seasonal labour migrants.[19]

It is not possible here to discuss the gradual transformation of migration history after the end of the Cold War in more detail. Although the field has been slow to respond to the rise of global and transnational history, several articles, monographs, and essay collections point at a new agenda that takes the close relationship between local, regional, continental, and transcontinental migrations into account.[20] In recent years a number of studies have provided a better understanding of the global dimension of mass migrations after 1800, notably in different parts of Asia.[21] The migration of large numbers of people, even over long distances, is not a new phenomenon. Dirk Hoerder's impressive survey *Cultures in Contact* demonstrates that high mobility rates were the norm around the globe long before 1800. This point is particularly germane because American and European migration scholars (and most studies with a transnational approach) tend to focus on Europe and North America. Mobility rates were high throughout the last thousand years in most parts of the world. Long before the tenth century sophisticated migration and trade networks stretched across the Eurasian landmass, throughout Southeast Asia, and around the Indian Ocean.[22] *Cultures in Contact* offers detailed descriptions of these movements and, in fact, of processes of global integration, placing the better-known history of free and unfree migration in the Atlantic world in a larger context.

The field of regional and global refugee studies is still dominated by publications focusing on recent events, written by political and social scientists.[23] An important exception is Michael Marrus' *The Unwanted*, an influential synthesis of the refugee crises affecting Europe in the aftermath of the two World Wars. Marrus' study transcends the traditional focus on nation states and on well-known members of the intellectual elites who were permanently exiled after 1918, notably from the Russian Empire. Instead he looked at the conditions refugees and permanently displaced people experienced, at the inability of most states to address the plight of refugees, at the establishment of a permanent High Commissioner for Refugees at the League of Nations (and after 1945) at the United Nations, and at the role of humanitarian NGOs.[24]

The scholarship about mass migrations after 1800 remains constrained by three closely related paradigms: the focus on specific states or regions, on specific ethnic or national groups, and on immigration (and to a lesser extent emigration) rather than the process of migration. Migrants who were and are crossing one country en route to another elude categorisations such as 'immigrant' or 'emigrant'. During the long nineteenth century most transmigrants spent a few days travelling through transit countries, usually by train. Some stopped over for a few weeks or months in cities such as Berlin or London to earn some money for continuing the journey, frequently without registering with the authorities. Persons who were not immigrants or emigrants in the narrow sense of the word were sojourners who stayed only for a short time, for instance seasonal agricultural workers, travelling salesmen, artistic performers or highly specialised artisans, visitors, especially tourists, and refugees. Few studies retrace the paths of migration across different countries and continents.[25] Researching the journey routes can be challenging because states along the travel routes categorised migrants according to different criteria (or did not formally register them). Materials relating to transit journeys are kept in public and private archives in different countries. Another challenge is that the undocumented and unwanted migrant was and is a legal construct. Restrictions in different parts of the world have driven migrants into the arms of sophisticated smuggling networks. Collapsed states such as Libya have emerged as stopovers for migrants from West Africa and the Middle East trying to reach Europe.[26] The contemporary discussion about criminal smugglers who overcharge and abuse migrants conveniently shifts attention away from the actual causes to the symptoms. A historical analysis of illegal border crossings along Prussia's eastern border between 1870 and 1914 illustrates that 'smugglers' and 'illegal' travel agents often were facilitators who enabled migrants to circumvent rigid restrictions, admittedly for a price. For instance, most migrants leaving the Russian Empire between the 1870s and 1914 depended on smugglers because it was difficult and costly to obtain the official permit to emigrate and too dangerous to cross the border alone.[27]

Transmigration is a complex movement of different groups and individuals that is not easy to disentangle. During the long nineteenth century the industrialisation of modern travel led to the commodification train and ship journeys. A steadily growing number of people covered long distances within days instead of weeks or months. Even in the cheapest class, transoceanic journeys on steamships became relatively comfortable and safe compared to the harrowing conditions on sailing vessels that dominated the transatlantic run until the 1850s. Routine journeys are by definition uneventful and thus not newsworthy. Ship disasters, train accidents, even smaller disturbances provide rare insights because newspapers published the names of passengers, their origins, and destinations.[28] A study about transmigration also allows for a different perspective on the points of passage, notably railroad hubs and major port cities.[29]

Following migrants across borders shows that the migration policies of different states were closely related.[30] One example highlights these links. Imperial Germany and to a lesser extent Britain served as major transit countries for Eastern Europeans moving to North America between the early 1870s and 1914. The passage of laws regulating and restricting immigration to the United States after 1880 led to more systematic controls and rejections of transmigrants by Prussia, which shared long land borders with the Russian and Austro-Hungarian Empires. As the United States began screening arriving immigrants more closely and returned Eastern Europeans categorised as 'undesirable' in growing numbers after the mid-1880s, the Prussian state had to cover rising costs for accommodating and transporting involuntary Eastern European return migrants (who were often destitute). To reduce costs and avoid lengthy negotiations with the Russian authorities, Prussian officials began to turn many transmigrants back during the transit journey after 1885. In 1887, however, Prussia relaxed its treatment of transmigrants from Eastern Europe following the intervention by Imperial Germany's two leading steamship lines. To safeguard their strong position in Eastern Europe, both lines promised the Prussian state to cover all costs for involuntary return migrants. In the mid-1890s, following the passage of even more restrictive U.S. immigration legislation that focused on the containment of contagious disease, the two steamship lines began to operate several control stations along Prussia's eastern border with the Russian Empire where transmigrants were disinfected. Transmigrants could only enter the control stations if employees of the steamship lines judged they would pass U.S. immigration controls. Otherwise they were deported back across the nearby border. In return, the Prussian state protected the de facto monopoly of the two German steamship lines of the Eastern European passenger markets. Migrants who wanted to travel through Prussia with the ticket of a non-German steamship line were frequently rejected at the control stations or forced to buy the ticket of a German steamship line. In 1904, Germany's main Jewish aid organisation, the *Hilfsverein der Deutschen Juden*, and the

Social Democratic opposition party publicised the rejections of Russian migrants with tickets of the British Cunard steamship line at the control stations. To protect their reputation and retain the lucrative Russian passenger business, the steamship lines allowed the *Hilfsverein* to post a representative at each control station.[31]

The de facto privatisation of Prussia's eastern border controls highlights the little noticed impact of non-state actors such as steamship lines but also humanitarian organisations that operated between the borders of states, almost literally in transnational space. The influential position of the German steamship lines depended on their ability to control migration across a long land border in East Central Europe that neither Prussia nor Russia, let alone the United States could systematically police. Stringent migration restrictions that were passed in the wake of the First World War and fiercely contested and thus closely guarded borders in post-1918 Europe deprived steamship lines of their position as private border guards.

A closer look at Prussia's eastern border controls before 1914 demonstrates why examining migration processes beyond the confines of the nation state paradigm provides a more differentiated perspective. An exclusive focus on migration policies and immigrants in a certain state has long defined the field of migration history. Comparative studies contributed to a more differentiated understanding of migration history in different parts of the world. Yet retracing major travel routes across national boundaries shows that the migration policy of one state was often influenced by those of other states. The transnational perspective also reveals the soft power of non-state actors, such as steamship lines, but also humanitarian organisations supporting or representing migrants.

The rise of critical migration historiography represented by Colin Holmes and others during the 1970s and 1980s was in part a response to a contemporary debate about the supposed threat of immigration. Their studies demonstrated that migration was not a new phenomenon and deconstructed negative images of immigrants as permanent strangers. The growing interest in the history of refugees and in transnational migration history in recent years also reflects the complexity of contemporary migration processes and renewed calls to close borders. In the current debate the contributions of Holmes and other historians remain timely because they showed that migration is the norm and not the exception in the history of most societies.

Notes

1 This essay is partly based on a review essay I published in 2010: Tobias Brinkmann, 'Taking the Global View: Reconsidering Migration History after 1800', *Neue Politische Literatur* vol. 55, no. 2, 2010, 213–232.
2 See the essays in: 'The Jews in the modern world: beyond the nation', *Journal of Modern Jewish Studies* vol. 8, no. 3, 2008, 283–376; Julia Phillips Cohen, *Becoming Ottomans: Sephardi Jews and Imperial Citizenship in the Modern Era* (Oxford: Oxford University Press 2014); Devi Mays, '"I killed her because I loved her too much": gender and violence in the 20th-century Sephardi diaspora', *Mashriq & Mahjar: Journal of Middle Eastern Migration Studies* vol. 2, no. 1, 2014, 4–28.

3 An exception: Vincent Viaene (ed.), *The Papacy and the New World Order: Vatican Diplomacy, Catholic Opinion, and International Politics in the Time of Leo XIII, 1878–1903* (Leuven: Leuven University Press 2005).
4 Ira Katznelson, Pierre Birnbaum (eds), *Paths of Emancipation: Jews, States, and Citizenship* (Princeton: Princeton University Press 1995); exceptions are: Jonathan Frankel, *The Damascus Affair: 'Ritual Murder', Politics, and the Jews in 1840* (Cambridge: Cambridge University Press 1990); Sarah Abrevaya Stein, *Making Jews Modern: The Yiddish and Ladino Press in the Russian and Ottoman Empires* (Bloomington: Indiana University Press 2004); Rebecca Kobrin, *Jewish Bialystok and Its Diaspora* (Bloomington: Indiana University Press 2010).
5 For a useful overview (in German) see: Klaus J. Bade, 'Historische Migrationsforschung', *IMIS Beiträge* vol. 20, 2002, 20–44.
6 Annemarie Steidl, 'Introduction', in Annemarie Steidl et al. (eds), *European Mobility: Internal, International, and Transatlantic Moves in the 19th and 20th Centuries* (Göttingen: V&R Unipress 2009), 7–16 (quote: 7).
7 Tara Zahra, *Great Departure: Mass Migration from Eastern Europe and the Making of the Free World* (New York: W.W. Norton 2016).
8 John Torpey, 'The Great War and the birth of the modern passport system', in John Torpey, Jane Caplan (eds), *Documenting Individual Identity: The Development of State Practices in the Modern World* (Princeton: Princeton University Press 2001), 256–270; the League of Nations held a series of meetings during the 1920s that led to the adoption of standardised international passports, see for instance: League of Nations, Organisation for Communication and Transit, *Passport Conference, held in Geneva from May 12th to 18th, 1926, Minutes of the Plenary Meetings of the Conference* (Geneva: Publications of the League of Nations 1926).
9 Caroline Brettell et al. (eds), *Migration Theory: Talking Across Disciplines* (New York: Routledge 2000).
10 For an excellent overview of changing trends in recent American immigration and ethnic history see: Russell Kazal, 'Revisiting assimilation: the rise, fall, and reappraisal of a concept in American ethnic history', *American Historical Review* vol. 100, no. 2, 1995, 437–71; an important exception is the influential study by an American scholar on emigration from Germany: Mack Walker, *Germany and the Emigration 1816–1885* (Cambridge, MA: Harvard University Press 1964).
11 James Grossman, *Land of Hope: Chicago, Black Southerners, and the Great Migration* (Chicago: University of Chicago Press, 1989).
12 For a study that simultaneously highlights the division along ethnic lines and attempts to overcome it see: Peter d'A. Jones et al. (eds), *Ethnic Chicago: A Multicultural Portrait* (Grand Rapids, MI: Eerdmans 1995).
13 Dirk Hoerder et al. (eds), *People in Transit: German Migrations in Comparative Perspective, 1820–1920* (Cambridge: Cambridge University Press 1995); for an innovative recent study that examines emigration and settlement in North America see: Jochen Krebber, *Württemberger in Nordamerika: Migration von der Schwäbischen Alb im 19. Jahrhundert* (Stuttgart: Franz Steiner Verlag 2014).
14 Walter Kamphoefner, *The Westfalians: From Germany to Missouri* (Princeton: Princeton University Press 1987).
15 Roger Daniels et al. (eds), *Japanese Americans: From Relocation to Redress* (Seattle: University of Washington Press 1991); Roger Daniels, *Prisoners without Trial: Japanese Americans in World War II* (New York: Hill and Wang 1993); Mae M. Ngai, *Impossible Subjects: Illegal Aliens and the Making of Modern America* (Princeton: Princeton University Press 2003); Erika Lee, *At America's Gates: Chinese Immigration During the Exclusion Era, 1882–1943*

(Chapel Hill: University of North Carolina Press 2003); David M. Reimers, *Other Immigrants: The Global Origins of the American People* (New York: New York University Press 2005).

16 Samuel P. Huntington, *Who Are We? The Challenges to America's National Identity* (New York: Simon & Schuster 2004); Samuel P. Huntington, 'The Hispanic challenge', *Foreign Policy* vol. 141, 2004, 30–45; Louis Menand, 'Patriot games: the new nativism of Samuel P. Huntington', *New Yorker*, 17 May 2004; Richard Alba, Victor Nee, *Remaking the American Mainstream: Assimilation and Contemporary Immigration* (Cambridge: Harvard University Press 2003); 'Chinese of Europe' quoted after: Donna Gabaccia, 'The "Yellow Peril" and the "Chinese of Europe": global perspectives on race and labor, 1815–1930', in Jan Lucassen and Leo Lucassen (eds), *Migration, Migration History, History: Old Paradigms and New Perspectives* (Berne: Peter Lang 1997), 177–196; see also: Nancy Foner, *From Ellis Island to JFK: New York's Two Great Waves of Immigration* (New Haven: Yale University Press 2000).

17 Gérard Noiriel, *Le Creuset français: Histoire de l'immigration XIXe-XXe siècle* (Paris: Seuil, 1988); Colin Holmes, *John Bull's Island: Immigration and British Society, 1871–1971* (London: Macmillan 1988), 3; Ulrich Herbert, *Geschichte der Ausländerbeschäftigung in Deutschland 1880 bis 1980: Saisonarbeiter, Zwangsarbeiter, Gastarbeiter* (Bonn: Dietz, 1986).

18 Leo Lucassen, *The Immigrant Threat: The Integration of Old and New Migrants in Western Europe since 1850* (Urbana: University of Illinois Press 2005).

19 Mark Wyman, *Round-trip to America: The Immigrants Return to Europe, 1880–1930* (Ithaca: Cornell University Press 1993); Samuel L. Baily, *Immigrants in the Lands of Promise: Italians in Buenos Aires and New York City, 1870–1914* (Ithaca: Cornell University Press 1999); Dirk Hoerder (ed.), *Labor Migration in the Atlantic Economies. The European and North American Working Classes During the Period of Industrialization* (Westport: Greenwood 1985); Dirk Hoerder et al. (eds), *Distant Magnets: Expectations and Realities in the Immigrant Experience* (New York: Holmes & Meier 1993); Jan Lucassen, *Migrant Labor in Europe 1600–1900. The Drift to the North Sea* (London: Croom Helm, 1987); Adolf Wennemann, *Arbeit im Norden: Italiener im Rheinland und Westfalen des späten 19. und frühen 20. Jahrhunderts* (Osnabrück: Universitätsverlag Rasch, 1997).

20 See especially Nancy Green, 'The comparative method and poststructural structuralism: new perspectives for migration studies', in Jan Lucassen and Leo Lucassen (eds), *Migration, Migration History*, 57–72; Leo Lucassen, 'Migration and world history: reaching a new frontier', *International Review of Social History* vol. 52, no. 1, 2007, 89–96; a detailed overview of the historiography on migration with a focus on Germany: Jochen Oltmer: *Migration im 19. und 20. Jahrhundert* (Munich: De Gruyter/Oldenbourg 2016); see also: Leslie Page Moch, *Moving Europeans: Migration in Western Europe since 1650* (Bloomington: Indiana University Press 1992); Page Moch treats the German states and Imperial Germany as part of 'Western Europe'; Klaus J. Bade, *Migration in European History* (Oxford: Blackwell 2003); for a similarly sweeping work see Lewis H. Siegelbaum and Leslie Page Moch, *Broad Is My Native Land: Repertoires and Regimes of Migration in Russia's Twentieth Century* (Ithaca: Cornell University Press 2014).

21 Adam McKeown, 'Global migration, 1846–1940', *Journal of World History* vol. 15, no. 2, 2004, 155–190; Adam M. McKeown, *Melancholy Order: Asian Migration and the Globalization of Borders* (New York: Columbia University Press 2008); Sunil S. Amrith, *Crossing the Bay of Bengal: The Furies of Nature and the Fortunes of Migrants* (Cambridge: Harvard University Press, 2013).

22 Dirk Hoerder, *Cultures in Contact: World Migrations in the Second Millennium* (Durham NC: Duke University Press 2002); see also: Patrick Manning, *Migration in World History* (London: Routledge 2004).

23 Jessica Reinisch and Matthew Frank, '"The story stays the same"? Refugees in Europe from the "Forty Years" crisis to the present', in Jessica Reinisch and Matthew Frank (eds), *Refugees in Europe, 1919–1959: A Forty Years' Crisis?* (London: Bloomsbury 2017), 1–19.
24 Michael R. Marrus, *The Unwanted – European Refugees in the Twentieth Century* (Oxford: Oxford University Press 1985); for a study with a focus on Britain: Tony Kushner, Katharine Knox, *Refugees in an Age of Genocide* (Abingdon: Routledge 1999); see also for a recent study with a similar broad focus see: Zahra, *The Great Departure*.
25 Zosa Szajkowski, 'Suffering of Jewish emigrants to America in transit through Germany', *Jewish Social Studies*, vol. 29, 1977, 105–116; Lloyd Gartner, 'Jewish migrants en route from Europe to North America: traditions and realities', *Jewish History* vol. 1, no. 2, 1986, 49–66; see also the essays in: Tobias Brinkmann (ed.), *Points of Passage: Jewish Transmigrants from Eastern Europe in Scandinavia, Germany, and Britain 1880–1914* (New York: Berghahn, 2013); for an account about transmigration from 1912 see: Franz Markitan, *Auswanderungsverkehrswege in Österreich, Vortrag gehalten vor der Generalversammlung des österreichischen St.-Raphael-Vereins am 19. März 1912* (Vienna: Verlag des österr. St. Raphael-Vereins, 1912).
26 'Travelling in Hope', *The Economist*, 22 October 2016, 51–53; Kornel Chang, *Pacific Connections: The Making of the U.S.-Canadian Borderlands* (Berkeley: University of California Press 2012); Grace Delgado, *Making the Chinese Mexican: Global Migration, Localism, and Exclusion in the U.S.-Mexico Borderlands* (Stanford: Stanford University Press 2012).
27 Tara Zahra, 'Travel agents on trial: Policing mobility in East Central Europe, 1889–1989', *Past and Present* vol. 223, 2014, 161–193.
28 Drew Keeling, *The Business of Migration Between Europe and the United States, 1900–1914* (Zurich: Chronos, 2012), 244–246; Per Kristian Sebak, *Titanic's Predecessor: The S/S Norge Disaster of 1904* (Laksevaag: Seaward, 2004).
29 Tobias Brinkmann, 'Strangers in the city: transmigration from Eastern Europe and its impact on Berlin and Hamburg 1880–1914', *Journal of Migration History* vol. 2, no. 2, 2016, 223–246.
30 Aristide R. Zolberg, 'The Great Wall against China: responses to the first immigration crisis, 1885–1925', in Jan Lucassen and Leo Lucassen (eds), *Migration, Migration History, History*, 291–315.
31 Tobias Brinkmann, 'Why Paul Nathan attacked Albert Ballin: the transatlantic mass migration and the privatization of Prussia's eastern border inspection, 1886–1914', *Central European History* vol. 43, no. 1, 2010, 47–83.

4

CLASS VS. ETHNICITY

Concepts of migrant historiographies in Britain and (West) Germany, 1970s–1990s

Christhard Hoffmann

Academic interest in migrant history in Western Europe first developed in the 1970s within the expanding fields of social and labour history. While pioneer studies on the history of immigration and emigration had originated earlier in some European countries, the breakthrough of migrant historiography occurred only in connection with general changes and innovations in the study of history, above all the rise of social history in the 1960s and 1970s. Challenging the established ways of historiography that focused on the reconstruction of political events and ideas, the new social history was interested in social structures and processes, such as urbanisation and industrialisation, inequality and class conflict, mobility and social change. It put in the limelight those social groups that traditional history writing had overlooked, above all workers, women, immigrants and ethnic minorities. Consequently, class, gender and ethnicity became central categories of historical analysis.[1]

Initiated by pioneer scholars such as Colin Holmes in Britain, Klaus Jürgen Bade in West Germany, Gérard Noiriel in France, Harald Runblom in Sweden and Jan Lucassen in the Netherlands, migration history as a field of research emerged in the 1970s and 1980s. It created informal networks of historians, meeting at conferences and contributing to new journals such as *Immigrant and Minorities*. As an academic field, migration history remained rather loosely institutionalised. It is symptomatic for the self-understanding of European migration historians as *social historians* that their most important transnational meeting place since 1996 has been the biennial European Social Science History Conference organised by the International Institute of Social History in Amsterdam.

An additional factor is important here: migrant historiography in Western Europe emerged against the background of contemporary immigration. After the Scond World War, West European countries recruited foreign workers from former colonies or as 'guest-workers' to fill the labour shortages in the growing economies. In the 1970s, at the latest, recruitment stopped but it became clear that many of these foreign workers and their families had come to stay. In the emerging public debates about immigration policies and the integration of newcomers, an historical perspective was often missing. By studying the immigration of the past and exploring general patterns of state and majority responses to newcomers and of minority integration into majority society, historians could fill this gap and thereby enlighten contemporary disputes on the immigration issue.[2]

A crucial question of any historiography is the use of analytical frameworks and explanatory concepts. I will have a closer look at how West German and British historians during the 1970s and 1980s applied the concepts of *class* and *ethnicity* in their narratives about immigrant workers of the late nineteenth and early twentieth centuries. While class and ethnicity are broad and complex analytical categories that have various meanings in different ideological and political contexts,[3] I will specify their significance for migrant historiography by looking at two opposing approaches that were dominant at the beginning of the 1970s.

In their influential book *Immigrant Workers and Class Structure in Western Europe*, published by the Institute of Race Relations in 1973, sociologists Stephen Castles and Godula Kosack introduced a Marxist analysis of contemporary labour immigration to West Europe. Explaining the import of foreign labour by the needs of the capitalist economy to maintain flexibility in the labour market, Castles and Kosack analysed the consequences of this immigration (such as a split labour market and a growing antagonism between indigenous and foreign workers) for the class structure of European countries. In their interpretation, the ethnicity of immigrant workers is completely insignificant:

> Immigrants [they claim], should be looked at not in the light of their specific group characteristics – ethnic, social, cultural – but in terms of their actual social position. Immigrant workers have come to form part of the class structure of the immigration countries. This in turn has effects on the economic, social, and political situation of all other classes.[4]

Castles and Kosack thus applied a traditional Marxist understanding of ethnicity as 'the mask that conceals class identity'.[5] Ethnicity is only of minor explanatory significance and needs to be 'stripped off in order to discover the "real" relations underneath'.[6]

By contrast, at the same time American migration scholars established *ethnicity* as their key frame of analysis. Based on new research on ethnic identities among minority migrant groups and their descendants in New York, political scientists Nathan Glazer and Daniel Moynihan, in their epoch-making book *Beyond the Melting Pot*, proposed a new conception of ethnicity. In contrast to a primordial definition of ethnicity as an ancient, unchanging and objective entity, Glazer and Moynihan viewed ethnicity as instrumental and situational. It is (in migrant groups) not identical with the ethnic culture of origin, but typically a post-immigration phenomenon. In ethnically pluralist societies, it serves as a means of mobilising immigrant groups to improve their socioeconomic position.[7] Glazer and Moynihan in this way defined ethnic groups as interest groups. They found that in the urban environment of New York City, 'ethnicity and class and religion are inevitably tied to each other'.[8] This conceptualisation opened up for an understanding of class and ethnicity as overlapping influences, rather than as opposites.

In what ways did European social historians, writing in the 1970s and 1980s about immigrant workers of the late nineteenth and early twentieth centuries, follow these two different paradigms – the class-based and the ethnicity-based approaches? Using the historiography on the Polish-speaking workers (*Ruhrpolen*) in the German Empire and on Eastern European Jewish immigrant workers in Britain as my main cases, I will argue that the predominance of the socioeconomic approach and the corresponding reluctance to use an American concept of ethnicity in European migrant historiographies may be understood in two broader contexts: 1. the historical European experiences of ethnic prejudice and ethnonationalistic conflict that culminated in the first half of the twentieth century; 2. the contemporary European experience of labour immigration that was evidently determined by the needs and business cycles of the capitalist economy.

Ethnicity as a relic or a resource? The historiography of the *Ruhrpolen*

The historiography of the Polish miners at the Ruhr developed parallel to the recruitment of foreign labour in West Germany. When the 'guest-workers' arrived from southern Europe in the 1950s and 1960s, a historical narrative gained prominence in the public that emphasised the successful integration of newcomers in German history. Communicated in public discourse, most prominently in political statements, speeches and in the media, this narrative emphasised the Huguenots of the seventeenth century and the Ruhr Poles of the nineteenth and early twentieth centuries as the most prominent examples of successful integration. It thereby bypassed the immediate experience and fresh memory of foreign slave labour in Germany during World War II.[9] The invention of a German tradition of tolerance and integration of foreigners projected an ideal onto the past that in reality never existed in such form and was rather a hopeful projection into the future.

It was only in the late 1970s that academic research on German migrant history gained momentum and social historians produced critical, differentiated and thoroughly researched accounts of the history of foreign labour in Germany. These showed a quite different picture compared to the idealised narrative of a German tradition of tolerance. In particular, the Prussian system of controlled importation of foreigners before the First World War was at the centre of scholarly attention.[10] This system allowed for the use of foreign labour (mainly as seasonal workers in agriculture) while preventing permanent settlement, and thereby introduced a tradition of institutionalised discrimination of foreign workers according to national origin and social status. These findings informed contemporary debates about the policy towards 'guest-workers' in West Germany.[11] In discussing the incorporation of newcomers, the *Ruhr Poles* (who were Prussian subjects and thus German citizens in the German Empire) became the main history of reference.

Christoph Kleßmann's important study on the Polish-speaking miners of the Ruhr area is a good example for the views of a new generation of West German social historians on questions of migrant labour and ethnicity.[12] In his book, Kleßmann focused on the tension between the social integration of the Polish miners on the one hand and the establishment of a national Polish subculture, with separate associations, schools, newspapers and even a Polish trade union, on the other. Between 1870 and 1914, almost half a million Poles moved from the agrarian Prussian Eastern provinces into the highly industrialised areas of the Ruhr. Why did they not assimilate to the same degree as other newcomer groups from the East, in particular the predominantly Protestant Masurians who spoke a Polish dialect? In his answer, Kleßmann points to the German 'Polish Question' and the politics of forced Germanisation and anti-Polish discrimination by the German government as the main barriers towards integration. Polish ethnic segregation, he argued, was primarily a response to the experience of anti-Polish oppression by the authorities. The bitter political conflict between German nationalists and the Polish minority that was virulent in the Eastern Prussian provinces also influenced the living conditions and identities of the Polish miners in the Ruhr area. It created a climate of ethnic demarcation and interfered with the 'natural' process of absorption of the Polish miners into the German working class and the local Catholic milieu. The consequences of this development were mostly negative. Kleßmann reads the Herne riots of 1899, caused by Polish wildcat strikers who protested against a rise in contributions to the miners' insurance fund, as proof of the lack of orientation, organisation and integration of the Polish workers. Following Shmuel N. Eisenstadt's 1951 model of the cultural and social adaptation of immigrants, he specified 'disorientation, delinquency, alcoholism and wildcat strikes' as indicators of deviant behaviour caused by a failed adaptation process, and established proof of all those criteria in the early phase of Polish settlement.[13] By subsequently building their own network of societies that paralleled the associational culture of their German-speaking environment, the Poles fostered group cohesion that, as Kleßmann suggested at one point, paradoxically may have contributed to their long-term integration.[14] Still, the main line of interpretation in Kleßmann and other German social and labour historians at the time followed an underlying model of historical evolution that classified ethnic identities among industrial workers as an obstacle to the development of a common working-class consciousness and coordinated action.[15] The 'retreat by the Poles into the defensive protection of their ethnic social milieu' (as Ulrich Herbert described the self-understanding of the Polish miners),[16] was therefore seen as dysfunctional and divisive, as an aberration from the normal path of modernisation and a weakening of the working-class movement.

The American historian Richard C. Murphy turned this pessimistic interpretation upside down in his 1983 book on the Polish migrant community in the town of Bottrop during the Wilhelmian Era. Viewing ethnicity as a resource rather than a relic, he maintained that the Polish efforts of community building should be understood as 'positive steps in the formation of the new urban society in the Ruhrgebiet', thus creating 'a German version of the plural society'.[17] Emphasising the upward social mobility and the active participation of the Polish coal miners in economic life, Murphy presented their history as a 'success story of American dimensions'.[18] By establishing their own trade union, the *Ruhrpolen* were able 'to force acceptance, not as assimilated in-migrants, but as a distinct ethnic group which formed a valuable part of the economic system of the city and the Ruhrgebiet as a whole'.[19] Murphy's optimistic interpretation met with harsh criticism by German labour historians, such as Klaus Tenfelde,[20] but in the 1990s, it was vindicated and elaborated on by the Polish-American labour historian John J. Kulczycki. Criticising West German historians as biased against the Polish immigrant workers when portraying them as unexperienced and non-committed towards class solidarity and collective action, Kulczycki presented a counter-narrative, based on a thorough analysis of four major strikes between 1893 and 1912, that was equally straightforward: it was the xenophobia of the German workers, not the ethnic segregation of the Poles that, at least initially, inhibited class solidarity in the Ruhr.[21] The Polish-speaking miners were (more than) committed to coordinated action with their German comrades and participated in strikes enthusiastically. Taking the lessons of these findings to the conceptual level, Kulczycki concluded that class and ethnicity should not be understood as opposites but rather as mutually reinforcing influences:

> [T]he evidence suggests that their [the Poles'] ethnic consciousness gave an edge to their class consciousness, which resulted in greater militancy in the cause of the working class than found among their fellow workers.

Consequently, Kulczycki used the term 'ethno-class consciousness' to describe the self-understanding of the Polish workers in the Ruhr.[22]

The differences of interpretation between West German historians on the one side and their two American colleagues on the other originated mainly from opposing views on ethnicity. While Murphy and Kulczycki understood ethnicity in an 'American' perspective and defined ethnic groups as interest groups in a pluralist migrant society, West German historians, by contrast, explained the ethnic segregation of the Polish workers primarily in the context of the bitter German-Polish ethno-nationalistic antagonism before 1945. Ethnicity was, for them, a relic of a past that should be overcome rather than serve as a model for the future.

Discovering the immigrant Jewish working class in Britain

British historiography on immigrants and minorities was more comprehensive, manifold and advanced than in Germany. This was partly due to the richer experience of Britain as a country of immigration. In contrast to Germany, a continuity of immigrant communities existed which preserved their own cultural legacy and produced community histories.[23] Emphasising intra-community solidarity and harmonising internal differences, these histories also fitted well into the hegemonic liberal narrative of Britain as a tolerant country of immigration. It was against this backdrop that a new social-historically (and sometimes Marxist) oriented migrant historiography in Britain developed in the early 1970s, challenging the Whig interpretation of British immigration history and introducing a class perspective to community history. The case of Jewish migrant historiography is most illustrating in this respect.

Already in 1960, in his pioneer study on the Jewish immigrant in England, the American scholar Lloyd P. Gartner had effectively challenged the liberal narrative of Anglo-Jewish community history by exploring the sensitive issue of immigration restriction within the Jewish community. In his portrayal of the immigrant Jewish worker, Gartner followed contemporary accounts that had described the Jewish worker as an economic individualist mostly interested in social advancement and lacking a strong sense of working-class solidarity.[24] In contrast to these earlier commentators, however, Gartner explained the differences between the Jewish and the English worker not by innate ethnic qualities, but by situational factors. 'His [the Jewish workman's] individualism in part reflected the instability of the immigrant trades, where the bridge from entrepreneur to workman and back was a short one'.[25] Because of the organisation of the (small) Jewish workshops in London and the anti-Jewish bias of English workers, unionisation among Jewish immigrant workers remained unstable.

Attacking Gartner and virtually all other historians working in the field as representatives of 'bourgeois historiography', Joseph Buckman, in his 1983 book *Immigrants and the Class Struggle* introduced a Marxist interpretation that resolutely put the Jewish worker to the fore and emphasised class, class conflict and socio-economic segregation within the Leeds Jewish community.[26] He placed the history of the Jewish immigrant worker into the broader context of contemporary developments in British economic and labour history and thereby brought 'the study of the Jewish community back into the mainstream of English historiography'.[27] Drawing on various sources, in particular the Yiddish socialist press, Buckman documented in close detail the bitter conflict between Jewish sweatshop masters and their Jewish workers in the Leeds clothing and slipper industries, emphasised the unionisation of the Jewish workers and concluded that the class struggle overrode ethnic-religious bonds.[28] Buckman founded his 'class not ethnicity' thesis solely on the antagonism at the workplace. He did not investigate whether the class conflict spilled over to non-economic spheres, into synagogues and other Jewish institutions. He simply assumed that proletarian loyalties and traditional ethnic-religions attachments were mutually exclusive and thereby ignored (as Todd Endelman put it in a critical review of Buckman's book): 'that workers could engage in trade union activity without completely abandoning traditional religious and ethnic sentiments'.[29]

With his narrow frame of interpretation and his snubbing attitude towards fellow historians, Buckman remained more of an outsider. His general approach, however, of researching class tensions within allegedly unified ethnic communities and, in particular, exploring Jewish trade unionism as a part of British working-class history was shared by several social historians, for example Bill Williams and Jerry White.[30] Studying the beginnings of Jewish trade unionism in Manchester in the broader perspective of English trade union history, Williams demonstrated the shortcomings of an isolated 'Jewish' perspective and showed the 'limitations of relying on real or supposed ethnic characteristics to interpret the labour history of minority groups'.[31] By rediscovering the lost history of the immigrant Jewish working class, these contributions aimed at integrating Jewish history into British labour history. The priority of 'class' over 'ethnicity' that was characteristic for these approaches became manifest in White's formulation that the immigrants formed 'a working class community that happened to be Jewish'.[32]

In her studies of trade unionism amongst Jewish tailoring workers of London and Leeds, Anne J. Kershen reached a different conclusion.[33] While she, too, saw the experiences and struggles of Jewish workers not in isolation but within the broader context of the British working class, she nevertheless maintained that *ethnicity mattered* in shaping the relations between Jewish employers and employees in the tailoring trades. Especially in the small-scale units of production where master and workers knew each other well and not only met in the workshop, but also in the synagogue or at other community events, 'class division did not always override communal ties ... but was at times blurred by the nexus of community'.[34] Personal contact and religious ties in small-scale workshop relations could thus weaken trade union affiliation. In contrast to earlier notions about the 'individualism' and 'lack of solidarity' of Jewish workers, this explanation did not argue with innate ethnic qualities, but with situational and organisational factors. Where the workforce was less fluctuant, and the infrastructure of the tailoring trade differently organised, the unionisation of Jewish tailoring workers was no less strong and successful than their English counterparts.

Criticising both an ethnic and a class perspective on Jewish immigrant labour as simplistic, David Feldman, in a critical historiographical review article of 1983,[35] and later, fleshed out in detail in his book *Englishmen and Jews* (1994), emphasised the 'plurality of axes of conflict and cooperation' that was characteristic for the experience of Jewish immigrant workers in London.[36] This experience was shaped by '[s]ectionalism and class conflict, collectivism and rivalry, worker militancy and cooperation with employers' and hence 'too diffuse to be captured by any single vision of collective interest and identity'.[37] In his view, not only the clear-cut alternative between class and ethnic identities was wrong, since historical studies found many overlaps in both class-based and ethnic affiliations, but also the attempt to understand the complexities of Jewish immigrant experience exclusively with the help of these two categories was reductive and led to distorted images of the past.[38]

Feldman's attempt to deconstruct the established class–ethnicity antagonism as the major frame of interpretation and to introduce a more sophisticated model of understanding Jewish immigrant identities represented a new historiographical approach of the 1990s. Influenced by the 'linguistic turn' in historiography, and the extension of labour-focused social history with a new cultural history, it questioned fixed and unambiguous definitions of identity of historical actors and rather stressed the complexities of multiple layers of social interaction. This new approach emphasised the fluidity of identity-formations and shaped the historiography not only of Jewish immigrants but of other immigrant groups as well. In his book *Class and Ethnicity: Irish Catholics in England, 1880–1939*, published in 1993, Stephen Fielding argued along these lines by demonstrating the shortcomings of a class-based narrative that had no room for the Irish Catholic identity within the conception of a homogeneous working-class culture.[39] In the same way, the introduction of 'equally homogeneous and static, ethnic cultures' seemed one-sided.[40] Fielding underlined that the experience of Irish Catholic immigrants was 'the result of a complex interweaving of ethnic and class influences'.[41] Rejecting both, full assimilation and complete separation, for them 'class and ethnicity formed a continuum, not mutually exclusive poles of attraction'.[42]

Conclusion

The dominant approach of migrant historiography in Britain and West Germany during the 1970s and 1980s was shaped by the conceptual framework of social history. It explored, often for the first time, the role of immigrants within the labour market, their settlement and housing conditions and their social mobility. Conflicts between majority societies and immigrant minorities that found its expression in xenophobic hostility and anti-immigrant discrimination were largely attributed to social, economic (and sometimes political) causes. In the same way, intra-community tensions within minority groups were explained by social differences and class conflict. In this manner, the social history approach to immigration aimed at deconstructing traditional views, in both historiography and the public, that were anchored in ethnic categories and used the 'innate character' of Poles, Jews or the Irish as an explanation. The priority of class over ethnicity was also apparent in the historiography on immigrant labour. Based on a progressive concept of historical development, labour historians had little understanding for the maintaining of religious or ethnic loyalties among immigrant workers, and often saw it as a regression, deviating from the 'normal' course of modernisation.

In the 1990s, ethnicity was (re)introduced as a concept to migrant historiography. This is more evident in Britain than in Germany, where it was, as we have seen in the historiography on the Polish miners at the Ruhr, only used by American historians. To be sure, this concept was very different from the older understanding of ethnicity as an objective, primordial affiliation. It was rather defined as subjective and ascribed, as situational and fluid. This concept of ethnicity was not seen as opposite to class. Accordingly, studies emphasised the interplay between ethnic and socioeconomic concerns in immigrant groups: John Kulczycki used the term 'ethno-class consciousness' and Panikos Panayi spoke of class-based ethnicity to emphasise that these two categories were not mutually exclusive.[43] The strict class–ethnicity dichotomy was undermined further by the introduction of other concepts to migrant historiography, in particular gender and religion. The 'linguistic turn' and the rise of cultural history also left its mark on migrant historiographies in the 1990s.

With its attention on concrete examples, the study of historiography provides many opportunities for methodological self-reflection and learning. The general question I have discussed here is about the significance of theory in the writing of history and, more specifically, about the application of modern sociological concepts to the often diverse experiences and conflicting self-understandings of historical actors. While this is a general challenge for historians, nobody, I believe, has made this point clearer with respect to migrant history than Colin Holmes. By cautioning the historian against the use of broad, all-encompassing sociological concepts, such as 'ethnicity' or 'racism' in a simplistic manner,[44] by carefully reconstructing the complexities of historical situations, and not least by insisting on precision and nuance in the historical narrative itself, his work has remained a model of migrant historiography.

Notes

1 See George G. Iggers, *New Directions in European Historiography*, revised ed. (Middletown CT: Wesleyan University Press 1984); Lex Heerma van Voss and Marcel van der Linden (eds), *Class and Other Identities: Gender, Religion and Ethnicity in the Writing of European Labour History* (Oxford and New York: Berghahn 2002).
2 Colin Holmes' participation in the TV programme *Passage to Britain* (Channel 4, 1984) is an early example for the public commitment of the migrant historian.
3 See Christopher McAll, *Class, Ethnicity, and Social Inequality* (Montreal and Kingston: McGill-Queen's University Press 1990).
4 Stephen Castles and Godula Kosack, *Immigrant Workers and Class Structure in Western Europe* (Oxford: Oxford University Press 1973), 5.
5 McAll, *Class, Ethnicity and Social Inequality*, 70.
6 Ibid., 75.
7 Nathan Glazer and Daniel P. Moynihan, *Beyond the Melting Pot: The Negroes, Puerto Ricans, Jews, Italians, and Irish of New York City*. 2nd edn (Cambridge MA and London: The M.I.T. Press 1970), 17.
8 Ibid., 5.
9 Karen Schönwälder, *Einwanderung und ethnische Pluralität: Politische Entscheidungen und öffentliche Debatten in Großbritannien und der Bundesrepublik von den 1950er bis zu den 1970er Jahren* (Essen: Klartext 2001), 168–170, 193, 203.
10 See Klaus J. Bade, '"Preußengänger" und "Abwehrpolitik": Ausländerbeschäftigung, Ausländerpolitik und Ausländerkontrolle auf dem Arbeitsmarkt in Preußen vor dem Ersten Weltkrieg', *Archiv für Sozialgeschichte*, vol. 24, 1984, 91–162; Ulrich Herbert, *A History of Foreign Labor in Germany* (Ann Arbor: University of Michigan Press 1990).
11 Klaus J. Bade, *Vom Auswanderungsland zum Einwanderungsland? Deutschland 1880–1980* (Berlin: Colloquium Verlag 1983); Friedrich Heckmann, *Die Bundesrepublik: Ein Einwanderungsland? Zur Soziologie der Gastarbeiterbevölkerung als Einwandererminorität* (Stuttgart: Klett-Cotta 1981), 146–149.

12 Christoph Kleßmann, *Polnische Bergarbeiter im Ruhrgebiet 1870–1945* (Göttingen: Vandenhoeck & Ruprecht 1978).
13 Christoph Kleßmann, *Polnische Bergarbeiter im Ruhrgebiet 1870–1945*, 74–82.
14 Ibid., 190.
15 See, for example, Klaus Tenfelde, 'Die "Krawalle von Herne" im Jahre 1899', *IWK – Internationale wissenschaftliche Korrespondenz zur Geschichte der deutschen Arbeiterbewegung*, vol. 15, 1979, 71–104 (90); Tenfelde, *Sozialgeschichte der Bergarbeiterschaft an der Ruhr im 19. Jahrhundert*, 2nd edn (Bonn: Verlag Neue Gesellschaft 1981), 246.
16 Herbert, *History of Foreign Labor*, 81.
17 Richard Charles Murphy, *Guestworkers in the German Reich: A Polish Community in Wilhelmian Germany* (Boulder CO: East European Monographs 1983), 7.
18 Ibid., 189.
19 Ibid., 78.
20 Klaus Tenfelde, 'Review of Guestworkers in the German Reich', *Archiv für Sozialgeschichte*, vol. 26, 1986, 659–661.
21 John J. Kulczycki, *The Foreign Worker and the German Labor Movement: Xenophobia and Solidarity in the Coal Fields of the Ruhr* (Oxford and Providence RI: Berg Publishers 1994), 152.
22 Ibid., 262.
23 See Tony Kushner (ed.), *The Jewish Heritage in British History: Englishness and Jewishness* (Abingdon: Frank Cass 1992); Panikos Panayi, 'The historiography of immigrants and ethnic minorities: Britain compared with the USA', in Martin Bulmer and John Solomos (eds), *Ethnic and Racial Studies Today* (London and New York: Routledge 1999), 60–72; Kathy Burrell and Panikos Panayi (eds), *Histories and Memories: Migrants and their History in Britain* (London and New York: Tauris 2006).
24 Lloyd P. Gartner, *The Jewish Immigrant in England, 1870–1914* (London: Allen & Unwin 1960), 64–66.
25 Ibid., 67.
26 Joseph Buckman, *Immigrants and the Class Struggle: The Jewish Immigrant in Leeds, 1880–1914* (Manchester: Manchester University Press 1983), viii–xii.
27 Bill Williams, 'Review Buckman', *Social History*, vol. 10, no. 1, 1985, 123–127 (125).
28 Buckman, *Immigrants*, 61, 162–165.
29 Todd Endelman, 'Review Buckman', *Victorian Studies*, vol. 29, no. 3, 1986, 473–474 (474).
30 Bill Williams, 'The beginnings of Jewish trade unionism in Manchester, 1889–1891', in Kenneth Lunn (ed.), *Hosts, Immigrants and Minorities: Historical Responses to Newcomers in British Society 1870–1914* (Folkestone: Dawson 1980), 263–307; Jerry White, *Rothschild Buildings: Life in an East End Tenement Block, 1887–1929* (London: Routledge and Kegan Paul 1980).
31 Williams, 'Beginnings', 298.
32 White, *Rothschild Buildings*, xv.
33 Anne J. Kershen, 'Trade unionism amongst the Jewish tailoring workers of London and Leeds, 1872–1914', in: David Cesarani (ed.), *The Making of Modern Anglo-Jewry* (Oxford: Basil Blackwell 1990), 34–52; Anne J. Kershen, *Uniting the Tailors: Trade Unionism amongst the Tailoring Workers of London and Leeds, 1870–1939* (Ilford: Frank Cass 1995).
34 Kershen, 'Trade unionism', 41.
35 David Feldman, 'There was an Englishman, an Irishman and a Jew …Immigrants and minorities in Britain', *The Historical Journal* vol. 26, no.1, 1983, 185–199 (193f.).
36 David Feldman, *Englishmen and Jews: Social Relations and Political Culture, 1840–1914* (New Haven and London: Yale University Press 1994), 256.

37 Ibid., 255–256.
38 Ibid., 256–257.
39 Stephen Fielding, *Class and Ethnicity: Irish Catholics in England, 1880–1939* (Buckingham and Philadelphia: Open University Press 1993), 3.
40 Ibid., 11.
41 Fielding, *Class and Ethnicity*, 12.
42 Ibid.
43 Panikos Panayi, *Immigration, Ethnicity and Racism in Britain 1815–1945* (Manchester and New York: Manchester University Press 1994), 77, 98.
44 See, in particular, Colin Holmes, *John Bull's Island: Immigration and British Society, 1871–1971* (Basingstoke and London: Macmillan 1988), 275–317.

SECTION 2
Places and spaces

Tony Kushner

Introduction

Drawing upon the classic work of anthropologist Mary Douglas, *Purity and Danger* (1966), David Sibley has emphasised how 'the boundaries of society are continually redrawn to distinguish between those who belong and those who, because of some perceived cultural difference, are deemed to be out of place'.[1] From at least the early modern era, and the creation of the Venetian ghetto in 1516,[2] there has been an often violent tradition of excluding those regarded as racially, ethnically and religiously different from certain areas regarded as 'pure' and 'clean'. These 'others' have then been removed totally or confined to lesser spaces so as to limit their contaminating influence. In turn, the contemporary and later representation of these 'polluting' minority groups has often been pathological too, legitimating, as Sibley notes, 'the boundaries of the acceptable' by portraying the 'other … as less than human'.[3]

The 'other', however, has not been without agency in both challenging the construction of boundaries – whether local, national or regional – and in restoring humanity through self-development and self-representation thus defying the negative mythology associated with them. The four chapters in *Places and Spaces* highlight such resistance either through sheer presence – what Peter Fryer famously labelled *Staying Power* in relation to black British history – or through cultural and artistic interventions relating to them – in short, how these 'real' places are constructed imaginatively and positively as migrant 'spaces'.[4]

Whilst Anne Witchard also explores the 'Chinatown' of Liverpool as well as Limehouse, there is a focus throughout this section on London and even then, certain areas within it, especially the East End. That the metropole of what became the world's largest modern empire should have a particularly rich immigrant history is unsurprising. But Panikos Panayi goes further and argues for the 'uniqueness' of London (embracing many different parts of the capital) in possessing a 'long term and continuous history of migrant settlement' leading to a 'superdiversity' not shared elsewhere in Britain. His model can be gently queried by highlighting that, even with all the progress made in migrant historiography, there are no intensively researched *local* versions of Colin Holmes' *John Bull's Island* – even for cities such as Manchester which have essentially been shaped by immigration. This lacuna is even more the case for small towns, villages and the countryside where the foundation myth of homogeneity is often shaken by the sympathetic interrogation of sources. As Caroline Bressey, who features in this section, has written elsewhere, 'white imaginaries of the English rural have ignored historical geographies of the black presence'.[5]

The 'place' index of *John Bull's Island* includes 169 British entries, only forty-seven of which relate to London.[6] Economic and other opportunities explain the specific attractions of the capital city to migrants and their descendants, and size enabled the flourishing of minority subcultures there, including divisions within them based on class, politics, gender, sexuality, age and religion. At particular moments, most British large towns and cities experienced at least one major migrant influx with the dynamism that then resulted. If Panayi is right that only a small number of urban sites witnessed multiple and continuous large-scale movements, all, or almost all, could locate a varied migrant presence in their histories once an effort was made to find it. Similarly, the East and Southern Europeans who are playing such a crucial role in British agriculture today are part of a longer-term rural tradition of settlement from overseas.

In her evocative and important historiographical intervention, *Lovers & Strangers* (2017), subtitled *An Immigrant History of Post-War Britain*, Clair Wills reveals a gap in her expertise when she suggests that those that came after 1945 came to a 'still largely ethnically homogenous Britain'. Wills rightly undermines the '*Windrush* myth' through which there has been a focus on (male) West Indian migrants to the exclusion of so many other arrivals in the 1940s and 1950s and then beyond.[7] She is, however, unconvincing when downplaying the significance of earlier arrivals, suggesting that 'previous waves of migrants such as the Irish and the Jews had either become ghettoized "local colour" or … absorbed into the English working class'.[8] Such marginalisation of the pre-1945 migrant presence is, as the contributions to this section make clear, unjustified but it reveals the need, even in the case of a sympathetic author, for more local studies to counter such assumptions.

The harder task still, given the power of xenophobic tendencies, is to challenge assumptions of the ethnic 'purity' of 'old England'. As Doreen Massey emphasised, 'The identity of places is very much bound up with the *histories* which are told of them, *how* those histories are told, and which memory turns out to be dominant'.[9] The articles in this section reveal the memory wars concerning migrants in particular places and spaces and how they have been represented. At a more basic level is the struggle to acknowledge the very presence of such groups who challenge the belief that the 'local' can somehow be isolated and kept pure from the 'global'. We must remember that 'Local uniqueness', as Massey again insisted, 'is always already a product of wider contacts; the local is … a product in part of "global" forces'.[10]

Bressey's chapter not only highlights the depth of presence, but the importance of specific spaces such as schools, bookshops and other less formal meeting places in the politics and culture of black London. She also reveals the potential of the digital revolution in recovering these histories and enabling spaces to be reclaimed, including those that witnessed intensely diverse working-class communities made up of many different migrant and non-migrant groups – and not simply more obvious ones such as the East End of London. Both her contribution and that of Anne Witchard outline how even when migrant histories are rediscovered, as with the *Windrush*, Massey's maxim can still operate. *Other* migrant stories and other chronologies can become lost or marginalised.

In her study of the 'Chinatowns' of London and Liverpool, Witchard shows the diversity of approaches contemporaries adapted to the Chinese presence. Although exclusion and deportation were ever present as part of the fears associated with the 'Yellow Peril', there were others who engaged more deeply and thoughtfully and were even inspired by the Chinese in their midst. For them, especially in the artistic and literary world, there was an awareness of commonality, and, as with the author Lao She, important interventions from Chinese writers themselves. Through studying such connections, Witchard argues for the 'transnational nature of literary modernism', reinforcing Massey's perspective on the intricate relationship between the local and the global.

The *particularity* of places runs through these four contributions, but so does their fluidity across time and space. How they were imagined becomes of equal importance and as Anne Kershen's chapter emphasises, all major migrant groups to the East End have done so themselves, if, tellingly, at different speeds and influence in wider society. Kershen brings in the work of sociologists, anthropologists and political scientists to understand patterns of migrant settlement in Spitalfields. She also shows the importance of literary sources in confronting an area – the East End – which itself has 'flexible boundaries' in the eye of the beholder. Taken together, these chapters emphasise the importance of the 'spatial turn' in studying migration and the necessity of bringing in as wide a range of sources as possible, 'traditional' and otherwise, to do so. Space, as Kershen insists, is often contested and these studies here, and the historiographies they critically build upon, do not always present a 'fluffy' multiculturalism. Indeed, they reveal hostility from the 'outside' and tensions from 'within'. But what they do illustrate collectively is the centrality of migrant resistance and the ongoing struggle against exclusion in the makings and remakings of places and spaces, including how they are remembered and represented.

Notes

1 Mary Douglas, *Purity and Danger: An Analysis of the Concepts of Pollution and Taboo* (London: Routledge 1996 [1966]); David Sibley, 'Outsiders in society and space', in Kay Anderson and Fay Gale (eds), *Inventing Places: Studies in Cultural Geography* (Melbourne: Longman 1992), 107.
2 Donatella Calabi, *Venice and Its Jews* (Milan: Officina Libraria 2017).

3 Sibley, 'Outsiders', 107.
4 Peter Fryer, *Staying Power: The History of Black People in Britain* (London: Pluto Press 1984).
5 Caroline Bressey, 'Cultural archaeology and historical geographies of the black presence in rural England', *Journal of Rural Studies* vol. 25, 2009, 386.
6 Colin Holmes, *John Bull's Island: Immigration & British Society, 1871–1971* (Basingstoke: Macmillan 1988), 430–435.
7 See Tony Kushner, *The Battle of Britishness: Migrant Journeys, 1685 to the Present* (Manchester: Manchester University Press 2012), chapter 7.
8 Clair Willis, *Lovers & Strangers: An Immigrant History of Post-War Britain* (London: Allen Lane 2017), 65.
9 Doreen Massey, 'Places and their Pasts', *History Workshop Journal* no. 39, 1985, 186.
10 Ibid., 183.

5

FROM THE PROFITABLE STRANGERS TO THE RESIDENTS OF BANGLATOWN

An exploration of the historiography of immigrants in London's East End

Anne J. Kershen

When asked to provide a chapter on the theme of the historiography of immigrants in the East End for this volume in celebration of the work of Colin Holmes – whose seminal historiographies have provided starting points for so many historians as well as those in other disciplines – I agreed with alacrity, and began compiling what rapidly, and not surprisingly, became an extensive bibliography. However, when I reviewed the ever-expanding list I realised that the nouns in my title required clarification. So before I launch into what is, by necessity, a brief survey of the historiography of immigrant settlement in London's East End, I intend to consider what is meant by 'historiography', 'immigrant' and 'East End' in the context of this chapter.

1

First, what do we understand by the term, historiography? For some it is, 'The study of the way history has been, and is, written ... the changing interpretation of events in the works of individual historians'.[1] As early as the 1960s, E. H. Carr recorded his belief that, when considering historiographies and historiographers, it was not enough to know the when and where of an event, it was necessary to have knowledge of the writers and of their stance on the subject under the microscope; thus embracing political bias, gender and race.[2] In addition, I would add that the reliability of the source material should be confirmed and the author's intended readership identified. Whenever consulting immigrant historiographies, the writer's insider or outsider status in relation to the people and place under investigation should be noted; variations of positionality create different nuances and emphases in the writing of migration history. For example, if it is a British-Jewish history, then the researcher should consider whether the author is British and/or Jewish; Geoffrey Alderman for example is both.[3] On the other hand, Todd Endelman is an American Jewish academic, whose work has mainly focused on the history of British Jewry.[4] While Colin Holmes, British but not Jewish, produced the seminal work on antisemitism in British society. In the book, Holmes references the Polish born historian Walter Laqueur whom, when referring to the writing of Jewish history in 1967, believed that, 'we could do with more studies of antisemitism and, in particular, accounts written by Gentiles'.[5] Holmes certainly fulfilled that requirement and produced an excellent study. Finally, when possible, those consulting historiographies should evaluate *what they know* to have been omitted, as well as that which has been included, for it has been known for historians to omit facts which might weaken their thesis.[6]

When looking at the range of narratives on immigrant settlement in the East End for the purposes of this chapter, I determined to include works of writers from disciplines other than history; particularly those of sociologists and anthropologists who, at the time of writing, were engaged in researching the present as opposed to the past. Their exclusion would have meant the omission of one of the earliest in-depth studies of an immigrant group in the post-Second World War East End: the account of the brief settlement of West Africans and West Indians in Cable Street, as recorded by the sociologist Michael Banton in the early 1950s.[7] When evaluating the changing attitudes to the writing of immigration history over the past sixty years, I would draw attention to the title of Banton's book which appeared in 1954, *The Coloured Quarter: Negro Immigrants in an English City*, the nouns used to describe both place and subjects being unacceptable in the twenty-first century. Significantly, Banton does admit to *disliking* the use of the nomenclature 'negro' and appears to apologise by claiming that repetition of the classifications 'West Indian' and 'West African' would have been, in his words, 'tiresome'.[8] Though his title may give pause for thought, the content provides an ideal template for the study of non-European immigrants in a metropolitan environment. This approach is also to be found in social anthropologist John Eade's seminal study of Bangladeshis in the East End, researched and written in the 1980s.[9] Accordingly I believe that this chapter would be diminished by my restricting analysis to one specific branch of learning.

An immigrant is a person who moves from one place to another, either to stay for a considerable period of time – at least one year – or to settle permanently.[10] There is some debate as to whether the descendant of immigrants – second and third generation – should be designated 'an immigrant by descent'. The *immigrants* I refer to here will be only those who *migrated*, their children will be referred to as 'first or second generation British born'. I have focused on all immigrants to the East End who arrived from outside mainland Britain, thus I include nineteenth-century Irish migrants, who crossed the water and became known as 'troublesome strangers' in London's East End.[11]

The East End is both a real and, in the literary sense, imagined space. Over the centuries it has been a place of flexible boundaries which has offered up a choice of identities to those who have sought to settle inside its space – East Ender, Cockney, insider, outsider, Huguenot refugee, Eastern European Jewish immigrant tailor, migrant Bengali restaurant owner/worker. If we apply the description Doreen

Massey put forward in her discourse on 'Places and Their Past', we can define the East End as '… a conjunction of many histories and many spaces'.[12] Within the East End is the 250-acre space of Spitalfields which has been a first place of immigrant arrival and settlement over the centuries. In each case, as the newcomers put down their roots, the landscape gradually takes on the character of the latest immigrant group, becoming in turn Petty France, Little Jerusalem and Banglatown. At each turn a new carapace is produced *almost* masking the one beneath. There is never complete coverage as, for example, in the case of the religious building on the corner of Brick Lane and Fournier Street; evidence of earlier communities seeps through. All the while, within the space that is the East End, indigenes and immigrants contest ownership of 'their' place.

Geographically, the area that is the East End evolved from the cluster of hamlets which had, centuries earlier, grown up on the outer edge of the eastern boundary of the City of London. Over time the hamlets expanded and fused to become one 'place' – the East End. Proximity to the capital's heartland led to the area becoming a first point of settlement for immigrants and refugees and a pattern of immigrant settlement was established by Huguenots and Jews from the mid-1600s onwards. By the close of the nineteenth century the East End was considered by outsiders to be both exotic and hazardous; in the eyes of some analogous with the African Jungle. Writing of the time he spent there in 1902, the social activist and journalist Jack London recounted having been told, 'You don't want to go down there … there are places where a man's life isn't worth tu'pence'. The East End was, according to London, in its darkest corners, an 'abyss'.[13] At the beginning of the twentieth century the novelist and historian Sir Walter Besant pinpointed East London (within which we find the East End), as the area which lay 'east of Bishopsgate Street Without and north of the River Thames, including the aggregation of crowded towns … formed of the once rural suburban villages called Hackney, Clapton, Stoke Newington, Old Ford, Stepney, Bow and Stratford'.[14] Currently the East End is accepted to be the area lying within the boundaries of the London Borough of Tower Hamlets, though some contend its spread is wider, extending to Hackney, Shoreditch, Hoxton and even parts of Newham. Others, such as Bill Fishman in his *The Streets of East London*, have used a much smaller parameter, focusing solely on Whitechapel or Spitalfields – 'the East End in the East End'.[15]

2

Though not directly referring to any resident 'immigrants' the East End makes its earliest appearance in literature in the General Prologue to Geoffrey Chaucer's *Canterbury Tales* (circa 1386–9); the Prioress is described as speaking 'French quite fluent after the style of Stratford atte Bow'.[16] More than two hundred years later in *Every Man in his Humour* (1601/1616), Ben Jonson makes malign references to Jews throughout the play – though the exact location of the characters is unclear. He also makes denigrating allusions to Houndsditch – that place which bounds the edge of the City and the East End. In the play's second act, he refers to '[A]

Houndsditch man, sir one of the devil's near kinsmen, a broker'; though the ethnic identity of 'the broker' is not stated, the insinuation is clear.[17] The East End is woven in and out of the works of Charles Dickens; in *Oliver Twist* (1841) Dickens describes the place where the Jewish 'receiver of stolen goods' Fagin was to be found, as a 'wretched place ... with filthy odours ... little knots of houses, where drunken men and women wallow in filth'.[18] Indeed, Sam Weller in *Pickwick Papers* (1837) considered Whitechapel, 'not a *wery* nice place'.[19] The nineteenth- and twentieth-century East End Jewish immigrant community appear in a number of literary works produced by co-religionists, these include Israel Zangwill's *Children of the Ghetto* (1892),[20] Simon Blumenfeld's *Jew Boy* (1935),[21] Wolf Mankowitz's *A Kid for Two Farthings* (1955)[22] and Alexander Baron's *The Lowlife* (1963).[23] The Chinese immigrant community of Chinatown have found their place in literature, appearing in Thomas Burke's 1916 short story collection, *Limehouse Nights*;[24] while Arthur Ward, under the pen name Sax Rohmer, was inspired by his visit to Limehouse to create the character Dr Fu Manchu, who first appeared in 1913 in *The Mystery of Dr Fu Manchu*.[25] More recently Monica Ali explored, or it could be said, *exposed*, the Bangladeshi community in her novel *Brick Lane* (2003);[26] a book which was praised by the critics but which did not meet with the approval of the East End Bengali residents. They complained that it 'greatly offended the hard-working, industrious Bangladeshi community'.[27] Arnold Wesker's trilogy, which begins with *Chicken Soup with Barley* (1958),[28] a play which traces the disintegration of an East End Jewish family from the Battle of Cable Street in 1936 to the Hungarian Revolution of 1956 and the failure of the socialist dream, and Bernard Kops' family melodrama, *The Hamlet of Stepney Green* (1957),[29] are amongst the plays that introduced wider theatre audiences to the twentieth-century immigrant Jewish community. In 2009, the playwright Richard Bean's *England People Very Nice* brought together the four major East End immigrant groups in a play which was criticised for being superficial and presenting general caricatures rather than in-depth studies of individual characters from the four groups – Huguenots, Irish, Jews and Bangladeshis.[30] Literature can add clarity but can also confuse and conflict with reality; a fact which should not be overlooked by those seeking to understand historiography and historiographers. However, East End literary works must not be ignored as they do provide an illustrative backcloth to the space Jack London, at the beginning of the twentieth century, considered 'The Abyss'.[31]

3

The historiography of immigration into the East End can be reviewed either chronologically or thematically. The latter demands the examination of a variety of themes: politics, gender, religion, social issues and race and ethnicity. The former enables a chapter such as this to cover more space in less time than the latter so, old-fashioned though it may be, for this purpose I will travel from the seventeenth century incomers – the Huguenots – through to the most recent arrivals who currently make up the largest non-white population of the East End, the Bangladeshis.

The Huguenots arrived in the East End from the late sixteenth century onwards, the majority both coming before and just after the Revocation of the Edict of Nantes in 1685. A number of factors have militated against their being the subject of historiographers in the same way as the Jewish and Bangladeshi immigrants to the East End. First, the East End was not their only first point of settlement, the more affluent refugees settled to the west of London, in and around the area known as Soho. Still others established themselves outside the capital in towns such as Canterbury and Norwich. Second, they were white, Christian and hardworking: ideal examples of the Protestant work ethic. By the end of the eighteenth century they were becoming increasingly integrated, many having moved their religious allegiance from their local French churches to Christ Church in Spitalfields;[32] by the second quarter of the nineteenth century the majority had left the East End. However, it should not be assumed that, though given the epithet 'Profitable Strangers', their presence went without condemnation. The Huguenots were just as capable of arousing feelings of xenophobia as did their later arrivals. The threats posed by the French silk weavers provoked their English counterparts in Spitalfields. In his doctoral thesis, the leading historian of the Huguenot settlement in England, Robin Gwynn, reports that in 1683 – two years before the Revocation of the Edict of Nantes – native apprentice weavers in Spitalfields warned the King that if he did not oppose the French weavers they would resort to violence and 'knock on the head' those who were undercutting wages locally.[33] Daniel Statt describes how, in 1675, the King's Guard was called out to prevent a massacre when English weavers in Spitalfields, protesting at the new weaving technology imported from France, resorted to violence against their French counterparts and savaged Huguenot homes and looms.[34] Yet it was not just the economic threat. In spite of the Huguenots being Calvinist refugees, fear of popery resulted in the spread of rumours that the new arrivals were crypto-Catholics, others rumoured that the Huguenots were responsible for the Fire of London. Poorer Huguenots, called wooden shoes, due to the clattering of their clogs, were considered to be of the 'meanest rank ... not much above common beggars'.[35] Almost a century later, at the time of the crisis over the 1753 Naturalisation Bill, both Huguenots and Jews were, unusually, brought together by those opposed to the bill, in the slogan, 'No Jews. No Wooden Shoes'.[36] The attitude towards the Huguenot immigrants is best summed up by looking at the behaviour and writing of the diarist Samuel Pepys who wrote: 'we do naturally all ... hate the French', whilst at the same time donating money to the Huguenot cause.[37]

The Jews that arrived after the Readmission of 1656 and the Huguenot refugees of the seventeenth century were laying the foundations of their communities at virtually the same time and in the same location. However, this coincidence has been overlooked as historians have rarely considered points of intersection between the two sets of incomers. There is another historical intersection in the history of immigration in the East End, that of the Irish and Eastern European Jewish communities during the second half of the nineteenth century. The 'Troublesome Strangers', as the Irish immigrants to East London became known, settled in the East End – in both Spitalfields and close to the docks – as well as in other parts of London, particularly St Giles, from the mid-nineteenth century onwards. Yet whilst there are historiographies which in their titles specifically record the Irish presence in Britain and London and essay titles which feature Birmingham, Bristol, Edinburgh, Liverpool, York and even Wolverhampton, I can find no trace of any published work which cites simply the 'Irish in the East End' in the title. In her chapter on 'Irish/Jewish diasporic intersections in the East End of London', Bronwen Walter highlights the fact that there has been 'a lack of attention to the parallels and intersections between the Irish and Jewish populations in Britain'.[38] However, while recording examples of Irish female domestics working in the homes of Jewish East Enders she makes no criticism of the fact there is a lacuna in this area of East End Irish/Jewish immigrant studies.[39] One of the exceptions to this is Lara Marks who, in her essay on 'Working Wives and Working Mothers', takes a comparative look at the experiences of Irish and Jewish women in the East End in the years when immigration from Eastern Europe was at its highest.[40] Whilst not providing a temporal intersection I take a comparative approach to female migrant economic activities in the East End in my chapter, 'Jewish and Muslim Married Women Don't Work'.[41] In this I highlight the fact that Eastern European Jewish husbands in the late nineteenth century and Bangladeshi husbands one hundred years later, discouraged their wives from working outside of the home, believing this was degrading and, in the case of the Bengali wife, created a danger that wives might stray beyond their ethnic community. Yet in both instances, in order to add to the household budget, these hidden other women were economically active in the privacy of the home. It is perhaps worth noting that, more recently, Muslim women are being encouraged to come out in into the open and take up employment in the economic mainstream.[42]

The economics and politics of the East End were responsible for other meeting points, and indeed cooperation between diverse contemporaries. Irish dockers and Jewish East End tailors supported each other during the strikes of 1889 and 1912,[43] and on 4 October 1936 stood together and confronted the police in order to prevent Oswald Mosley and his Blackshirts marching through the East End. This event has become one of the most powerful myths in East End history and one so frequently recorded by historiographers that it is redundant to delve more deeply here.[44]

4

The Jewish immigrants of the East End have featured in innumerable texts yet here again the appearance of both subjects and place together in a volume's title is rare. Indeed, in his celebratory *A History of the Jews in England* (1949), Cecil Roth glosses over the late nineteenth-century immigrants as though they were an embarrassment.[45] Other pre-1970s histories, such as Charles Russell and Harry Lewis' *The Jew in London* (1901),[46] Lloyd Gartner's *The Jewish Immigrant in England 1870–1914*[47] and Vivian Lipman's *Social History of the Jews in England 1850–1950*

(1954),[48] though each almost entirely devoted to East End Jewry avoided including that specific 'on the edge' location in their title. It was Bill Fishman who, in the 1970s, brought the Jewish East End to the title page of history books; his prize winning *East End Jewish Radicals* (1975) left his readers in no doubt as to the where and the who, whilst his *Streets of East London* (1979) and his *East End 1888* (1988), in addition to expanding on the East End Jewish experience, provided navigational information for readers who wished to learn and see more. In 1981 Aubrey Newman edited a volume which clearly annunciated the subject of his book. *The Jewish East End* is a collection which embraces the broad spectrum of the Eastern European Jewish immigrant experience between 1840–1939. In his all-embracing essay on Anglo-Jewish historiography produced in 1986, Gartner is somewhat critical of the Newman collection, considering the articles to be of 'varying quality'.[49] He also considered that the majority of those Anglo-Jewish historians he was referring to were, in the main, not members of university faculties, insinuating that they were amateurs. However, while he made less than gracious comments about some of those I have named above, I should add that he was particularly complimentary about the individual honoured in this *festschrift*.

While Gartner was researching and presenting his paper to the Jewish Historical Society of England, a school of 'young historians'[50] were engaged in researching and writing Eastern European Jewish immigrant histories, warts and all.[51] At the same time, a new wave of migrants were arriving to take the place of their Jewish counterparts, the latter by this time having moved out to the suburbs of London – only a small number of residual, mainly elderly, members of the East End Jewish community remained behind. The newcomers were from East Pakistan, which, after a bloody civil war, became the independent state of Bangladesh in 1971. And the Bangladeshis rapidly became the focus of research for anthropologists, sociologists, geographers, medics and, eventually, historians.

5

Immigrant settlement in the East End created a tradition of research and publication. But whereas in the case of earlier settlers there had been, with certain exceptions (for example Charles Booth's survey of poverty in the East End which examined the impact of the Eastern European immigrants and the already mentioned Russell and Lewis exploration)[52] a considerable time gap between settlement and published works, there was far less of an interval between the entry of Bangladeshis and their appearance in print. It was the 1962 Commonwealth Immigrants Act which galvanised South East Asian migrant entry to the United Kingdom. Amongst those early arrivals were the men who would lay the foundations of the East End Bangladeshi community. A community created as the 'myth of return'[53] gradually took over from the determination to return to Bangladesh as 'rich men of high status' faded. In 1985 Sean Carey and Abdus Shukur published an essay which presented a profile of the burgeoning community, providing concise information on economic activity, education, religious practices and politics.[54] Though at the time a contemporary study, and running to only twelve pages, it provided a basic insight into the East End's newest immigrant population. This was followed two years later by Caroline Adams' 'life histories' of Syhetti settlers in Britain.[55] Though neither an academic nor an historian, and not focusing solely on East End immigrants, Adams' book has become a standard in the bibliography of Bangladeshi East End studies. In 1989 John Eade published the first in-depth account of the Bangladeshi community in the East End; this created the benchmark for those keen to examine the development of what was to become the largest concentration of Bangladeshi people outside of Bangladesh. His seminal work was, as described by Eade himself, 'one which engaged with the current debates concerning political representation, ethnicity and race'.[56] Though contemporary at the time of publication, it has become a standard in *historical* studies of Bangladeshi settlement in England.

From the 1990s onwards the study of Bangladeshis in East London was on the agenda of a multiplicity of disciplines, the range of topics including politics, racism, religion, health and welfare, education and more recently radicalisation.[57] Yet whereas early studies were male-centric, the twenty-first century has seen the focus shift to the 'hidden other' of the Bangladeshi community in East London, with studies which have explored the complex assimilation process of first generation migrant women and their experiences in the labour market. More recently, the growing library of work on Bangladeshi immigrants in the East End has been added to by an examination of the political mobilisation of the Bengali population of East London,[58] and an analysis of the complexity of British-Islamic identity in a post-9/11 world.[59] As with early East End migrant studies, insider and outsider writings provide different interpretations of the arrival and settlement of Bangladeshis in the area; works which give contemporary readers comparative food for thought. Whatever the variations, they are all texts which, in the future, will provide nourishment for another generation of East End immigration historians.

6

Some closing points: first, though I have concluded this account of immigrants in the East End of London with the arrival and settlement of Bangladeshi migrants this is not to suggest that they will be the final newcomers to the area. The East End has always been a magnet for immigrants and it would be surprising if the influx of Eastern Europeans does not make an impact, though arguably less than that of previous arrivals. Much has been written about contemporary Eastern European immigration but not as yet specifically related to the East End and it remains to be seen if their presence will be permanent, or transitory as was the case in Banton's 'coloured quarter'. Second, whilst the East End has attracted immigrant settlement – or as Massey has described them, 'intrustions'[60] – for more than three hundred years, one questions whether these are a combination of the global and the local and thus become glocal, or has the global *become* local. Finally, I believe it has been vital in this account of East End immigrant historiography to reference texts other than just pure histories. As I hope to have shown, historians owe a debt to a multiplicity of disciplines for laying down the frameworks and benchmarks from which to proceed. However, this raises two questions, at what point does a contemporary study become a history? And what ownership can history claim of the sources referred to in this chapter?

Notes

1. Michael Salevouris with Conal Furay, *The Methods and Skills of History: A Practical Guide* 2nd edn (Wheeling IL: John Wiley 1988), 223.
2. See Edward Hallett Carr, *What Is History* (London: Pelican 1985), 3–35.
3. See for example, Geoffrey Alderman, *Modern British Jewry* (Oxford: Clarendon Press, 1992), and *British Jewry Since Emancipation* (Buckingham: University of Buckingham Press 2014).
4. See for example, Todd Endelman, *The Jews of Britain 1656–2000* (Berkeley, Los Angeles, London: University of California Press 2002) and *The Jews of Georgian England 1714–1830: Tradition and Change in a Liberal Society* (Ann Arbor: University of Michigan Press 1999).
5. Colin Holmes, *Anti-Semitism in British Society 1876–1939* (London: Edward Arnold 1979), 1.
6. It would be invidious to name names!
7. Michael Banton, *The Coloured Quarter: Negro Immigrants in an English City* (London: Jonathan Cape 1955).
8. Ibid., 4.
9. John Eade, *The Politics of Community: The Bangladeshi Community in East London* (Farnham: Avebury 1989).
10. The UNO/ONS define a, 'long-term migrant as someone who moves to a country other than his/her place of residence for at least a year'. Those that stay for less are deemed 'switchers'. www.migrationobservatory.ox.ac.uk/resources/briefings/who-counts-as-a-migrant-definitions-and-their-consequences/ (accessed 22 November 2016).
11. In the mid-nineteenth century the Irish were the largest immigrant group in London, numbering some 109,000; by 1901 the number of Irish-born living in London had reduced to 60,000. www.oldbaileyonline.org/static/Irish.jsp# (accessed 12 December 2016).
12. Doreen Massey, 'Places and their pasts', *History Workshop Journal*, vol. 39, 1995, 191.
13. Jack London, *The People of the Abyss* (London: Journeyman Press 1977), 11.
14. Walter Besant, *East London* (London: Chatto & Windus 1901), 4.
15. William J. Fishman, *The Streets of East London* (London: Duckworth 1979), 7.
16. http://english.fsu.edu/canterbury/general.html line 125 (accessed 12 December 2016).
17. https://archive.org/stream/worksbenjonsonw09giffgoog/worksbenjonsonw09giffgoog_djvu.txt (accessed 8 January 2017).
18. www.gutenberg.org/files/47529/47529-h/47529-h.htm line (accessed 14 December 2016).
19. www.gutenberg.org/files/580/580-h/580-h.htm (accessed 8 January 2017).
20. See Israel Zangwill, *Children of the Ghetto: a Study of a Peculiar People* (London: Macmillan 1898).
21. See Simon Blumenfeld, *Jew Boy* (London: Lawrence and Wishart 1986 edition).
22. See Wolf Mankowitz, *A Kid for Two Farthings* (London: Bloomsbury Group 2011 edition).
23. See Alexander Baron, *The Lowlife* (London: Black Spring 2010 edition).
24. See Thomas Burke, *Limehouse Nights* (Rockville MD: Wildside Press 2003 edition).
25. See Sax Rohmer, *The Mystery of Dr. Fu Manchu* (London: Titan 2012 edition).

26 Monica Ali, *Brick Lane* (London and New York: Doubleday 2003).
27 http://news.bbc.co.uk/1/hi/uk/5229872.stm (accessed 11 December 2015).
28 See Arnold Wesker, *Chicken Soup with Barley* (London: Penguin 1966 edition of all three plays in the triology).
29 See *New English Dramatists 1* (Penguin Plays), *Each His Own Wilderness: The Hamlet of Stepney Green; Chicken Soup with Barley* (London: Penguin 1959).
30 Richard Bean, *England People Very Nice* (London: Oberon Books 2009).
31 London, *The People of the Abyss*, 11.
32 See in Anne J. Kershen, *Strangers, Aliens and Asians: Huguenots, Jews and Bangladeshis in Spitalfields 1660–2000* (Abingdon: Routledge 2005), ch. 4.
33 Robin Gwynn, 'The Ecclesiastical Organisation of French Protestants in England in the late 17th Century, with special reference to London', PhD thesis, University of London, 1976, 240.
34 Daniel Statt, *Foreigners and Englishmen: The Controversy over Immigration and Population 1600–1760* (Newark: University of Delaware Press 1995), 183.
35 Ibid., 138.
36 Kershen, *Strangers, Asians and Aliens*, 198.
37 Ibid.
38 Browyn Walter, 'Irish/Jewish diasporic intersections in the East End of London: paradoxes and shared locations', in Michel Prum (ed.), *La Place de l'Autre* (Paris: L'Éditions L'Harmattan 2010), 60.
39 Ibid., 53–67.
40 Lara Marks, *Working Wives and Working Mothers: a Comparative Study of Irish and Eastern European Married Women's Work and Motherhood in East London 1870–1914* (London: P.N.L.P. 1990).
41 Anne J. Kershen, 'Jewish and Muslim married women don't work', in *Home Cultures* vol. 8, no. 2, 2011, 119–132.
42 See Ibid., and also Naila Kabeer, *The Power to Choose: Bangladeshi Women and Labour Market Discourses in London and Dhaka* (London: Verso 2000).
43 Anne J. Kershen, *Uniting the Tailors: Trade Unionism Amongst the Tailoring Workers of London and Leeds 1876–1939* (Ilford: Frank Cass 1995), 126–162.
44 For a discussion on the differing accounts of the Battle of Cable Street, see Daniel Tilles, 'Winning the battle, but what about the war? Cable Street in context', in Colin Holmes and Anne J. Kershen (eds), *An East End Legacy. Essays in Memory of William J Fishman* (Abingdon: Routledge 2017).
45 Cecil Roth, *A History of the Jews in England* (Oxford: Clarendon 1949).
46 Charles Russell and Harry Lewis, *The Jew in London* (London: Fisher Unwin 1901).
47 Lloyd P. Gartner, *The Jewish Immigrant in England 1870–1914* (Liverpool and London: George Allen and Unwin 1960).
48 Vivien D. Lipman, *Social History of the Jews in England 1850–1950* (London: Watts & Co. 1954).
49 Lloyd P. Gartner, 'A quarter of a century of Anglo-Jewish historiography', *Jewish Social Studies*, vol. 48, no. 2, 1986, 105–126.
50 In some cases a description of stage of work rather than age!
51 These included David Cesarani, Bryan Cheyette, Todd Endelman, David Feldman, Anne Kershen, Tony Kushner as well as Bill Williams known for his work on Manchester Jewry and, of course, William J. Fishman. Not all these historians were engaged on specific East End studies but their research and subsequent publications were to inform and influence students and researchers in the decades that followed.

52 Charles Booth, *Life and London of People in London: First Series Poverty* (London: Williams and Norgate 1889).
53 For the myth of return see, Muhammad Anwar, *The Myth of Return: Pakistanis in Britain* (London: Heinemann Educational Books 1979).
54 Sean Carey and Abdus Shukur, 'A Profile of the Bangladeshi Community in East London', *Journal of Ethnic and Migration Studies* vol. 12, no. 3, 405–417.
55 Caroline Adams, *Across Seven Seas and Thirteen Rivers* (London: Thap Books 1987).
56 John Eade's description of his book, *Politics of Community*, in an email to the author, 9 August 2016.
57 See for example the works of: Claire Alexander, Halima Begum, John Eade, David Garbin, Katy Gardner, Sarah Glynn, Naila Kabeer and Georgie Wemyss.
58 Sarah Glynn, *Class, Ethnicity and Religion in the Bengali East End: A Political History* (Manchester: Manchester University Press 2015).
59 See for example, Kabeer, *The Power to Choose*; Chris Phillipson, Nilufar Ahmed and Joanna Latimer, *Women in Transition; A Study of the Experiences of Bangladeshi Women Living in Tower Hamlets* (Bristol: Policy Press 2003) and Aminal Hoque, *British-Islamic Identity: Third Generation Bangladeshis in East London* (London, Stoke on Trent: Trentham Books 2015).
60 Massey, 'Places and their past', 9.

6

THE CHINESE CONNECTION

An historiography

Anne Witchard

In the twenty or so years since Colin Holmes published 'The Chinese Connection' the subject of the Chinese in Britain has come so far in terms of scholarship and general attention that as of September 2016 it has been included as a component of the national GCSE history syllabus.[1] Back in the early 1990s that essay was pretty much the standalone work on the subject and it remains a foundational source for the wide range of studies that have come since (one of many such testaments to Holmes as Professor Fishman's worthy successor). 'The Chinese Connection' pulled together Holmes' previous attention to the Chinese in *John Bull's Island: Immigration and British Society, 1871–1971*.[2] It also built on an earlier article by J. P. May that Holmes had published a decade before in the edited volume, *Immigrants and Minorities in British Society*.[3]

While the title of May's chapter, 'The Chinese in Britain, 1860–1914', would seem to indicate a general attention to the late nineteenth-century period of emigration from China, his aim was chiefly to examine the manifestations of an apparent animosity directed towards the Chinese in Britain in the first decade of the twentieth century. Given the amount of sensational media directed at this relatively tiny immigrant community, May begins, the subsequent lack of attention paid by social historians to the Chinese presence in Britain would appear 'at first sight ... strange'.[4] He pinpoints three key events which prompted alarmist newspaper coverage: a Commission of Inquiry into Liverpool's Chinese appointed by the city council in 1906, party political contention during the 1906 General Election over the use of Chinese 'coolie' labour in South African mines, and rioting and arson attacks during the seamen's strike of 1911.

May assesses the factors which conditioned relations between Chinese settlers and British society, showing how press reportage, irrespective of political position – from *The Times* to radical socialist journals such as *Commonweal* – followed United States precedent. From the early 1870s few reports of Chinese settlement in

America omitted to mention (in pecuniary detail) the fractional wages for which they were prepared to work and the subsistence levels at which they could survive. Coupled with increasingly low costs of mass transportation, Chinese immigration was posed as a looming threat to British labour interests. As early as 1873, Thomas Wright in 'The Journeyman Engineer' had noted: 'the wholesale importation of coolie and Chinese labour going on in some parts abroad is a thing to "give pause" to the thoughtful among the working classes'.[5] In 1882, George Sala deliberated the American phenomenon in his *Illustrated London News* column: 'are we really in danger of being invaded by the "Heathen Chinee", not in his hundreds, but in his tens of thousands'.

> Are Betsy Jane the cook and Sarah Ann the housemaid to be ousted by the yellow men with the pig-tails who cook so cleverly, make beds so neatly and scrub floors so conscientiously; while Mrs Tearall, the washerwoman is ousted from her tub by Ah Sing, the laundryman from Canton.[6]

By the end of the century, the British working class was thoroughly instructed in the threat to its interests posed by immigrant Chinese labour. And, again following U.S. precedent, newspaper stories focused on their 'alien' characteristics – addiction to opium smoking, inveterate gambling and perhaps most worryingly of all, consorting with white women.

Britain's first Chinese residents were seamen who settled in the dock neighbourhoods of London, Cardiff and Liverpool. In June 1907 the Council Proceedings of the Committee investigating Liverpool's Chinese, set up to investigate allegations of opium smoking and illicit liaisons with underage English girls, failed to find much justification for these charges. May observes that 'uncertainty about the origin and nature of any opposition to the Chinese was reflected in the general nature of the questions asked about them and the speculative and diverse nature of the conclusions offered'.[7] He cites a letter to the Home Secretary from Liverpool's Chief Constable: 'opium smoking is no doubt common among them, but it amounts to no offence against the law and no crimes due to it have come to the knowledge of the police … As to gambling, whenever Chinese get together they will gamble.'[8] The letter concludes: 'there is no evidence to show that their morals are any worse than those of the rest of the community'.[9] The Chinese were found to be peaceable, industrious and to 'treat their women well, they are sober, they do not beat their wives and they pay liberally for prostitution'.[10] May notes a tone of indifference in the Chief Constable's letter, together with bewilderment as to the raising of the inquiry in the first place: 'I cannot help thinking that what is really at the bottom of most of it is the competition of the Chinese with the laundries and boarding-house keepers'.[11] What becomes evident, May surmises, is that this purported tension or hostility between the Chinese and their host community indicated by reports of 'exotic or potentially provocative habits such as opium taking, gambling and sexual relations with "white women" and girls' was not the whole picture.[12] His investigation concludes that the aforementioned media-hyped instances were localised, whether in Liverpool, Cardiff or Limehouse, they were geographically contained, of not much concern to their neighbours and of little significance to the police. The 'possibility' of discovering 'an interesting tension between Britain's first Chinese residents and the wider community' being refuted accounts then, May suggests, for subsequent socio-historical disinterest.[13]

May's conclusion to his opening query regarding the lack of attention paid by social historians to the Chinese presence in Britain is entirely framed by its late-1970s discursive context, namely that minority communities necessitate a 'problem'. He references Ng Kwee Choo's summing up of his brief statistical account, *The Chinese in London* (published in the same year as Enoch Powell's 'Rivers of Blood' speech): 'they have not appeared to pose any sort of minority problem'.[14] Indeed, by the late 60s and 70s, concerns regarding a disruptive immigrant presence had long shifted away from the Chinese.

'The Chinese Connection' published some fifteen years later in 1993 opens with an ironic inversion of May's starting point. Rather than academic disinterest, Holmes describes an ongoing evasion by the 'unco-operative' Chinese of scholarly attention to their presence.[15] His declared intention in reconsidering those disproportionally hostile early responses is to attempt to understand the nature of opposition encountered by minority groups generally. Holmes pays attention first to the specifics of claims made against the Chinese and then to their mobilisation in a general 'dynamics of racial hostility'.[16] Despite the fact that of all foreign workers, the Chinese were statistically a very small group, just 480 out of 15,246 (1911 census), unlike other foreign seamen they were regularly employed as strike breakers, so anti-Chinese hostility from dockers and seamen was unremitting. Yet if, as May had noted, resentment of the Chinese was related to specific contexts, why did it develop and spread? Holmes makes connections with reactions to other racial groups. While waves, floods and swamps are often threatened, hostility is rarely relative to numbers, the most beleaguered group between 1904 and 1906, he points out, were one hundred or so German Gypsies who encountered considerable violence, were rounded up and deported from England en masse. Indeed the Chinese faced greatest hostility when their numbers were smallest. As Holmes goes on to illustrate, small groups come under hostile scrutiny when they become linked to issues of national economic or social concern. While the cheapness of Chinese labour provoked localised anger, this was exacerbated by broader claims of anti-social habits, illegal gambling, illicit sexual relations and recreational drug use. Holmes continues the story where May leaves off, at the outbreak of the First World War.

As May had observed, the policing of drugs had until then been pretty relaxed, both in Liverpool and London. The 1916 Defence of the Realm Act (DORA) with its new strictures on drug use brought Britain's Chinatowns under the social microscope once again. In the face of war the very existence of foreign quarters threatened the idea of 'a nation wish[ing] to believe itself socially and ethnically homogenous'.[17] The Chinese were portrayed as agents of Germany, and London's Limehouse as an alien underworld. Late nineteenth-century notions of a Yellow

Peril were revitalised and in the strained aftermath of war, depictions of their immoral or treacherous qualities continued to grow in significance. The increased strictures of the 1919 Aliens Act confirmed the escalation of post-war anxiety. Any acknowledgement of Chinese assistance in the war effort evaporated while random incidences combined to consolidate the mythology of London's Chinatown, most notorious being the case of the fatal overdose of starlet Billie Carleton, fictionalised in Sax Rohmer's *Dope: A Tale of Chinatown* (1918). Holmes emphasises the role of popular culture in disseminating anti-Chinese sentiment, examining the interplay of the daily press, literary potboilers and lurid films, with police and government reports, a potent brew that filtered into a popular consciousness in which the Chinese presence, tiny though it was, loomed large.

In his close attention to the operation of anti-Chinese discourses in early twentieth-century Britain, Holmes' work troubled the accepted narrative of multicultural Britain, challenging the dominance of the arrival of the *SS Empire Windrush* at Tilbury Docks in 1948 and the attendant conflicts that came to a head in the Notting Hill race riots of 1958. The historiography that took from 1948 to 1958 as originary in terms of 'coloured' immigration and its attendant racial antagonisms not only 'forgot' earlier settlements but had served also to repress the unoriginality of the period's racialised rhetoric. What 'The Chinese Connection' renders striking about the newspaper articles and government reports about 'coloured British subjects' involved in pimping, gaming and drug trafficking, is how precisely they replicated the early twentieth-century deployment of a Yellow Peril. The same discursive matrix of urban squalor, transgressive sexuality and drug abuse that formerly constructed the Chinese as unalterably alien and unassimilable was deployed anew. The 'coloured' dope fiends were black rather than Yellow, marijuana replacing opium as the agent that facilitated undesirable sexual contact between the races.

'The Chinese Connection' makes the final point that the kind of racial antipathy predicated upon vice and immorality serves at the same time to attempt to subordinate its potential victims. Those newly enfranchised young women such as Billie Carleton were offered a stark reminder of the pitfalls of courting independence by headlines declaring the 'moral suicide' of sensation-seeking flappers, just as their granddaughters, liberated by the Pill, would be warned to beware the marijuana menace.

In unpicking the workings of anti-Chinese discourse in early twentieth-century Britain, 'The Chinese Connection' mapped out a broad terrain of future study, much of it then 'murky and uncharted'.[18] Refraining from speculation on the consequences for Chinese immigration of the upcoming Hong Kong Handover of 1997, already prompting panicky parliamentary reports of an impending influx of 'a quarter or half a million more people ... a store of problems for our children' which needless to say never materialised, Holmes could not then have predicted the massive economic boom that would put China at centre stage of global attention and the early history of Sino-British relations under the spotlight.[19] Certainly the projects of cultural historians like myself were to benefit from establishment interest in fostering improved relations with China by addressing the myths and stereotypes, slights and humiliations of former times. In what follows I will outline some of the key works of recent decades to which I have been indebted, the disciplinary range of which bears witness to the breadth of approaches suggested by the scope of Colin Holmes' early attention.

First, *Dope Girls: The Birth of the British Drug Underground*, Marek Kohn's inimitable study which compellingly connected the racial demonisation of drugs with the emergence of female autonomy at the start of the twentieth century is the definitive book on the moral panics around immigration that gave birth to Britain's present-day drug laws. My own interest in the Chinese in Britain began with postgraduate research into literary representations of nightlife and drug subcultures in London around the time of the First World War. I was perusing Chinatown press clippings in the Museum of London when a thoughtful librarian placed Kohn's book on my desk as possibly of interest. The blow of finding my research ambitions redundant was ameliorated by a reference in *Dope Girls* to Thomas Burke's *Limehouse Nights: Tales of Chinatown*.[20] It struck me that this forgotten work was a key to the complexities of this cultural moment. An oddly benign version of the Yellow Peril thriller, Burke's *Limehouse Nights* eschews the straightforward racism of the Fu Manchu model for a self-contradictory fantasy of a world both squalid and sumptuous, both frightening and alluring – and, perhaps most importantly, both foreign and British. In *Thomas Burke's Dark Chinoiserie: Limehouse Nights and the Queer Spell of Chinatown* I read Burke's Chinatown fiction in the tradition of literary chinoiseries, and make a case for chinoiserie as an essential vein of modern British culture, albeit in forms that have served differing ideological purposes.[21]

The first monograph-length study regarding not just the complexities of British Chinese identities but broader cultural questions around hybridity and Otherness vis-à-vis China and Britain was published in the mid-1990s, Gregory B. Lee's *Troubadours, Trumpeters, Troubled Makers: Lyricism, Nationalism, and Hybridity in China and Its Others* investigates twentieth-century Chinese literary culture in terms of its relation to diasporic notions of Chineseness.[22] His subsequent book, *Chinas Unlimited: Making the Imaginaries of China and Chineseness*, further examines ways of perceiving and projecting notions of Chineseness.[23] Lee's maternal grandfather was a Chinese who emigrated to Liverpool and worked as a laundryman and here he clears up any confusion regarding the motivation behind the 1906 Liverpool Inquiry into Chinatown vice. It had been instigated by none other than James Sexton, General Secretary of the National Union of Dock Labourers. Sexton had won St Anne's ward in 1905 on an overtly anti-Chinese manifesto and he also happened to sit on the Liverpool city council.[24] The Chief Constable's suspicions had been justified.

The quantity as well as the impact of popular cultural representation of the Chinese in early twentieth-century Britain finds its most detailed account in Robert Bickers' *Britain in China: Community, Culture and Colonialism, 1900–49*.[25] While this is a study of British incursion in China, the first chapter 'China in Britain, and in the British imagination' is concerned with how the colonial mindset was informed by its 'mental baggage'.[26] Bickers details the films, plays and fiction, both for children and adults, in which the cruelty and wickedness of 'China and the Chinese – and the Chinese in Britain too – were represented to the extent that those pleading for improvements in relations between Chinese and Britons routinely joked about it'.[27] He draws our attention to what was then a little known novel *Er Ma* (1929), an early work by the renowned Chinese novelist, Lao She (1899–1966). *Er Ma* was based on the author's experience of living and working in London during the 1920s and describes the pernicious effects of current popular sinophobia on the everyday lives of both native and immigrant Londoners. Bickers' preliminary research on Lao She's London years, together with the late sinologist William Dolby's then unpublished translation of the novel, was an invaluable source for my book *Lao She in London* in which I make a case for the transnational nature of literary modernism as well as drawing attention to this sole Chinese fictional response to the immigrant experience of the interwar years.[28]

When Thomas Burke published *Limehouse Nights*, Pennyfields in London's Limehouse district was inhabited almost entirely by Chinese. 'Chong Ching, Chong Sam, Wong Ho, Yow Yip, Choi Sau, Ah Chong Koon, Pong Peng, and Cheng Pong Lai' are a few names taken at random from a collection of application forms for ration books during the First World War.[29] By 1934, the Register of Electors shows that of twenty-seven houses listed in the street only one was inhabited by a Chinese family. The combined pressures of the Alien Restriction Acts of 1914 and 1919, together with police harassment, were partly responsible for the decline. Limehouse Causeway was widened in 1934 and a maze of alleys, courts and side streets, including several occupied by Chinese shops and lodging-houses, was demolished to make way for blocks of flats. So-called 'slum clearance', together with the effects of the Depression and a slump in international trade, further diminished the Chinese population. Thomas Cook's suggested charabanc route for an 'East End Drive' no longer made an 'attraction' of Limehouse. The myth of London's nefarious Chinatown declined along with the reality. Now newspaper stories reported the 'dwindling population' of Chinese Limehouse and sympathised with 'the sensational writer bereft of one of his more thrilling scenarios'.[30] Census figures from the 1930s indicate an acceleration of movement of Chinese to the West End and the outer suburbs. The Blitz helped finish the work begun by the London County Council clearances. Two important works, each indebted to Holmes, explore the 'facts', as far as they can be gleaned, of London's early Chinatown in relation to the fantasies it engendered. John Seed's article 'Limehouse Blues: looking for Chinatown in the London Docks, 1900–1940' utilises census and other recently accessible data to attempt an assessment of the actual numbers of Chinese in the Limehouse area, the discrepancy between exotic reportage and drab reality.[31] Sascha Auerbach's *Race, Law, and 'The Chinese Puzzle' in Imperial Britain* examines the manner in which derogatory media representation influenced the treatment of Chinese immigrants in the British judicial system and how the reports of these legal judgments in turn reinforced the ways in which the Chinese in Britain were depicted in the media.[32] Auerbach argues that the creation of a negative cycle of representation was significant in the development of race as a category in British culture, law and politics. Finally, with *The Chinese in Britain, 1800-Present: Economy, Transnationalism, Identity*, Gregor Benton and E. T. Gomez addressed the 'critical lacuna' as Auerbach described it, with the most ambitious study to date of the long history of Chinese migration to Britain. Most significantly, Benton and Gomez revise previous accounts that treated all Chinese emigrants as one unified diaspora.[33] The Chinese in Britain are a highly diverse group, divided by points of origin, reasons for leaving, linguistic differences and intra-ethnic conflicts.

The most recent developments in the history of the Chinese in Britain have been prompted by the centenary of the Great War. A series of Penguin Specials to commemorate China's neglected involvement include Mark O'Neill's *The Chinese Labour Corps: The Forgotten Chinese Labourers of the First World War* (2014) and my own *England's Yellow Peril: Sinophobia and the Great War* (2014).[34] The contribution of Chinese labour to the Allied war effort is still not widely known. How aware the British public at the time were of China's part in the war one can only surmise. As Britain suffered heavy casualties at the front during World War One, the nation closed ranks against outsiders and the Chinese in London were the principal scapegoat for anti-foreign sentiment. As Mark O'Neill points out, the recruitment of a 135,000 strong Chinese Labour Corps to the Allied battlefront, beginning in July 1916, was a plan that the government kept secret as British trade unions vehemently opposed the import of Chinese labour, wartime or not. In September 1916 the Trades Unions Congress hit newspaper headlines across the country with dramatic accusations of Chinese opium trafficking and the takeover of British maritime jobs. The Congress moved that the government introduce a bill to halt the alarming increase in employment of Chinese labour on British ships 'almost as important a matter as the war'.[35] Inevitably, conditions in Liverpool and London Chinatowns were raised. It was claimed that 'over 4000 Chinese' were 'living in Liverpool in places such as no boarding-house or lodging-house keeper should be allowed to keep' and that of even more astounding a character were 'the "hop-joints" (opium dens) and gaming houses in East London' where opium was being 'openly manufactured' and 'smuggled abroad in large quantities'. James Sexton, now acknowledging his part, reminded the Congress that nine years previously he had raised the Liverpool Commission of Enquiry to draw public attention to 'this horrible state of affairs'. Sexton accused the Aliens Acts of fraudulence, claiming the Chinese, 'the most dangerous of all aliens', were selling 'their wives and daughters before leaving their own country to ship as crew at a shilling a month'.[36]

It is satisfying to give the last word to the Chinese who did not take this slander quietly. A spirited defence from 'the leading Chinamen of Liverpool', as the *Liverpool Post and Mercury* styled them, was published in that paper the following week.[37] The letter contested the figure of 4,000 Chinese residents in Liverpool, stating there were no more than 4,000 Chinese across the country and besides 'our opponents say nothing of the 20,000 or 30,000 Britishers who are occupying good positions and enjoying peaceful dwellings in China and who do not want to come home'.[38] The Commission of 1906 was referred to which had entirely refuted accusations of insanitary boarding houses in Liverpool's Chinese quarter – and as for opium: 'Who began the opium traffic? ... Who first forced opium into our country against our wish and will and made us poor as a nation? ... the truth is opium is now entirely stopped, as our critics ought to know, both in London, Liverpool, Cardiff and everywhere else, and Chinese have bid farewell to the habit.' Chinese seamen were employed because shipowners found them steady and reliable and 'to get Britishers to work on ships is almost impossible, unless it is they cannot work on land'. The letter concluded by asking that 'Messrs Cotter, Sexton ... and all other slanderers feel thoroughly ashamed of themselves for insulting a class of people who have never harmed them but give proof after proof of their friendship towards Great Britain and her Allies'. It was signed Lum Lie, Chow Chee, Sing Tai, A. Keow, F. Ah Pooh, Wong York, Cheong Ping, Yuan Time, Lai Kee, Wo Fat, Leo Chu and Yee You Kee.[39]

As 'The Chinese Connection' made clear, a combination of propaganda and popular culture, from the breakfast newspaper to the latest West End stage sensation, worked to fan the flames of local resentment into a national sinophobia. London's Limehouse Chinatown became a byword for miscegenation, gambling and opium smoking, exoticised by Sax Rohmer's evil mastermind, Fu Manchu and Thomas Burke's best-selling tales of lowlife romance. England's Yellow Peril exploded in the midst of a catastrophic war and would define the representation of Chinese in the decades to come. While recent publications such as Ross Forman's *China and the Victorian Imagination: Empires Entwined*, Christopher Frayling's *The Yellow Peril: Dr Fu Manchu and the Rise of Chinaphobia* and Phil Baker and Antony Clayton's edited collection *Lord of Strange Deaths: The fiendish world of Sax Rohmer* thoroughly excavate the popular Yellow Perilism of turn-of-the-century pulp, critical appreciation is also being paid to an arguably more productive and less considered legacy of Sino-British encounter.[40] Patricia Lawrence's *Lily Briscoe's Chinese Eyes: Bloomsbury, Modernism and China*, Eugenia Zuroski Jenkins' *A Taste for China: English Subjectivity and the Prehistory of Orientalism*, Elizabeth Chang's *Britain's Chinese Eye: Literature, Empire, and Aesthetics in Nineteenth-Century Britain* and my own edited collection, *British Modernism and Chinoiserie*, each explore the ways in which the visual iconography and style of China constituted a precursor of literary and visual modernism within the Victorian realist regime.[41] Chinese aesthetics primed British eyes for European modernism, a cultural counterpoint to the more familiar negative narrative. Lastly, Wendy Gan's *Comic China: Representing Common Ground, 1890–1945* (forthcoming Temple University Press) takes a refreshingly positive look at what we share rather than what divides us.

Notes

1 Colin Holmes, 'The Chinese Connection' in idem. and Geoffrey Alderman (eds), *Outsiders and Outcasts: Essays in Honour of William J. Fishman* (London: Duckworth 1993); Runnymede Trust, 'Our Migration Story: The Making of Britain' to support GCSE History module 'Migration to Britain c.1000 to 2010, The Impact of the Empire on the British Isles 1688-c.1730'.

2 Colin Holmes, *John Bull's Island: Immigration and British Society, 1871–1971* (London: Macmillan Education 1988).
3 Colin Holmes, *Immigrants and Minorities in British Society* (London: Allen & Unwin 1978).
4 J. P. May, 'The Chinese in Britain, 1860–1914', in Colin Holmes (ed.), *Immigrants and Minorities in British Society* (London: Allen & Unwin 1978), 111.
5 Ibid., 113.
6 George Sala, *Living London* (London: Remington 1883), 425.
7 May, 'The Chinese in Britain, 1860–1914', 114.
8 Ibid., 123, footnote 28, Letter from the chief constable, Liverpool, to the Home Secretary, 8 December 1906, HO45 11843/139147/8
9 Ibid., 119.
10 Ibid., 123, footnote 28.
11 Ibid.
12 Ibid, 111.
13 Ibid.
14 Ibid. Ng Kwee Choo, *The Chinese in London* (London: Oxford University Press for The Institute of Race Relations 1968).
15 Colin Holmes, 'The Chinese connection', 76.
16 Ibid.
17 Marek Kohn, *Dope Girls: The Birth of the British Drug Underground* (London: Lawrence & Wishart 1992), 30.
18 Ibid.
19 Cited in Anne Witchard, 'Limehouse, Bloomsbury, and *Piccadilly*: A Chinese sojourn in the Twenties', in Pallavi Rastogi and Jocelyn Fenton Stitt (eds), *Before Windrush: Recovering an Asian and Black Literary Heritage within Britain* (Newcastle: Cambridge Scholars Press 2009).
20 Thomas Burke, *Limehouse Nights: Tales of Chinatown* (London: Grant Richards 1916).
21 Anne Witchard, *Thomas Burke's Dark Chinoiserie: Limehouse Nights and the Queer Spell of Chinatown* (Farnham: Ashgate 2009).
22 Gregory B. Lee, *Troubadours, Trumpeters, Troubled Makers: Lyricism, Nationalism, and Hybridity in China and Its Others* (Durham NC: Duke University Press 1996).
23 Gregory B. Lee, *Chinas Unlimited: Making the Imaginaries of China and Chineseness* (Honolulu: University of Hawaii Press 2003).
24 Ibid., 30.
25 Robert Bickers *Britain in China: Community, Culture and Colonialism, 1900–49* (Manchester: Manchester University Press 1999).
26 Ibid., 22.
27 Ibid., 23.
28 Anne Witchard, *Lao She in London* (Hong Kong: Hong Kong University Press 2012). Dolby's translation of Lao She's *Er Ma* is now published in a Penguin Modern Classic edition as *Mr Ma and Son* (2013).
29 See Witchard, *Thomas Burke's Dark Chinoiserie*, 254.
30 'Limehouse debunked' unattributed newspaper clipping, 1934. Chinatown File, Local History Archive, Tower Hamlets Central Library.
31 John Seed, 'Limehouse blues: looking for Chinatown in the London Docks, 1900–1940', *History Workshop Journal*, vol. 62, 2006, 58–85.
32 Sascha Auerbach, *Race, Law, and 'The Chinese Puzzle' in Imperial Britain* (London: Palgrave 2009).
33 Gregor Benton and E. T. Gomez (eds), *The Chinese in Britain, 1800-Present: Economy, Transnationalism, Identity* (London: Palgrave Macmillan Transnational History Series 2008).

34 Mark O'Neill, *The Chinese Labour Corps: The Forgotten Chinese Labourers of the First World War* (Beijing: Penguin China 2014); Anne Witchard, *England's Yellow Peril: Sinophobia and the Great War* (Beijing: Penguin China 2014).
35 *Devon and Exeter Gazette*, 9 September 1916.
36 Ibid.
37 *Liverpool Post and Mercury*, 15 September 1916.
38 Ibid.
39 Ibid.
40 Ross Forman, *China and the Victorian Imagination: Empires Entwined* (Cambridge: Cambridge University Press 2013); Christopher Frayling, *The Yellow Peril: Dr Fu Manchu and the Rise of Chinaphobia* (London: Thames and Hudson 2014); Phil Baker and Antony Clayton (eds), *Lord of Strange Deaths: The Fiendish World of Sax Rohmer* (London: Strange Attractor Press 2015).
41 Patricia Lawrence, *Lily Briscoe's Chinese Eyes: Bloomsbury, Modernism and China* (Columbia: University of South Carolina Press 2003); Eugenia Zuroski Jenkins, *A Taste for China: English Subjectivity and the Prehistory of Orientalism* (Oxford: Oxford University Press 2013); Elizabeth Chang, *Britain's Chinese Eye: Literature, Empire, and Aesthetics in Nineteenth-Century Britain* (Stanford CA: Stanford University Press 2010); Anne Witchard (ed), *British Modernism and Chinoiserie* (Edinburgh: Edinburgh University Press 2015).

7
THE UNIQUENESS OF LONDON

Panikos Panayi

There are many ways to write immigration history in Britain but we can identify the following. First, a small number of general histories of migration to the country.[1] Second, studies of particular groups who have settled in Britain, an approach which has a long tradition dating back to the nineteenth century in the case of Jewish and Irish communities in particular[2] but which has also led to similar studies of a variety of other more recently arrived groups from the second half of the twentieth century.[3] These two approaches have distinct aims in mind. The general histories, written against the background of migration taking place at the time of their writing and, perhaps more importantly, the widespread newspaper-led hostility which migrants face, wish to demonstrate that Britain has a long tradition of migration stretching back centuries and even millennia. The histories of particular migrant groups also emerge against a background of hostility but have the key aim of proving that the particular group under consideration, usually written by somebody with the same ethnic identity as the group about which they write, has not only made a significant contribution to the history of Great Britain but also has a long history of settlement in the country. Such narratives play a central role in the development of an ethnic consciousness whether in the case of the Irish, Jews, black people or Asians, to simply name four of the most visible and politically active ethnic communities in Britain.[4] Both of these approaches essentially react against a dominating British nationalism which, unchallenged, leaves little space for any type of ethnic difference.

Several problems emerge when approaching migration on a national basis. Most obviously, it limits the room for examining both local and personal experiences. At the same time, such histories also tend to impact on the scope for international comparison. Great Britain may have specific features in its migration history but movement to the country reflects the globalisation of the world which has not simply taken place over the past twenty years or even in the age of Empire during the nineteenth century. The presence of migrants in Britain, as the general studies by Walvin, Holmes, Winder and Panayi have demonstrated, has a long history.

As well as these national studies of migration to Britain, others have taken a more focused urban approach. Some concentrate upon the general history of a group in a particular town or city, such as, to give a couple of examples, Manchester Jewry[5] or the Germans in Glasgow.[6] Others have tackled a more specific location. We can point, for example, to a concentration on the impact of Jews on the East End of London, from the end of the nineteenth century.[7] The approach remains the experience of one group in one location, just more focused. Such narratives, while they may have the underlying desire of proving a point about the value and longevity of a group, which would apply to the studies of Margoliouth,[8] Visram or Fryer,[9] for example, remain driven by a more purely scholarly driven agenda.

In contrast to national studies of migration, we have few studies which have taken a long-term perspective on the immigration history of one town or city. In the case of Manchester, for example, there only exists an unsatisfactory, if useful and interesting, edited volume issued by the city's education committee as long ago as 1963.[10] Nothing similar has emerged for other major multicultural urban environments in Britain. The explanation for this may lie in the fact that few cities have a long-term and continuous history of migrant settlement as well as the fact that much migrant history emerges from the pen of those writing about the group from which they emerge. Few Britons have a multicultural consciousness.

We should expect London to be historiographically different but no single authored work has emerged on the history of migration to the city in contrast to the studies of specific groups in London or individual locations within it, especially the East End. While *The Peopling of London*, edited by Nick Merriman, took a big step towards filling this lacuna by bringing together a wide range of scholars who demonstrated the diversity and longevity of migrant settlement in London, it only covered seventeen different groups, although this seventeen would multiply further if broken down into countries of origin as they include 'Arabs', 'Latin Americans' and 'South Asians'.[11] The scholar who has especially concentrated upon the immigration history of London consists of Anne J. Kershen. She has written focused studies on Jews,[12] produced an important work on the immigration history of Spitalfields[13] and brought together academics and others in a series of edited books which have looked at migration from a historical and contemporary perspective.[14]

While the absence of immigration histories of some of the major British cities of Britain proves surprising, this statement applies especially to London because of the centrality of migration in the history of British and former imperial capital. Kershen has pointed to the importance of migrants in contemporary London. In 2011 'almost three million of the capital's total population of eight million were born outside the United Kingdom',[15] while in 'London as a whole by 2015, 44 percent of the population are of black or minority ethnicity'.[16] Despite the work she has carried out on the history of immigration into London, Kershen sees the past decades as unique in this history, pointing to the fact in '1951, one in twenty Londoners was born outside the UK, by 1991 one in five and by 2011 more than one in three. In just the decade 2001–11, the non-UK population increased by 1 million'.[17]

While we cannot take issue with the increased proportion of Londoners born abroad, the longevity and continuity of migration to the British capital represents one of its unique features, both on a national and an international scale. Other cities in the globe may have a similar percentage of their populations born abroad, but London would appear almost unique in the fact that it has attracted migrants for so much of its history. Clearly, great US cities such as New York or Chicago have evolved as a result of migration over the last two centuries, while, for example, German urban concentrations such as Berlin or Frankfurt have similar multicultural histories since the Second World War, but none of these four examples can compare with the British capital in terms of the longevity of migration, dating back millennia. Perhaps the only European settlements which have comparable experiences consist of the imperial capitals of Rome and Paris, which have a similar long-term history to London.

The volume edited by Nick Merriman on *The Peopling of London* carried the subtitle of *Fifteen Thousand Years of Settlement from Overseas*. While most of the essays which followed focused upon communities which evolved during the preceding two centuries and, more especially, the period since the Second World War, Merriman's introductory piece 'From Prehistoric Times to the Huguenots' looks at Roman London as a 'cosmopolitan city', but also points to its importance under Saxons and Vikings, indicating its essence as a city created and ruled in its early days by invaders/migrants.[18]

From the Norman invasion, London became a city which attracted a series of migrant communities (in contrast to invaders) which established its history as a migrant hub until the present day.[19] The level of persecution may differ[20] from that experienced by newcomers in the post-War period, but the increasing level of control which newcomers to London face,[21] resembles that of their medieval predecessors.[22]

Those who moved to the capital until the eighteenth century divide into a series of categories. Jews constitute a fairly unique grouping because of the continuity of their presence, despite their absence from the capital between 1290 and 1655 as a result of their expulsion. They include an elite group of money lenders yet, on the other hand, some of them formed part of the medieval underclass, confined to their ghetto in Old Jewry.[23] Following readmission, Jews have formed a key element in the demographic, cultural and economic history of London with a presence on all parts of the economic spectrum since that time (although social mobility characterises the Jewish history of London).[24]

The rest of the migrant groupings which have settled in London since the Norman period divide into three categories. First, banking, business and financial elites, with origins in the medieval Jews and Lombards who helped finance the English state and the development of banking in London.[25] At the same time, London served as a major headquarters of the Hanseatic League with its base in the Steelyard, although the Hansa provide just the most famous example of medieval merchants in London.[26] More recently, German businessmen and financiers (both Jewish and gentile) settled in nineteenth-century London,[27] while post-War and, more especially, post-Thatcher and post-economic liberalisation London has, genuinely, become the playground of the wealthy.[28] The continuity in this city of global importance from the sixteenth-century age of exploration followed by the nineteenth-century age of Empire and European importance in the middle ages, needs emphasising. Because of this international importance, it has attracted banking, trading and business elites during the past millennium.

London has also acted as an important magnet for refugees and other political elites, even though their numbers have declined in recent decades because of the increasing control exercised over migration by the British state and the desire to disperse refugees away from areas with high concentrations of ethnic minorities. An important turning point in the history of refugee movements to London consisted of the Reformation when Protestant exiles from a variety of origins flocked to London and established the Austin Friars Church.[29] Similarly, the English capital also became a major focus for the settlement of Huguenots.[30] From the end of the eighteenth century, London attracted political exiles in the age of revolution and nationalism. The imperial capital became a major centre for the evolution of Marxist ideology acting as long-term home to Karl Marx and the birthplace of the First International. London has also played a central role in the development of nationalist movements whether as a home to Polish exiles[31] or as a major focus for the birth of Pan-Africanism and, therefore, the ideologies which destroyed the British Empire.[32] During the twentieth century, London attracted refugees during the 'Age of Extremes'.[33]

London has also acted as a magnet for mass migration of manual labourers. The Irish have settled in London from the middle ages and developed distinct communities from the eighteenth century onwards although the migration of people from the 'New Commonwealth' meant they became increasingly invisible after 1945.[34] While, as Kershen has demonstrated, the Huguenots developed a distinct community in Spitalfields from the end of the seventeenth century, the kaleidoscope of settlements which characterise the capital today really began to evolve from the nineteenth century. While the three major groups which emerged in London before the First World War in the form of the Irish, Germans and Jews may all have developed a major focus on the East End, this remained one of several locations for their settlement. By the Victorian period black and Asian people also lived in the capital, although the former had reached their peak during the height of the eighteenth-century slave trade.[35] The 'age of migration'[36] transformed London after the Second World War as the capital became a multicultural kaleidoscope, a fact which became increasingly apparent as the twentieth and twenty-first centuries progressed.[37]

The above survey of the history of migration to London might also appear to apply to other parts of Britain. Most of the groups outlined above would not simply have settled in the capital, but would also have moved to cities throughout the country, whether Hanseatic merchants, Jews, the Irish or Germans. But clear differences exist. The first consists of the continuity of settlement to return to our original point about the longevity of London as a migrant metropolis. For example, while a significant Jewish community has always existed in London, the history of provincial Jewry has no other continuous focus. Medieval Jews settled in Bristol, Cambridge, Exeter, Gloucester, Lincoln, Oxford and York,[38] but even the rise of provincial Jewry as identified by Cecil Roth[39] did not revive some of these communities. Similarly, the centres of Hanseatic England in the high middle ages such as Ipswich, Yarmouth, Hull and York do not constitute major areas of migrant settlement in recent centuries. Outside London the major Jewish communities of the nineteenth and twentieth centuries emerged in the major industrial cities of Manchester, Leeds and Glasgow which became major urban centres as a result of the industrial revolution. At the same time, the nineteenth-century Irish settled in major cities such as Liverpool and Newcastle-upon-Tyne which have not become significant locations of post-War migration since 1945. This is not to deny a continuity of migrant settlement in these big British cities, especially Liverpool, which witnessed black settlement because of its role in the slave trade.[40] Clearly London is different because it has *always* acted as the main area of settlement for most migrant groups who have made their way to Britain. No break exists in this history. This essentially receives explanation from the centrality of London in the economic, political and cultural history of Britain. While the industrial revolution gave birth to new urban centres, important medieval and early modern towns such as York, Norwich or Bristol did not experience significant growth. London, on the other hand, grew at the same time as the great industrial cities mushroomed during the nineteenth century.[41]

The British capital has acted as the focal point for at least half of the population of most migrant groups settled in Britain and a much higher proportion for others. Most of the larger groups who moved to Britain in the nineteenth and early twentieth centuries concentrated upon London. This applies particularly to the 50–60,000 German immigrants in the late Victorian and Edwardian period, fifty percent of whom always lived in the capital, with much smaller concentrations in northern cities such as Liverpool, Manchester, Hull and Bradford.[42] The Italian community also focused upon the capital (between 5,000 and 10,000 people) throughout the nineteenth and early twentieth centuries, with smaller concentrations in Edinburgh, Glasgow, Liverpool, Manchester and South Wales.[43] Most of the smaller European groups also tended to concentrate on central London.[44] While provincial Jewry has a long and diverse history, the evolution of Anglo-Jewry remains closely linked with London. In the middle of the nineteenth century about two-thirds of British Jews resided in the imperial capital. By 1900 about 135,000 Jews lived in London, a figure which increased to almost 200,000 by 1929, when Jews made up four percent of the city's population.[45] While dispersal has taken place since the interwar years and while traces of this history become increasingly hard to locate, the Jews in London remain especially closely linked with the East End, dating back to the eighteenth century.[46] While the Irish may have become one of the most widely spread groups in Britain, they also have a major concentration in London dating back to the middle ages and increasing during the eighteenth and nineteenth centuries so that in 1851 108,548 people born in Ireland resided in the capital, making up 4.6 percent of the total population. While the proportion of Irish living in several industrial towns in Victorian Britain may have stood at a higher rate, London always counted the largest total.[47]

Although the East End housed a significant percentage of most migrant communities in London before 1945, settlement also spread to most parts of the capital. This increasing dispersal becomes more apparent after 1945. Bangladeshis may have taken the place of Jews in the East End, but other newcomers did not automatically settle here so that West Indians developed concentrations in Brixton and Notting Hill in particular,[48] while also residing elsewhere in the capital. Sikhs have concentrated in the Southall heartland, while Gujuratis have settled slightly further north in Wembley, with another concentration around Tooting. Pakistani communities, meanwhile, have largely evolved outside the capital.[49] Irish settlement in post-War London has concentrated in north and north-west London, especially Brent, Camden, Islington and Ealing. If an Irish heartland in London has existed, it may consist of Kilburn.[50] The post-war Greek Cypriot settlement has predominantly focused upon North London, initially in inner London in Camden Town, although its members have increasingly moved to the northern suburbs, initially Haringey, but then further out to Enfield. Nevertheless, like other post-War migrant groups, while Greek Cypriots have concentrations, they are represented in most London boroughs from Hackney, one of the poorest, to Barnet, one of the richest.[51] The increase in immigration which has taken place to Britain recently, particularly from the European Union, has focused especially upon London, even though newcomers from the nation states which joined the EU in 2004 have settled throughout the whole of Britain. In 2010 thirteen percent of the population of the UK consisted of people born abroad whereas the percentage for London stood at more than 34 or 39 for inner London. The closest to this figure outside the capital consisted of Leicester (34.5 per cent), with Manchester at 25 per cent and Birmingham at 20.2 per cent.[52] These figures mask local variations and do not refer to ethnic identity (which would include the second and subsequent generations).

These figures do not reveal the increasing diversity of London, which makes it a perfect example of what Steven Vertovec has described as 'super-diversity', using London as his case study, but also viewing it as part of wider developments in Britain. Vertovec focuses upon the range of countries from which the population of the British capital has originated as well as the range of languages spoken and religious pluralism.[53] Migrants to the capital and, to a lesser extent, the rest of the country, do not simply stem from the West Indies, South Asia and the EU but also from a range of other locations which, in recent years, have especially included Africa, particularly Ghana, Kenya, Nigeria, Somalia, South Africa and Zimbabwe (all with British imperial connections).[54] By 2001 the number of black Africans in London (378,933) had overtaken the number of black Caribbeans (343,567).[55] Some communities, especially Latin Americans, remain overwhelmingly concentrated upon London.[56]

Importantly, for a social scientist, Vertovec recognises the long history of migration to London, while stressing the post-1945 years,[57] as well as focusing upon interaction. On the one hand London may resemble a kaleidoscope of differing ethnic groups, with their own constructed identities, living in particular locations. Certainly, an examination of London settlement patterns during any period in the last two hundred years and before would reveal ethnic concentrations.[58]

On the other, London has evolved a type of multiculture because of the level of ethnic diversity, which is not necessarily unique either in the British case or in comparison with other global capitals. The evolution of the restaurant in London would demonstrate this both in terms of the range of different foods available, the development of fusion food, beginning with fish and chips (Jewish in origin) in the East End, and the fact that much of the population of London, whatever their ethnic origins, sample all types of cuisine.[59] Multiculture also becomes inevitable in everyday interaction whether in terms of working, schooling or the development of relationships, which have increasingly become inter-ethnic in the case of London. The difference between London and the rest of Britain lies precisely in the range of different ethnic groups which live in the capital, which contrasts with some provincial towns such as Nottingham with a tradition of African Caribbean settlement,[60] or Bradford, with a preponderance of Pakistanis.[61] These locations certainly differ from the global superdiverse London.

Both superdiversity and multiculture have roots in the history of migration to the capital. As we have seen, while the range of groups may have increased in the twenty-first century, they build upon longer-term traditions of settlement. Some apparently newer communities have long histories of settlement in London. Poles emerged during the nineteenth century, increasing in numbers at the end of the Second World War and expanding significantly after 2004.[62] Similarly, ethnic interaction in London, while often driven by native Londoners displaying hostility towards newcomers, has evolved over centuries, indicated by Jewish and Irish experiences.

The uniqueness of London therefore lies in its long history of immigration, the fact that it counts far more migrants than other British cities as a percentage of its population, and, in the twenty-first century, increasing diversity. Alternatively, we could argue that the British capital forms a central point in the system of international migration in the modern world, because of its importance as a global capital, in which its role as the centre of a global empire proved the decisive turning point, whether during the nineteenth century, or even dating back to the eighteenth century or before.

Ultimately, the history of London and the history of migration, both from other parts of the world, from Europe and from the rest of Britain, remain inextricably linked. As the largest city in Britain and before, during and after the age of Empire, it attracted a wide range and vast numbers of people unique in Britain and replicated in few places in the world. Not only have economic growth and migration developed simultaneously in London since the arrival of the Irish in the middle of the nineteenth century, but European elites have played a central role in its development since the middle ages. The character of London has become deeply multicultural, despite anti-immigrant hostility dating back centuries. The arrival of hundreds of thousands of Irish and Jews from the middle of the nineteenth century acted as a turning point in the development of the increasingly metropolitan and global metropolis. While London may have become the epitome of superdiversity, this development has a long history.

Notes

1 Jim Walvin, *Passage to Britain: Immigration in British History and Politics* (Harmondsworth: Penguin 1984); Colin Holmes, *John Bull's Island: Immigration and British Society, 1871–1971* (Basingstoke: Palgrave 1988); Robert Winder, *Bloody Foreigners: The Story of Immigration to Britain* (London: Little Brown, 2004); Panikos Panayi, *An Immigration History of Britain: Multicultural Racism Since c1800* (London: Longman 2010).
2 Studies of the Jews in Britain which appeared before the First World War include: Moses Margoliouth, *The History of the Jews in Great Britain*, 3 volumes (London: Richard Bentley 1851); John Mills, *The British Jews* (London: Houlston & Stonemann 1853); A. M. Hyamson, *The History of the Jews in England* (London: Jewish Historical Society of England 1908). For the Irish see: John Denvir, *The Irish in Britain* (London: Kegan Paul, Trench, Trübner & Co. 1892).
3 See especially the pioneering and now classic: Peter Fryer, *Staying Power: The History of Black People in Britain* (London: Pluto 1984); and Rozina Visram, *Ayahs, Lascars and Princes: Indians in Britain 1700–1947* (London: Pluto 1986).
4 Kathy Burrell and Panikos Panayi, 'Immigration, history and memory in Britain', in Kathy Burrell and Panikos Panayi (eds), *Histories and Memories: Migrants and their History in Britain* (London: I.B. Tauris 2006), 3–17.
5 Bill Williams, *The Making of Manchester Jewry, 1740–1875* (Manchester: Manchester University Press 1985).
6 Stefan Manz, *Migranten und Internierte: Deutsche in Glasgow, 1864–1918* (Stuttgart: Steiner 2003).
7 The three classic studies remain: Lloyd P. Gartner, *The Jewish Immigrant in England, 1870–1914* (London: George Allen & Unwin 1960); John A. Garrard, *The English and Immigration, 1880–1910* (London: Oxford University Press 1971); Bernard Gainer, *The Alien Invasion: The Origins of the Aliens Act of 1905* (London: Heinemann Educational 1972). Despite their titles, these three studies remain focused upon the East End of London, illustrating the point made below, about the false conflation of the London metropolitan experience with the national picture.
8 Margoliouth, *History of the Jews in Great Britain*.
9 Fryer, *Staying Power*; Visram, *Ayahs, Lascars and Princes*. These two volumes remain deeply scholarly.
10 N. J. Frangopoulo, *Rich Inheritance: A Guide to the History of Manchester* (Manchester: Manchester Education Committee 1963).
11 Nick Merriman (ed.), *The Peopling of London: Fifteen Thousand Years of Settlement from Overseas* (London: Museum of London 1993).
12 Anne J. Kershen, *Uniting the Tailors: Trade Unionism Amongst the Tailors of London and Leeds, 1870–1939* (London: Routledge 1995).
13 Anne J. Kershen, *Strangers, Aliens and Asians: Huguenots, Jews and Bangladeshis in Spitalfields, 1660–2000* (London: Routledge 2005).

14 Anne J. Kershen, (ed.): *The Promised Land: The Migrant Experience in a Capital City* (Aldershot: Ashgate, 1997); and *London the Promised Land Revisited: The Changing Face of the London Migrant Landscape in the Early 21st Century* (London: Routledge 2015).
15 Anne J. Kershen, 'Introduction: London the Promised Land Revisited: The Migrant Landscape in the 21st Century', in Kershen, *London the Promised Land Revisited*, 13.
16 Anne J. Kershen, 'Foreword', in Kershen, *London the Promised Land Revisited*, xvii.
17 Ibid.
18 Nick Merriman, 'The invisible settlers: from prehistoric times to Huguenots', in Merriman, *Peopling*, 29–34.
19 Ibid., 34–41.
20 See, for example, Martin Holmes, 'Evil May-Day 1517: The story of a riot', *History Today*, vol. 15, 1965, 642–650.
21 See, for example, Tendanyi Bloom, 'London's "Ghosts": The Capital and UK Policy of Destitution of Refused Asylum-Seekers' and Parvati Nair, 'Undocumented and Unseen: The Making of the Everyday in the Global Metropolis of London 2015', in Kershen, *London the Promised Land Revisited*, 77–111.
22 See, for example, T. H. Lloyd, *Alien Merchants in England in the High Middle Ages* (Brighton: Harvester 1982), 22–34.
23 W. D. Rubinstein, *A History of the Jews in the English-Speaking World: Great Britain* (Basingstoke: Macmillan 1996), 36–40.
24 David Cesarani, 'A funny thing happened on the way to the suburbs: social change in Anglo-Jewry between the wars, 1914–1945', *Jewish Culture and History* vol. 1, 1998, 5–26.
25 Merriman, 'Invisible Settlers', 34–9; Terri Colpi, *The Italian Factor: The Italian Community in Great Britain* (Edinburgh: Mainstream 1991), 25–6.
26 T. H. Lloyd, *England and the German Hanse, 1157–1611: A Study in their Trade and Commercial Diplomacy* (Cambridge: Cambridge University Press 1991).
27 Panikos Panayi, *German Immigrants in Britain during the Nineteenth Century, 1815–1914* (Oxford: Berg 1995), 139–142.
28 An indication of this can be found in the annual *Sunday Times Rich List*.
29 Panayi, *German Immigrants*, 7–8.
30 Kershen, *Strangers*.
31 As an indication of refugee activity in nineteenth century London see Sabine Freitag, ed., *Exiles from European Revolutions: Refugees in Mid-Victorian England* (Oxford: Berghahn 2003).
32 Marc Matera, *Black London: The Imperial Metropolis and Decolonization in the Twentieth Century* (Berkeley: University of California Press 2015).
33 See, especially, Martin A. Conway and Jose Gotovitch (eds), *Europe in Exile: European Exile Communities in Britain 1940–45* (Oxford: Berghahn 2001).
34 Lynn Hollen Lees, *Exiles of Erin: Irish Immigrants in Victorian London* (Manchester: Manchester University Press 1979); Martin Mac an Ghaill, 'The Irish in Britain: the invisibility of ethnicity and anti-Irish racism', *Journal of Ethnic and Migration Studies* vol. 26, 2000, 137–47.
35 Fryer, *Staying Power*, 67–236.
36 Stephen Castles, Hein de Haas and Mark J. Miller, *The Age of Migration: International Population Movements in the Modern World* 5th edn (Basingstoke: Palgrave 2013).
37 Kershen, *London the Promised Land Revisited*.
38 H. G. Richardson, *The English Jewry under Angevin Kings* (London, 1960), 6–14.
39 Cecil Roth, *The Rise of Provincial Jewry: The Early History of the Jewish Communities in the English Countryside* (London: Jewish Monthly 1950).

40 Ray Costello, *Black Liverpool: The Early History of Britain's Oldest Black Community 1730–1918* (Liverpool: Picton 2001), 8–10.
41 Jerry White, *London in the Nineteenth Century: 'A Human Awful Wonder of God'* (London: Jonathan Cape 2007).
42 Panayi, *German Immigrants*, 92–107.
43 Lucio Sponza, *Italian Immigrants in Nineteenth Century Britain* (Leicester: Leicester University Press 1988), 322–325; Terri Colpi, *The Italian Factor: The Italian Community in Great Britain* (Edinburgh: Mainstream 1991), 74.
44 Panikos Panayi, *Immigration, Ethnicity and Racism in Britain, 1815–1945* (Manchester: Manchester University Press 1994) 56–57.
45 Geoffrey Alderman, *Modern British Jewry* (Oxford: Oxford University Press 1992), 118; H. L. Trachtenberg, 'Estimate of the Jewish population of London in 1929', *Journal of the Royal Statistical Society* vol. 96, 1933, 87–98 (96).
46 As an introduction see, the admittedly now dated, Aubrey Newman, *The Jewish East End* (London: Jewish Historical Society of England 1981).
47 Panayi, *Immigration, Ethnicity and Racism*, 53.
48 Edward Pilkington, *Beyond the Mother Country: West Indians and the Notting Hill White Riots* (London: I. B. Tauris 1988); Sheila Patterson, *Dark Strangers: A Sociological Study of the Absorption of a Recent West Indian Migrant Group in Brixton, South London* (London: Tavistock Publications 1963); Ruth Glass, *Newcomers: The West Indians in London* (London: Allen & Unwin 1960), 32–40; Richard Skellington with Paulette Morris, *Race in Britain Today*, 2nd edn (London: Sage 1996), 58.
49 Panikos Panayi, 'Cosmopolis: London's ethnic minorities', in Andrew Gibson and Joe Kerr, *London from Punk to Blair* (London: Reaktion 2003), 67–71; Gurharpal Singh and Darshan Singh Tatla, *Sikhs in Britain: The Making of a Community* (London: Zed 2006), 62–63; Muhamad Anwar, *British Pakistanis: Demographic, Social and Economic Position* (Coventry: Centre for Research in Ethnic Relations 1996), 16–19.
50 Bronwen Walter, 'Contemporary Irish settlement in London: women's worlds, men's worlds', in Jim Mac Laughlin, (ed.), *Location and Dislocation in Contemporary Irish Society: Emigration and Identities* (Cork: Cork University Press 1997), 67–68; Judy Chance, 'The Irish in London: an exploration of ethnic boundary maintenance', in Peter Jackson (ed.), *Race and Racism: Essays in Social Geography* (London: Allen & Unwin 1987), 142–160.
51 Robin Oakley, *Changing Patterns of Distribution of Cypriot Settlement* (Coventry: Centre for Research in Ethnic Relations 1987).
52 Office for National Statistics, www.ons.gov.uk/peoplepopulationandcommunity/populationandmigration/internationalmigration/datasets/populationoftheunitedkingdombycountryofbirthandnationality, Population of the United Kingdom by Country of Birth and Nationality, Data Set, 2010 (accessed 28 February 2017).
53 Steven Vertovec, 'Super-Diversity and its implications', *Ethnic and Racial Studies* vol. 30, 2007, 1024–1054.
54 Ibid., 1031–1032.
55 Leo Benedictus, 'Every race, colour, nation and religion on earth: Part 1', *Guardian*, 21 January 2005.
56 C. McIlwaine, J. C. Cock and B. Linneker, *No Longer Invisible: The Latin American Community in London* (London: Trust for London 2011).
57 Vertovec, 'Super-Diversity', 1026–1028.
58 Panayi, 'Cosmopolis'.
59 Brenda Assael, 'Gastro-Cosmopolitanism and the restaurant in late Victorian and Edwardian London', *Historical Journal*, vol. 56, 2013, 681–706; Panikos Panayi, *Spicing*

Up Britain: The Multicultural History of British Food (London: Reaktion 2008), 65–94, 124–180; Panikos Panayi, *Fish and Chips* (London: Reaktion 2014), 43–76.
60 Daniel Lawrence, *Black Migrants, White Natives: A Study of Race Relations in Nottingham* (Cambridge: Cambridge University Press 1974).
61 See, for example, Ikhlaq Din, *The New British: The Impact of Culture and Community on Young Pakistanis* (Abingdon: Routledge 2006).
62 Kathy Burrell, 'Migration to the UK from Poland: continuity and change in East-West European mobility', in Kathy Burrell (ed.), *Polish Migration to the UK in the 'New' European Union: After 2004* (Farnham: Ashgate 2009), 2–11.

8

SPACES OF BLACK HISTORY

Caroline Bressey

In 2015, at the London Guildhall Art Gallery's exhibition 'No Colour Bar: Black British Art in Action 1960–1990', a recreation of the Bogle-L'Ouverture/Walter Rodney bookshop was placed at the heart of the exhibition.[1] Founded in 1968 by Jessica and Eric Huntley, Bogle-L'Ouverture would become one of the best-known radical black publishers in Britain, though its activities have now ceased and its archive deposited with the London Metropolitan Archive.[2] Two years before the Huntleys opened their bookshop, New Beacon Books was founded by John La Rose and Rachel White, establishing Britain's first black bookshop and publishing house. Both organisations provided places in which readers could find works by writers from Africa, the Caribbean, Asia and 'Black Britain'.[3] As the poet Linton Kwesi Johnson recalled, when as a young man he became interested in literature, access to the material published and presented by New Beacon Books and Bogle-L'Ouverture 'was like discovering an oasis in a desert of knowledge because at school, there was nothing in the school curriculum that told you anything about yourself'. For Johnson, these organisations created a space where a 'whole new world opened up for me'.[4]

Accessing 'black history' has been and remains an important part of political activism and a search for a sense of belonging for black people in Britain. Linton Kwesi Johnson was recalling his time as a pupil in Britain during the 1960s, an era when black children were routinely marginalised in the school system. This is examined in Bernard Coard's book *How the West Indian Child is Made Educationally Subnormal in the British School System* published by New Beacon Books in 1971. Some parents concerned about the knowledge their children were receiving through the state education system turned to supplementary schools. First established in the 1950s, these are mostly small organisations, run after school or on weekends in a variety of spaces from private front rooms to council accommodation.[5] The schools are 'spaces and places in which counter-hegemonic discourses of blackness can be created' and as one mother recalled, the first time she took her son to Saturday school he was inspired by learning history: 'He loved it, he was really excited. He said I know all about so and so and about so and so, all these people from black history'.[6] I began my own research into black Victorian women in London in the archives of the children's Barnardo's. As a geography undergraduate I was keen to understand my place in the historical geography of the city I had grown up in. I had studied the nineteenth century at both school and university, but not the history of the black presence within it.[7] Over twenty years has passed since I began my undergraduate studies, and in that time, despite the lobbying of parents, teachers and scholars, black history – the history of black people *in* Britain – has remained largely absent from the school curriculum, and research into the black presence in Britain remains largely undertaken by those working outside academia and 'mainstream' publishing houses.

Research to date indicates that M. Dorothy George was the first modern historian to note the historical presence of black people in Britain.[8] In her 1925 depiction of London life in the eighteenth century, George examined the presence of 'negroes in London' alongside Jewish, Irish and South Asian lascar communities.[9] George paints with a broad brush the 'London Immigrants' she focuses on. There were, she writes, many types of Irish in London, coal-heavers and ballast-men based in Wapping and Shadwell, settlements in Whitechapel, Poplar and Southwark and St Giles, which she described as 'a centre for beggars and thieves and the headquarters of street sellers and costermongers'.[10] The history of poorer London Jews and the Irish she found in Session papers and records from the Old Bailey. These, along with runaway slave notices, are the same sources from which she drew out the black presence in the city. George reflects that as black people 'did not live in colonies with their countrymen', their lives 'must have been strangely friendless and anomalous'.[11] Yet the inclusion of a petition by the wife of John Caesar suggests more complexity than George's analysis suggests.

According to his wife's case, Caesar had been serving Benjamin and John Wood, printers and embossers in Whitechapel, as an enslaved man without wages for fourteen years. For much of this time he had been forced to remain within the confines of their home. Unless her husband was released from his enslavement his wife was likely to have to rely upon relief from the Parish. The conclusion of the case was for the Woods to come to an arrangement with Caesar regarding the payment of wages. Though the saga continuing into the next sitting of the Sessions suggests that such cases were not easily resolved, Caesar's wife's petition speaks to the intimate historical geographies of marriage, family and kinship networks among working people.[12] George hints at these again when reporting on the presence of 'lascars, who apparently began to be conspicuous in London about 1783', a community who she viewed as being 'in many ways in a more unfortunate position than the Negroes'.[13] Employed by the East India Company and abandoned in London before being re-employed on a return voyage, these men were apparently 'exploited by each other and by the worst products of the riverside slums of Wapping and Shadwell and Poplar'.[14] Some of them though found shelter in the common lodging-houses of St

Giles – the home of the Irish 'beggars and thieves' George identified earlier in the chapter and suggestive of a rather less ghettoised city than George seems to assume.

George's observations have been enriched and challenged by research on the black presence undertaken since her publication. Norma Myers' investigation of criminal records, parliamentary reports and baptism records between 1780 and 1830 gives insight into the experiences of the poor, their kin and accomplices.[15] The Northamptonshire Black History Association is one example of research being undertaken outside academia by groups interested in their local histories. The stories uncovered by the Northamptonshire collective include that of the Dare family based in Gretton, a village on the northern border of their county. Here, in 1749 a black man named Richard Dare married Ann Medwell. The couple had twelve children, and one of their sons, Robert, married locally and in turn he and his wife Elizabeth baptised seven children as recorded in Gretton Parish Records between 1784 and 1797.[16] Kathleen Chater's work on the black presence in Britain between 1660 and 1807 also mined the records of the Old Bailey to unearth the experiences of black people who found themselves before the courts as victims, perpetrators and witnesses. Among these and other archives she found a sense of ordinariness of her subjects, men and women living simple lives and raising families as best they could.[17]

The permanent residence of black communities in Britain appears to have begun with the development of the transatlantic slave trade, and the greatest knowledge of the lives of black people in British history before the twentieth century is bound to the period of forced migration between the sixteenth and nineteenth centuries. Although Britain's involvement in the slave trade did not develop to a mass scale until around the 1660s, in 1554 John Lock sailed back from the West Coast of Africa with a cargo of black slaves though in his 1947 study *Negroes in Britain*, Kenneth Little believed it doubtful that black men or women would have been common until later in the century.[18] Peter Fryer and Paul Edwards located a number of black people in Britain in the early part of the century, including black ladies in the Scottish court in 1513, and a black trumpeter in the courts of Henry VI and Henry VII; Miranda Kaufmann has since found evidence of over 360 Africans living in Renaissance Britain.[19]

Peter Fryer (1984) noted towards the end of the sixteenth century it became fashionable for those who could afford it to have one or two black slaves among their household servants and this remained popular well into the seventeenth, with George observing that in the early eighteenth century 'little black boys as pages or playthings' remained 'favourite appendages of fashionable ladies or ladies of easy virtue'.[20] As evidence of this, George possibly had in mind William Hogarth, the artist most commonly associated with work in this context. Hogarth used images of black men, women and children in his representations and caricatures of eighteenth-century urban life; his series of *The Harlot's Progress* and *Marriage A La Mode* perhaps the most famous and re-examined through a black history lens by David Dabydeen.[21] Perhaps now better known is the 1779 portrait of Dido Elizabeth Belle with her cousin Lady Elizabeth Murray, both young women are depicted exquisitely dressed in the grounds of Kenwood, then the country home of the women's uncle and guardian Lord Mansfield. But it is more usually the presence of anonymous 'pages or playthings' that are found in depictions of the British aristocracy such as Pierre Mignard's 1682 portrait of the Duchess of Portsmouth with an unidentified servant, which hangs in the National Portrait Gallery, London. Another example is Edward Smith's 1773 depiction of an angling party, in which a small black servant boy is seen peering into a pond. Little argued that there is not much reason to doubt that by 1770 there were a fair number of black people working on country estates, and portraits such as these support his supposition. They also locate black people beyond the urban imaginative geographies with which they are usually associated.

Complementing evidence from visual sources in the eighteenth century, Paul Edwards took more seriously the works of anti-slavery activists Olaudah Equiano and Ottobah Cugoano. An abridged edition of Olaudah Equiano's *Narrative* was published as *Equiano's Travels* in 1967, later followed by full editions of the *Narrative* and Ottobah Cugoano's rather more radical *Thoughts and Sentiments on the Evils of Slavery*. With David Dabydeen he drew together an anthology of works by black writers in Britain between 1760 and 1890; a collection of the letters of Ignatius Sancho, dismissed by George for writing letters in a 'rather painful imitation of the manner of Sterne', he prepared on his deathbed.[22] Equiano's *Interesting Narrative* of his life first published in London in 1789 has now been reissued many times, with critical analysis being undertaken of his travels, the politics of his writings and his construction of identity. Vincent Caretta's thesis that Equiano was born in the United States and not in Africa (and thus did not experience the middle passage as his 'memoir' vividly describes) remains contentious for some, but the debates reflect how well known Equiano now is, but also suggest Equiano's understanding of oral testimony and narrative frameworks.[23] Research examining his friendship with Thomas Hardy, a founding member of the radical working-class group the London Corresponding Society, has drawn attention to the politics of solidarity in the eighteenth century and these complexities only add to the importance of Equiano's writings in the canon of black British history.

Radical politics was at the heart of Peter Fryer's seminal 1984 work *Staying Power*. He began this with the bold statement that 'There were Africans in Britain before the English came here' – a reference to the soldiers who served as part of the Roman army when it was stationed in Britain during the second century AD.[24] The presence of Septimus Severus, the Libya-born emperor who spent his last three years in Britain before he died in York, inspired Bernardine Evaristo's novel in verse about Zuleika, the daughter of Sudanese immigrants living in Londinium in 211 AD.[25] There are claims for an even earlier record of a black presence. Based on his readings of Tacitus, John Rogers argued that Tacitus' mention of 'the swarthy faces of the Silures, the curly quality, in general of their hair, suggested a black presence in pre-Roman times'.[26] Little reported this proposition in his study of *Negroes in Britain*, but rejected Rogers' reading, arguing that a black presence could really be traced only to the sixteenth century.

With *Staying Power*, Fryer, a left-wing journalist, produced a history of black Britons just shy of 600 pages, including over 100 pages of notes. I cannot remember where I bought my now well-worn and discoloured copy. It was an essential companion during my early research, though in part I chose to focus on the history of black women in Victorian Britain because they were not well covered by Fryer. Fryer was not alone in wondering what became of the community of black people, thought be numbering around 10,000, who were living in Britain at the beginning of the nineteenth century. Fryer's supposition was that as the majority of these were men, they married white women and their grandchildren became an indivisible part of the urban poor, the records of their lives now 'obscure and scattered' and 'for the most part forgotten by their descendants'.[27] Their records certainly remain 'obscure and scattered' amongst the vast amount of printed material the Victorians created from the national census to penny dailies. The ongoing digitisation of these archives now makes it possible for me to draw out their stories and consider their lives among the urban poor in a way that was unimaginable when I began my own research and certainly not possible when Fryer completed his work. Within these new archival spaces, the fragments of lives published in nineteenth-century newspaper advertisements has been particularly striking; they allude to experiences of belonging and not belonging, similarity and difference one advert among many, part of a crowd of men and women looking for work.

FIGURE 8.1 'Wanted'

Sheffield Daily Telegraph
9 April 1872

Staying Power remains an important text, but it has limitations. For example Fryer's conception of 'black people' included the South Asian diaspora. This reflected both anti-racist strategies of the new-left during the 1980s and his experience of utilising historical sources. He maintained that 'if you go back to the seventeenth century, those pageant performers, you cannot tell very often whether they were Asians or Africans'.[28] In my research of the nineteenth century I have also found this to be the case, and certainly when Charles Dickens reflected on the presence of 'The Black Man' in 1875, he had both African and Indian men in mind, writing: 'Doubts exist as to the time when, and the place where, the first black man came amongst us. Nor is it distinctly certain whence he came, of whether his nationality was of Asia or of Africa'.[29] He concluded that it did not seem very probable that 'the black man either of East Indian or West Indian origin was not a very familiar figure in England until the seventeenth century'.[30] But though Fryer held this political and methodological commitment to a broad understanding and exploration of Blackness, the majority of the book does focus on the experiences of those from the African diaspora.

Forged as a political intervention into the politics of the 1980s, *Staying Power's* 'courage and clarity' remain inspiring.[31] It was certainly inspiring for me and Fryer is not the only author to find it difficult to realise a black history of the Victorians. In Peter Ackroyd's London biography their presence was accorded just a few lines in which he informs the reader that in the nineteenth century black people 'rarely appear in novels or narratives, except as occasional grotesques, and their general fate seems to have been one of settlement among the urban poor'.[32] Kenneth Little acknowledged that if the evidence of late nineteenth-century commentators was to be believed then by the 1870s the black man or woman had virtually disappeared except for crossing-sweepers and an occasional black bishop – as asserted by Dickens in his 1875 essay. Dickens reported that there had been a 'considerable departure of the "black man" from among us'. Could it be, he asked, that 'He fills no longer the place he once occupied in our English domestic life. Can it be that when it was firmly established, not so very long since, that the negro was "a man and a brother" he forthwith ceased to be a friend?'.[33] There has been a persistent assumption among historians that by the end of the nineteenth century there was 'only a small black population in London, desperately poor, composed largely of West Indian sailors living in Canning Town in the East End'.[34] This is despite Ian Duffield's early scepticism of this stance. He argued in 1981 that far more 'patient, dogged work' needed to be done on black local history and biography to reveal what happened to black people in the nineteenth century.[35] There is still much of this work to be undertaken, and my own research on the black presence in the late Victorian period suggests that there is a far greater historical geography of the black presence to be uncovered. This is especially true of black women who I have found to be working as domestic servants, on stage, as cooks and barmaids across the country.[36]

There are now some well-known Victorian characters including the Jamaican nurse Mary Seacole and the Chartist William Caffay, deported for treason in

1848. Fryer celebrates Caffay's contribution to radical British politics in *Staying Power*, including his speech from the dock. Caffay's experience speaks to another important avenue of black British history that was uncovered by Ian Duffield's research into the journeys of forced migration from Britain to Australia. The detailed, and racialised, records of the prisoners' arrivals made in Australia enabled Duffield to reconstruct aspects of their lives before they left Britain. Of the just over 200 individuals he found in the archives, six were women and all worked as domestic servants including Charlotte Claydon, an unmarried mother who stole £6 in London's Bethnal Green and arrived in Sydney in 1837.[37]

Since Fryer's expansive history of a black presence from the Romans to 'resistance and rebellion' in the 1970s and early 1980s, researchers have tended to focus on providing greater detail of focused periods in history. Jeffrey Green introduced us to the diverse membership of the black community in the early part of the twentieth century with his work on *Black Edwardians* in addition to a biography of the composer Samuel Coleridge-Taylor, a Pan-Africanist whose cantata for Hiawatha's Wedding Feast made him one of the most popular musicians of the era.[38] Stephen Bourne was inspired to write about the black presence through conversations with his adopted black Aunt Esther who was born in London in 1912.[39] Since writing about her Edwardian childhood he has written about entertainers who worked in British theatre and film and the experiences of black men and women on the home front during the First and Second World Wars.[40] In 1909 A. B. C. Merriman-Labor published his vision of *Britons Through Negro Spectacles*, which gives some insights into the expectations and experiences a black middle-class man had. Written in the 'guise of a jester' Merriman-Labor's claim that there were not many more than one hundred blacks living in London at the time of his writing seems quite an underestimate given the insights of Green and Bourne.[41]

Alongside these works of social history are the examinations of political black life in interwar Britain. *The Black Jacobins*, C. L. R. James' groundbreaking account of the Haitian revolution fought by enslaved Africans in the Caribbean, inspired many; Linton Kwesi Johnson recalled it being required reading as a member of the Black Panther Movement.[42] It is the radical anti-racist and anti-colonial and pan-African activists such as C. L. R. James who lived in Britain during the interwar years who have drawn most attention from scholars in recent years, including Christian Høgsbjerg's account of *Chris Braithwaite* and Leslie James' work on George Padmore and his Pan-Africanist activism.[43] Marc Matera's work on anti-colonial activists includes a welcome focus on women such as Amy Ashwood Garvey as well as women who worked in the WASU (West African Students Union) and those involved in the Abyssinian campaign, a rallying point for many black activists in Britain. He highlights the importance and challenges faced by Una Marson, a poet and BBC broadcaster who worked for the League of Coloured Peoples and was the subject of Delia Jarrett-Macauley's biography.[44]

Hakim Adi's work on the African diaspora has informed a number of these studies through his work on interwar Pan-Africanist politics, including *West Africans in Britain 1900–1960* and *Pan-Africanism and Communism*.[45] Hakim Adi was one of the founding members of an organisation which became known as BASA (the Black and Asian Studies Association), focused on fostering and disseminating research on the history of African and Asian diasporas in Britain. A collective of teachers, archivists, activists, parents, community scholars and some academics such as myself, BASA held conferences, lobbied curators, archivists and governments for better representations of black history in libraries, museums and schools and was a vital support for me and others undertaking research, regularly publishing early findings by members in its *Newsletter*. Marika Sherwood, a co-founder of BASA and editor of the *Newsletter* for many years, has published numerous papers and books focusing on the biographies of politically active individuals including Claudia Jones, founding editor of the *West Indian Gazette*, and Pastor Daniels Ekarte who started the African Churches Mission in Liverpool in 1931.[46] Sherwood has also explored the early histories of Pan-Africanism, writing a biography of Henry Sylvester Williams and with Hakim Adi a book on the 1945 Pan-African Congress, published by New Beacon Books in 1995.[47] Three years later the fiftieth anniversary of the arrival of the *Empire Windrush* was celebrated but, as Linda Bellos pointed out, not only did commentators promote these celebrations in the context of the 'first arrival' of black peoples in Britain and the beginning of a multicultural nation, but many black people who had lived and worked in Britain before 1948 were excluded.[48] The focus on these post-war migrants re-emphasised the temporal divide that British national memory insists upon building and rebuilding. In a post-Brexit Britain this melancholic condition re-imagines a mythical time when a white homogeneous land 'stood on its own two feet'.[49]

The relaunch of the works of black writers like Sancho, Equiano, Cugoano and Mary Seacole provided examples of an articulate black membership of British society.[50] But their place in Britain is still often viewed through their individual experiences, and it is unclear how broad the communities from which they came were. We still know little about the members of the Sons of Africa who worked on anti-slavery campaigns with Equiano or how a group of black people attending a christening in the Parish Church of St Giles' in 1726 came to be friends or acquaintances, nor how well they knew the members of Irish and lascar communities who lived close by.[51] There is still plenty of critical enquiry as well as recovery work to be undertaken within British black history and particularly at the scale of local history. David Killingray has reflected on the lack of ethnic and immigrant minority histories in local history research and writing.[52] He observes that it is those in other disciplines, including geography, who have largely taken this lead on this research.

As a cultural and historical geographer, space, place and time have always been tightly intertwined in my work. I have observed with interest the 'spatial turn' in history and the histories of immigration will surely be beneficiaries of any greater concern and attention to place and scale. The importance of place comes through strongly in Matera's book as he explicitly sets out to examine black London through his exploration of spaces of exchange, networks and communities operating at varying scales and topographies in interwar London.[53] These include the sounds of black London and the international migrations of musicians and political activists that came together in the public spaces of clubs and bars and the private living rooms of London. The need to draw on a broad range of sources in order to 'see' colour in the Victorian archive means my own research has also sought the black experience in archives from asylums to children's homes and prisons, in archives created by pen, print and the photographic studio.[54] The structure of the Victorian archive means I have often been researching people who were captured at a moment not of their choosing and thus are recovered from the margins of a marginalised history. But even from opaque records it is possible to glean intimate moments of family life and map them within broader histories of regional, national and global migrations. For me the work of feminist geographers, historians and critical race theorists was also essential for creating a framework that could begin to reconstruct the fragmented and intersected lives of black women – and black men.[55]

There is more research to be done for all periods of Britain's black history, and new themes of recovery and analysis such as queer black histories are emerging.[56] Yet, the diversity of British history that has been uncovered to date is hardly reflected in sites of Britain's heritage, and when attempts are made to change this they are challenged by those who object to their 'political correctness'. Naming a road after Mary Seacole caused a row in one London borough because some residents objected to its 'political correctness' and similar feelings seem to have been behind the criticism of the unveiling of a statue to Seacole in the grounds of St Thomas' hospital in 2016.[57] In this respect, the undertaking of black historical research continues to be seen as, and can often feel like, a radical undertaking, with black heritage sites remaining sites of resistance and controversy. The ongoing challenge of black history to ideas of 'our history' in a post-Brexit Britain makes the threatened closure of New Beacon Bookshop announced in December 2016 all the more poignant – the surge of support it received a reflection of how important such spaces still are.[58]

This is not an exhaustive account of historical scholarship of black history in Britain, but is suggestive of the breadth of research that has been undertaken and been influential on my own work on the long nineteenth century. Recently I have returned to the focus of my PhD research, the forgotten geographies of black women in Victorian and Edwardian London. I am seeking to make their lives a lens through which we can reconsider the structures of working-class culture as their stories, along with those of their Irish, Asian and Jewish neighbours, give us a sense of how people in Britain lived together before the arrival of the *Windrush*. On completing my PhD I had assumed that in 'the future' black history would have a strong presence in academic historical scholarship, at heritage sites and within popular history and school history, but it remains marginalised in all these places, even for many young black school children, for whom it can prove to be such an inspiring subject.[59]

Notes

1 The exhibition was held between July 2015 and January 2016.
2 Philippa Ireland, 'Laying the foundations: New Beacon Books, Bogle-L'Ouverture Press and the politics of black British publishing', *E-rea. Revue électronique d'études sur le monde anglophon*, vol. 11, no. 1, 2013.
3 Ruth Bush, 'African Connections at New Beacon Books: a conversation with Sarah White and Ali Hussein', *Wasafiri* vol. 31, no. 4, 2016, 3–8.
4 Alex Wheatle, 'A conversation with Linton Kwesi Johnson', *Wasafiri* vol. 24, no. 3, 2009, 35–41 (35).
5 Heidi Safia Mirza and Diane Reay, 'Spaces and places of black educational desire: rethinking black supplementary schools as a new social movement', *Sociology* vol. 34, no. 3, 2000, 521–544 (533).
6 Ibid.
7 Caroline Bressey, 'Conversations with Caroline' in Antoinette Burton, and Dane Kennedy (eds), *How Empire Shaped Us* (London: Bloomsbury 2016), 183–193.
8 As undertaken by Kathleen Chater. 'Making History: Black British History', available at www.history.ac.uk/makinghistory/resources/articles/black_history.html#2 (accessed 22 August 2017).
9 M. Dorothy George, *London Life in the Eighteenth Century* (Chicago: Academy Chicago Publishers 1985), 184.
10 Ibid., 121.
11 Ibid., 139.
12 Ibid., 141.
13 Ibid., 143.
14 Ibid.
15 Norma Myers, 'Servant, sailor, soldier, tailor, beggerman: black survival in white society 1780–1830', *Immigrants and Minorities* vol. 12, no. 1, 1993, 47–74. See also Norma Myers, 'The black presence through criminal records 1780–1830', *Immigrants and Minorities* vol. 7, no. 3, 1987, 292–307.
16 Northamptonshire Black History Association, *Sharing the Past: Northamptonshire's Black History* (Northampton: Northamptonshire Black History Association 2008).
17 Kathleen Chater, *Untold Histories: Black People in England and Wales during the Period of the British Slave Trade* (Manchester: Manchester University Press 2009).
18 Ian Duffield, 'History and the historians', *History Today* vol. 31, 1981, 34–36.
19 See Duffield, 'History and the historians', 34–36; Peter Fryer, *Staying Power: This History of Black People in Britain* (London: Pluto Press 1984); Miranda Kauffman, *Black Tudors: The Untold Story* (London: Oneworld 2017).
20 George, *London Life in the Eighteenth Century*, 142.
21 David Dabydeen, *Hogarth's Blacks: Images of Blacks in Eighteenth Century English Art* (Kingston-upon-Thames: Dagaroo 1985).
22 Christopher Fyfe, 'Paul Edwards – A tribute', *Slavery & Abolition*, vol. 19, no. 3, 1998, 134–139; George, *London Life in the Eighteenth Century*, 142. Ian Duffield (1981), in *History Today* which that year produced a special issue on 'The History of Black People in Britain', notes that before his death Edwards was also using his knowledge of Old Norse, Old Irish and Old English to trace black people who lived in Britain during the Dark Ages.
23 Vincent Caretta, *Equiano, the African: Biography of a Self-Made Man* (Athens: University of Georgia 2005). For an outline of the controversy see David Dabydeen, 'Poetic licence', *The Guardian*, 3 December 2005.

24 Fryer, *Staying Power*, 1.
25 Bernardine Evaristo, *The Emperor's Babe* (London: Penguin 2001).
26 Kenneth Little, *Negroes in Britain: A Study of English Race Relations in English Society* (London and Boston: Routledge and Kegan Paul 1972), 187.
27 Fryer, *Staying Power*, 235.
28 Quoted in Rob Waters, 'Thinking black: Peter Fryer's *Staying Power* and the politics of writing black British history in the 1980s', *History Workshop Journal* vol. 82, no. 1, 2016, 104–120 (109).
29 Charles Dickens, 'The Black Man', *All The Year Round*, 6 March 1875, 489–493 (489).
30 Dickens, 'The Black Man', 490.
31 Rob Waters, 'Thinking black: Peter Fryer's *Staying Power* and the politics of writing black British history in the 1980s', 104.
32 Peter Ackroyd, *London: The Biography* (London: Chatto and Windus 2000), 714.
33 Dickens, 'The Black Man', 492.
34 Jonathan Schneer, *London 1900: The Imperial Metropolis* (New Haven and London: Yale University Press 1999), 203.
35 Ian Duffield, 'History and the historians', *History Today* vol. 31, 1981, 34–36, (36).
36 Caroline Bressey, 'Four women: black women writing in London between 1880 and 1920', in F. Paisley and K. Reid, (eds), *Critical Perspectives on Colonialism: Writing the Empire from Below* (Oxford: Routledge 2013), 179–198 and 'Black women and work in England, 1880–1920', in M. Davis (ed.), *Class and Gender in British Labour History: Renewing the Debate (Or Starting It?)* (London: Merlin Press 2011), 117–132.
37 Ian Duffield, 'Skilled workers or marginalised poor? The African population in the United Kingdom 1812–1852', *Immigrants and Minorities* vol. 12, no. 3, 1993, 49–87.
38 Jeffrey Green, *Samuel Coleridge-Taylor: A Musical Life* (Basingstoke: Routledge 2011).
39 Stephen Bourne, with Esther Bruce. *Aunt Esther's Story* (Hammersmith and Fulham Ethnic Communities Oral History Project 1996).
40 Stephen Bourne, *Black in the British Frame: The Black Experience in British Film and Television* (London: Continuum 2001); *Mother Country: Britain's Black Community on the Home Front 1939–45* (Stroud: The History Press 2010); *The Motherland Calls: Britain's Black Servicemen and Women 1939–1945* (Stroud: The History Press 2012); *Black Poppies: Britain's Black Community and the Great War* (Stroud: The History Press 2014).
41 A. B. C. Merriman-Labor, *Britons Through Negro Spectacles* (London: Imperial and Foreign Company 1909).
42 Wheatle, 'A conversation with Linton Kwesi Johnson', 35–41.
43 Christian Høgsbjerg, *Mariner, Renegade and Castaway: Chris Braithwaite: Seamen's Organiser, Socialist and Militant Pan-Africanist* (London: Redwoods 2013). Leslie James, *George Padmore and Decolonization from Below: Pan-Africanism, the Cold War, and the End of Empire* (Basingstoke: Palgrave Macmillan 2015). See also Daniel Whitall, 'Creolising London: Black West Indian activism and the politics of race and empire in Britain, 1931–1948', Ph.D. thesis, Royal Holloway University of London, 2012.
44 Marc Matera, *The Imperial Metropolis and Decolonization in the Twentieth Century* (Oakland: University of California Press 2016). Delia Jarrett-Macauley, *The Life of Una Marson* (Manchester: Manchester University Press 1998).
45 Hakim Adi, *Pan-Africanism and Communism: The Communist International, Africa and the Diaspora, 1919–1939* (Trenton NJ: Africa World Press 2013); *West Africans in Britain 1900–1960: Nationalism, Pan-Africanism and Communism* (London: Lawrence and Wishart 1998).
46 Marika Sherwood, *Pastor Daniels Ekarte and the African Churches Mission* (London: The Savannah Press 1994); *Claudia Jones: A Life in Exile* (London: Lawrence and Wishart 1999).

47 Marika Sherwood, *The Origins of Pan-Africanism: Henry Sylvester Williams and the African Diaspora* (London: Routledge 2010); Hakim Adi and Marika Sherwood, *The 1945 Manchester Pan-African Congress Revisited* (London: New Beacon Books 1995).
48 Linda Bellos, 'History' in Courttia Newland and Kadija Sesay (eds) *IC3: The Penguin Book of New Black Writing in Britain* (London: Hamish Hamilton, 2000) 120–121.
49 David Davis, 'Britain is not like other countries', 27 May 2016, available on the *Daily Telegraph* website, www.telegraph.co.uk/news/2016/05/27/britain-is-not-like-other-countries--even-the-sclerotic-eu-will/ (accessed 22 August 2017). On 'melancholia' see Paul Gilroy, *Postcolonial Melancholia* (New York: Colombia University Press 2005).
50 See Ziggi Alexander and Audrey Dewjee (eds), *Wonderful Adventures of Mrs Seacole in Many Lands* (Bristol: Falling Wall Press 1984) and Paul Edwards and David Dabydeen (eds), *Black Writers in Britain, 1760–1890: An Anthology* (Edinburgh: Edinburgh University Press 1991).
51 Gretchen Gerzina, *Black London: Life Before Emancipation* (New Brunswick NJ: Rutgers University Press 1995).
52 David Killingray, 'Immigrant communities and British local history', *The Local Historian* vol. 41, no. 1, 2011, 4–12. He has also written extensively on African histories, for example 'African slaves in Britain in the early modern period' in Klaus Bade, Pieter Emmer, Leo Lucassen and Jochen Oltmer (eds), *The Encyclopaedia of Migration and Minorities in Europe. From the Seventeenth century to the Present* (Cambridge: Cambridge University Press 2011), 211–213 and David Killingray, 'Significant Black South Africans in Britain before 1912: pan-African organisations and the emergence of South Africa's first Black lawyers', *South African Historical Journal* vol. 64, no. 3, 2012, 393–417.
53 Caroline Bressey, a review of *Black London: The Imperial Metropolis and Decolonization in the Twentieth Century* by Marc Matera, *Twentieth Century British History* vol. 28, no. 1, 2017, 143–145.
54 Caroline Bressey, 'Seeing colour in black and white: the role of the visual in diversifying historical narratives at sites of English heritage', *Critical Social Policy* vol. 32, no. 1, 2012, 87–105.
55 As examples, Linda McDowell, *Gender, Identity and Place: Understanding Feminist Geographies* (Cambridge: Polity Press 1999); Catherine Hall, 'Introduction: thinking the postcolonial, thinking the empire', *Cultures of Empire: A Reader* (Manchester: Manchester University Press 2000) 1–33; bell hooks, *Black Looks: Race and Representation* (Boston: South End Press, 1992).
56 See Gemma Romain's *Race, Sexuality and Identity in Britain and Jamaica. The Biography of Patrick Nelson, 1916–1963* (London: Bloomsbury Academic 2017).
57 Caroline Bressey, 'Radical history then and now', *History Workshop Journal* vol. 83, no. 1, 2017, 217–222.
58 www.thebookseller.com/news/afro-caribbean-bookshop-new-beacon-books-close-444436; www.standard.co.uk/news/london/uk-s-first-black-bookshop-is-fundraising-to-save-finsbury-park-premises-a3493161.html; The bookshop continued fundraising: www.thebookseller.com/news/ swell-support-new-beacon-books-helps-raise-10k-513551
59 Hakim Adi's project 'History Matters' seeks to enable young people to engage with history within their schools. See: www.chi.ac.uk/department-history-and-politics/research/history-matters.

SECTION 3
Community history

Christhard Hoffmann

Introduction

In the historical representation of the migrant experience in Britain, community histories of immigrant groups have played a popular and influential role. Mediating between the cultural heritage of origin and present life in the country of settlement, these histories essentially fulfil a dual function. Directed to the inside (immigrant) group, they present the rupture in the immigrant's biography as a meaningful process, thereby fostering acculturation, identity and ethnic pride; directed to the outside world, community histories substantiate the claim for recognition and special status of the particular immigrant group by emphasising its contributions to and sacrifices for the adapted country.[1] Consequently, histories of immigrant communities tend to focus on the success stories of integration and social advancement, downplaying negative experiences of discrimination, hostility and exclusion. In the same way, they stress ethnic cohesion and solidarity, disregarding internal divisions, inequality and conflict. Seeking to present a usable past, they do not explore community history in its entirety, but focus on a 'harmonious' and 'respectable' selection of it. While academic studies of immigrant communities since the 1970s certainly have widened the perspectives and addressed many of the 'blind spots' of community history, tendencies towards 'sanitised accounts' (Kevin Myers) and 'ethnic cheerleading' (Tony Kushner) are prevalent in public heritage culture, for example in recent historical narratives celebrating the ethnic diversity of multicultural Britain.[2] In a corresponding way, majority societies often convey a positive self-image by constructing one-sided and celebratory narratives of immigration history. The Whig interpretation of Britain as a 'tolerant country of immigration' thus became commonplace and served as a useful formula in public debates on national identity and immigration policy.

It was against this backdrop that historians such as Colin Holmes and the Sheffield School started in the 1970s to explore the history of newcomers and their reception in British society beyond the limitations of a self-gratulatory consensus. Within the historiography of immigrant communities, younger historians challenged cherished views of social harmony and ethnic solidarity. Introducing a class perspective to Jewish community history, Bill Williams and Joseph Buckman, for example, addressed the social conflicts between established and immigrant Jews in Manchester and Leeds. Another pioneer in criticising and transgressing the self-imposed limitations of established Jewish historiography in Britain is Geoffrey Alderman. His chapter, which starts this section, is a revised and updated version of a 'classic' article, first published in 1994, that has not lost its significance today. It presents an inside view of the tension between 'academic duty' and 'communal obligation' in the field of Anglo-Jewish history and frames it as a question of professional integrity for the historian. Criticising some of the pioneers of Jewish community historiography for tiptoeing around controversial topics and some community officials for trying to control and confine independent historical research, Alderman forcefully argues that a historian should never compromise on seeking the truth out of regard that it might be unfavourable to the community. Together with other historians, mentioned in the chapter, he has lived up to this maxim and thereby changed Jewish community historiography. In 2017, Alderman received a five-year Senior Research Fellowship at the Institute for Historical Research (London) to undertake research into the Jewish contribution to crime in the United Kingdom since the Cromwellian Readmission.

In her critical analysis of the historiography on the Italian immigrant community in Britain, Wendy Ugolini shows how celebratory narratives, emphasising the long-established, well-integrated and well-liked Italian 'model minority' in Britain, have obscured incidents of racism, hostility and conflict, especially during the Second World War. Highlighting the histories of victimhood and suffering while marginalising the influence of fascism within the Italian diaspora in Britain and, on the other hand, excluding the experiences of second generation Italian immigrants who served in the British Army, these accounts, she argues, presented the wartime history of the Italian community in a highly selective way. Trying to balance the picture, the works of Ugolini and other historians have focused on the topics missing in these narratives and have thereby shown the plurality and heterogeneity of the Italian diaspora experience in Britain.

The selectivity of migrant representations in cultural memory is also a central topic in Jennifer Craig-Norton's illuminating chapter on the historiography of Jewish refugees from fascism who came to Britain in the 1930s. For a long time, the story of their immigration was told in a purely celebratory way, as a heroic tale of rescue and redemption and as an example of British humanitarian exceptionalism. Accordingly, the focus of public historical interest was on the *Kindertransports* of 1938/39 that brought nearly 10,000 Jewish children to Britain (while their parents were left behind) or on the (famous) refugee intellectuals, who enriched British academic life. As Craig-Norton shows in detail, the conduits of the celebratory historical narrative did obscure the uncomfortable aspects of the refugee experience in Britain and exclude all those from public memory who did not fit in, such as the refugee domestics and nurses. Challenging these limitations, historians such as Louise London and Tony Kushner, and those who followed them, have placed the reception of the Jewish refugees of the 1930s into the broader context of (restrictive) British immigration politics and have tried to explore the complexities of their experiences more fully – 'beyond the celebratory'.

In her study of the East African Asians who settled in Britain after having been displaced from Uganda, Kenya and Tanzania during the 1960s and 1970s, Saima Nasar highlights the 'frightening elasticity' (Colin Holmes) by which this group was defined in the British public and, correspondingly, defined itself. Although holding the status of Citizens of the UK and Colonies, the East African Asians were classified as 'refugees' and put in the same category as earlier exiles (Huguenots, Jews) that found refuge in Britain. This outward definition exercised an influence on the self-representation of the migrants that found its expression in a 'rags to riches' narrative of resettlement, emphasising the successes and the social, cultural and economic contributions of a 'model minority'. While this proud self-representation of the East African Asian community dominates public heritage projects and exhibitions, professional historians have been interested in the complexities of post-imperial and transnational belongings of this group between Britain, India and Africa. As Nasar concludes, the relationship between the two – community memory and the academic study of history – remains an uneasy one.

Notes

1 On the use of 'home-making myths' in the memory culture of European immigrant groups in the United States, see Orm Øverland, *Immigrant Minds, American Identities: Making the United States Home, 1870–1930* (Urbana: University of Illinois Press 2000), 8ff.
2 See the articles by Tony Kushner and Kevin Myers in Kathy Burrell and Panikos Panayi (eds), *Histories and Memories. Migrants and their History in Britain* (London and New York: Tauris Academic Studies 2006), 18–34, (Kushner) and 35–53 (Myers).

9

ACADEMIC DUTY AND COMMUNAL OBLIGATION REVISITED[1]

Geoffrey Alderman

In 1992 Oxford University Press published my book *Modern British Jewry*. The volume may be regarded in some sense as a sequel to another book, published by Oxford a half-century ago. I refer, of course, to the late Dr Cecil Roth's *History of the Jews in England*, which first appeared in 1941 and which went into three editions.

It has become fashionable now to dismiss this work. Professor David Katz has pointed out that Roth's writings in the field of Anglo-Jewish history were 'full of mistakes, undocumented assertions, and numerous gaps'.[2] So they were. It is the fate of all pioneers to have their mistakes uncovered by those who come after them, and to have their theories cast aside. But to say these things is to miss the point. Yes, Roth's *History* was sanitised, apologetic, complacent; it stopped with Emancipation, in 1858, in part because Roth wished, for propaganda purposes, to end on a note of triumph; he felt uncomfortable dealing with the era of the great immigration of Jews to Britain in the 1880s and 1890s, and with the anti-Jewish prejudice in Britain which this immigration triggered. As Professor Katz himself rightly observes,

> Roth was a pioneer who worked very largely during the blackest era of Jewish history, when it seemed that the very last thing the Jews needed was avoidable criticism from within, supplying genuine arguments to even more genuine anti-Semites.[3]

1941 was not a good year for the Jews. Roth, like so many other British Jews, did not know how to cope with the reality of the Holocaust. He adopted a then conventional explanation, that the sufferings of the Jews were a test. He was right to contrast these sufferings, ordered by Nazi Germany but carried out with the help of many other European nations, with the relative tranquillity of the Jews in Britain; here was a debt that had to be acknowledged and paid. Roth saw it as a solemn duty to pay it. But even in so doing, he wrought a sea-change in the researching and writing of British-Jewish history.

History is the collective memory of a people and in large measure shapes their view of the present and of the future. That is why I devote some space, in my book, to the way in which Jews in Britain have approached and interpreted their past.

The first history of Anglo-Jewry to be written by an Anglo-Jewish writer appeared in 1847, a slim pamphlet, published in *Chambers's Miscellany*, the work of a woman of Marrano descent, Grace Aguilar (1816–47). 'Jews,' she declared, 'are still considered aliens and foreigners ... little known and less understood. Yet they are, in fact, Jews only in their religion – Englishmen in everything else.'[4] 'A Jewish murderer, adulterer, burglar, or even petty thief,' she added coolly, 'is actually unknown.' We may smile at the sweeping superficiality and patent dishonesty of such statements. There were plenty of Jewish criminals in Britain in the 1830s and 1840s, and it is difficult to believe that Aguilar did not know about them. Criminality among the Jewish poor obsessed the communal grandees at this time: the dramatic escape from police custody in 1827 of Ikey Solomons, on whom Dickens is thought by some to have modelled Fagin; the trial of Sol Litsenberg, indicted at Marlborough Street Police Court in 1830 for running a gang of twenty juvenile thieves in the vicinity of Leicester Square; the scandals which arose from cases of Jewish-run houses of easy virtue, condemned by Ashkenazi Chief Rabbi Hirschell in 1836. The Jewish 'fence', dealing in stolen property, was a feature of Petticoat Lane market throughout the mid-Victorian period, and its eradication was felt by many of the lay leaders of British Jewry to be an essential pre-requisite of full political emancipation. Considerations of image obsessed the leadership then, just as considerations of image obsess the leadership now.

Historians were expected to play their part in maintaining the image intact. In 1993 the Jewish Historical Society celebrated its centenary. It is worth recalling that the notion of establishing a society devoted to Anglo-Jewish history was viewed with not a little misgiving, and that those who established it and who supported its establishment were at pains to justify its existence in terms of the good account it would give, to the Gentiles, of the Jewish people.

In his inaugural address to the Society the journalist Lucien Wolf, its first president, gave this assurance. Wolf wrote extensively on Anglo-Jewish historical themes, concentrating especially upon the period of the Resettlement, and writing in the style of an earlier generation of Anglo-Jewish historians (principally Myer Davis and James Piciotto), whose work in the 1870s forms the bridge between Grace Aguilar and Lucien Wolf himself. Cecil Roth learned his craft from Lucien Wolf, to whom he referred, in adulatory terms, in his last address to the Jewish Historical Society, in 1968.

Roth felt the weight of this responsibility very heavily and very personally. But he gave to the researching and writing of Jewish history a scholastic basis which it had not had hitherto. As the late Professor Lloyd Gartner observed, 'Jewish history as a profession virtually did not exist during the 1920s', when Roth made that fateful decision to turn from the history of Renaissance Italy to that of Italian Jewry and then of Anglo-Jewry.⁵ The researching and writing of Anglo-Jewish history had hitherto been the preserve of non-scholastic apologists like Grace Aguilar and Lady Magnus, gifted amateurs like Davis and Wolf, and ministers of religion who, as Roth himself observed, regarded Jewish history 'almost as a branch of theology'.⁶ Roth, single-handedly, transformed Anglo-Jewish historiography into a scholarly activity worthy of pursuit at the highest university levels.

British Jewry recognised his achievements, and marked them. The Readership in Post-Biblical Jewish Studies which he held at Oxford from 1939 to 1964 was created for him through a communal benefaction. But he had to sing – so to speak – for his supper. Approached by the then President of the Federation of Synagogues (the crook Morry Davis) to write the Federation's jubilee history (1937), Roth was obliged to pen what can only be described as a pamphlet, so superficial and wanting in scholastic rigour that he was too ashamed to include it in a list of his own publications. It is, I think, quite well known that the celebratory centenary history of the *Jewish Chronicle*, which appeared in 1949, was written by Roth; but he would not permit his name to appear in the title page.

I was a student of Cecil Roth, and I remain an admirer. But I am in no sense an imitator, less still a disciple. Disciples and imitators there certainly were. Foremost amongst these were Albert Hyamson (1875–1954) and Vivian Lipman (1921–90). Hyamson's history of *The Sephardim in England*, which appeared in 1951, was written very much in the Roth mould: apologetic, highly selective, uncritical. The volume was meant to cover the centuries from 1492 to 1951; in fact precisely twenty pages, in a work of over 460, were devoted to the twentieth century, and much was left unsaid into the bargain. The controversial reign of Moses Gaster as *Haham* – that is, supreme rabbinical authority of the Spanish and Portuguese Jews' Congregation of London – from 1887 to 1918 – was totally unexplored; nothing was said, that is, about the man who was Theodor Herzl's staunchest and earliest ally in Britain. Hyamson's excuse for all these omissions – 'The historian ought never to deal or attempt to deal with events of which he has a personal knowledge' – strikes me as lame indeed. But it was an excuse which Roth himself had proffered more than once to explain his own reluctance to deal with twentieth-century problems.

The late Vivian Lipman was a pupil of Roth, and a disciple in every sense of the word. As is well known, Lipman was a distinguished civil servant who rose to become Director of Ancient Monuments and Historic Buildings at the Department of the Environment. He was an expert on medieval Anglo-Jewry – in some respects more of an expert than his teacher. But he was also more establishment-minded than his teacher, willing to curry favour with the communal grandees even if this meant being economical with the truth. When the then Jewish Board of Guardians, founded in 1859, decided to commission a centenary history, Vivian was not their first choice. They turned initially to a young Anglo-Jewish academic, an objective scholar in every sense of the word; this young man produced a chapter for the consideration of the grandees. They were horrified, for he had told the truth, the whole truth and nothing but the truth. The commission was naturally taken from him and given to Vivian Lipman instead. And the work which Vivian published, in

1959, is distinguished chiefly by its meticulous attention to detail, its highly descriptive approach and its signal failure to explore, let alone explain, the abominable treatment, by the Jewish Board of Guardians, of Jewish refugees to Britain in the l880s and 1890s.

Lipman's last book, his *History of the Jews in Britain since 1858*, was published posthumously a few months after his death. The bulk of the work was devoted to the period 1858 to 1939; precisely fifteen pages address the post-1945 period. The treatment throughout is descriptive, uncritical, highly selective and outrageously partial. Let me give a few examples.

When Russian persecution and economic hardship drove millions of Jews westwards in the 1880s and 1890s, the communal leadership did its best to prevent any but the most affluent of them from ever settling permanently in Britain. To this policy Lipman accorded just three inadequate sentences. In the 1930s a not entirely dissimilar policy was invoked to hinder the entry into Britain of refugees from Nazism. Vivian hinted darkly at this, but on the whole peddled the now discredited apologia of Norman Bentwich (*They Found Refuge*, 1956), whose defence of Otto Schiff, the man whom the Home Office trusted to select the 'right' type of German Jew to be permitted to enter Britain, has crumbled as archival material (of which Lipman was, I know, well aware) has become available for public inspection. Nor, except in terms of unashamed bias and lack of professionalism, is it possible to explain the complete absence, in Lipman's book, of any allusion to the stratagems devised by the leadership of the United Synagogue in the interwar period, to prevent Zionism becoming official United Synagogue policy. It is, incidentally, worth remarking that the official historian of the United Synagogue, Professor Aubrey Newman, was himself strangely silent on this subject.

It would be comforting to think that we have heard the last of the 'Whig' historians of Anglo-Jewry, whose writings have been characterised as apologetic, sanitised, triumphant, uncritical, even 'cosy'.[7] I fear not, for I have recently (July 2016) been asked to referee for a commercial publishing house a manuscript in which all these hallmarks appear in ample measure, as if the revolution of the past 40 years in Anglo-Jewish historiography had not taken place.[8]

I am proud to think that I played a part in that revolution. But I was not its prime mover. It cannot be without significance that the scholar who broke the mould of what had passed for Anglo-Jewish historiography hitherto, the late Professor Lloyd Gartner, was an American, a pupil of the great Salo Baron. Gartner's monograph *The Jewish Immigrant in England* first appeared in 1960. Gartner's view of the immigrants in the period 1870 to 1914 was that, at bottom, they had much less in common with the non-Jewish manual working classes amongst whom they dwelt than with the Jewish bourgeoisie to whose status and lifestyle they aspired. It is a view that has come under serious challenge, notably from Dr Joseph Buckman in relation to Leeds Jewry and from Professor David Feldman and the late Professor William Fishman, whose use of Yiddish sources has set new standards for the study of the Anglo-Jewish proletariat.

My view is that both sides of the argument are right. In the short term, the immigrants had to confront life as they found it. This meant that they had to meet and make friends with the British proletariat, of which, perforce, they became a part. But we must remember that many of the Jewish immigrants who came to this country in states of penury had, in fact, been members of a petty bourgeoisie in Russia, Poland, Galicia and Romania. Their undoubted motivation for self-improvement derived in part from their ambition to recapture in Britain the status they had lost in Eastern Europe. The average British trade unionist saw his or her life as beginning and ending in a working-class milieu; this was not a vision shared by Anglo-Jewish trade-unionists.

The major impact of the immigrants is to be found in the challenge they mounted to the rule of the so-called Cousinhood, that small group of interrelated monied families which affected to rule Anglo-Jewry in the age of emancipation. It has become fashionable to contrast the process of emancipation in Britain with that on the European mainland, where Jewish communities often had to undergo a formal renunciation of their separate ethnic and often internally self-governing status; as individuals Jews were offered absolute equality before the law, that is, but only on condition that communal rights were severely delimited. On the face of it, no such demand was ever made of the Jews in Britain.

In fact, we would be very wrong to conclude from the absence of a formal emancipation 'contract' that no concessions were extracted from British Jewry in return for the grant of civic rights. Emancipation, which Cecil Roth saw as the triumphant culmination of the Jewish existence in Britain, was bought at a very considerable cost, no more so than in the religious sphere.

For example, it was no coincidence that Reform Jews were to be found at the very forefront of the emancipation struggle, actually arguing, in a petition to Sir Robert Peel, the Prime Minister, in 1845 that emancipation should be granted as a reward, so to speak, for reform of the synagogue service to make it somewhat less Jewish and more English in form. Another example is provided by the status, in English law, of a rabbinically sanctioned divorce. When the Matrimonial Causes Act was passed in 1857, it was assumed that the hitherto undisputed freedom of the Jews to dissolve marriages contracted under rabbinical auspices would continue. But then another argument was heard: if the Jews wanted equality before the law, so be it – in every sphere. So the supremacy of the civil divorce court over the *Beth Din* (the Jewish ecclesiastical court) was established. How much less intractable would have been the present difficulties over Jewish divorce had this form of 'equality' not been imposed!

The generation of the emancipation wished for nothing better than to be accepted by the host society as Britons of the Jewish persuasion. The immigrants mounted a sustained challenge to this assimilatory view, by insisting upon the preservation of their separate ethnic identity and (worse still!) by parading it for all to see. For some, this ethnic separatism took a religious form – the establishment of the Federation of Synagogues in 1887 and of the Union of Orthodox Hebrew

Congregations in 1926; for others it took a political form – the formation of Jewish trade unions and of a uniquely Jewish species of socialism and Labourism; for still others it took a cultural form – the maintenance of a rich Yiddish culture, theatre and newspaper press; and for others it took a geopolitical form – the assertion of provincial autonomy and rebellion against the rule of the London grandees.

All these discontents were exploited by the Zionists, who until the 1930s were really a very small band operating if not on the periphery of the Anglo-Jewish world then certainly at a remarkable distance from its centre. Our view of the Zionist dimension in Anglo-Jewish history has been transformed through the researches of Professor Stuart Cohen of Bar Ilan University and the late Professor David Cesarani of Royal Holloway University of London. It is, I fear, still but little understood now how very fashionable anti-Zionism was within British Jewry before 1939. The Zionist view was that the emancipation of the Jews in Europe had failed and was destined to fail because, at the end of the day, the Jews were simply not capable of assimilation within European societies. This was precisely the view of the Nazis. The established Jewish communities in Britain, obsessively anxious to maintain the image of British Jewry totally at one with its British environment, opposed both Zionism and Nazism for the same reason. So we encounter and enter upon one of the blackest phases of British-Jewish history, the reaction of British Jews to fascism at home and to Nazism abroad.

As to the former, in respect of which our knowledge has been immeasurably transformed by Professor Colin Holmes, the world's leading authority on anti-Jewish prejudice in Britain, by his pupil Professor Tony Kushner, and by my pupil Dr Thomas Linehan (now of Brunel University), it is clear now that the community, certainly as represented by the Board of Deputies of British Jews, was concerned less about protecting Jews from Gentiles than about protecting Gentiles from Jews. That is, the Board, in its communal defence policy, accepted and acted upon the view that Jews, by their behaviour, fostered and fomented antisemitism.

Here I must pay tribute to the work of Dr Louise London, whose London University doctoral thesis I was privileged to examine, and also to the work of my own postgraduate student, Dr Paula Hill. I do believe that in the immediate post-war period, and aided particularly by the euphoria generated by the re-establishment of the Jewish State so soon after the catastrophe of the Holocaust, there developed within British Jewry a collective amnesia (the guilt of those who survived, perhaps) about the precise nature of its own reaction to news of the Final Solution and to the plight of its Jewish victims. All I wish to say here is that I trust I have not disappointed those many Jewish fugitives from Nazism who hoped they would find a welcome from their British co-religionists, whose hopes were brutally dashed, and who have waited for over half a century for the truth to be told.

I have stressed that the preservation of image has been the uttermost priority of the Anglo-Jewish leadership through the ages. In *Modern British Jewry*, and its sequel *British Jewry Since Emancipation* (published by the University of Buckingham Press in 2014) I attempt to show how very divided the Jewish communities of Britain have become since the disappearance of the self-discipline imposed by the

Holocaust years. The last Chief Rabbi who could truly claim to speak as the religious head of the Jews in Britain was Dr Hertz, who held the office from 1913 to 1946. Hertz had problems coping with the left, so to speak, the Reform and Liberal movements, and from the right, the Union of Orthodox Hebrew Congregations and the Gateshead community. But in the shadow of the Nazi menace the various factions tacitly agreed to sink their differences. Under his successor, Israel Brodie, the fabric of religious unity so carefully constructed by the Adlers, father and son, during the nineteenth century began to fall apart, and during the tenure of office of his successor, Lord Jakobovits, the fabric was rent asunder. As I say in *British Jewry Since Emancipation*, Jakobovits bequeathed to Rabbi Dr Jonathan Sacks 'an office less recognised throughout Jewish Britain than at any time since the Emancipation'.

Even before Sacks' election, the suzerainty of the Chief Rabbinate had been publicly repudiated by the Federation of Synagogues, the Union of Liberal and Progressive Synagogues and the Assembly of Conservative Synagogues; subsequently it was repudiated also by the Reform Synagogues of Great Britain; it had never been recognised by the Union of Orthodox Hebrew Congregations or by the Spanish and Portuguese Jews. Professor Barry Kosmin, then Director of the Research Unit of the Board of Deputies, calculated that in 1982 that the communities and congregations which acknowledged the authority of Jakobovits amounted to only 62 per cent of synagogue members in the UK as a whole, and to only 53 per cent in London; the proportions over whom Dr Sacks could claim authority were certainly smaller, and diminished still further – to barely 50 per cent – in the early years of the new millennium.

In my books I try to explain how and why this has happened, but I also emphasise that it is a development parallel to and not unconnected with a similar loss of prestige, status and, ultimately, authority, suffered by the Board of Deputies of British Jews. In times gone by, the wealthy within British Jewry played their part and took their place in the circles of the Board. That past is dead. There is now a more or less wholesale divorce between those who claim to speak as the representatives of British Jewry and those who control its purse strings, some of whom have defected to the upstart Jewish Leadership Council.

The Board is also a victim of the religious polarisation of Anglo-Jewry: it cannot claim to speak on behalf of the secular Jews, nor on behalf of the sectarian orthodox, represented by and through the Union, which walked out of the Board in 1971 and which has shown no sign of wanting to return. The Board has tried to paper over these fissures, but in so doing has been driven to ever more desperate remedies. The truth was – and is – bound to get out in the end. During the very bitter controversy between the Board and the Chief Rabbinate on the one hand, and a loose alliance of orthodox synagogal groupings, led by the Spanish and Portuguese Jews, the Union and the Federation on the other, over the protection of '*shechita*' (the Jewish humane method of slaughter of food animals) in the late 1980s, the claim of the Board to 'represent' British Jewry was effectively quashed. It is now nothing more than a gigantic bluff.

In some respects it is true that the publication of Professor Gartner's *Jewish Immigrant in England* proved to be a false dawn.[9] Why was this? In the first place we must remember that this work came from the pen of an American scholar, thoroughly at home with the Hebrew and Yiddish sources as well as the English, and free from the subtle inhibitions and somewhat less subtle communal constraints that obtained in the United Kingdom. In the second, whereas the American university world was glad to offer homes to young scholars who had served their academic apprenticeships within the world of Jewish history (and, more generally, of Jewish studies), no such opportunities existed in the UK. Outside of the universities of Oxford, Cambridge and London Jewish history was hardly taught; where it was taught, it was likely to be only within departments of theology, classics and ancient history.

Happily, this is no longer the case. Modern Anglo-Jewish history has benefitted from the increasing interest in 'ethnic' studies, and in the experience and impact of immigrant minorities in British – and more generally in European – urban communities. British Jewry itself has matured: it is no longer reluctant to confront its recent past. Scarcely less important has been the willingness of communal philanthropists to fund university posts in and university-level research into this recent past.

The history of the Jews has been recognised as a subject in its own right within the scope of the quinquennial government-mandated Research Assessment Exercises involving the taxpayer-funded higher education sector in the UK. In the early 1990s the University of London approved the history of the Jews in Britain as a discrete optional subject within its Bachelor's programme in modern history. Today there is scarcely a university in the UK where it is not possible to study modern Anglo-Jewish history in some form. Of particular note – but this list is far from exhaustive – are the Oxford Centre for Hebrew and Jewish Studies, the Department for Hebrew and Jewish Studies at University College London, the Centres for Jewish Studies at the University of Manchester and at the School of Oriental and African Studies, and the Parkes Institute and Library at the University of Southampton, which houses the largest single collection of private archives bearing upon the history of the Jews in the UK. We might also note that a number of leading communal bodies have been persuaded to transfer their own archives (often inadequately housed hitherto) to the expert care of London Metropolitan Archives.

At the same time the academic study of Anglo-Jewish history has flourished in the United States of America, where some of its most brilliant contemporary expositors – I am thinking particularly of Professor Todd Endelman – are to be found. It is a particular tribute to these expositors that they, and their students, have managed to maintain and expand this scholarship in spite of the ocean that separates them from their subject matter.

In my writings I have built on foundations dug by others, but the building is mine, and I am responsible for its faults and imperfections. With whatever shortcomings its detractors may find fault, it is my child, and I shall extend to it the full measure of my protection. Some of you may wonder why I speak in these terms. I choose my words carefully and I voice them with good reason. Any professional historian working in the field of British-Jewish history knows that he or she walks in a minefield, and that the assertion of too independent a judgment can bring down communal wrath in full measure.

I well recall how in the spring of 1989 my satisfaction in accepting an invitation from the Jewish Historical Society of England to deliver a paper to it was rudely interrupted when the then Programme Committee of the Society expressed its displeasure on learning that I proposed to talk on the career of Morry Davis, the aforementioned crook, one of the most important figures in Labour politics and political corruption in Stepney between the two World Wars. Their objection appears to have been not that I would say things about Davis that were untrue, or could not be supported by the evidence, but that what I would say would be only too true. I stood my ground, the Programme Committee backed off, and the paper was delivered – and printed.

In the inaugural lecture which I was privileged to give following my elevation to a Personal Chair at Royal Holloway College in 1989 I drew attention to this incident, but omitted to cite another, far graver, which had occurred but a few months previously. I had wished to examine a particular archive of the Board of Deputies.[10] Because of its antisemitic nature I well understood the sensitivity of the Board on this matter, which I had raised, as a Deputy, on the floor of the Board. When, therefore, in October 1986, the then President of the Board, Dr Lionel Kopelowitz, wrote offering me access to this archive, on conditions which included an undertaking that I would not divulge anything from this archive without the prior permission of the President, I readily assented.

This agreement, as come to in October 1986, was never carried out. A series of bureaucratic and other obstacles was placed in the way of its implementation until, in May 1988, it was made clear to me by Dr Kopelowitz that access to the archive would depend not merely upon my adhering to conditions to which I had already agreed, but also upon my agreeing to other, new conditions which had nothing remotely to do with the archive itself, but which pertained to my role and profile in a quite different communal matter. In other words, my access to the archive was now dependent upon my keeping my mouth shut on a current matter then of great communal interest and importance.

Was there ever, I wonder, such pressure put upon a professional historian working in the field of Anglo-Jewish history as was put upon me at that time? And could there, I wonder, be a more perfect example of the contempt in which British Jews – at least as represented by the Board – holds those who seek the truth of its history?

Throughout all these – and other – trials and tribulations I was constantly assailed by members of Anglo-Jewry. I was told to be careful what I wrote and how I wrote it. I was enjoined to present Anglo-Jewry in a favourable light. I was told not to say anything that might be used as ammunition by antisemites.

I replied, and I reply, as follows. If, as I sit in front of my laptop, my constant intent is not to write anything that may be used by the detractors of the Jewish people, then the detractors have already, thereby, won a victory. That is not a victory I propose or have ever proposed to give them.

I recall, and commend, some words penned by one of the greatest novelists and poets to write in the English language, Thomas Hardy. In the 'Explanatory Note' to the first edition of his great novel *Tess of the D'Urbervilles*, written in November 1891, Hardy felt it prudent to remind his audience of some words of St Jerome. I repeat them now, and I have no qualms about doing so since I follow the maxim of the late Chief Rabbi Hertz, who enjoined his fellow Jews to accept the truth from whatever source it comes.[11]

The words of St Jerome quoted by Hardy run thus: 'If an offence come out of the truth, better is it that the offence come than that the truth be concealed.'[12]

Notes

1 This is a revised and updated version of a paper first delivered and published under the auspices of the Centre for Jewish Studies, University of London, 1994.
2 David S. Katz, 'The marginalization of Early Modern Anglo-Jewish history', *Immigrants and Minorities* vol. 10, 1991, 61.
3 Ibid.
4 Grace Aguilar, 'History of the Jews in England', *Chambers's Miscellany of Useful and Entertaining Tracts* vol. 18, no. 152, 1847, 1–32.
5 Lloyd. P. Gartner, 'Cecil Roth: historian of Anglo-Jewry', in Dov Noy and Issachar Ben-Ami, *Studies in the Cultural Life of the Jews in England* (Jerusalem: Magnes Press 1975), 69–86 (71).
6 Quoted in ibid., 83.
7 Todd M. Endelman, 'English Jewish History', *Modern Judaism* vol. 11, 1991, 92.
8 I recommended the manuscript's rejection. The publisher ignored my advice!
9 Geoffrey Alderman, 'The Canon', *Times Higher Education*, 28 May 2009, 49.
10 On this episode see Geoffrey Alderman and Colin Holmes, 'The Burton Book', *Journal of the Royal Asiatic Society*, vol. 18, no. 1, 2008, 1–13.
11 Joseph Herman Hertz (ed.), *The Pentateuch and Haftorahs* 2nd edn (London: Oxford University Press 1969), vii: from the preface to the first edn, 1936: 'Accept the true [sic] from whatever source it come, is sound Rabbinic doctrine – even if it be from the pages of a devout Christian expositor or of an iconoclastic Bible scholar, Jewish or non-Jewish.'
12 Thomas Hardy, *Tess of the D'Urbervilles* (London: Penguin 1985), 35.

10
WEAVING ITALIAN EXPERIENCE INTO THE BRITISH IMMIGRATION NARRATIVE

Wendy Ugolini

Colin Holmes' pioneering work encouraged the emergence of a substantial historiography which testifies to historical traditions of intolerance towards different immigrant communities in Britain since the mid-nineteenth century. Yet, traditionally, there has been a tendency within British Italian texts dedicated to recovering the histories of the Italian presence in the United Kingdom to portray the Italians as somehow immune from the difficulties faced by other ethnic minority groups. For example, one of the leading commentators, Terri Colpi, once defined the Italian community as being 'in an unique and aristocratic position amongst the immigrant populations of this country', whilst Umberto Marin, writing in 1975, described the Italians in Britain as 'a privileged collectivity' which represented 'a kind of Eden within the troubled emigration front'.[1] Furthermore, academic and popular representations have often converged to present a largely celebratory – and at times almost saccharine – overview of the Italian presence in Britain which arguably serves to obscure historical incidences of racism and hostility. This is typified in an example from a local Scottish newspaper which asserts,

> They bought us restaurants, ice cream sold from street vending vans ... 'They' are the Italians whose humour is as rich as their wine and whose charm is as warm as the sun in any vineyard. They are a gregarious race, who, since arriving in Scotland, have become as closely entwined with Scots society as spaghetti lengths in a bowl.[2]

I have tried to interrogate and challenge this rather cosy reciprocity in my own work, published from 1998 onwards and, more recently, historians working in Wales such as Marco Giudici, have further attempted to complicate the notion of a 'tolerant' response to the Italian presence within the constituent nations of Britain.[3] This chapter will track the evolution of the historiography of the British Italian migrant experience, acknowledging the groundbreaking contributions of scholars such as Terri Colpi and Lucio Sponza whilst also mapping more recent works which focus on questions of war, identities and memory.

The Italians are considered a long-established migrant group, having started to arrive in Britain in significant numbers in the mid-nineteenth century. The 1871 census records an Italian population of just over 5,000 present in Britain. By 1911, this figure stood at 25,365 with around one-fifth in Scotland.[4] As Sponza notes, a unique feature which distinguished Italian settlement in Britain was the concentration in the catering professions which occurred at the end of the nineteenth century and enabled Italian families to remain largely self-employed.[5] However, their sense of belonging within the wider British community was substantially eroded during the Second World War – and the fragility of their status clearly underlined – when Italy declared war on Britain in June 1940 and Italian nationals were categorised as 'enemy aliens', leading to state-sponsored policies of internment, deportation and relocation as well as outbreaks of anti-Italian violence in British cities and towns. For many decades the history of the Italian presence in Britain was relatively neglected, although there were some early and interesting exceptions such as a social anthropological study by Philip Garigue and Raymond Firth undertaken in 1956. This explored the experiences of 'persons of Italian nationality ... and persons of British nationality, born of parents or grandparents of Italian nationality living in London', categorising this inter-generational cohort as 'Italianates' displaying kinship ties with relations in Italy.[6] In the aftermath of the Second World War, they noted the 'operation of discrimination' against those living in London which, in turn, served to reinforce a strong sense of 'Italianness'.[7] The sociologist Anne-Marie Fortier notes how a focus in the early 1970s on white ethnic groups, so-called 'invisible immigrants', stimulated fresh interest in the Italian community in Britain.[8] An insightful study of Italians in London by Robin Palmer in 1977 followed Garigue and Firth in picking up on a 'slow rate of assimilation'. Palmer also alluded to the 'traumatic' wartime history of the community in London and the 'disastrous' attachment within the diaspora to Italian Fascism in the interwar period.[9] Another formative text to emerge at this time was Marin's 1975 study, *Italiani in Gran Bretagna*, although the fact that it was produced in the Italian language arguably limited its wider circulation. Much of the early recovery work of Italian migrant experience in Britain was undertaken by geographers rather than historians.[10] In 1979, there was an edition of the *Association of Teachers of Italian Journal* devoted to Italian immigration which was followed in 1993 by a supplement to the *italianist* recording 'a century of Italian emigration to Britain'.[11] In Scotland, the scholar Andrew Wilkin has been particularly assiduous in tracking the early origins of Italian settlers in Scotland,[12] and Sandra Chistolini addressed post-war female experience in Scotland in her Italian-language study, *Donne italoscozzesi*.[13] In the same year, an edited collection on Italian language and culture in Scotland was published.[14] There was also an influential chapter by Murdoch Rodgers entitled '*Italiani in Scozzia* [sic]' which drew upon a BBC Radio Scotland broadcast programme.[15] The 1980s witnessed the emergence of a broad range of local studies, which helped to map the experiences of different communities across the United Kingdom, beginning with Bruno Bottignolo's study of Italian immigrants in south-west England, *Without a Bell Tower*, in 1985.[16] A number of autobiographies and memoirs have also been published, primarily reflecting two key constituencies: those who have achieved commercial success within the community or those who feel compelled to 'tell' the story of their wartime experiences.[17] In 1991, Colin Hughes produced a detailed overview of the Italian community in South Wales with the typically evocative title, *Lime, Lemon and Sarsaparilla*. Whilst Hughes' book includes considered analysis, particularly when acknowledging the emergence of Italian Fascism within interwar diasporic communities, the general tone adopted is one of celebration, with Hughes making claims for the Italians as a long-established, well-'integrated' migrant group.[18] Fortier points out that the leading British Italian texts appeared at a time of wider public discourse on the general desirability (or not) of different immigrant groups.[19] In participant observation fieldwork undertaken with the London Italian community at the close of the twentieth century, Fortier notes how, 'In a country and continent where "immigrant" means black and foreigner', there was a keenness within the present-day Italian community not to emphasise their marginal status as members of a minority group within British society.[20]

One figure who has made a significant and pioneering contribution to British Italian historiography is Terri Colpi, a geographer, who published an extensive range of journal articles from 1979 onwards before finally producing her groundbreaking text, *The Italian Factor*, in 1991 which was accompanied by a photographic collection, *Italians Forward*.[21] Another leading figure is Lucio Sponza who produced a comprehensive scholarly work on Italian immigrants in nineteenth-century Britain which he followed with *Divided Loyalties*, examining the experience of Italian internees and Italian Prisoners of War in Britain during the Second World War.[22] Together, their published oeuvre constitutes an impressive contribution to British Italian historiography although both contain some flaws and omissions which will be discussed below. In light of the general paucity of material on the Italian presence in Britain, Colpi's book, in particular, became influential. However, an interesting intervention was made in 2000 by Fortier. In her book, *Migrant Belongings*, Fortier points out that although much of the literature on Italians in Britain 'depicts a collectivity characterized by a high degree of diversity within', the very fact of producing 'written renditions of the Italian presence' means that 'some kind of coherence is created' from the disparate histories, social relations and social positions of Italian migrants and therefore constructions of a one-dimensional Italian 'community' emerge.[23] The very act of writing the history of the Italian presence in Britain, argues Fortier, means that ultimately these texts and publications 'produce what they claim to be re-presenting and re-covering'.[24] Furthermore, she notes how most of the books are produced by Italians who have, in one way or another, a personal commitment to the British Italian 'community'.[25] For example, Sponza is Italian and at the time of writing, a Professor Emeritus of Italian Studies at the University of Westminster whereas Colpi is a self-styled 'third-generation Italian

Scot' who writes as 'a proud member of the Community'.[26] Significantly, Colpi's book *The Italian Factor* was launched at the National Library of Scotland's 1991 exhibition *The Italian Scots*, legitimising Colpi's status as an 'authority' on the community, and in 1995 she received the title of *Cavaliere* from the Italian government for her contribution to the advancement of the community in Britain.[27] Yet, as Fortier points out, *The Italian Factor* stands out as a 'highly normative' representation where the Italian 'Community' 'is given as a unified "thing", the membership of which is policed by the degree of *conformity* to its cultural contents'.[28] Indeed, Colpi's book 'consistently objectifies and normalizes *what it means to be and act Italian*: from *campanilismo* to *compadrismo*, family loyalties and first communions'.[29] In the introduction to her 1991 book, Colpi admits that it 'is not directly concerned with those who have opted or drifted out of the Community; it is concerned with those who have *an Italian way of life*' but it is not entirely clear what this assertion means in the context of the late twentieth century when Italian families have been settled in Britain for many generations.[30]

As a social and cultural historian, I am particularly interested in the ways in which Colpi narrates the impact of the Second World War on the Italian diasporic community. For example, it is striking that, in the chapter addressing the war Colpi states her intention to explain events '*from the Italian point of view*' [my emphasis] which, again, seems to suggest a normative way of behaving to which 'Italians' should have conformed in wartime.[31] Colpi writes that by 1939, the Italians in Britain were 'well integrated, respected and often prosperous members of British society', the war had a devastating impact but the community managed to successfully rebuild their businesses and relations with the local community in the post-war period.[32] As Bill Williams identifies in his work with Jewish immigrants, communal myth often promotes the idea of a 'socially coherent and harmonious' community, an image which is absorbed over time by the immigrants themselves and later repeated by historians.[33] As I have stated in my own work, it has arguably been in the interest of those once most actively involved in the interwar Italian Fascist clubs, the more successful, commercially based members of the Italian community, to reconstruct the past to suit the needs of the present day, where they, in Colpi's own phrase, 'trade on their ethnicity'.[34] In the post-war era, where the entrepreneurial members of the community have 'often concentrated on selling some aspect of their Italianness',[35] it has been important to construct narratives which emphasise the bonds of friendship and ignore the 'tangled' histories of the past.[36] In this interpretative context, the Italophobia of the Second World War becomes dismissed as a 'one-off' event, a regrettable disruption in a long history of cordial relations. This tendency to downplay anti-Italian hostility can be seen in the production of an article by Sponza on the anti-Italian riots of 1940 in Scotland in which he downplayed their 'xenophobic' dimension, alluding to the importance of the 'depressed socio-economic conditions of the Scottish youth'.[37] This seems to deny the insight of David Cesarani on incidences of racial violence which warns against the temptation 'to localise these occurrences and thus foreclose an appreciation of how anti-alienism was a universal phenomenon' in Britain.[38] It can also be countered to some degree by my own research on the riots which, drawing upon the oral testimonies of British Italians, highlights their profoundly unsettling racialised nature and the long-term psychological impact upon many of those who witnessed the violence at first hand.[39]

The desire to 'gloss over' difficult issues such as racial violence, Fascist membership and split allegiances leads to partial or even misleading accounts of British Italian experience.[40] Both Colpi and Sponza foreground the experience of male internees when discussing the impact of the war on the Italian community with the net result that a narrow stratum of experience becomes representative of the community as a whole and difference on the grounds of class, gender or political allegiances is overlooked. In particular, this dominance of a singular elite narrative, focusing on internment, has silenced the memories of different groups within the community. Major aspects of British Italian experience – service in the British Armed Forces, life on the home front for women and children, essentially the memories of *non-internees* – have been marginalised in the traditional historiography.

A notable absence from the work of both Colpi and Sponza are the experiences of second generation Italians who enlisted in the British Armed Forces and auxiliary services. It would appear that the act of British-born Italians serving in the British Forces, raising difficult questions of loyalties and allegiances, has resulted in them being excluded from historiographical representations of the community's past.[41] In *The Italian Factor*, Colpi asserts that the generation of British-born Italians 'who served in the *fiercely anti-Italian* British Armed Forces' during the war were 'forced to throw off their heritage, shake themselves adrift of their roots and *pretend to be something they were not*' [my italics].[42] In sharp contrast, the actions of the far smaller group of 'British-born Italians' who were interned, usually because of their involvement in the *Fasci*, were commended for being 'determined to go with "the Italians" and to remain united with their roots and their Community'.[43] Thus, traditional historiography, by neglecting those who served in the British Forces, makes an implicit judgement about their claim to being a 'good Italian' and itself draws upon wartime dichotomies when, as Colpi acknowledges, 'the community became deeply split into the so-called "good Italians" (the Fascists) and "bad Italians" (the others)'.[44] This disavowal of British Italian military service runs counter to wider trends within immigration historiography which acknowledge how migrant communities often foreground military participation in wartime in order to lay claim to a sense of citizenship and national belonging in Britain.[45]

My own research aimed to rebalance the picture by investigating the experiences of second generation Italians who served in the British Forces. Based on an analysis of the Second World War Roll of Honour, I calculated that over 7,000 men of Italian origin served in the British Army alone.[46] My book, *Experiencing War as the Enemy Other*, which incorporates the recorded oral testimonies of British Italians, attempted to foreground the lived experiences of those who served in the British Armed Forces and auxiliary services. This research illuminated the extent to which the accommodation of British-born Italians within the UK military structure encouraged the formulation of a distinctive dual-identity, which rested on identification with both Britain and Italy. Amongst second generation Italians who lived through the war, there is a strong sense of hybridity, of belonging to two cultures at once, highlighting the plurality of the Italian diaspora space in Britain. However, due to some anti-Italian discrimination faced in the British Forces, it could also be argued that second generation veterans often emerged with a strong sense of 'otherness'.[47]

Experiencing War also addressed memorialisation of the war with the British Italian community, noting the emergence of 'narratives of victimhood' surrounding the sinking of the deportation ship the *Arandora Star* by a German U-boat in July 1940 when around 446 Italian internees were drowned.[48] In Fortier's view, 'the British Italian community still defines itself by the grief over the lives lost in the *Arandora Star*'.[49] Those on board the ship had been categorised as the 'most dangerous' of the internees in the sense that they had been members of Italian Fascist clubs in Britain. However, unlike with German and Austrian refugees, there had been no attempts to 'screen' or classify members of the Italian community via tribunals, leading to an over-reliance on the racialised views of the security authorities. In recent years there has been a burgeoning of interest in this event, underlined by a range of commemorative activities, including the production of populist histories and fictional novels.[50] However, I have argued that the constant emphasis on the tragedy within communal discourse, drawing upon the symbolism of victimhood and suffering, functions to distract attention away from political, class and generational differences in the interwar period and, in particular, the fact that a small but significant minority of the Italian diasporic elite embraced Fascism.[51] My book traces how, after a relative silence of seven decades, organised elements within Italian communities from across Britain started to claim their own sites of memory to commemorate the disaster with the parallel development of campaigns for an apology or compensation for wartime Italian internment.[52]

In recent years there has been a burgeoning of more critical work on Italian experience in Britain which acknowledges complexity. Claudia Baldoli's work, *Exporting Fascism*, made a refreshing addition to the historiography by mapping the process through which Mussolini's Italy attempted 'to transform its emigrants in Britain into enthusiastic Fascists'.[53] This countered historiographical trends which tended to downplay the political dimensions of Italian Fascism in Britain in the interwar period. Tony Kushner provides a fresh analysis of the anti-Italian riots in *We Europeans?* which, by making use of contemporaneous Mass Observation diaries, uncovers evidence of 'bonding with the British Italians' and suggests that local knowledge often gave 'a sophisticated insight into the dynamics of ordinary Italians in Britain and the ambiguities and tensions caused by the pull of family, politics and patriotisms in creating a place called home'.[54] There has also been interesting work by Deianira Ganga on the 'new' post-war Italian community in England, focusing on those who settled in Nottingham and addressing transnational ties in the modern era. Ganga explores the numerous motivations lying behind the choice of older Italians to remain in the United Kingdom and effectively highlights the 'portability' of present-day identity, with many older Italians commuting regularly between Italy and England.[55] As noted above, there is also a body of research emerging from Wales, most notably the work of Bruna Chezzi and Marco Giudici. Both have produced thoughtful work addressing memorialisation as well as wider reflections on the place of Italians within Britain. In his study of museums and memorials in post-devolution Wales, for example, Giudici notes that the Italians have been portrayed as being a successful 'model minority'. Being an allegedly integrated, successful and 'popular' migrant group, he argues, the Italians have offered an ideal narrative to reach out to other migrants and encourage them to get civically engaged in Welsh society. He shows how devolved nations such as Wales make use of their immigrant past to construct a tolerant and inclusive image of themselves that suits their current political aims.[56] This idea of demonstrating a 'unique tolerance' toward minority groups is also present within the Scottish Government which actively engages with the Italian diasporic community, lending its own 'institutional aura' to campaigns such as that for an *Arandora Star* memorial in Glasgow.[57] Chezzi provides an analysis of the recent campaign for an *Arandora Star* memorial in Wales, arguing that recent memorialisation within the United Kingdom reflects 'an attempt to create a platform for the generation of memories after nearly seven decades of silence'.[58] It is worth noting however that Chezzi, an Italian scholar, was actively involved in the campaign itself and states in her article: 'I strongly sympathised with my Welsh-Italians friends who had lost family members on the ill-fated ship, and I wanted to help raise awareness of those events and their significance for posterity.'[59] Here, Chezzi is adopting what Pamela Ballinger terms the 'solidarity-rapport model' of ethnography.[60] However, as Fortier has acknowledged, there are inherent challenges within critical scholarship if academics position themselves as advocates for the 'cause' of the migrant group which they are studying.[61]

Conclusion

The distress Italian families experienced during the wartime period, as well as the fact that they have been settled in Britain for over a hundred and fifty years, has produced what Fortier characterises as 'a distinctly Italian form of belonging *in Britain*'.[62] I have suggested elsewhere that it was perhaps only in the closing decades of the twentieth century, with domestic hostility focusing on more 'visible' immigrant groups and with Italian popular culture widely celebrated, that Italian identity in Britain could be more safely articulated.[63] Writing in 1991 Colin Holmes warned that 'Hostility towards immigrant groups "sleeps lightly"'.[64] Whilst there is an understandable tendency – particularly evident within devolved governments – to promote inclusivity and to celebrate the successful integration of the Italian community in Britain, there is also the danger that if we fail to address the more negative aspects of British Italian experience, then we will continue to feign surprise at the readiness of British society to target the internal 'other' at times of adversity.

Notes

1. Terri Colpi, 'Italian migration to Scotland: settlement, employment and the key role of the padrone'. Paper given at the *Race, Curriculum and Employment Conference*, University of Glasgow 8 March 1986, 1; Umberto Marin, *Italiani in Gran Bretagna* (Roma: Centro Studi Emigrazione 1975), 104 (translation by Anne-Marie Fortier, *Migrant Belongings: Memory, Space, Identity* (Oxford: Berg 2000), 39.
2. Frank Hurley, 'The incomers. They gave us the ice cream vendors', *Edinburgh Evening News* 3 February 1973, 87–8. See Wendy Ugolini, '"Spaghetti lengths in a bowl"? Recovering narratives of not "belonging" amongst the Italian Scots', *Immigrants & Minorities* vol. 31, no. 2, 2013, 214–234.
3. Wendy Ugolini, 'Re-inforcing Otherness? Edinburgh's Italian community and the impact of the Second World War', *Family & Community History* vol. 1, 1998, 57–69; Wendy Ugolini, *Experiencing War as the 'Enemy Other': Italian Scottish Experience in World War II* (Manchester: Manchester University Press 2011); Marco Giudici, 'Discourses of identity in post-Devolution Wales: The case of Welsh-Italians', *Contemporary Wales* vol. 25, no. 1, 2012, 228–47.
4. Terri Colpi, *The Italian Factor* (Edinburgh: Mainstream 1991), 48.
5. Lucio Sponza, 'Italians in Great Britain', in Melvin Ember, Carol R. Ember and Ian Skoggard (eds), *Encyclopaedia of Diasporas: Immigrant and Refugee Cultures around the World, Vol. 2* (New York: Springer 2005), 874–83 (880). This has allowed some historians to argue that Italians have been largely protected from discrimination rooted in labour tensions. See Murdoch Rodgers, 'Italiani in Scozzia', in Billy Kay (ed.), *Odyssey. Voices from Scotland's Recent Past* (Edinburgh: Polygon 1982), 13–21 (15).
6. Philip Garigue and Raymond Firth, 'Kinship organisations of Italianates in London', in Raymond Firth (ed.), *Two Studies of Kinship in London* (London: Athlone Press 1956), 67–93 (67).
7. Ibid., 69.
8. A term first coined in a 1972 statistical survey on Italians, Spanish and Portuguese immigrants by MacDonald & MacDonald. See Fortier, *Migrant Belongings*, 21.
9. Robin Palmer, 'The Italians: patterns of migration to London', in James Watson (ed.), *Between Two Cultures* (Oxford: Blackwell 1977), 242–268 (243; 266).
10. See Russell King, 'Italian migration to Great Britain', *Geography* vol. 62, no. 3, 1977, 176–186.
11. *Association of Teachers of Italian Journal* no. 29, 1979; Lucio Sponza and Arturo Tosi (eds), *A Century of Italian Emigration to Britain 1880–1980s. Five Essays,* Supplement to *The Italianist* vol. 13, 1993.
12. Andrew Wilkin, 'Origins and destinations of the early Italo-Scots', *Association of Teachers of Italian Journal* no. 29, 1979, 52–61; Andrew Wilkin, 'Defined origins of the earliest Italo-Scots', in Andrew Wilkin (ed.), *Mosaico. A Miscellany of Writings Presented to Cav. Uff. Dr Enrico Cocozza* (Glasgow: Strathclyde University 1985); Andrew Wilkin, 'Further definition of the origins of the earliest Italo-Scots', in Eileen A Millar (ed.), *Renaissance and Other Studies* (Glasgow: University of Glasgow 1988), 348–59; Andrew Wilkin, 'Introducing the Italo-Scots', *Vector* vol. 2, 1990, 15–23.
13. Sandra Chistolini, *Donne Italoscozzesi. Tradizione e cambiamento* (Roma: Centro Studi Emigrazione 1986).
14. Mario Dutto (ed.), *The Italians in Scotland: Their Language and Culture* (Edinburgh: Edinburgh University Press 1986).
15. Rodgers, 'Italiani in Scozzia'.

16 Bruno Bottignolo, *Without a Bell Tower* (Roma: Centro Studi Emigrazione 1985). See also David Green, 'Little Italy in Victorian London: Holborn's Italian community', *Camden History Review* vol. 15, 1988, 2–6; Anthony Rea, *Manchester's Little Italy* (Manchester: Neil Richardson 1988) and, more recently, Doreen Hopwood and Margaret Dilloway, *Bella Brum. A History of Birmingham's Italian Community* (Birmingham: Birmingham City Council 1996); Giancarlo Rinaldi, *From the Serchio to the Solway* (Dumfries: Dumfries and Galloway Council 1998); Terry Cooke, *Little Italy: A History of Liverpool's Italian Community* (Liverpool: Bluecoat Press 2002).

17 Peppino Leoni, *I Shall Die on the Carpet* (London: Leslie Frewin 1966); Bruno Sereni, *They Took the Low Road* (Glasgow: Casa d'Italia 1974); Charles Forte, *Forte. The Autobiography of Charles Forte* (London: Pan Books 1997); Piero Tognini, *A Mind at War: An Autobiography* (New York: Vantage Press 1990); Joe Pieri, *Isle of the Displaced* (Glasgow: Neil Wilson 1997); Joe Pieri, *Tales of the Savoy. Stories from a Glasgow Café* (Glasgow: Neil Wilson 1999); Enrico Cocozza, *Assunta – The Story of Mrs Joe* (New York: Vantage Press 1987).

18 Colin Hughes, *Lime, Lemon and Sarsaparilla. The Italian Community in South Wales 1880–1945* (Bridgend: Seren Books 1991). In books addressing the Italian diaspora, there is often a tendency to adopt a rather nostalgic approach rooted in the cultural appeal of the ice cream seller or café owner. See, here, Hughes' comment: 'One of my earliest recollections is of learning to read the words on the wrappers and boxes in the window of an Italian shop in the village where I was born in South Wales.' Colin Hughes, 'The Italian community in South Wales from 1880 to the Second World War', in Sponza and Tosi (eds), *A Century of Italian emigration to Britain 1880–1980s*, 43–58.

19 Fortier, *Migrant Belongings*, 38–39.

20 Ibid., 120.

21 Terri Colpi, 'The Italian community in Glasgow, with special reference to spatial development', *Association of Teachers of Italian Journal*, no. 29, 1979, 62–75; Terri Colpi, 'The Italian migration to Scotland: fact, fiction and the future', in Dutto (ed.), *Italians in Scotland*; Terri Colpi, 'The impact of the Second World War on the British Italian community', in David Cesarani and Tony Kushner (eds), *The Internment of Aliens in Twentieth Century Britain* (London: Frank Cass 1993) 167–187; Colpi, *Italian Factor*, Terri Colpi, *Italians Forward. A Visual History of the Italian Community in Great Britain* (Edinburgh: Mainstream 1991); Terri Colpi, 'The Scottish Italian Community: senza un campanile?', *The Innes Review*, XLIV, no. 2, 1993, 153–167.

22 Lucio Sponza, *Italian Immigrants in Nineteenth-Century Britain: Realities and Images* (Leicester: Leicester University Press 1988); Lucio Sponza, *Divided Loyalties. Italians in Britain during the Second World War* (Bern: Peter Lang 2000).

23 Fortier, *Migrant Belongings*, 37.

24 Ibid., 38.

25 Ibid., 40.

26 Colpi, *Italian Factor*, 5.

27 Fortier, *Migrant Belongings*, 41.

28 Ibid., 42.

29 Ibid., 168.

30 Colpi, *Italian Factor*, 16.

31 Ibid., 99.

32 Ibid., 101. Fortier defines this as an 'entrepreneurial narrative', adopting a narrowly capitalistic definition of success. Fortier, *Migrant Belongings*, 46.

33 Bill Williams, 'The Jewish immigrant in Manchester: the contribution of oral history', *Oral History* vol. 7, no. 1, 1979, 43–53 (43).

34 Colpi, *Italian Factor*, 196. See Ugolini, *Experiencing War*, 65.
35 Colpi, *Italian Factor*, 256.
36 Angelo Principe, 'A tangled knot: prelude to 10 June 1940', in Franca Iacovetta, Roberto Perin and Angelo Principe (eds), *Enemies Within. Italian and Other Internees in Canada and Abroad* (Toronto: University of Toronto Press 2000), 27–51 (27).
37 Lucio Sponza, 'The anti-Italian riots, June 1940', in Panikos Panayi (ed.), *Racial Violence in Britain in the Nineteenth and Twentieth Centuries* (London: Leicester University Press 1996), 131–149 (146).
38 David Cesarani, 'An alien concept? The continuity of anti-alienism in British society before 1940', in Cesarani and Kushner (eds), *Internment of Aliens*, 25–52 (38).
39 Ugolini, *Experiencing War*, 118–143.
40 For a global perspective of this phenomenon see Franca Iacovetta and Roberto Perin, 'Introduction. Italians and wartime internment: comparative perspectives on public policy, historical memory, and daily life', in Iacovetta, Perin and Principe (eds), *Enemies Within*, 3–21.
41 Ugolini, *Experiencing War*, 15.
42 Colpi, *Italian Factor*, 193.
43 Ibid., 111.
44 Ibid., 100.
45 Wendy Ugolini, 'The embodiment of British Italian war memory? The curious marginalization of Dennis Donnini, VC', *Patterns of Prejudice* vol. 46, nos. 3–4, 2012, 397–415 (406–9).
46 Ugolini, *Experiencing War*, 144.
47 Ibid., 194–5. See also Wendy Ugolini, '"The sins of the fathers": The contested recruitment of second-generation Italians in the British Forces 1936–43', *Twentieth Century British History* vol. 24, no. 3, 2013, 376–397.
48 Ugolini, *Experiencing War*, 224.
49 Fortier, *Migrant Belongings*, 57.
50 Pietro Zorza, *Arandora Star* (Glasgow: Italiani in Scozia 1985); Des Hickey and Gus Smith, *The Star of Shame – the Arandora Star* (Madison Publishing 1989); Maria Serena Balestracci, *Arandora Star. From Oblivion to Memory* (Parma: Monte Università 2008). The *Arandora Star* retains its magnetic hold on popular imagination. See Natalie Dye, *Arandora Star* (London: Peach Publishing 2014). The experience of Italian Prisoners of War is another heavily romanticised aspect of British Italian experience. See Philip Paris, *Orkney's Italian Chapel: The True Story of an Icon* (Edinburgh: Black & White Publishing 2013).
51 Ugolini, *Experiencing War*, 233.
52 For more on this, see Ugolini, *Experiencing War*, 223–250.
53 Claudia Baldoli, *Exporting Fascism. Italian Fascists and Britain's Italians in the 1930s* (Oxford: Berg 2003), 1.
54 Tony Kushner, *We Europeans? Mass-Observation, 'Race', and British Identity in Twentieth-Century Britain* (Aldershot: Ashgate 2004), 181–182.
55 Deianira Ganga, 'Reinventing the myth of return: older Italians in Nottingham', in Kathy Burrell and Panikos Panayi (eds), *Histories and Memories. Migrants and Their History in Britain* (London: Tauris Academic Studies 2006), 114–130 (127).
56 Marco Giudici, 'Immigrant narratives and nation-building in a stateless nation: the case of Italians in post-devolution Wales', *Ethnic and Racial Studies* vol. 37, no. 8, 2014, 1409–1426; Marco Giudici, 'Migration history and nation-building: the role of museums and memorials in post-devolution Wales', in Lawrence Gourievidis (ed.), *Museums and Migration History: History, Memory and Politics* (Abingdon: Routledge 2014), 216–226.

57 Giudici, 'Migration history', 217; 'New memorial plan for WWII tragedy', *Scotsman*, 28 May 2008.
58 Bruna Chezzi, 'Wales breaks its silence: from memory to memorial and beyond. The Italians in Wales during the Second World War', *Italian Studies* vol. 69, no. 3, 2014, 376–393 (376).
59 Ibid., 378. See also Bruna Chezzi, *Italians in Wales and their cultural representations, 1920s–2010s* (Newcastle: Cambridge Scholars Publishing 2015).
60 Pamela Ballinger, *History in Exile. Memory and Identity at the Borders of the Balkans* (Princeton: Princeton University Press 2003), 271.
61 Fortier, *Migrant Belongings*, 9.
62 Ibid., 164–165.
63 Ugolini, *Experiencing War*, 12–13.
64 Colin Holmes, *A Tolerant Country?* (London: Faber & Faber 1991), 95.

11

JEWISH REFUGEE HISTORIOGRAPHY

Moving beyond the celebratory?

Jennifer Craig-Norton

In 1956, Viscount Herbert Samuel wrote in the introduction to one of the first books devoted to telling the story of Jewish refugees in Great Britain:

> The duty of help and rescue, so far as any was possible, lay upon the Jewish communities … It is right that we of this generation should leave to posterity an authentic record of those tragic events, and the way they were faced … It is a poignant story; but consoling also as a tale of devoted human service … And that service was by no means limited in Great Britain to the Jews. The whole nation rose to the occasion. The statesmen – Lord Baldwin … Sir Samuel Hoare … and Lord Gorell … all the Christian Churches also, with that noble body of philanthropists – the Quakers – as always in the forefront; the professional classes, who made room … for thousands of scientists and other refugees; and a great multitude of the rank and file of the people, who gave … hospitality … to children.[1]

With these words, Samuel, who had himself been involved in Anglo-Jewish efforts to help Jews fleeing Fascist oppression, exemplified the celebratory narrative that dominated Britain's emerging historiography of Jewish refugees in the 1930s. Samuel sketched an unequivocal tale of heroism on the part of Anglo-Jewry, the British government and people, the Christian churches, philanthropists and the professional classes in rescuing thousands of scientists, children and other refugees. The title of the volume in which Samuel's introduction appears, *They Found Refuge*, exemplifies the dominant theme that characterised these early studies. Other similarly themed volumes, A. J. Sherman's *Island Refuge* and Naomi Shepard's *A Refuge from Darkness*, appeared in the succeeding two decades, signifying how salient and persistent the notions of asylum, protection, shelter and sanctuary were in prevailing interpretations of Britain's role in the refugee crisis brought about by the rise of Nazism.[2]

About a decade after the publication of Bentwich's laudatory volume, American scholars began to critically examine US responses to the refugee crisis. A flourishing historiography, with works by David Wyman, Henry Feingold and Saul Friedman, among many others, critiqued the Roosevelt administration for actively impeding the flow of Jewish refugees to America and indicted Americans' passivity, apathy and indifference and American Jewry's impotence in responding adequately to both the refugee crisis and the Holocaust.[3] Conversely, in Britain, such critical works did not begin appearing until a decade later, heralded by Bernard Wasserstein's *Britain and the Jews of Europe 1939–1945* in 1979.[4] While this was a landmark publication in the historiography of official and governmental British responses to the Holocaust, it did not explicitly address Britain's response to the refugee crisis, taking as its starting point the beginning of the war. Similarly, the somewhat later *British Jewry and the Holocaust* by Richard Bolchover offered a much-needed critical appraisal of Anglo-Jewish responses to the Holocaust, but did not include the pre-war years in its remit.[5]

It would not be until the 1980s, with the emergence of the Sheffield School, led by Colin Holmes, that a critical approach to the subject of Britain and Jewish refugees from fascism entered the mainstream. In works such as *John Bull's Island* and *A Tolerant Country*, Holmes pioneered the contextualisation of Jewish refugees of the 1930s within the broader continuum of British migration experiences, opening the door for the more specialised studies that would follow.[6] In 1984, both the Gerhard Hirschfeld edited *Exile in Great Britain: Refugees from Hitler's Germany* and Marion Berghahn's *German-Jewish Refugees in England* signalled a new and more critical focus on the subject of Jewish refugees from fascism.[7] In chapters authored primarily by scholars of German history, the Hirschfied volume explored a range of subjects including immigration policy, settlement problems, internment and refugee contributions to Great Britain, suggesting new avenues for further investigation. Berghahn, a German social anthropologist, was one of the first to use interviews with former Jewish refugees – rather than the perspectives of British rescuers – as the lens through which to examine their reception, adaptation and assimilation in Britain. Both of these studies broke new ground in expanding the scope and range of Jewish refugee scholarship, but it remained, like Holocaust studies generally, largely dominated by German academics until the late 1980s when a more Anglo-centric outlook emerged with the scholarship of Tony Kushner and others of the Sheffield School.

British social and cultural historians such as Kushner have made invaluable contributions to the historiography of refugees and migrants and offered new and insightful critiques that have continued to place the Jewish refugee crisis of the 1930s in the context of British attitudes to 'the other' and questioned the unambiguously redemptive and celebratory narratives of the past.[8] This critical turn added complexity and nuance to the study of British responses to the Jewish refugees of the 1930s and broadly interpreted such responses as a mixture of pragmatic and humanitarian impulses that put perceived British interests ahead of altruistic concerns, undercutting national self-imaginings of Britain as a haven of refuge and asylum. The 1990s were a fertile period of reappraisal of British-Jewish history generally, and produced a number of seminal works on

Anglo-Jews and Jewish refugees and migrants including Geoffrey Alderman's *Modern British Jewry*, and the Werner Mosse edited volume *Second Chance: Two Centuries of German-speaking Jews in the United Kingdom*.[9] These efforts promised the development of such research into full monograph-length studies of official and Anglo-Jewish responses to Jewish refugees as well as targeted studies of various refugee groups, biographies of refugee activists and other microhistorical approaches. In some respects, this promise has been realised, but in other areas, it remains unfulfilled.

One of the contributors to the Werner Mosse volume was Louise London who, a decade later, would produce a landmark volume in the historiography *Whitehall and the Jews*, which remains the definitive study on the subject of British immigration policy from 1933–1948.[10] London's authoritative command of official papers and other archival sources supports her carefully shaded conclusions that both censure a government policy that was all too often illiberal and exclusionary, while commending those groups and individuals whose humanity and compassion allowed for the emigration of 60–70,000 Jewish refugees. Additional scholarship produced around the turn of the twenty-first century included Amy Zahl Gottlieb's *Men of Vision* – an update of *They Found Refuge*, using the recently discovered records of the Central British Fund – and works by Ken Lunn, Panikos Panayi and others as well as revisions and republications of many of the definitive texts already noted.[11] This scholarship has countered many of the earlier uncritical commemorative narratives and in turn weathered a round of revisionism and reinterpretation notably by William Rubinstein and Pamela Shatzkes who contested the interpretations of Bolchover, Alderman, Kushner and others.[12] Rubinstein argued provocatively and with questionable success against the 'Myth of the Closed Doors' and Shatzkes against the argument that Anglo-Jewish leadership reacted to the refugee crisis with timidity, indifference and fear.

As encouraging as this trend towards scholarly engagement with refugee histories has been, the tendency toward the celebratory still persists. At the end of the twentieth century, Louise London wrote:

> A gulf exists between the memory and history of [Britain's refugee] record. British kindness towards Jewish refugees is remembered fondly by those who gave generously ... and the refugees who benefitted from such kindness. We remember the touching photographs and newsreel footage of unaccompanied Jewish children arriving on the Kindertransports. There are no such photographs of the Jewish parents left behind in Nazi Europe, and their fate has made minimal impact. The Jews excluded from entry to the United Kingdom are not part of the British experience because Britain never saw them ... the story of exclusion and failure is not part of what most people remember ...[13]

While London and other scholars have critically examined government policy and the actions and attitudes of the Anglo-Jewish community, the impulse to selectively remember, to commemorate and to celebrate the positive aspects of the migratory experience of continental Jews is still present in the historiography of Jewish refugees to Britain in the 1930s. Louise London rightly singled out the *Kindertransports* for special mention in this respect, for the historiography of this select group of Jewish refugees is particularly subject to forgetting the difficult parts of the story.

Louise London followed her observations about the gulf between history and memory by noting the perils for historians who focus on the story of the excluded Jewish refugees of the 1930s. She suggested that 'the historian who tells it may well be accused of neglecting the positive experience of refugees who came to Britain and the help they received from the British people and their government'.[14] This is especially true for critiques of the *Kindertransport*, as it has been dominated by discourse of gratitude and salvation. Tony Kushner was one of the earliest to challenge this narrative and his work, especially the chapter 'The Kinder: A Case of Selective Memory?' in *Remembering Refugees Then and Now*, blazed a path for more critical study of the *Kindertransport*, which had been stuck in the limbo of popular history for far too long.[15] Still, to date, only a few scholarly works have appeared, and many of these have perpetuated the portrayal of the *Kindertransport* in *A Great Adventure: The Story of the Children's Refugee Movement*:

> It is not a small thing in these years of suffering without parallel, to have given ten thousand children the opportunity to grow up in an atmosphere of decency and normality, to work, play, to laugh and be happy and to assume their rightful heritage as free men and women.[16]

In this telling, the children (whose suffering had all occurred before arrival in Britain) were saved and lived 'happily-ever-after', and a mantle of exceptionalism is placed on the British government, the refugee agencies and the British people, air-brushing the lapses in after care, the children's trauma and the lost families out of the narrative. The popular histories ...*And the Policeman Smiled* and *Into the Arms of Strangers* fall into this frame, while scholarly works by Doris Whiteman and Vera Fast and Frances Williams also fail to challenge the triumphant paradigm.[17] Studies that have interrogated aspects of the *Kindertransport* more critically have also appeared within the last fifteen years, largely in collections such as a 2004 edition of the journal *Shofar*, a recent German and Austrian Exile Studies Yearbook, *The Kindertransport to Britain 1938/9: New Perspectives*, and an issue of the journal *Prism*, presenting some promising new research directions.[18] Nearly eighty years on, however, there remain only a few critical monograph treatments of the *Kindertransport*, including an untranslated volume in German by Claudio Curio, and a specialised psychological study by Iris Guske.[19] Most recently, *Never Look Back* by Judith Baumel-Schwartz, does not ignore the less palatable aspects of the *Kindertransport* but takes a more conciliatory and less interrogative approach than her 1982 MA dissertation upon which the book is based.[20]

Kindertransport research, and indeed scholarship on all Jewish refugees to Great Britain in the 1930s, has been hampered by a lack of access to the archival records held by the successor agency to the Central British Fund. This has limited researchers to administrative records and testimonial archives, which are themselves dominated by narratives of rescue and gratitude. My own research on the *Kindertransport*, based on the newly discovered case files of a about 100 children brought to Britain by the Polish Jewish Refugee Fund, a small independent relief agency, challenges these redemptive interpretations. As Louise London pointed out, silences about the parents and their fates – like silences about all the refugees not welcomed into the UK – have contributed significantly to the persistence of predominantly celebratory discourses about the *Kindertransport*. Thus, my own contribution to this body of scholarship devotes an entire chapter to the parents, whose story remains largely untold.[21] Though it is tragic and makes for uncomfortable reading, in order for the parents to be seen, as Louise London suggested, they must assume a prominent role in *Kindertransport* historiography and thus be made a part of the British experience. I have occasionally encountered resistance to a more nuanced and less redemptive telling of the *Kindertransport* story, most often from the families of the Kinder. However, the Kinder I have spoken to appreciate a greater focus on the uncomfortable aspects of the child refugee movement, especially the absence of the *Kindertransportees*' parents in the discourse. For example, at a conference honouring Eleanor Rathbone, at which I delivered a paper on the absent parents to caution against using the *Kindertransport* as a model for current refugee crises, a former *Kindertransportee* in the audience came up to me later and said, 'I have been waiting seventy years for someone to say the things that you just said.'

The impulse to celebrate and commemorate the Jewish refugee experience of the 1930s extends to another select group of refugees – the scientists, intellectuals, cultural leaders, doctors and other professionals who were brought to Britain under the aegis of the Society for the Protection of Science and Learning. Although they represented only about two to three percent of all the refugees from fascism who successfully entered the UK in the 1930s, the literature devoted to them, their rescuers and their impact on British intellectual and cultural life is relatively large. This commemoration began quite early, with the publication of Norman Bentwich's *The Rescue and Achievement of Refugee Scholars* in 1953 but really gained traction in the past fifteen years with Daniel Snowman's *The Hitler Emigrés* in 2002, Jeremy Seabrook's *The Refuge and the Fortress* in 2008 and the edited volume *In Defence of Learning* in 2011.[22] The efforts of those who sought to rescue Europe's Jewish scientific and cultural intelligentsia are certainly laudable and the visible achievements and contributions of these refugees have undoubtedly enriched the cultural and intellectual fabric of the nation. However, the attention devoted to these refugees is far from proportionate to their numbers and has tended to reinforce a narrative of celebration and unadulterated humanitarian rescue.

Notwithstanding the attention paid to the two most visible and easily celebrated groups of refugees, children and intellectuals, it is encouraging to note that other specialised studies have entered the historiography as well. Susan Cohen's critical work on Eleanor Rathbone, *Rescue the Perishing*, is a welcome addition to the genre, and suggests the need for additional research on other individuals from the period who worked closely with and for Jewish refugees. Another figure deeply involved in refugee work, Solomon Schonfeld, though the subject of several monographs has thus far not been subjected to a truly critical academic investigation. Schonfeld was a polarising figure, and the works devoted entirely to him have tended to be hagiographic, while he has often been vilified in more generalised studies of refugee work in the 1930s and 1940s.[23] If it has been difficult to produce an even-handed treatment of a controversial figure such as Solomon Schonfeld, it remains to be seen whether a universally lauded rescuer such as Nicholas Winton, a nationally beloved figure dubbed 'Britain's Schindler', will ever garner a more than hagiographic account. Winton's life story and rescue activities fit neatly into paradigmatic *Kindertransport* narratives of deliverance and redemption and achieved a level of fame that even he would have probably agreed was disproportionate to his role in the *Kindertransport*, completely overshadowing the work of his fellow rescuers Trevor Chadwick and Doreen Warriner. Chadwick, whose work getting children out of Czechoslovakia was even more extensive than Winton's, but whose life story does not conform so tidily to images of heroic rescuers, has been particularly sidelined in *Kindertransport* historiography.[24]

Individuals active in the effort to bring Jewish refugees to Britain deserve greater attention in the historiography, and so too do individual communities' responses to the refugee crisis of the 1930s. The outstanding academic contribution to this endeavour is Bill Williams' *Jews and Other Foreigners*, a comprehensive compendium of the groups and individuals in Manchester who worked to aid Jewish refugees and of many of the refugees who were aided by this community.[25] One of the first in this category was Zoe Josephs' *Survivors: Jewish Refugees in Birmingham 1933–1945*, published in 1988. Based almost entirely on survivor testimony, it covers a wide range of refugee experiences specific to Birmingham and the efforts of its Jewish community to help refugees.[26] All the major cities in the United Kingdom and hundreds of smaller ones formed refugee committees, and there is an enormous scope for further area studies of the kinds pioneered by Williams and Josephs.

Zoe Josephs' work crossed genres, incorporating at a very early stage the perspectives of the refugees themselves. Testimony, memoir, oral history and other ego-documentation now represents a substantial part of the historiography concerning Jewish refugees from fascism. In Britain, the Association of Jewish Refugees, the Research Centre for German and Austrian Exile Studies, the Imperial War Museum and the British Library have gathered the largest collections. These provide a uniquely British perspective to questions of refugee experience, but other large oral history collections – the USC Shoah Foundation Visual History Archive, the Fortunoff Video Archive for Holocaust Testimonies, the United States Holocaust Memorial Museum and Yad Vashem – also contain significant numbers of testimonies from those who came to the UK as refugees in the 1930s. Most of this material has been gathered in the past thirty years, and it has become an increasingly important source for constructing histories of the 1930s refugee crises. Nevertheless, while refugee perspectives are enormously important, to date, this material has often been presented with minimal interpretive commentary. The paucity of archival documentation, the influence of relief agencies and imperatives of gratitude have all exerted considerable force in limiting the incorporation of these resources critically into the historiography to challenge the dominant narratives.

The persistence of the celebratory impulse in the historiography of Jewish refugees from fascism is perhaps best illustrated by the near total silence, both in the historiography and in national memory, on the single largest group of refugees to enter this country between 1933 and 1939: refugee domestics and nurses. Approximately 20,000 mainly Jewish women between the ages of 16 and 50 came to Great Britain on the only visas available to them – visas that required them to take positions as live-in servants in private English residences. Another 1,000 or so, mostly young Jewish women under the age of 25, took jobs as trainee nurses, often in care facilities for the chronically sick and mentally ill. To date, only one professional journal article, written in 2003, has addressed these nursing refugees, though their numbers are similar to those who came as part of the intelligentsia. And with respect to the refugee domestics, who made up nearly half of all adult refugees to enter the UK before the war, there exists in Britain only the pioneering scholarship of Tony Kushner, who has been writing about them in selected contexts for the past twenty-five years, including two chapters in his most recent monograph, *Journeys from the Abyss* (2017).[27] Other than this, there has been very little scholarship on this forgotten group of refugees, despite the existence of hundreds of testimonies and other archival documentation detailing every aspect of their pre-emigration, refugee and post-war experiences.

The lack of scholarship on these refugee groups speaks to several gaps in the historiography of Jewish refugees. Mirroring British social history more generally, there has been relatively little academic interest in the domestic and serving professions in the interwar period, and within refugee historiography, scholarship is only now emerging on women refugees and their experiences from a gendered perspective.[28] Despite a vast memory record from these former refugees, and significant archival resources, interest in their lives and experiences have not gained the traction that children and intellectuals have enjoyed. Perhaps the most compelling reason for the lack of attention to refugee domestics and nurse trainees is that their rescue cannot be framed as an uncomplicated narrative of humanitarian salvation. Unlike images of sweet, vulnerable children, or accounts of Nobel scientists and famous academics, there was nothing glamourous in images of refugee women scrubbing floors on their knees or emptying bedpans in mental hospitals. Their 'rescue' came at the price of servitude – an institution that is still regarded with a mixture of fascination and discomfort. The survival of Jewish refugee domestics and nurses was predicated on a *quid pro quo* arrangement that obscured their status as victims and denied their employers the mantle of altruism conferred upon those who took in children or helped intellectuals escape persecution.

Although the treatment of Jewish refugees from Nazism in the historiography of interwar Britain has undergone several shifts in critical analysis over the past sixty years, the celebratory narrative has proven to be both resilient and persistent. Within this historiography, both critics and defenders have evaluated the responses of the British government, voluntary organisations and Anglo-Jewry to the refugee crisis of the 1930s, resulting in an increasingly nuanced analysis of this aspect of the history. The work of British social and cultural historians such as Colin Holmes, Tony Kushner and others in the Sheffield School was crucial in the development of the critical turn in the historiography of Jewish refugees in the 1930s. However, the study of local responses and refugee perspectives has lagged behind and the scholarship on individual groups of refugees has been unevenly concentrated on children and intellectuals and remains largely redemptive and triumphant. Major refugee groups, including transmigrants, students, trainees and, most notably, refugee domestics and nurses, have largely been left out of the picture. Their lack of representation in the historiography is perhaps the clearest indication that, although it has achieved much in terms of critical discourse, it still has some distance to go in moving beyond the celebratory.

Notes

1 Norman Bentwich, *They Found Refuge: An Account of British Jewry's Work for Victims of Nazi Oppression* (London: Cresset 1956), xi–xii.
2 A. J. Sherman, *Island Refuge: Britain and the Refugees from the Third Reich, 1933–39* (Berkeley: University of California Press 1978), Naomi Shepard, *A Refuge from Darkness: Wilfrid Israel and the Rescue of the Jews* (New York: Pantheon 1984).
3 David Wyman, *Paper Walls: America and the Refugee Crisis 1938–1941* (Amherst: University of Massachusetts Press 1968), Henry Feingold, *The Politics of Rescue: The Roosevelt Administration and the Holocaust 1939–1945* (New Brunswick: Rutgers University Press 1970), Saul Friedman, *No Haven for the Oppressed; United States Policy toward Jewish Refugees, 1938–1945* (Detroit: Wayne State University Press 1973).
4 Bernard Wasserstein, *Britain and the Jews of Europe 1939–1945* (London: Clarendon 1979).
5 Richard Bolchover, *British Jewry and the Holocaust* (Cambridge: Cambridge University Press 1993).
6 Colin Holmes, *John Bull's Island: Immigration and British Society, 1871–1971* (Basingstoke: MacMillan 1988), and *A Tolerant Country?: Immigrants, Refugees and Minorities* (London: Faber and Faber 1991).
7 Gerhard Hirschfeld, (ed.), *Exile in Great Britain: Refugees from Hitler's Germany* (Leamington Spa: Berg 1984) and Marion Berghahn, *German-Jewish Refugees in England* (Basingstoke: Palgrave MacMillan 1984).
8 Tony Kushner, *The Persistence of Prejudice: Antisemitism in British Society during the Second World War* (Manchester: Manchester University Press 1989), Tony Kushner and Katharine Knox, (eds), *Refugees in an Age of Genocide: Global, National Response in the Twentieth Century* (London: Frank Cass 1999).
9 Geoffrey Alderman, *Modern British Jewry* (Oxford: Oxford University Press 1993) and Werner E. Mosse, Julius Carlebach, Gerhard Hirschfeld, Aubrey Newman, Arnold Paucker and Peter Pulzer (eds), *Second Chance: Two Centuries of German-speaking Jews in the United Kingdom* (Tübingen: Mohr Siebeck 1991).
10 Louise London, *Whitehall and the Jews 1933–1948: British Immigration Policy and the Holocaust* (Cambridge: Cambridge University Press 2000).

11 Amy Zahl Gottlieb, *Men of Vision: Anglo-Jewry's Aid to Victims of the Nazi Regime 1933–1945* (London: Weidenfeld and Nicolson 1998), Panikos Panayi, *Immigration, Ethnicity and Racism in Britain 1815–1945* (Manchester: Manchester University Press 1994), Tony Kushner and Ken Lunn (eds), *Traditions of Intolerance: Historical Perspectives on Fascism and Race Discourse in Britain* (Manchester: Manchester University Press 1989) and by the same authors, *The Politics of Marginality: Race, the Radical Right and Minorities in Twentieth Century Britain* (Abingdon: Routledge 1991).
12 William Rubinstein, *The Myth of Rescue: Why the Democracies Could Not Have Saved More Jews from the Nazis* (Abingdon: Routledge 1996) and Pamela Shatzkes, *Holocaust and Rescue: Impotent or Indifferent? Anglo-Jewry 1938–1945* (New York: Palgrave MacMillan 2002).
13 London, *Whitehall and the Jews*, 13.
14 Ibid.
15 Tony Kushner, *Remembering Refugees: Then and Now* (Manchester: Manchester University Press 2006).
16 John Presland [Gladys Skelton Bendit], *A Great Adventure: The Story of the Children's Refugee Movement* (London: Bloomsbury House 1944).
17 Barry Turner *...And the Policeman Smiled: 10,000 Children Escape Nazi Germany* (London: Bloomsbury 1990), Mark Jonathan Harris and Deborah Oppenheimer, *Into the Arms of Strangers; Stories of the Kindertransport-The British Scheme that Saved 10,000 Children from the Nazi Regime* (London: Bloomsbury 2000), Dorit Bader Whiteman, *The Uprooted: A Hitler Legacy – Voices of Those Who Escaped before the 'Final Solution'* (New York: Plenum Press 1993), Vera K. Fast, *Children's Exodus: A History of the Kindertransport* (London: I. B. Tauris 2011) and Francis Williams, *The Forgotten Kindertransportees: The Scottish Experience* (London: Bloomsbury 2014).
18 *Shofar: An Interdisciplinary Journal of Jewish Studies* vol. 23 no. 1, 2004, Andrea Hammel and Bea Lewkowicz, (eds), *The Kindertransport to Britain 1938/9: New Perspectives, The Yearbook of the Research Centre for German and Austrian Exile Studies* vol. 13, 2012, and *PRISM: An Interdisciplinary Journal for Holocaust Educators* vol. 5, 2013.
19 Claudia Curio: *Verfolgung, Flucht, Rettung. Die Kindertransporte 1938/39 nach Großbritannien* (Berlin: Metropol 2006) and Iris Guske, *Trauma and Attachment in the Kindertransport Context: German-Jewish Child Refugees Accounts of Displacement and Acculturation in Britain* (Newcastle-upon-Tyne: Cambridge Publishing 2009).
20 Judith Tydor Baumel-Schwartz, *Never Look Back: The Jewish Refugee Children in Great Britain, 1938–1945* (West Lafayette IN: Purdue University Press 2012).
21 My own publications on the Kindertransport include: 'Contesting the Kindertransport as a "model" refugee response', *European Judaism* vol. 50, no. 2, 2017, 'From dependence to autonomy: Kinder, refugee organisations and the struggle for agency', *Prism: An Interdisciplinary Journal for Holocaust Educators* vol. 5, 2013 42–51, 'Polish Kinder and the struggle for identity', *The Kindertransport to Britain 1938/39: New Perspectives, Yearbook of the Research Centre for German & Austrian Exile Studies* vol. 13, 2012, 29–46, 'The Kindertransport: History and Memory', MA thesis, California State University Sacramento, 2010, and my forthcoming work, tentatively titled *Contesting Memory: New Perspective on the Kindertransport*.
22 Norman Bentwich, *The Rescue and Achievement of Refugee Scholars; The Story of Displaced Scholars and Scientists 1933–1952* (Houten: Springer Netherlands 1953), Daniel Snowman, *The Hitler Émigrés: The Cultural Impact on Britain of Refugees from Nazism* (London: Chatto & Windus 2002), Jeremy Seabrook, *The Refuge and the Fortress: Britain and the Flight from Tyranny* (Basingstoke: Palgrave MacMillan 2008), Shula Marks, Paul

Weindling and Laura Wintour (eds), *In Defence of Learning: The Plight, Persecution and Placement of Jewish Refugees 1933–1980s* (Oxford: Oxford University Press 2011).

23 For hagiographies see David Kranzler, *Holocaust Hero: The Untold Story and Vignettes of Solomon Schonfeld, an Extraordinary British Orthodox Rabbi who Rescued 4000 Jews during the Holocaust* (Jersey City: KTAV 2004) and Derek Taylor, *Solomon Schonfeld: A Purpose in Life* (London: Valentine Mitchell 2009). Slightly more critical is Chanan Tomlin, *Protest and Prayer: Rabbi Dr Solomon Schonfeld and Orthodox Jewish Responses in Britain to the Nazi Persecution of Europe's Jews 1942–1945* (Bern: Peter Lang 2006). For the most vilifying treatment, see Turner, *…And the Policeman Smiled*. Schonfeld is characterised as primarily oppositional in Gottlieb, *Men of Vision* and Williams, *The Forgotten Kindertransportees*. The studies in which his refugee work is most objectively appraised are Baumel-Schwartz, *Never Look Back* and Fast, *Children's Exodus*.

24 An autobiographical account of Chadwick's work appears in Karen Gershon (ed.), *We Came as Children: A Collective Autobiography of Refugees* (London: Victor Gollancz 1966) and the only one work, authored by his son, has been published about Chadwick's Kindertransport work. William Chadwick, *The Rescue of the Prague Refugees 1938–39* (Leicester: Troubadour 2010).

25 Bill Williams, *Jews and Other Foreigners: Manchester and the Rescue of the Victims of European Fascism 1933–1940* (Manchester: Manchester University Press 2011).

26 Zoe Josephs, *Survivors: Jewish Refugees in Birmingham 1933–1945* (Oldbury: Meridian 1988).

27 Tony Kushner, 'Asylum or servitude? Refugee domestics in Britain, 1933–1945', *Bulletin of the Society for the Study of Labour History*, vol. 53 no. 3, 1988, 19–27; 'Politics and race, gender and class: Refugees, Fascists and domestic service in Britain, 1933–1940', in Tony Kushner and Kenneth Lunn (eds), *The Politics of Marginality: Race, the Radical Right and Minorities in Twentieth Century Britain* (Abingdon: Routledge 1990), 49–58; 'An Alien Occupation – Jewish Refugees and Domestic Service in Britain, 1933–1948', in Mosse et al. (eds), *Second Chance: Two Centuries of German-speaking Jews in the United Kingdom*, 553–578; *Journeys from the Abyss: The Holocaust and Forced Migration from the 1800s to the Present* (Liverpool: Liverpool University Press 2017).

28 Bea Lewkowicz, 'Does gender matter? Reflections on the role of gender in women's oral history narratives', in Charmian Brinson, Jana Barbora Buresova and Andrea Hammel (eds), *Exile and Gender II: Politics, Education and the Arts. The Yearbook of the Research Centre for German and Austrian Exile Studies*, vol. 18, 2017, 231–246.

12

WE REFUGEES?

Re-defining Britain's East African Asians

Saima Nasar

As a coda to decades of Africanisation policies, thousands of East African Asians were confronted with mass displacement during the 1960s and 1970s.[1] Popularly associated with the Ugandan Asian expulsion in 1972, when Idi Amin enforced a series of presidential decrees that called for all South Asians to leave Uganda within just ninety days, this displacement took place irrespective of citizenship status. It followed the propagation of inflammatory rhetoric, such as the notion that South Asians were a self-segregating community of 'bloodsuckers' that had 'sabotaged the economy'.[2] Patterns of Ugandan Asian deracination could be traced, and indeed were mirrored elsewhere in the region. Faced with social, ethno-political and economic persecution, South Asians were also excluded from the new nation states of Kenya and Tanzania. Altogether, approximately 103,500 East Africa Asians relocated to Britain during this period.

In *John Bull's Island* Colin Holmes described the 'frightening elasticity' with which immigrants have been defined and classified.[3] This elasticity is strikingly evident in the historiography of Britain's East African Asian population. In the chaotic politics of decolonisation, border enforcements were used to order populations and to redesign the parameters of national citizenship. As imperial power diminished and post-independent nation states emerged, Britain, alongside Kenya, Uganda and Tanzania, exercised the power to exclude. Accordingly, over the last sixty-year period, East African Asians have been discursively constructed and then reconstructed as subjects, citizens, aliens, exiles, others and refugees. Their narratives of multiple migrations have been told and re-told by all kinds of social and political actors, be that behind official parliamentary doors, at the European Court for Human Rights or in community centres, museums and living rooms across continents. More recently, there has been an attempt by community historians to re-fashion popular projections of the 'East African Asian refugee' as a 'model minority'. In the process of doing so, and as this chapter will set out, they have variously questioned, reinforced, absorbed, challenged and subverted the refugee label. Much like Hannah Arendt sets out in her influential essay 'We Refugees', which lends its title to this chapter, East African Asians have sought to re-define their ascribed refugee status on their own terms.[4] In particular, commemorative projects have been used to reproduce the Mr Cohn character, which Arendt describes as the ideal transnational multiple migrant who, having shed the deficiencies of refugeedom, is deeply patriotic in every country he resides. Having faced the realities of statelessness, the migrant is recognised as a *zoon politikon*, a political animal.

Contemporary historians have inherited from these synchronic and diachronic perspectives an extraordinary archive of mostly untapped private papers, reports, petitions and conversations. The processes of East African Asian identity formulation will therefore be used to shed light on the re-negotiation of minority identities. This chapter begins by exploring the historiography on Britain's East African Asians and the elasticity with which they have been classified. It elaborates on the ways in which scholarly analysis, and broader political discourse, has evolved since the 1960s. It then turns to forms of self-representation and British East African Asian attempts to question the refugee label and establish a new identity as a 'model migrant'. In so doing, this chapter interrogates the role of migrant classifications in the struggle for meaning and belonging.

From subject to citizen

Prior to their forced migration in the 1960s and 1970s, East African Asians were deemed British subjects and imperial citizens of the Commonwealth. With the passing of the 1948 British Nationality Act, a new identity was brokered for British subjects. The concept of a shared Commonwealth citizenship was espoused, which privileged Britishness above any and all other national affinities. Residents of the Empire swore allegiance to the crown – they were British subjects and Commonwealth citizens first, and local citizens second.

While as a common status Commonwealth citizenship served to hold together the 'octopus power' and sought to invoke a shared identity, the uncoupling of citizenship from national identity in this way meant that, technically, the British government inadvertently opened the door to any person who was living anywhere in the Empire.[5] East African Asians were no exception. Britain pledged responsibility for East Africa's minority South Asian population and repeatedly assured them that their citizenship status was not under threat – even in the event that they were displaced. As set out by Ann Dummett and Andrew Nicol, 'subjecthood signified a personal link. It was a vertical relationship between monarch and individual, not a horizontal one between members of a nation or citizens of a body politic.'[6] In an attempt to consolidate and espouse British imperial strength, the British East African Asian subject was born.

Refugee creation

As New Commonwealth immigration increased throughout the 1950s, its visibility within the public imagination helped to further racialise issues of immigrant citizenship and belonging.[7] The notion that the Empire was striking back quickly gained currency as 'floods' of South Asian migrants were supposedly entering Britain's borders every year. East African Asians resettling in Britain therefore attracted extensive coverage in media and political circles. In connection to the so-called Kenyan exodus that took place from the late 1950s to the 1960s, the *Daily Mirror* led with: 'Britain to face illegal flood of Asians'. The article discussed the ways in which 'a group of wealthy Asians were planning to flood Britain with illegal refugees'. It explained that: 'They are to charter a shop or place within the next few weeks and land a load of Asians on Britain's doorstep. The refugees, all carrying British passports, will come from East Africa.'[8]

Anxieties in connection to the latent citizenship of 'coloured imperial subjects' were reflected within broader public rhetoric at the time. Viewed as part of a foreign invasion, the negative coverage focused on four key tropes: housing shortages, unemployment, the perceived strain on social services and the notion that Asians did not fit in with 'our way of life'.[9] These tropes are captured for instance in a report published by the Community Relations Commission. One contributor revealed: 'Nationals of ours will be pushed even further down the long, long, housing and employment registry of this country to make way for the unwanted ethnic groups of our country.'[10] Another commented on the state of welfare provisions: 'Our medical services can barely cope with the present population, and yet we gladly welcome 50,000 more immigrants. What a mad hatter's tea party.'[11] In connection to the need for strong leadership and control, one commentator stated: 'What a pity we have not got a man of the calibre of Sir Winston Churchill to come to our aid in this moment of crisis.'[12]

Although the *Guardian* criticised Britain's 'shameful' treatment of the newcomers it nonetheless acknowledged that East African Asians were simply 'Britain's unwanted citizens'.[13] In political circles, this popular hostility culminated in the steady erosion of the progressive ideals of imperial unity, and resulted in increasingly restrictive immigration legislation. Specifically, Britain passed the Commonwealth Immigrants Acts of 1962 and 1968.[14] These Acts amended earlier statutes that bestowed Citizens of the UK and Colonies (CUKC) with an automatic right of entry into Britain. They applied restrictions to citizens who were not born, adopted, registered or naturalised in the UK, or who did not have such a parent or grandparent. British East African Asians were thereby controversially restricted from entering the UK.

From a policy of 'free passage' to controlled migration, policymakers not only entered the complex political game of citizenship that would go on to have profound consequences, but they also tinkered with the goalposts of imperial, and postimperial, belonging. This shift from a pan-British imperial identity espoused in the 1940s to local 'national' affinities in the 1960s meant that East African Asians were reconceptualised first as national 'Others' and resident aliens in the East African context, and then as Commonwealth migrants that required entry visas to enter the UK. This 'Otherness' was reflected in academic discourse as well as popular rhetoric at the time. Colonial historiography and African national histories, as outlined by Donald Rothchild in *Racial Bargaining in Independent Kenya: A Study of Minorities and Decolonisation*, frequently touched upon the socially isolated and endogamous nature of South Asian communities in East Africa.[15] They emphasised the economic dominance of a handful of Asian entrepreneurs, meanwhile glossing over the complex history of civic participation and intercultural exchange that had developed over decades of interactions.[16] As such, in an era of decolonisation and postcolonial nation-building, East African Asians were refused the right to live and settle in not only their ancestral homes, but also the nation states that had administered their passports, which in most cases was Britain. Squeezed by the metropole and the postcolony, the stateless figure of the East African Asian emerged.[17]

It was in this context that the 'East African Asian refugee' was created. As holders of British passports, Britain had a responsibility to its global citizens under both national and international law. The government's initial response was that of administrative foot-dragging. It hesitated when it came to accepting its obligation to its passport holders. As the crisis deepened, political agitation to reassess Britain's stance increased, and reports from non-governmental organisations, such as the Joint Council for the Welfare of Immigrants and the National Council for Civil Liberties, emerged. Depictions of the destitute, homeless and victimised East African Asian eventually elicited compassion and media representation altered accordingly. National newspapers came to adopt a more sympathetic, conciliatory tone. *The Times* warned that 'Gen Amin planned concentration camps for Asians after deadline' and that is was Britain holding up the exodus.[18] The *Daily Telegraph* labelled the Asians as 'Uganda's Huguenots'.[19] While the *Telegraph* communicated the 'Pogrom by Expulsion',[20] the *Guardian* explained how Britain's quota was keeping '20,000 Asians in ghettos'.[21] Also viewed as 'The Jews of East Africa' a number of news outlets including the *Sunday Times* drew upon post-war liberal sentiments and reported that:

> The position of the Indians in East Africa grows every day more strictly comparable to that of the Jews in Eastern Europe round the turn of the century. They are the traders whom everyone despises because they are good at trade. Their fate is not yet as terrible, but it can become so at any moment.[22]

Even when both the British government and the media recognised that the displacement and relocation of East African Asians to Britain was inevitable, rather than recognising their status as Citizens of the UK and Colonies, East African Asians were rendered a refugee community. This not only served to de-politicise their citizenship status, but it helped to depict Britain's response as one of discretionary humanitarianism – that is, what Didier Fassin describes as the process that offers aid on a discretionary basis and serves to regulate and define migrant-refugee status.[23]

The rendering of East African Asians as refugees in this way is instructive. It is especially useful here to turn to the work of Jordanna Bailkin. Bailkin has noted the enormous public interest in migration in the wake of the Second World War. As Britain's apparent historic tolerance of migrant populations was tested by a 'flood' of newcomers from the former colonies, migration, she argues, was one of the largest growth areas of expertise.[24] As the groups entering and leaving Britain diversified, 'experts' contributed to a 'framework of visibility and invisibility, in which only some population transfers warranted the state's attention'.[25] Experts created elaborate classificatory systems to understand and order these population transfers. According to Bailkin, in an age of decolonisation, the migrant was the ultimate expert creation used by different parties to capture their own missions and methods, to secure state resources and to offer their own distinctive interventions.[26] Britain's East African Asians provide a fitting case study of this.

Model minority

The elasticity with which East African Asians have been classified has strongly informed not only state responses but also the ways in which the immigrant trajectories of Britain's East African Asians have been understood over time. While scholarly analysis produced in the 1970s and 1980s has traditionally been limited and confined to sociological accounts which tend to focus on refugee experiences of resettlement in Britain in the aftermath of forced migration,[27] more recent offerings have begun to reveal and interrogate the complexities of post-imperial, transnational belonging. Parminder Bhachu's research on Punjabi Sikhs from Kenya, for example, most notably questions the assumption that all South Asians in Britain subscribe to the myth of return to India and emphasises East African Asians' commitment to Britain as a homeland.[28] Moreover, Divya Tolia-Kelly has examined multiple connections by drawing on material and visual cultures, such as artefacts from East Africa, to explore East African Asians' emotional connections to 'home'.[29] In so doing, Tolia-Kelly, alongside scholars such as H. Ramji, has revealed a complex transnational relationship to Britain, India and East Africa.[30]

Yet, the popular imagination and some historical studies have emphasised the 'subject-citizen-refugee' trajectory despite the fact that many East African Asians were British passport holders and thus metropolitan citizens. For instance, in a 2012 article in the *Spectator* titled 'Ugandan Asians Are Part of Britain's Secret Weapon of Success', Baroness Warsi, then senior Foreign Office Minister and Minister for Faith and Communities, exalted: 'So let's, all of us, be inspired by the people who turned dispossession into prosperity and setback into success: our British Ugandan Asians.'[31] This suggests that this 'subject-citizen-refugee' narrative has been used to applaud Britain's role as a refugee island.

Significantly, among East African Asian communities, this image has been mobilised to stress a 'rags to riches' story of resettlement.[32] In exhibition spaces across the country, East African Asians are retelling this narrative in a sequence of settlement, persecution, flight, exile and resettlement so as to renegotiate past and present identities.[33] The cultural landscape has in many ways been used to promote a proud narrative of resettlement. The 'Kampala to Leicester' exhibition launched in Leicester in July 2012, for instance, accommodated the prevalent notion that Ugandan Asians are important contributors to Britain's social, cultural and economic life. Having accepted a *former* refugee status, the exhibition proudly proclaimed East African Asians' prior access to metropolitan citizenship rights, as well as their cultural and linguistic affinity with Britain. In the process of doing so, these acts of remembrance have paradoxically challenged East African Asians' refugee status and have cultivated the notion of an East African Asian 'model minority' – that is, a minority that has added and continues to contribute to civic life while possessing the ability to persevere and succeed in times of hardship. They have depicted a high achieving, successful, professional East African Asian character that serves as an example of 'the good migrant'. This was mirrored elsewhere, including the visual exhibition 'Ugandan Stories' held in Nottingham and an 'Exiles' project conducted in London.[34] Used as a rhetorical device, here notions of the model citizen were refracted and East African Asians asserted their profound work ethic as well as their tendency toward self-sufficiency. Economic productivity was stressed alongside qualities of proto-citizenship such as intellect, morality, a tendency to abide by the law and being able to offer cultural enrichment.

Community versus history

What then is the relationship between community and history, and what do commemorative projects tell us about individual and collective memory? Although knowledge encoded in images and the memories that they trigger open up multiple cultural readings, what recent projects of commemoration illustrate is that public histories have adopted a pattern in their narrative construction of migration whereby East African Asians have shed their refugee status and are fashioning a new identity, that of the model migrant. Much like Arendt's account of refugees of the Nazi period, East African Asians have actively chosen to tell their own story in a way that best serves their individual and collective interests.

In light of this, it is useful to draw on Pierre Nora's theorisation on history and memory. Nora claims that 'modern memory is above all archival. It relies entirely on the materiality of the trace, the immediacy of the recording and the visibility of the image.'[35] Memory thus exists though its exterior scaffolding and outward signs: its 'new vocation is to record'.[36] For Nora, real, spontaneous memory no longer exists and so sites of memory such as archives and memorials are constructed artificially. While it would be unwise to unthinkingly follow Nora in discounting these projects of commemoration as memories that are not real, his work is valuable in that it provides an explanation for why popular memory, or community histories like these do not easily translate into veridical, exact histories. The primary concern of these projects is not to relay a factual, historical account. For most, the popularisation of self-representations has been more concerned with negotiating the past and articulating present identities. This does not necessarily correlate with professional history. For instance, the 'Kampala to Leicester' project began by explaining that Ugandan Asians came to Britain in 1972.[37] It did not clarify that some Ugandan Asians had migrated prior to the expulsion while others took a different route, like the 'Kampala to Leicester' project lead who had gone to study in India when the edict was announced and joined her family in England a year later. Furthermore, the focus on Kampala where just over half of Ugandan Asians resided, overlooks other urban and rural areas of settlement that inevitably shaped everyday life in different ways.

While the positive contributions of Britain's diasporic Ugandan Asian population is certainly not refuted, the emphasis on the East African Asian as the good or model migrant, however, overlooks a more nuanced history of colonial and postcolonial interactions and power relations. It is important to note here that not all East African Asians came to Britain during the period of crisis as patterns of migration began in the 1950s, and while some Ugandan Asians came to the UK with very little money or material possessions, this cannot be said about all East African Asian migrants. Earlier migrancy allowed the acquisition of housing and the establishment of small to large businesses. It was often East African Asian landlords that offered medium-to-long-term housing to those affected by the expulsion. This suggests that while British East African Asian trajectories are subject to diverse readings, individuals and groups seek safety in semi-public processes of selective narrative formation.

Thus, as much as the relationship between public heritage projects and professional history is an uneasy one, these interactions with immigrant narratives shed light on how immigrants self-identify and understand the world around them. Public history can be used to broker new identities. This is because over time immigrant populations undergo a complicated process of identity reformulation. In the case of East African Asians in Britain, they have at various points absorbed, reinforced, contested and subverted the refugee label. Ultimately, they have set this detachment in motion in order to collapse the boundaries between 'us' (the receiving society) and 'them' (the refugee other). This shows that individuals and groups are just as important in mediating the processes of identity formation. Constructions of the self are not fixed or passive but are contingent to change 'from below'. While public policy, governments and the media can ascribe the 'refugee' label, so too is it possible for groups and individuals to challenge it. History, to use the words of Arendt, 'is no longer a closed book to them'.[38]

Conclusions

In sum, a number of conclusions can be drawn from this case study. First, in an era of globalisation, East African Asians have been variously constructed as subjects, citizens, aliens, others, refugees and model migrants. The articulation of these identities is complicated by the rhetoric of nationalism advanced at times of nation-building. Yet an accurate historical reading of imperial and post-imperial subjectivity dislodges the dominance of linear narratives, and allows for a deterritorialised understanding of global exchanges. It is in this context that diasporic groups draw on multiple vectors of identity.

Second, alongside the construction of nations, states and peoples, it is instructive to take into account the state's power to derail, fragment, shape and reshape. In response to the political manoeuvrings that served to order and classify citizens and non-citizens, crises, and their long-term effects, involve a vast body of social and political actors, ranging from political leaders, human rights agencies, aid organisations and volunteers, to archivists, curators and individual migrants. Each actor in the British East African case has in some way contributed to the co-construction of migrant (post-imperial) identities and the negotiation of modern citizenship. As such it is important to acknowledge that the recognition of migrant-refugees is protean, contingent and subject to re-definition. Migrant classifications, even those incorrectly ascribed such as the East African Asian refugee label, are selectively applied irrespective of context and composition. The great force of public opinion encouraged a negotiation to take place, one which Arendt describes as blurring the distinction between the 'conscious pariah' and the 'social parvenus'.[39] Immigration histories are therefore anchored in both immigrant experiences and in structures of political power, which operate in symbiosis.

Notes

1 Africanisation-as-indigenisation policies were adopted by many African countries in an attempt to raise the profile of African culture and language. They were also used to transfer wealth and the ownership of the means of production to indigenous Africans. This resulted in the introduction of increasingly restrictive policies relating to immigration as well as business enterprise whereby Asians in East Africa were excluded from civil servant positions and saw the nationalisation of their private assets. This compelled many Asians to relocate.
2 *Uganda Argus*, 5 August 1972.
3 Colin Holmes, *John Bull's Island: Immigration and British Society, 1871–1971* (London: Routledge 2015), 4.
4 See Hannah Arendt, 'We refugees' in Marc Robinson (ed.), *Altogether Elsewhere: Writers in Exile* (Harcourt Brace 1996), 110–119.
5 For more on Britain as an 'octopus power' see: John Darwin, *The Empire Project: The Rise and Fall of the British World-System, 1830–1970* (Cambridge: Cambridge University Press 2009).
6 Ann Dummett and Andrew Nicol, *Subjects, Citizens, Aliens and Others: Nationality and Immigration Law* (London: Weidenfeld and Nicolson 1990), 22.
7 It is important to note that while a pan-imperial identity was being projected, considerable fear concerning 'coloured' colonial migrants remained. As Brian Harrison has observed, 'the right of entry under the 1948 British Nationality Act was seen as a welcome free movement between Britain and the old white dominions'. See Brian Harrison, *Seeking a Role: The United Kingdom 1951–1970* (Oxford: Oxford University Press 2009), 82.
8 *Daily Mirror*, 2 February 1970, 3.

9 There is extensive archival and newspaper material that documents this. See: Saima Nasar, 'Subjects, Citizens, and Refugees: The Making and Remaking of Britain's East African Asians', Ph.D. thesis, University of Birmingham, 2016.
10 *Observer*, 22 October 1972, 41.
11 Ibid.
12 Ibid.
13 *Guardian*, 20 March 1970, 13.
14 See James Hampshire, *Citizenship and Belonging: Immigration and the Politics of Demographic Governance in Postwar Britain* (Basingstoke: Palgrave Macmillan 2005) and Randell Hansen, *Citizenship and Immigration in Postwar Britain* (Oxford: Oxford University Press 2000).
15 Donald Rothchild, *Racial Bargaining in Independent Kenya: A Study of Minorities and Decolonisation* (London: Oxford University Press 1973).
16 See Saima Nasar, 'The Indian voice of East Africa: connecting self-representation and identity formulation in diaspora', *History in Africa* vol. 40, 2013, 99–124.
17 Anneeth K. Hundle, 'The Politics of (In)security: Reconstructing African-Asian Relations, Citizenship and Community in Post-Expulsion Uganda', Ph.D. thesis, University of Michigan, 2013, 21.
18 *The Times*, 14 September 1972.
19 *Daily Telegraph*, 17 August 1972.
20 Ibid., 21 August 1972.
21 *Guardian*, 19 March 1971.
22 *Sunday Times*, 2 February 1969.
23 Didier Fassin, 'Policing borders, producing boundaries: the governmentality of immigration in dark times', *Annual Review of Anthropology* vol. 40, 2011, 213–226.
24 Jordanna Bailkin, *The Afterlife of Empire* (Berkeley: University of California Press 2012), 37.
25 Ibid., 38
26 Ibid., 67.
27 See for example the works of Michael Twaddle (ed.), *Expulsion of a Minority: Essays on Ugandan Asians* (London: Athlone Press 1975); William G. Kuepper, G. Lynne Lackey and E. Nelson Swinerton, *Ugandan Asians in Great Britain: Forced Migration and Social Absorption* (London: Croom Helm 1975); and Valerie Marett, *Immigrants Settling in the City* (London: Leicester University Press 1989).
28 Parminder Bachu, *Twice Migrants: East African Sikh Settlers in Britain* (London: Tavistock 1985).
29 Divya P. Tolia-Kelly, 'A journey through the material geographies of diaspora cultures: four modes of environmental memory', in Kathy Burrell and Panikos Panayi (eds), *Histories and Memories: Migrants and Their History in Britain* (London: Tauris Academic Studies 2006), 149–170.
30 H. Ramji, 'Engendering diasporic identities', in Nirmal Puwar and Parvati Raghumram (eds), *South Asian Women in the Diaspora* (London: Bloomsbury Academic 2003).
31 *Spectator*, 6 December 2012.
32 While Warsi is a direct Pakistani migrant, her article was quoted and used by East African Asians, especially in oral history interviews carried out in 2012. See: Nasar, 'Subjects, Citizens, and Refugees'.
33 Tony Kushner, *The Battle of Britishness* (Manchester: Manchester University Press 2012).
34 'Ugandan Stories' was hosted by the New Art Exchange arts space in Nottingham in 2015. The project 'Exiles: The Ugandan Asian Story' was hosted by the Royal Geography Society in 2013.

35 Pierre Nora, 'Between memory and history: les lieux de mémoire', *Representations* vol. 26, 1989, 7–24.
36 Ibid.
37 The 'From Kampala to Leicester: The Story of Leicester's Ugandan Asian Community' exhibition took place in Leicester's New Walk Museum and Art Gallery in 2012.
38 Arendt, *We Refugees*, 118.
39 Ibid., 119.

SECTION 4
Racisms and anti-migrant politics

Christhard Hoffmann

Introduction

One of the characteristic features of the work of Colin Holmes and the Sheffield School is that it combined the study of migrant history with a strong interest in the traditions of intolerance in British society, focusing on antisemitism, fascism and the radical right. A number of key historians of the school, including Holmes himself, Kenneth Lunn and Tony Kushner, worked first on the history of antisemitism in Britain before they turned to the history of immigrants and minorities. Important publications by these historians, such as *Traditions of Intolerance* (1989), *The Politics of Marginality* (1990) and *A Tolerant Country?* (1991), explored hostile reactions towards newcomers within the broader historical context of fascism and race discourse in British society.[1] Based on a historical perspective of the *longue durée*, these studies sought to uncover the roots of long-term prejudice and to analyse the social and political conditions that produced restrictive and exclusionary measures towards migrants and minorities. Opening a wide historical horizon in studying immigration and intolerance in Britain, historians of the Sheffield School have emphasised the variety of racialist discourses and different forms of racism.[2] In their perspective, the persuasive and popular 'Windrush narrative' of British multiculturalism was inadequate since it reduced British immigration history to the post-1948 arrivals of Blacks and Asians, and, consequently, defined hostility towards newcomers almost exclusively as racism of white people towards people of colour.

The four chapters of this section address different aspects of this broader topic. Taking up the issue of race and colour in the post-1945 period, Gavin Schaffer takes a closer look at how white (Irish and Jewish) immigrant communities positioned themselves towards the politics of race relations that evolved in the 1960s. While the Irish community in Britain fought for minority recognition that would enable state support against discrimination, the Jewish community was supportive of the

Race Relations Act but did not consider it as a means for its own protection. These differing positions towards the programme of race relations, Schaffer argues, can be attributed to differences in social status and integration. Moreover, the experience of discrimination was more critical for the Irish community, which in the conflict with the IRA often was presented as a 'fifth column' and especially targeted in the fight against terrorism. Schaffer does not call into question that the racialisation of the Irish and Jewish communities (whose 'whiteness' was always taken for granted) was essentially different from the racialisation of the black and Asian immigrants that was based on skin colour. He concludes, however, that the experiences of white immigrant communities can contribute to a more complex and nuanced picture of the mechanisms and varieties of racism and, therefore, should be included in the historiography of multicultural Britain.

Turning to the mainstream of British racism, Barbara Bush provides an insightful study of the continuities of racial myths from the colonial context to the establishment of West Indian migrant communities in Britain. Looking at welfare policies that were set up in the 1950s and 1960s in order to help West Indian migrants integrate into British society and thus improve 'race relations', she finds the liberal discourse of racial equality and welfare intervention deeply ingrained with stereotypical notions of the 'dysfunctional' black family as main course of poverty and 'backwardness'. Addressing black migrant women, welfare interventions tried to promote assimilation to the family ideals of the white middle class and thereby ignored the significance of Afro-Caribbean cultural practices and family organisation. This form of gendered cultural racism, Bush emphasises, was based on supposedly objective academic research, spread in popular media and thus widely accepted as common knowledge.

In a different way, the role of academically trained specialists and officials is also crucial in Krista Maglen's chapter on British immigration and disease control. In contrast to the United States, which in the last quarter of the nineteenth century established a 'medicalised border', i.e. a quarantine system for immigrants to prevent the importation of infectious diseases, the 'English system' was much less rigid. It did not prevent immigrants who arrived on 'infected' vessels from entering the country and relied on the local public health infrastructure to monitor the disease. While this flexible approach was challenged and partly modified during the 1892 cholera epidemic when medical categories increasingly determined the desirability of immigrants and anti-alienists demanded the adaptation of the American quarantine system, Maglen shows that public health officials defended the existing system as sufficient to prevent the spread of disease and declined a routine screening of immigrants. The 'medical clause' of the Aliens Act in 1905 was introduced against the explicit recommendations of the medical community.

Demands for quarantine and internment found their echo in more radical circles. Focusing broadly on the anti-immigration rhetoric of extreme right-wing political organisations, Graham Macklin gives a survey of the historiography on fascism in Britain and traces the major stages of this evolving field of research. In its early stages, it frequently had to defend its relevance against the widespread national consensus that fascism was essentially 'alien' to British traditions, therefore an 'inevitable failure' and consequently no significant subject of study. As other fields of history writing, the development of fascism historiography has been influenced by the availability of fresh sources, the stimulation of new scholarly approaches (such as cultural or transnational perspectives) and not least by contemporary events (such as the rise of right-wing parties). With an eye to the work of Colin Holmes, especially his *Antisemitism in British Society* (1979) and *Searching for Lord Haw-Haw: The Political Lives of William Joyce* (2016), Macklin highlights the centrality of antisemitic conspiracy theories for British fascists. Antisemitism not only served as a tool to mobilise support, but also provided an interpretative ideological frame 'through which the nation's ills were diagnosed and its "cure" prescribed'.

As the chapters in this section have illustrated, whether through state, society or racist organisations, the range of migrant groups and the way they have been attacked has been and continues to be wide-ranging and often severe in its impact.

Notes

1 Tony Kushner and Kenneth Lunn (eds), *Traditions of Intolerance: Historical Perspectives on Fascism and Race Discourse in Britain* (Manchester: Manchester University Press 1989); Tony Kushner and Kenneth Lunn (eds), *The Politics of Marginality: Race, the Radical Right and Minorities in Twentieth Century Britain* (London: Routledge 1990); Colin Holmes, *A Tolerant Country? Immigrants, Refugees and Minorities in Britain* (London: Faber and Faber 1991).
2 See for example, Panikos Panayi, *An Immigration History of Britain: Multicultural Racism since 1800* (Pearson: Harlow 2010).

13

RACE AND COLOUR REVISITED

White immigrants in post-war Britain

Gavin Schaffer

In recent years, prominent historians of British immigration have emphasised the value of looking at movement and settlement over the *longue durée*, producing far-reaching studies which push beyond the construction of migration as a post-1945 phenomenon. Scholars, most obviously Panikos Panayi in his *An Immigration History of Britain*, have argued that the tendency of popular histories (Phillips and Phillips' *Windrush* would be a good example)[1] to present the development of British multiculturalism as a black post-war history has served to silence much more complex trajectories of movement, displacement and racialisation over hundreds of years of British history.[2] Recent interventions by Panayi, and Tony Kushner, reveal something of their personal historical training, studying under the supervision of Colin Holmes, whose substantial contribution to immigration history, *John Bull's Island*, insisted on a far-reaching analysis of a wide selection of migrant groups over one hundred years.[3]

This approach to immigration avoids all-too-evident pitfalls in analysis. Reducing British Black history to stories about post-1948 migrants is problematic for several reasons, most obviously because it silences centuries of the Black British past, as all scholarship that follows Peter Fryer's *Staying Power* should be aware. The famous first line of that book, 'There were Africans in Britain before the English came here', remains a rallying call for those who should, by now, know better.[4] But the privileging of *Windrush* narratives as storyboards of British multiculturalism also silences longer trajectories of immigration more broadly, especially that which was white and European (which dominated immigration before the Second World War).[5] Indeed, the focus on *Windrush* in school and university curricula, and in heritage and culture, has created considerable misunderstandings about immigration, which all too often is understood in terms of black and Asian migrants arriving in a white country. This analysis bears little resemblance to the realities of British history. As Colin Holmes pointed out in *John Bull's Island*, 'down to 1971 the Irish remained the largest single immigrant group in Britain'.[6] Following in the tradition of Colin Holmes (of looking at racialisation and immigration as issues which relate to colour, but cannot be reduced to it) I want to use this chapter to think through the reasons why segregated histories of immigration have been so prominent, why it has been felt appropriate to focus immigration narratives primarily on black immigration, and what that says about British society – then and now. But specifically, I want to focus on white migration within that period of post-war migration which is so often silenced by Windrush narratives.

The first and most obvious explanation for the foregrounding of black histories in the post-war era is that scholars and other observers have believed that immigrant reception and outcomes were significantly shaped by colour.[7] Put simply, white post-war immigrants were perceived to have faced lesser challenges, less racism, both in society and from the state.[8] The most obvious and frequently visited example of this relates to the first significant restrictive legislation in the post-war period, the Commonwealth Immigrants Act, 1962. Nearly every scholar who has studied this legislation (as well as most commentators at the time) observed that the new law was not designed to stop immigration from the Commonwealth *per se*, but specifically black and Asian immigration.[9] I myself have taken this position, and it would be perverse to take any other. Stopping black immigrants, quite clearly, is what the Commonwealth Immigrants Act was primarily designed to do. As Michael Dummett put it: 'It was how the country at large took it and was meant to take it.'[10]

A note prepared for the Home Secretary in 1961, explaining the aims of the new legislation, couldn't have been much clearer: 'We must recognise that although the scheme purports to relate solely to employment and to be non-discriminatory, its aim is primarily social and its operation is intended to, and would in fact, affect coloured people almost exclusively.'[11] Put even more starkly by the Inter-Departmental Working Party on Immigration a few months later, the Commonwealth Immigrants Act was specifically designed to 'leave the door wide open' for white immigration.[12]

The most frequently cited evidence of colour prejudice in the design of the Commonwealth Immigrants Act relates to its treatment of Irish immigration. In practice, if the Act was designed to stem the flow of unskilled Commonwealth immigrants, Ireland should have fallen directly under its purview, but in actuality, citizens of the Republic were exempted from the immigration controls.[13] This exemption was clearly influenced by perceptions of race. Instead of facing a voucher system for their citizens, the Irish government were asked to support Britain's attempt to keep out other immigrants, by imposing controls on entry to Britain through the Republic.[14]

The view that colour was *the* marker of difference in a multicultural society had a resonance beyond Westminster and became a pillar of 'race relations' initiatives designed to support migrants and smooth tensions. For example, when in 1965 the BBC was persuaded to produce television programmes to support the integration of South Asian migrants (teaching English and how to function in British society to viewers and listeners in radio and television programmes) no parallel efforts were made to help similarly vulnerable white immigrants.[15]

This approach was brought clearly into focus in 1966 when the Archbishop of Britain's Greek Orthodox community wrote to the Director General of the BBC to ask if Cypriot migrants might also be afforded their own programme on television. The Director General's reply emphasised the importance of blackness to the BBC's understanding of immigration problems in Britain. He told the Archbishop: 'We introduced the special programmes for Indians and Pakistanis very largely because the colour problem made the integration of the people concerned particularly difficult'.[16]

White immigrants and race relations: the Irish in post-war Britain

Whiteness scholars, placing nearly all their focus on the USA, have made the case that colour was not an unmovable reality, but instead a malleable category, from which groups could move in and out.[17] On these terms, Jewish and Irish migrants have been analysed in terms of ascending to whiteness as their status in new societies became more secure.[18] This idea, though, has provoked something of a backlash, as other scholars have pointed out the extent to which black and Asian migrants have faced challenges rooted in the impossibility of their 'passing', confronted as they were with racism based upon their skin colour.[19] Here, there seems to be an important difference, as Karen Brodkin has asserted, between race as an 'ethnoracial assignment' and race as an 'ethnoracial identity'.[20] Jews, Irish and other white migrants might well identify (or not) as racialised, and they may also be assigned to a specific space on the racial hierarchy, but these are not the same thing. In post-war Britain, I argue, the racial assignment of white migrants was not really comparable with black and Asian people (which is not to say that white migrants were never racialised), yet Jews and Irish engaged their ethnoracial identities in the context of their potential assignment, and attempted to exert agency around it. Here, the example of the Greek Archbishop offers a case in point. The BBC did not assign the Greek Cypriot minority to racialised status, and denied any such assignment (comparable to black and Asian people) was taking place within society. Yet the Archbishop aspired to identify in these terms, and wanted to gain extra provision for his flock on this basis.

For some white immigrant communities, denial of status as racial minorities (in comparison to black and Asian groups) became totally unacceptable. Most significantly, Britain's Irish community fought long and hard for minority recognition, mindful that such status could open up avenues of state support (notably at local government level), which were being denied to them. In 1981, the Greater London Council (GLC) belatedly recognised 'the Irish as an ethnic minority'. This change of stance empowered local Irish groups to apply for new funding streams, so that by 1985 around thirty Irish community projects in the London area were being funded by the GLC.[21] The GLC's stance, however, was not the norm in Britain. In the late 1990s, Mary Hickman and Bronwen Walter were employed by the Commission for Racial Equality to write a report on 'Discrimination and the Irish Community', which emphasised the continuing parlous position of Irish people in Britain as white migrants. The report argued, regarding the position of the Irish, 'they meet the situation where they are not seen as being entitled to the same rights as the national population, but are also not represented as sufficiently "different" to have their particular needs recognized'. What was needed, the report concluded, was 'an Irish dimension in all equal opportunity policies' and 'in any resource allocation which specifically targets ethnic minority groups'.[22]

By the 1980s and 1990s, Britain's Irish communities certainly had their fair share of problems. Conflict with the IRA, and specifically terrorism in British cities, had led to draconian legislation in 1974 (the Prevention of Terrorism Act or PTA) which almost exclusively targeted Irish people and operated as a state channel of retribution and racialisation. As Hillyard explained, 'the most important feature of the operation of the PTA has been the way in which it has constructed a suspect community in Britain'.[23] 'This community', he continued, was 'treated in law and in police practices very differently from the rest of the population', a tendency which led the public 'to do the same'.[24]

Looking back, it is hard not to see the PTA of 1974 and subsequent legislation as primarily an instrument of anti-Irish intimidation. Really, the Acts did nothing for security, as evidence from parliament at the time illustrated. By May 1978, 3,235 people had been detained under the legislation in Britain. These arrests, nearly all Irish, only led to 142 charges and only twenty of these offences were under the Acts themselves.[25] The Irish Embassy raised this issue in correspondence with the British government in January 1978. They observed: 'Over 96% of persons detained under the Acts have not been charged with any offences, and only 0.56% have been charged with offences under the Acts.'[26]

If then the PTA was a tool of racial intimidation, and a reflection of the racialisation of the Irish in Britain, it was hardly the first time the British Irish community had been racialised. In actuality, the racialisation of Irish people in Britain long preceded 1970s terrorism. As Jordanna Bailkin has recently explained, while the Irish may have been excluded from immigration restriction in the Commonwealth Immigrants Act, they were susceptible for deportation under it – and were disproportionately targeted as racial undesirables.[27] Of course, work on Irish racialisation in modern Britain (Don MacRaild and Enda Delaney in particular) shows long trajectories of prejudice going back into the nineteenth century.[28] My question, in this context, is how did communities, and how should historians, understand this prejudice in relation to attitudes towards black and Asian immigrants? For the Irish, there is considerable evidence of a desire to be pulled into a similar frame of reference. And, as we have seen, Greek Cypriots too could feel deserving of additional protection and support. But the responses of Britain's Jewish community to race relations in this period offers a slightly different example.

Jews and race relations in post-war Britain

For sure, in the 1960s, Britain's Jews still felt that they needed protection from racism and used their institutional leadership to achieve it, playing a large role in making the case for the Race Relations Act 1965, which outlawed discrimination in public places and the incitement of racial hatred. In January 1965, following Harold Wilson's election victory in 1964, a Board of Deputies delegation went to see Frank Soskice (the new Home Secretary) to lobby for the Race Relations Act, telling him that the 'cold-blooded slaughter of millions of Jews' informed their desire for legislation.[29]

Neither the action of the Deputies, nor the prominent parliamentary use of the Holocaust in advocating for legislation, should be taken as evidence of a disregard for other minorities, and especially for black Britons, but I do think it is clear that the Deputies were significantly worried about their own people as they lobbied for the Race Relations Act. That said, another agenda was clearly emerging in an increasingly confident Anglo-Jewish community, an agenda that saw race relations primarily as the problem of other people, an issue for black, and Asian Britons (where the Jewish role was that of an experienced predecessor). In 1969 the Board of Deputies produced a Working Party Report on race relations, which had grown out of separate committees set up by the Chief Rabbi, and the Jewish Defence Committee, in 1968. The Report, 'Improving Race Relations: a Jewish Contribution', was a document which presented Britain's Jews as advisors on racial problems, not as victims.

The terms of reference of the Working Party, for example, set out their task as 'to consider the most appropriate means for the Anglo-Jewish community to assist in the integration of the coloured people in this country, to improve race relations, and to report and recommend accordingly'.[30] The Report noted the Board's role in supporting Jewish immigrants at the turn of the century in the face of prejudice and commented (in capitals): 'SIMILAR MISLEADING ALLEGATIONS AGAINST COLOURED IMMIGRANTS TODAY MUST BE CONSTANTLY CHALLENGED'.[31]

The Board distributed 50,000 copies of this report, which was assembled from 800 questionnaires sent out to Jewish groups, asking what they were doing about race relations in their local communities. The Board of Deputies, the report claimed, was being used as an example of communal leadership by recently formed 'commonwealth immigrant associations'. 'Its methods in presenting aspects of Jewish life have been studied as a guide in the presentation of religions and cultures of commonwealth immigrant groups.'

The report recommended cooperation in local race relations initiatives from local rabbis and teachers, the holding of special Race Relations Sabbaths in synagogues, lectures for the community 'at every educational level' and advised Jewish communities to make contact and work with immigrant groups. One member, from the Union of Liberal and Progressive Synagogues, told a Board of Deputies meeting that the Brent Friendship Council had opened up their premises to host events for 'local Indian groups' and provided them with helpers.[32] Two years later, Rabbi Leigh from Edgware Reform Synagogue reported that his Women's Guild was looking into the possibility of teaching English to immigrants.[33] John Raynor, liberal Rabbi from London, marked Race Relations Sabbath in 1971 with a sermon, in which he told the congregation that 'To harbour [racist] thought is to be less than Jewish; to act on such a thought is to commit a crime against Judaism.'[34] These enthusiastic interventions, however, did not characterise the response of Britain's Jewish communities writ large.

Of the 800 surveys sent out by the Board, only forty ended up being completed by local communities.[35] This, of course, does not in and of itself prove that communities weren't acting on race relations but it suggests that it wasn't too high on lists of priorities. The Chief Rabbi's office, in private, described the community response as 'rather disappointing'.[36] For Britain's Jews, by the 1970s, the situation seems to have been that they could, for obvious historical reasons, sometimes be harnessed into a united front for racial equality, but, more than anything, that most Jews no longer saw race relations as having anything to do with them.

And, of course, Jews were just as susceptible to racism as everyone else. One response to the Chief Rabbi's survey was telling. This respondent, from Sheffield, told the Board of Deputies that he was returning the questionnaire 'as a matter of principle'. Race relations, he argued, was 'not our direct concern' and 'can only produce great harm to ourselves'.[37] He continued:

> In the first instance, in England there is no race problem. Please do not confuse it with the colour problem ... We do not need, nor shall we make these black people to be our champions but at the same time we are alienating the legitimate decent white natives of this liberty loving country whose future we seem to be generously giving away to the black.[38]

Conclusion

Of course, the differing positions of the Jewish and Irish communities as regards race relations can be explained easily enough on some levels. On average, the British-Jewish community by the 1970s and 1980s was settled and increasingly middle class. Few Jews had migrated to Britain since 1939 so there were hardly new immigrants as such. In contrast, there had been a huge wave of Irish immigration through and after the Second World War (over half a million new migrants arrived between 1951 and 1961).[39] While these new migrants did join established communities, the volume of Irish migration created considerable housing problems, leaving new arrivals often vulnerable and in need of welfare support.[40] In the aftermath of IRA campaigns, these communities were also much more susceptible to construction as a fifth column.[41]

These differences go some way to account for the fact that while the British Irish community was trying, in this period, to pull itself within the protective framework of race relations, British Jews were increasingly comfortable outside it. As one community pulled one way, and the other in the opposite direction, it is worth observing that both communities considered their starting position as different to black and Asian migrants.

Setting this story in the context of American immigration histories, one may be tempted to see these responses as stages in aspirations towards 'whiteness'. Scholars like Brodkin and Ignatiev, for example, have famously argued that, respectively, Jews and Irish became white, and secured preferential outcomes as a result. I, though, am not convinced. As Arnesen's critique of whiteness studies suggested, this kind of analysis seems to me to over-simplify the complexities of racialisation, and also to over-emphasise the idea of colour as a choice.

For Jews and Irish in post-war Britain, whiteness was not a choice or a strategy. While of course I accept that skin colour in a huge number of cases is not an objective marker, all communities involved read it in this way. Jews and Irish were both racialised and these racialisations were anything but trivial, but the whiteness of both sets of immigrants was taken for granted in discussions at every level in this period. In post-war Britain, white immigrants did not experience the same discriminations levelled everyday at black and Asian groups, which is not to say that they did not experience discrimination. Instead, levels of discrimination and racialisation were tied at every stage both to discourses of race and class, and, specifically, societal position. From this vantage point, one racialised community pulled towards racial minority status while the other hoped to transcend it, all the while both were still frequently constructed as different to other white Britons. While in and of itself these varying responses cannot speak to white migration writ large, I hope that future research on the interactions of race and multiculturalism in white immigrant communities might enhance historical debate about the importance of skin colour in shaping immigrant outcomes in British society.

Looking at the migration experiences of white migrants alongside black and Asian histories will not only help to tease out the importance of colour in shaping British understandings of race and belonging, but will also facilitate a clearer and more nuanced history of migration to Britain. While the colour of migrants' skin often did determine specific responses at every level, writing history that is itself segregated into racial categories may serve to entrench racialisation, but also to oversimplify it. If, instead, migration histories probe commonalities and differences across communities and generations, we may open the historical process to new understandings of race, racism and multiculturalism. In the wake of *John Bull's Island*, the work of Colin Holmes and subsequent generations of scholars of race and Britain have provided strong foundations for doing so.

Notes

1 See Mike and Trevor Phillips, *Windrush: The Irresistible Rise of Multi-Racial Britain* (London: Harper Collins 1998). For more recent high-quality scholarship of this migration see Kennetta Hammond Perry, *London is the Place for Me: Black Britons, Citizenship and the Politics of Race* (Oxford: Oxford University Press 2016).
2 See Panikos Panayi, *An Immigration History of Britain: Multicultural Racism since 1800* (Pearson: Harlow 2010) and Tony Kushner, *The Battle of Britishness: Migrant Journeys, 1685 to the Present* (Manchester: Manchester University Press 2012).
3 Colin Holmes, *John Bull's Island: Immigration and British Society, 1871–1971* (Basingstoke: Macmillan 1988).
4 Peter Fryer, *Staying Power: The History of Black People in Britain* (London: Pluto 1984), 1.

5 Panayi, *An Immigration History*, 23. For a more nuanced reading of *Windrush* itself, see Kushner, *The Battle of Britishness*, 163–185.
6 Holmes, *John Bull's Island*, 271.
7 John Rex and Robert Moore, *Race, Community and Conflict: A Study of Sparkbrook* (London: Oxford University Press 1967).
8 See Mary Daly, *The Slow Failure: Population Decline and Independent Ireland, 1920–73* (Madison: University of Wisconsin Press 2006), 154.
9 Similar views have been expressed by a disparate range of scholars of post-war British racism. See Fryer, *Staying Power*, 372–399, Kathleen Paul, *Whitewashing Britain: Race and Citizenship in the Postwar Era* (Ithaca and London: Cornell University Press 1997), 111–130, Ian Spencer, *British Immigration Policy Since 1939: The Making of Multi-racial Britain* (London: Routledge 1997), 129–133, John Solomos, *Race and Racism in Britain* (Basingstoke: Macmillan 1989), 61–63, and Harry Goulbourne, *Ethnicity and Nationalism* (Cambridge: Cambridge University Press 1991), 87–125. For my work in this area see Gavin Schaffer, *Racial Science and British Society, 1930–62* (Basingstoke: Palgrave 2008), 156–157.
10 A. Dummett and M. Dummett, 'The role of government in Britain's racial crisis', in C. Husband (ed.), *Race in Britain: Continuity and Change* (London: Hutchison 1982, (97–127) 103.
11 National Archives, Kew, London (NA), CAB21/4774, Memorandum for the Home Secretary, October 1961.
12 NA, CAB21/4774, Report by the Working Party on Immigration, 28/7/1961.
13 Significantly, Bailkin has pointed out that measures in the Act to enable deportations were targeted at Irish migrants. See Jordanna Bailkin, *The Afterlife of Empire* (Berkeley: University of California Press 2012), 203.
14 NA, DO175/121, Report by D. M. Cleary on a memorandum by the Home Secretary, 28/9/61.
15 See Gavin Schaffer, *The Vision of a Nation: Making Multiculturalism on British Television* (Basingstoke: Macmillan 2014).
16 Ibid.
17 David Roediger, *Working Towards Whiteness: How America's Immigrants Became White. The Strange Journey from Ellis Island to the Suburbs* (New York: Basic 2005).
18 Noel Ignatiev, *How the Irish Became White* (New York and London: Routledge 1995) and Karen Brodkin, *How Jews Became White Folks and What that Says about Race in America* (Rutgers University Press: New Brunswick 1998).
19 In particular see Eric Arnesen, 'Whiteness and the historians' imagination', *International Labor and Working-Class History*, vol. 60, 2001, 3–32.
20 Brodkin, *How Jews Became White Folks*, 173.
21 Liz Curtis, Jack O'Keeffe and Claire Keatinge, *Hearts and Minds: The Cultural Life of London's Irish Community* (London: Strategic Policy Unit 1989), 19.
22 Mary Hickman and Bronwen Walter, *Discrimination and the Irish Community in Britain: A Report of Research Undertaken for the Commission for Racial Equality* (London: CRE 1997), 230–235.
23 Paddy Hillyard, *Suspect Community: People's Experience of the Prevention of Terrorism Acts in Britain* (London and Boulder CO: Pluto 1993), 257.
24 Ibid., 259.
25 Hansard (Commons), Vol: 950, Col:772, 26/5/78.
26 NA, FCO 87/800, Note by the Irish Embassy 'The Prevention of Terrorism (Temporary Provisions) Acts 1974 and 1976', 24/1/78.

27 Bailkin, *The Afterlife of Empire*, 203.
28 See Enda Delaney, 'Almost a class of helots in an alien land': The British state and Irish immigration, 1921–45', *Immigrants & Minorities*, vol. 18, nos. 2–3, 2010, 240–265 and *Demography, State and Society: Irish Migration to Britain, 1921–71* (Liverpool: Liverpool University Press 2000), G. K. Peatling, 'The whiteness of Ireland under and after the Union', *Journal of British Studies*, vol. 14, no. 1, 2005, 115–133 and Donald MacRaild, *The Irish diaspora in Britain, 1750–1939* (Basingstoke: Palgrave 2010) and *The Irish in Britain, 1800–1914* (Dublin: Economic and Social History Society of Ireland 2006).
29 Board of Deputies MSS, ACC/3121/E4/403, London Metropolitan Archive, Memorandum sent to Soskice prior to meeting, 'Observations on Racial Discrimination and Incitement to Racial Hatred', 6/1/65.
30 Board of Deputies MSS, ACC/3121/E4/289, A Report and Recommendations by the Working Party on Race Relations: the Board of Deputies of British Jews (1969).
31 Ibid.
32 Board of Deputies MSS, ACC3121/E4/80, 'Meeting to Consider Report on "Improving Race Relations: the Jewish Contribution" and Follow-Up Activities', 10/12/69.
33 Board of Deputies MSS, ACC3121/E4/80, Rabbi Leigh to M Domitz (Board of Deputies), 4/5/71.
34 Board of Deputies MSS, ACC/3121/E4/80, Sermon of Rabbi John Rayner, 20/3/71.
35 Board of Deputies MSS, ACC/3121/E4/289, Letter from Rabbi AM Rose (from Office of the Chief Rabbi) to Alderman M Fidler President of the Board of Deputies, 15/10/69.
36 Ibid.
37 Board of Deputies MSS, ACC/3121/E4/80, Respondent to Survey, 16/4/69.
38 Ibid.
39 Mary J. Hickman, *Religion, Class and Identity* (Aldershot: Avebury 1995), 207.
40 E. Delaney, *Demography, State and Society: Irish Migration to Britain, 1921–71* (Liverpool: Liverpool University Press 2000), 213.
41 See Barry Hazley, 'Re/negotiating "suspicion": exploring the construction of self in Irish migrants' memories of the 1996 Manchester bomb', *Irish Studies Review*, vol. 21, no. 3, 2013, 326–341 and Louise Ryan, 'Who do you think you are? Irish Nurses encountering ethnicity and constructing identity in Britain', *Ethnic and Racial Studies*, vol. 30, no. 3, 2007, 416–438.

14

FAMILY MISFORTUNES?

Gendered perspectives on West Indian migration, welfare policies and cultural racism in post-Second World War Britain

Barbara Bush

In redefining national identity in the era of imperial decline, new West Indian migrant communities were a perceived threat to British culture. Negative perceptions of African Caribbean culture in popular, academic and official discourse reinforced racial myths which were long-rooted in the white collective consciousness. This powerful misreading of African Caribbean culture was highly gendered and informed differing responses to male and female migrants. Fundamental to understanding British responses to West Indian migration are the welfare and development policies introduced after the serious protests against poverty and neglect in the West Indies in the 1930s. 'Modernisation' of the 'backward' cultural beliefs and practices of the poorer African Caribbean majority and population control were now advocated in academic and official circles as the key to development. Perceptions of the 'dysfunctional' black family as a central problem were given academic credibility in sociological and population studies conducted in the 1940s and 1950s that targeted illegitimacy, female fecundity, 'looseness' of family life and poor parenting as major causes of poverty.[1] Such interventions demonstrate the durability of a transnational discourse of the 'dysfunctional' black family and the way it has migrated with African diaspora peoples across time and space.

Research into African Caribbean culture generated in the colonial context, particularly Jamaica, arguably influenced interventions into the most intimate areas of the private domestic life of early West Indian migrants. Pioneering migrants were colonial citizens and, up to independence in the early 1960s, primarily the responsibility of West Indian colonial governments and the Colonial Office. 'West Indian' thus denotes a generalised political identity as opposed to an African Caribbean cultural identity associated with the black peasantry and working classes. Given this colonial context, as noted in contemporary studies, migration is a more appropriate term than immigration which implies movement across political boundaries.[2] In colony and 'Mother Country' academic research, official policies and voluntary initiatives centred on the African Caribbean family dovetailed into a powerful agenda of interventionist welfare policies. Inherent to this agenda were assumptions about the superiority of the middle-class European culture of modernity. Hence, from their inception, social policies and initiatives favoured by British government officials and agencies involved in the welfare of migrants in British cities reflected a cultural racism, masked by a liberal discourse of racial equality, that permeated the new genre of race relations literature. Given the perceived problems related to black family life, welfare initiatives were directed primarily to female migrants and thus some consideration of gendered perspectives on migration is required to contextualise such initiatives. This is followed by a discussion of welfare interventions and, finally, an assessment of the impact of the cultural racism that informed public and official responses to migration on black family and community life.

Gendered perspectives on migration

Early West Indian migration to Britain was represented as masculine enterprise and gendered perspectives on migrant experiences are relatively recent.[3] Between 1953 and 1956, 162,000 migrants arrived, of which 52 percent were men, 40 percent women and 8 percent children. After 1956, more women and children began to arrive and by 1960 at least 50 percent of incomers from the West Indies were female. Oral testimony reveals that women, as well as men, were caught up in the infectious 'fever' to migrate and found it an 'exciting' prospect.[4] Many black women, like Irish women, came as independent migrants: some were single but others left behind partners and children, an additional stress on their difficult existence in England. Others migrated with their husbands or common law partners. The first West Indian female migrants found it more difficult to find suitable employment than men and were generally employed in the lowest grades of factory work and public domestic labour and excluded from shop and office work, that is 'meeting the public' jobs. Those who had skills worked mainly in the garment trade, often working long hours at home in busy periods.[5] According to an officially sponsored consultative committee into 'Immigrant Problems in London', West Indian women were 'very difficult to place, largely because of lack of skills and unwillingness to entertain certain forms of employment (e.g. domestic service) or to travel more than short distances to work'.[6] Unaccompanied girls and pregnant women faced particular difficulties in finding employment and places to live and were warned of the ulterior motives of some men offering them accommodation.[7]

For new migrants, the high cost of living and low wages meant that both husband and wife had to work. Budgeting was stringent and allowances had to be made for remittances to support children left in the West Indies. Childcare was a problem for working mothers. Nancy Foner observed that urban life in England 'dramatically' improved the lives of Jamaican female migrants, who came primarily from poor rural backgrounds, but child rearing was more difficult due to lack of family support.[8] Working full or part time (if they had children) black women had higher economic activity rates than white women which, arguably, excluded them from the white domestic ideal that dominated in the 1950s.[9] Single women on low wages reportedly found supporting themselves in London very difficult, especially if they had commitments to children left in the West Indies or gave birth to additional children in London. The 'economic plight' of such female migrants led to 'casual associations' with male migrants (who might already be married), cohabitation, pregnancy and loss of employment. If 'putative' fathers shirked responsibility and costs of childminding could not be found, children had to be taken into care.[10]

Migration was thus a gendered process as were experiences of racism. In the 1950s there was also an increase in female migrants with professional qualifications, such as teachers and nurses, but they also faced racial discrimination at work or had to take less qualified jobs.[11] Women's identities became homogenized and they had to negotiate new identities as migrants and members of a racialised minority group; the colour/class hierarchy that structured West Indian colonial societies became less relevant although lighter coloured women remained favoured over black. When Sheila Patterson interviewed employers and supervisors for her study of the Brixton migrant community, darker West Indian women were described as slow workers with a high degree of absenteeism and 'colossal' pregnancy rate.[12] Thus, as in the West Indian colonies, black women were embedded in public discourse primarily in terms of profligate childbearing and their contribution to the perceived instability of black family life associated with illegitimacy and single motherhood. Conversely, newer post-war male migrants (in contrast to the respectable 'old timers'), demonised as a sexual threat to respectable white womanhood, were associated with paternal irresponsibility and the emergent black 'ghetto' characterised by clubs, prostitution, drugs and gambling.

These gendered representations of new West Indian migrants arguably tell us more about anxieties about post-war transformations in British society and 'white' culture than the nature of the migrant experience. Migrant experiences were negatively affected by redefinitions of whiteness and white ethnicity mirrored against a new and 'threatening' black presence in an age of imperial decline. West Indian migrants, argued the social researcher Sheila Patterson, more so than any other migrant group, 'signally failed to conform to the white mores of the respectable British upper working-class with their strict codes of cleanliness, propriety and privacy'.[13] In liberal race relations discourse the solution was the stabilisation of black family life through welfare interventions to facilitate cultural assimilation into white norms and values of marriage and parenting. This would promote integration into British communities and reduce potential for racial conflict.

Welfare interventions in black family life

During the war, in response to greater numbers of West Indian and West African students in Britain, the Colonial Office recognised the need to expand welfare provision. In the post-war period the welfare remit extended to new West Indian migrants and the British Caribbean Welfare Service (BCWS) was established in 1956 based at the Colonial Office to assist new arrivals with entry requirements, advice and information. On the recommendation of a report sponsored by the Jamaican government a Migrant Services Division of the Commission in the UK for the West Indies, British Guiana and the Honduras (MSD) replaced the BCWS in 1958 as the prime organisation responsible for migrant welfare.[14] The MSD was divided into welfare, industrial relations and community relations divisions and liaised with other organisations involved in migrant social problems such as local Councils for Social Service and voluntary support agencies including the Citizens Advice Bureau and the Family Welfare Association. Trained social workers were employed, including welfare workers seconded from Jamaica, to 'study migrant problems' and reduce 'friction and misunderstandings' on both sides (migrants and agencies).[15]

The work of the MSD became more pressing as numbers of migrants and racial tensions increased, erupting in the 1958 anti-black riots in Notting Hill and Nottingham. The Colonial Office now demonstrated greater concern about the social problems of migrants, including housing and family problems. In a draft report on agencies involved with 'assimilation', officials recognised the role of the MSD but stressed that the chief responsibility rested with 'local social workers' despite the fact many such workers who 'came up against [immigrant] problems' knew 'relatively little' of the West Indian background.[16] This attempt to shift responsibility for migrant welfare reflected financial and organisational problems that undermined the MSD's effectiveness. Until funding ceased in 1962 with the collapse of the West Indian Federation the Colonial Office had argued that, as five percent of the West Indian population was now in the UK, the Federal Government in Trinidad should financially support the MSD before the UK considered a subsidy. When funding was cut, despite the increase in migrant numbers and related social problems, Colonial Office officials proposed that migrant welfare should be the responsibility of the Home Office and funded accordingly.[17]

Government officials regarded welfare as crucial to the integration of migrants into local communities but funding was sparse and policy making haphazard. No comprehensive study of migrant experiences and problems existed. This gap was filled by the London Family Welfare Association who sponsored a three-year 'Project for the Welfare of Coloured People', published in 1960, to address the problem of the 'large influx of coloured people' into London and to promote assimilation.[18] The FWA (1946–1965) evolved from the Charity Organisation Society (1843–1946) but by the 1950s its work was increasingly dominated by salaried professional social workers involved primarily in family casework. The research concluded that family and personal problems were like those experienced by white families but complicated by 'the strains of overcrowding', the separation of families, 'different attitudes to illegitimacy' (regarded as a shame on a respectable white family), the 'cultural background of migrants' and 'differences in their personalities'.

The solution to these problems was to provide West Indian men and women with 'preventative knowledge' and instruct them on 'questions relating to the social and moral attitudes of the society in which they live'.[19]

Migrant women received particular attention. The FWA study asserted that after housing and unemployment (which increased after the Suez crisis in 1956), 'the problem of West Indian mothers appears to be next in ... importance'.[20] As in the times of slavery black women were insensitively condemned as neglectful mothers, further reinforcing contrasts with 'good' white mothers. This arguably reflected the fact that more migrant women had to work outside the home at a time when the 'Janet and John' image of the nuclear family, with the stay-at-home mother, was central to the 1950s discourse of cosy domesticity (which poorer white families were also unable to attain). Of specific concern were single parents and pregnant women who came in search of husbands or mates who had migrated to England and not heard of since. Such women were in 'serious difficulties' if the man could not be found or, if found, did not want to renew the relationship. Additionally, pregnant migrants had difficulties finding a hospital to give birth in as there was insufficient provision even for 'local' women. When born, the child could not remain with its mother, who had to work to support herself, and was 'invariably' sent to an institution 'to the horror of most of the mothers'.[21] Such illegitimate children were regarded as a particular social problem as reflected in a conference organised by the London Council of Social Service to address 'the care and protection of coloured illegitimate children' in September 1960.[22] Interracial relationships between West Indian men and white women, rare in the Caribbean, also resulted in desertion of some black women and their children for white women.[23] Given the burden of employment and childcare combined with race and gender oppression and, in some cases, separation from children, it was inevitable that some women were susceptible to stress and depression.

In the new child-centred ethos of the post-war era, differing attitudes to child rearing amongst West Indian migrants also resulted in accusations of cruelty to children. It was difficult for black women to attain the white middle-class ideal of motherhood as it was normal for most mothers, married or single, to work long distances from home, often having to do overtime. Women, observed the FWA study, were often reliant on inadequate nursery provision but frequently blamed for being 'dilatory in calling for their children'. West Indian parents, the researchers concluded, were 'so absorbed in their own personal difficulties' that they had little time to devote to their children and added that the strains of adjusting to a new situation and culture could result in mental breakdown. Child neglect was, nevertheless, rare despite family and personal problems resulting from overcrowding and poor housing conditions, particularly when welfare workers 'instructed' mothers on 'proper childcare' to overcome any problems related to their 'cultural background'.[24] A report published in the late 1960s observed that, in reality, allegations of poor parenting reflected the multiple pressures on migrant lives, including 'maternal depression, economic pressures on parents, mothers too exhausted to give time to or enjoy their children, inadequate housing, inadequate care of children and multiple fostering'. Furthermore, West Indian parents retained the 'Victorian values' of the British 'Motherland' that permeated the imperial curriculum in West Indian schools and instilled strong discipline at home in contrast to the more lax modern British parenting.[25]

From the mid-1960s, white liberals and sociologists were keen to demonstrate that social policies of assimilation and integration were working and changing attitudes to marriage, legitimacy and parenting indicated that West Indian families now conformed more to the values and culture of the white working class.[26] Yet preoccupations with the 'pathological' black family centred on the matriarchal norm of mother and children born to several partners and high levels of illegitimacy persisted.[27] But what did white researchers and social workers really know about the black family? Given the denigration of African Caribbean culture and the general disapproval of illegitimacy and 'serial unions' which informed the attitudes and practice of such professionals (which included more middle-class 'respectable' West Indians), it is not surprising that migrants had a 'tendency to be secretive' in discussing intimate personal details.[28] In addition, such 'stranger' interventions were culturally alien to West Indians. This raises the question of how migrants responded to welfare interventions and official policies to promote integration in an implicitly racist environment. What was the reality of their lives 'Ina England'?

Rhetoric versus reality: cultural racism, migration and black family and community life

The reality of black family life, as opposed to the rhetoric of dysfunction and deviance from the acceptable white norm, was a struggle to keep the family together despite the pressures and stresses of migration. These stresses included the fact that many children had been behind in the care of grandmothers or aunts until such a time as it was feasible to bring them over to Britain. According to Elaine Arnold, between 1955 and 1960 adult migrants brought an estimated 6,500 children to the UK but left 90,000 behind; and the stress of broken attachments through separation, combined with problems of reunion and the racism experienced by their children in the UK, put additional pressures on black mothers.[29] There is evidence that before restrictions were introduced under the proposed Commonwealth Immigration Bill, West Indian migrants made every effort, at considerable cost, to bring their children (and elderly relatives) to the UK. In response to fears about migrant numbers, however, the authorities tightened up on procedures. Colonial Office concern about 'young persons' arriving at ports and airports 'unescorted or found abandoned by the person who might have been in charge during the journey' (thirty-seven in 1961) led to stricter arrangements for issuing children and young persons with passports in Jamaica (where most West Indian migrants came from) and their reception and welfare in the UK. The bureaucracy necessary to ensure children had the right documents to come to travel now led to 'considerable delays'. Moreover, passports could not be issued until authorised by the MSD which allegedly failed to respond to requests. Frustrated parents thus tried to speed up the passport application process by adopting the 'wrong procedures' in contacting the Home Office, solicitors and MPs but the Colonial Office stressed that passports could only be issued in the home territory.[30] These policies asserted the FWA caused 'great anxiety and distress due to protracted separation and wasted payments to escorts who could not wait indefinitely'.[31]

When families were reunited problems persisted as children had to adjust to a different culture and an education system pervaded by racism. After the 1958 riots West Indian parents feared that their children might experience 'anti-colour feeling' at school. In response to enquiries by the Ministry of Education, education departments claimed that problems were exaggerated and even after the riots relations between white and coloured children were 'good'; a teachers' union representative, in an implicitly racist tone, reported that in London schools there were 'no signs of racial prejudice' except for 'an occasional fight between 'coloured children' over legitimacy reflecting a 'superiority complex of those born in wedlock'.[32] Given these attitudes it is unsurprising that West Indian children were stigmatized by white teachers as 'backward', 'sullen', 'disruptive' and unresponsive. In effect, as a pioneering study observed, they faced problems of 'language, identity and race' that contributed to underperformance and reached 'crisis' proportions in secondary schools by the 1970s.[33] West Indian youths also found it difficult to get employment and experienced police harassment and racist attacks which adversely impacted on black family and community life.

Since the 1970s, failed by the education system and alienated from mainstream society, some poorer black males have identified with a 'hyper masculinity' of gang culture and violence, including domestic violence.[34] Black male machismo as expressed through men taking pride in 'babymothers', with whom they frequently do not live, has perpetuated negative ideas of pathological black family life. It has fuelled a street gang culture that embroils black children and young adults in poorer areas. The threat of gang killings, so-called 'black on black' violence, combined with racial attacks on black children and police harassment, has placed additional strain on black families. Moral panics about the black family now centre on absent fathers, who take little responsibility for their children, a perceived crisis in black masculinity, and single mothers dependent on the welfare state whose sons lack paternal controls. Despite legislation and improved life chances for black British citizens, such moral panics flag a continuing problematic relationship between black families and the state.[35] This stems in part from social research and welfare policies from the 1940s onwards that had conceptualised the black family as different and culturally inferior. As Aminatta Forna has argued, white society has failed to acknowledge the African-based values, common across the diaspora, around which black family life is organised, in particular the importance of motherhood.[36]

From arrival in the UK the West Indian migrant experience was affected by cultural racism, disguised in the language of assimilation, that informed state policy and voluntary initiatives related to family, marriage and parenting. Negative perceptions of black family life and gender relations obscured diversity in class, aspirations, adjustment to migration and other factors that influenced the migrant experience. Family and marital problems within the West Indian migrant community must also be contextualised in the wider framework of poverty and racial exclusions. In effect, as Kennetta Hammond Perry has demonstrated, migrants and their black British descendants consistently challenged racism and asserted their right to belong.[37] Men and women worked hard to build better lives for themselves and their children: with support of their communities many families survived and prospered, despite prejudice and racism, laying the foundations for a permanent British Caribbean community. This flags the importance of migrants' agency in building meaningful lives for themselves and their children in a generally hostile white society. Women developed strong female support networks, mostly ignored in sociological studies of migration, and were crucial to sustaining West Indian families and communities in Britain. Women's province, when not working, was home and reconstituted elements of Caribbean community life; church, market, dressmakers and hairdressers. Women migrants were also instrumental in administering pardner or *sou-sou* schemes, a means of acquiring deposits to buy houses and, as women's testimonies recorded by Wendy Webster confirm, 'home' was very important in black women's strategies for survival in a hostile world.[38] Apart from in the workplace, women were less publicly visible than men. Pubs and other public social arenas were male provinces. As one female British Jamaican woman recollected, women '… just didn't hang out at those places [and] never really socialized with white people.' For these reasons women were regarded as less of a threat, and more 'assimilable' than male migrants.[39] In effect, however, it was women who protected and preserved key elements of African Caribbean culture and identity and transmitted these to their children.

Much has changed in the transition from first generation migrants to established British Caribbean communities. Welfare and educational policies directed to West Indian migrants in Britain in the 1950s and 1960s derived from a discourse of cultural difference that failed to understand and/or acknowledge the strength and resilience of African Caribbean cultural practices and family organisation. Social research projects sponsored by colonial governments targeted the 'dysfunctional' African Caribbean family as a key barrier to modernisation and development. With an increase in migration to Britain, state concern, and related academic research, now focused on the problems of new migrant communities. Official policies and related voluntary initiatives confirmed durable, negative and gendered interpretations of black family and community life that seeped into the popular media and contributed to the deeper institutionalisation of racism. The interventions of the modern British state were based on supposedly objective academic research but perpetuated deep cultural tensions that led to alienation and resentment in British Caribbean communities, and entrenched the economic and social divide between white and black Britain.

Notes

1. See Thomas A. Simey, *Welfare and Planning in the West Indies* (Oxford: Clarendon 1946) 4, 88–90. Other influential studies include Edith Clarke, *My Mother Who Fathered Me: A Study of the Family in Three Selected Communities in Jamaica* (London: George Allen and Unwin Ltd 1957); Madeleine Kerr, *Personality and Conflict in Jamaica* (Liverpool: Liverpool University Press 1952); J. Mayone Stycos and Judith Blake, 'The Jamaican Family Life Project: some objectives and methods', *Social and Economic Studies*, vol. 3, nos. 3 & 4, 1954, 342–349. For a fuller discussion of government sponsored research into African Caribbean culture, see Barbara Bush, 'Colonial research and the social sciences at the end of empire: The West Indian Social Survey, 1944–57', *The Journal of Imperial and Commonwealth History* vol. 41, no. 3, 2013, 451–474.
2. As in Clarence Senior and Douglas Manley, *A Report on Jamaican Migration to Great Britain* (Kingston, The Government Printer 1956), ii.
3. See, for instance, Mary Chamberlain, *Narratives of Exile and Return* (London: Macmillan 1997); Nancy Foner, 'Gender and migration: West Indians in comparative perspective', *International Migration* vol. 47, no. 1, 2008, 3–29. Early migrant experiences are also recorded in oral interviews conducted by Mike and Trevor Phillips in *Windrush: The Irresistible Rise of Multi-Racial Britain* (London: Harper Collins 1999), 46–93.
4. Jamaican migrant to Britain, 1958 cited in Karen Flynn, '"I'm not your typical nurse": Caribbean nurses in Britain and Canada', in *Women's History Magazine* (now *Women's History*) Issue 69, 2012, 26–36 (28). Statistics cited in S. K. Ruck (ed.), *The West Indian Comes to England: A Report Prepared for the Trustees of the London Parochial Charities by the Family Welfare Association* (London: Routledge Kegan and Paul 1960), 88 and Elaine Arnold, *Working with Families of Caribbean Origin: Understanding Issues around Immigration and Attachment* (London and Philadelphia: Jessica Kingsley Publishers 2012), 44.
5. Ruck (ed.), *The West Indian*, 72, 105; Sheila Patterson, *Immigration and Race Relations in Britain, 1960–1967* (Oxford: Oxford University Press 1969), 136.
6. 'Draft Notes' April 1960 in CO 0 31/ 3941 'Consultative Committees to deal with Immigrant problems in London, 1960–62', National Archives (henceforth NA).
7. Senior and Manley, *A Report on Jamaican Migration*, 36–37.
8. Nancy Foner, 'Women work and migration: Jamaicans in London', *New Community* vol. V, nos. 1–2, 1976, 85–99 (89–90).
9. Wendy Webster, *Imagining Home: Race, Class and National Identity, 1945–64* (London, UCL Press 1997), 41–44, 92–93, 122.
10. Ruck (ed.), *The West Indian*, 75–77.
11. See Beryl Gilroy, *Black Teacher* (London: Bogle-l'Ouverture Press, 1976); Flynn, '"I'm not your typical nurse"'.
12. Sheila Patterson, *Dark Strangers: A Study of West Indians in London* (London: Pelican Books 1965. (First published 1962)), 96, 125.
13. Patterson, *Dark Strangers*, 198.
14. Senior and Manley, *A Report on Jamaican Migration*, 50–52.
15. 'Welfare arrangements for West Indians in the UK (Marked Confidential)'; 'Minutes of meeting in the Colonial Office, 24 November 1958', in CO O31/2945, 'Migrant Services Division for West Indians in the United Kingdom of the West Indies Commission, 1957–9', NA.
16. 'Memo from M. Z. Terry, 15 June 1960'; 'Draft Notes' prepared for circulation to Home Office and Ministry of Housing and Local Government', April 1960 in CO 031/3941, 'Consultative committees to deal with immigrant problems in London, 1960–1962', NA.

See also Ruck (ed.), *The West Indian*, 92 for problems of communication between social workers and migrants.

17 'Extract from CO minutes, 4 August, 1960'; 'E M Mackintosh to Mr Thomas, 30 December 1960', in CO 1031/4219, 'Migrant services Division of the Commission in the UK for the West Indies, British Guiana and British Honduras, 1960–1962', NA.

18 Ruck (ed.), *The West Indian*, v. For the importance of this study, see a review article by Harold Pollins, *Social Work* vol. 17, no. 2, 1960, 34–37.

19 Ruck (ed.), *The West Indian*, 87–88, 119, 127–137.

20 Ibid., 122.

21 Senior and Manley, *A Report on Jamaican Migration*, 36–37.

22 'Memo from M Z Terry, 15 June, 1960', in CO 031/3941. Edward Brathwaite, the British Guianan author of *To Sir With Love* (1959) was a London County Council social worker responsible for finding foster homes for non-white children, 1958–60 (E R Brathwaite, Obituary by John Mair, *Guardian*, 15 December 2016).

23 Ruck (ed.), *The West Indian*, 129–130.

24 Ruck (ed.), *The West Indian*, 119, 137–139. For issues of racism and mental health see James Y. Nazroo, 'Understanding the poorer health of black people in Britain', in Kwesi Owusu (ed.), *Black British Culture and Society: A Text Reader* (London: Routledge 2000), 311–323 (319).

25 E. J. B. Rose and Associates, *Colour and Citizenship: A Report on British Race Relations* (London and Toronto: Oxford University Press 1969), 210–212, 423.

26 Rose et al., *Colour and Citizenship*, 349, 431–433; Clifford S Hill, *How Colour Prejudiced is Britain?* (London: Victor Gollancz 1965), 172–173.

27 For instance, Special Report, 'Unmarried black mothers: problems and prospects', *Race Today*, vol. 5, 1973, 208–209.

28 Ruck (ed.), *The West Indian*, 144.

29 Arnold, *Working with Families of Caribbean Origin*, 44 and Ch. 4 'Narratives of African Caribbean mothers, separated from and reunited with their children', 71–91.

30 'Report by Miss M. Z. Terry, 20 November, 1961,' in CO 1031/3944 'Emigration of Children and Young Persons from the West Indies to the United Kingdom, 1960–2', NA.

31 'Ian Macleod to Sir Robert Carey MP, Letter about complaints from the Manchester FWA, 21 September, 1961', in CO 1031/4219, 'Migrant services Division 1960–1962', NA.

32 Internal memo, 12 September 1958; Draft reply to the Secretary of State for Colonies, 15 September 1958, in Ed 147/612, 'Miscellaneous: West Indian Children in Schools, Anti-semitism, 1958–60', NA.

33 CK3/123, 'University of Bristol (West Indian) Children in Schools-Report, 1974', NA. For a damning polemical critique from the West Indian perspective see Bernard Coard, *How the West Indian Child is Made Educationally Subnormal in the British School System* (London: Caribbean Education and Community Workers' Association 1971).

34 Amina Mama, 'Woman abuse in London's black communities' (1996) reproduced in Owusu (ed.), *Black British Culture*, 89–110.

35 Deborah A. Thomas, 'The violence of diaspora: governmentality, class, cultures and circulations', *Radical History Review*, Issue 103, 2009, 83–104 (84).

36 Aminatta Forna, 'Mothers of Africa and the diaspora: shared maternal values among black women', in Owusu (ed.), *Black British Culture*, 358–373 (363–364).

37 Kennetta Hammond Perry, *London is the Place for Me: Black Britons, Citizenship and the Politics of Race* (Oxford: Oxford University Press 2016).

38 Wendy Webster, *Imagining Home*, 180. For women's part in building communities see Claudette Williams, 'We are a natural part of many different struggles: black women

organising', in Clive Harris and Bob Carter, *Inside Babylon: The Caribbean Diaspora in Britain* (London: Verso 1993) 154; Valentina Alexander, 'A mouse in the jungle: the black Christian woman's experience in the church and society in Britain', in Delia Jarrett-Macauley (ed.), *Reconstructing Womanhood, Reconstructing Feminism* (London: Routledge 1996). Several works exist which draw on women's oral testimonies of life in England including Elyse Dodgson, *Motherland: West Indian Women to Britain in the 1950s* (London: Heinemann 1984).

39 Ruck (ed.), *The West Indian*, 129; Recollections of Celia Robinson cited in Jean Simpson and Helen Kolowole 'Exodus: movement of the people', *Pride*, January/February, 1997, 115.

15

INSIDE, OUTSIDE, AND IN-BETWEEN

Shifting borders in British immigration and disease control

Krista Maglen

The June 2016 Brexit referendum brought with it a need to reconsider the geopolitical shape of Britain. What would removal from the European Union do to the United Kingdom and its borders? For European immigrants at the centre of the Brexit vote, the borders of Britain that were once open to them have begun to close, shrinking the frontiers of inclusion back towards the island littoral. Immigration border controls that have been carried out across the English Channel in France or Belgium under agreements such as the Treaty of Le Touquet may be pushed back to Britain in the Brexit negotiations;[1] while 'Britain is seeking to shift the frontline of immigration controls to Ireland's ports and airports to avoid having to introduce a "hard border" between north and south after the UK leaves the European Union'.[2] These readjustments to the placement of openings and edges to the country are not new, however. Britain's border has been a malleable construct for a long time, expanding to embrace the world beyond its shores, as well as contracting to tighten around internal apprehensions. Border flexibility has perhaps been most clearly displayed in the ways that prevention and management strategies have been applied to the importation of infectious disease, particularly among immigrant communities. This chapter reviews some of the literature that has spoken to migrant public health from the nineteenth century, and explores the interdependence of and interfacing between disease control and immigration control in the defining of national space and those who could enter it.

Beginning in the nineteenth century in response to increased global trade and migration, public health officials, dealing with the control of disease, began to consider the parameters that defined what pathogens were domestic and endemic, and what were imported and 'exotic'. Until the third quarter of the century, British laws and the local and national authorities that enforced them tended towards approaches that sought not to exclude or close access to people or ships that arrived carrying either category of disease, but rather relied upon the growing domestic sanitary infrastructure to manage outbreaks. With the exception of people and ships that arrived with either of the two diseases named in the 1825 Quarantine Act, plague or yellow fever (which were nearly non-existent in Britain in the nineteenth century), the law did not prevent anyone from entering the country. Even those who arrived carrying smallpox or tuberculosis could enter through ports overseen primarily by the Customs authorities, and a handful of sanitary officers. This was because the traditional approach to imported infections, quarantine, was increasingly marginalised in British ports due to the costly delays it demanded of 'infected' or 'suspected' merchant ships. Instead, a system known to contemporaries as the 'English System' combined sanitary regulations, procedures, and surveillance at the ports and in port towns and cities to serve as a less disruptive alternative to quarantine. It brought maritime disease management under the control of domestic public health infrastructure, merging port health with urban health. People who arrived on an infected ship were permitted to disembark and disperse to lodgings or homes throughout the port city once they had provided health authorities with their addresses. Infected people were kept in hospital isolation, but healthy passengers and crews from the same ship were monitored by sanitary officers in their homes and accommodation, so that the health control of immigrants and international arrivals occurred inland from the ports, in neighbourhoods, reception rooms and lodging-houses. Rather than marking a biopolitical perimeter around the littoral, like quarantine did, the new system identified a particularly 'English' public health zone that was more elastic and could be both stretched out to sea and to the colonial diaspora (where sanitary inspections and regulations sought to prevent the movement of disease from one place to another) or it could contract into the streets and domestic spaces of coastal towns and cities.[3]

So, in Britain, unlike in the United States and elsewhere, the association between quarantine and immigration was not being made during most of the nineteenth century. This came later. Rather quarantine was almost exclusively and intimately connected to commerce and diplomacy and it was administered and challenged through these channels. As immigrant numbers began to increase in the final decades of the century, any diseases found among them on arrival were dealt with within this 'sanitary zone' of the domestic public health and sanitary infrastructure and not at the ports and borders.[4]

This separation of quarantine from issues of immigrant health is reflected in much of the scholarship in which historians of late nineteenth-century immigration into Britain have tended to concentrate more specifically on the economic effects, responses and restrictions to immigration, and particularly to European immigrants.[5] This focus on European migrants is likely because, despite the longevity of black and Asian immigration to Britain, between 1800 and 1945 the number of non-European migrants to Britain barely reached beyond a few thousand. So, the majority of migrants during the nineteenth century were variously European with the largest groups coming from Ireland, primarily until the 1860s and then Eastern Europe from the beginning of the 1880s. Where the historiography has focused on their health, some important work on this period has been produced, but these studies have focused on the health of immigrants after arrival and settlement in Britain. Historians such as Lara Marks, Bernard Harris and Anne Hardy in the 1990s and early 2000s examined comparative infant mortality rates, life expectancy, nutrition and instances of disease among immigrant communities in England,[6] while Kenneth Collins explored similar themes in Glasgow.[7] Hardy shows, for example, that while outbreaks of typhus in the 1850s and 1860s were often blamed on Irish immigrants, there was little evidence to show that the disease had been brought from Ireland. Rather it flourished in crowded and unsanitary conditions of the poorer neighbourhoods of the large cities where immigrants tended to live.[8] On the other hand, Marks demonstrates the superior health and wellness of Jewish immigrants in London's East End compared with their Polish and Italian counterparts and the native born population of the same neighbourhoods.[9] Yet while these studies were critical to our understanding of nineteenth-century migrant health, in comparison with the ever increasing literature on twentieth-century and particularly post-war migrant health, there is a much feebler body of scholarship on the century prior to the passing of the 1905 Aliens Act. These studies also did not explore the medical inspection of immigrants as they arrived into British ports or how perceptions of risk, relating to immigration, affected existing practices in port prophylaxis. Aside from my own book, which sought to redress this imbalance, historians of the nineteenth century have only examined disease control at ports of entry in more general studies of disease intervention, quarantine or seamen's health, for example, rather than focusing on immigrants in particular.[10]

Where nineteenth-century scholarship of immigrant port health screening is most vibrant is in relation to the United States with scholars such as Howard Markel, Alan Kraut, Amy Fairchild and Nyan Shah, forging a strong historiographical foundation for the period.[11] Howard Markel has argued, for example, that immigration and disease control in United States ports became integrated both conceptually and in practice during the nineteenth century, explaining: 'In many respects, the movement to restrict immigration to the United States during this period was a call for quarantine in its broadest sense against undesirable immigrants.'[12] And, Amy Fairchild showed how medicalised borders functioned not only as exclusionary but also as inclusionary apparatuses. United States immigration medical examinations were, she explains, not only intended to keep out those people who arrived with threatening illness but were also 'shaped by an industrial imperative to discipline the labouring force in accordance with industrial expectations'. So, American medical frontiers had the dual purpose of prohibiting the entry of 'foreigners' into the national 'body' as well as regulating the admission of those deemed beneficial to it.[13]

The significance of the United States in this period is not only the value of its historiography though, as it was in many ways transformational to the way that Britain came to think about and regulate the bodies of immigrants to its own shores. This was the consequence both of Britain being an important 'transmigration' country, meaning that the majority of migrants who arrived at British ports in the final decade of the nineteenth century and first decade of the next were transiting on their way to America, as well as the growing concern that those migrants unable to gain admission to the United States were being returned to

Britain or had resigned to stay in Britain without even attempting the transatlantic voyage. The increasingly medicalised categories of 'desirability' and 'undesirability' that were being created at, and were creating, the United States border only emphasised the lack of such categories or controls in British ports. The strict quarantine imposed against cholera vessels in New York in 1892 and the harsh medical restrictions of the 1891 US Immigration Act received both admonition and admiration in Britain. However, the growing desire among anti-alienists to adopt measures against migrants similar to those in the United States was incompatible with the successful systems and narratives of sanitary regulations and surveillance that had been employed through much of the century, and which had prevented the importation of dangerous infections like cholera without the need to exclude anyone from arriving or detaining ship-loads of immigrants in quarantine.

However, the 1892 cholera outbreak was the first real test of the English System, and while it proved to be hugely effective in preventing the disease from entering into the population, it was not strong enough to counter the widespread perception that Eastern European, primarily Jewish, immigrants and transmigrants (en route to America) were the prime conduits of the disease. The confidence that 'anti-quarantinists' had displayed both internationally and at 'home' in the prophylactic capacities of the sanitary zone began to falter as the disease approached, and even the most stalwart proponents of British public health infrastructure began to lose their nerve. Previous cholera epidemics had arrived in Britain on trading vessels from Egypt and the Mediterranean. Then, the source of the disease appeared sufficiently far removed and that meant that Britain could, as Peter Baldwin argues, safely eschew quarantine, confident in the protective bulwark of other countries closer to the source.[14] But, in 1892, the 'source' of the disease was believed to be those people who were congregating in ports on the western edge of Europe, fleeing pestilence and persecution in the east, their eyes firmly set on America. This time the disease appeared to be on the doorstep, and what's more, the transportation of thousands of migrants from Russia, west through Europe and ultimately, for most migrants, to the United States, was big business. An operation that was quickly and, on the whole, efficiently managed using the latest technologies of rapid steam travel. It was the numbers and speed with which these migrations appeared to move across Europe with the added tinder of deep and existing prejudices associated with them that fuelled the perception that this was a different kind of disease, requiring a different type of response.

Demonstrating the anxiety of those monitoring the outbreak, an article in *The Lancet* claimed that the migrants did not import the disease through any process of contagion, as upheld in the new science of bacteriology, but rather that they themselves embodied the 'foreign' origin of cholera, bring with them the 'locality' within which disease could generate:

> A number of immigrants arriving from an infected district – possibly dirty as regards their persons, and still more so as regards their clothes – may be provisionally regarded as so many minute migratory fragments of the locality whence they came.[15]

So, despite a continued rhetoric which rejected quarantine, the notion that the very bodies of immigrants were 'migrating locations' of disease meant that existing sanitary systems, which controlled the health of port and urban spaces, might not be enough to hold back the disease. In response, temporary measures were introduced that in effect renewed a type of quarantine for the poorest class of migrants. The surveillance that had previously relied on the collection of information about accommodation in the days that followed arrival of an infected ship became the mechanism for monitoring all immigrants whether they had arrived on an infected vessel or not. The new regulations insisted that onward addresses of all migrants were 'correct' and that proof of financial independence could be provided. For many immigrants this was very difficult, if not impossible. Numerous lodging-houses in London had been placed on a Port Medical Inspector 'watch list', so that even migrants who arrived with an onward address – and many did not – found themselves temporarily denied entry. One man, who arrived in London during the epidemic, described the moment at which the Port Medical Officer denied him entry on the basis of his onward address:

> The Captain presented to the Dr. a list of all the passengers with the address of their proposed destinations, reading my name with 28 Finsbury Square as my proposed address. This address did not appear to be satisfactory to the Dr. but the Captain urged very strongly that the address was quite suitable and the Dr. asked me thro' the Captain from whom I got the address and I replied, from a similar home in Hamburg. The Dr. shrugged his shoulders and said I can't pass your address, but gave no reason.[16]

These temporary preventive measures against cholera, which were later incorporated into permanent Port Sanitary regulations, were aimed directly at steerage class passengers and particularly migrants. They contradicted the long-standing commitment to open and fluid port spaces. Instead, migrants began to be seen as a different subset within the categorisation of imported diseases, allowing for new concepts of 'place' and 'locality' that underpinned a sanitary response to disease, and requiring expanded powers among Port Medical Officers. They represented the beginning of a different approach to the movement of (certain) people within and through the ports. Immigrants, as 'migratory fragments' of 'infected' foreign places, could contaminate the sanitary zone, and needed to be kept away from known 'problem' localities. Expressing the 'danger' this way was different from the idea of potential contagions needing to be quarantined. It was not a reversal of position or policy. It was the construction of a 'new' type of threat to the carefully managed sanitary zone established by the English System and public health infrastructure. Yet, even with these changes, immigrants were only ever delayed in their arrival. They were not prohibited from landing – eventually – and were not, as in the United States, turned around at the ports.

Ultimately, and beyond the initial panic of the 1892 cholera epidemic, the port and urban medical and sanitary officers who oversaw the arrival and health of immigrants in their first days and weeks in the country did not consider them to pose a problem that could not be dealt with within existing public health systems. This was despite the increasing volume of anti-alien rhetoric that was beginning to echo American notions of medical categories of 'undesirability'. Rather, the emphasis remained focused on the sanitary conditions of the places into and through which immigrants moved, and once the cholera scare had passed, the focus returned to 'infected' ports and shipboard sanitation, rather than to the bodies of people who disembarked in London and elsewhere. Once again, ships, rather than the immigrants who filled their hulls, were seen as the 'migrating localities' of disease. As Katherine Foxhall has shown for an earlier period, ships were seen to be 'not simply a vector for disease' but were themselves potentially productive disease environments.[17] So, for the medical men and public health officials who were concerned with the arrival of increasing numbers of immigrants, urban localities and maritime spaces were yet again the focus of their efforts – what they kept under sanitary surveillance, and what they made conform to sanitary norms. Herbert Williams, Port Medical Officer of Health of the Port of London from 1901 to 1916, declared that immigrants were only of interest where they entered into or linked these environments.[18] The English System was, they were once more confident, a sufficient instrument for preventing the spread of any disease that may arrive among immigrant passengers. To this they testified in a unified voice before the 1903 Royal Commission on Alien Immigration, stating that disease among immigrants required no special measures beyond those that were in place for the 'native' population. The most senior Medical Officer summoned before the Commission, Shirley Murphy, Medical Officer of Health for the Administrative County of London, said flatly: '… my feeling is this, that I should be indisposed to put these people under any different law from that which relates to our English population with regards to such matters'.[19]

So, it was not the will of the medical community, nor the public health concerns of the expansive sanitary system, that was behind the inclusion of a medical clause in the 1905 Aliens Act. In fact one of the sitting members of the Royal Commission, Lord Rothschild, declared in a memorandum to the recommendations of the Commission that:

> It has been proved in evidence … that there is very little illness amongst these immigrants, and that they are not found to have introduced any infectious or contagious disease. There is little or no evidence that lunatics come over with them, and the health of the immigrants after arrival here as proved by the Vital statistics given in evidence appears to be superior to that of the native population. No case therefore seems to have been made for any special measures for exclusion at the port of landing on the ground of health.[20]

He, and fellow Commission member Kenelm Digby, recommended that as the problems of disease were essentially local they should be dealt with as such and not through national legislation or regulation. They thus, in effect, concurred with the idea that a firm border around the littoral, excluding those who did not conform to medical concepts of 'desirability', was not needed to protect the public health. And yet, their entreaties fell on deaf ears, and the Commission ultimately recommended a focused medical examination of immigrants at ports of arrival, and the deportation of those 'found to be suffering from infectious or loathsome disease, or mental incapacity' to their port of embarkation at the expense of the shipping company that had brought them.[21]

It was this recommendation that in due course shaped the medical clause of the Aliens Act, replicating American legislation by making 'desirability' and 'undesirability' characteristics that could be located in an immigrant body (or mind) as well as in economic status. It also mirrored US practice by ensuring that carriers, now liable for the return passage of 'rejected' migrants, undertook their own pre-screening of potential passengers. Thus, the new law pushed the surveillance of migrant bodies outside and beyond the ports into a broader regulatory space distinct from the reaches of the sanitary zone.

Today, UK border and health controls continue to reach beyond the English Channel, with pre-entry tuberculosis screening required for residents of 101 countries applying for visas of more than six months, and all other passengers pre-screened by airlines before departure. With the exception of special orders given at times of a particular disease threat, such as Ebola, little medical screening is carried out as a matter of course at the major ports of entry. Economic screening is now the primary tool of border control in both external and internal border control. Where those borders lie is a central question in the continuing Brexit negotiations. However, the durable elasticity of the UK border, that has shifted and modified numerous times since 1905, should mean that any changes brought with Britain's new relationship to Europe will not be fixed in place.

Notes

1 France 'will definitely close UK border at Calais', BBC News, 16 November 2016, www.bbc.com/news/uk-politics-37921598.
2 'Britain to push post-Brexit UK immigration controls back to Irish border', *Guardian*, 10 October 2016.
3 Krista Maglen, *The English System: Quarantine, Immigration and the Making of a Port Sanitary Zone* (Manchester: Manchester University Press 2014).
4 Ibid.
5 Geoffrey Alderman and Colin Holmes (eds), *Outsiders and Outcasts – Essays in Honour of William J. Fishman* (London: Gerald Duckworth & Co 1993); Geoffrey Alderman, *London Jewry and London Politics 1889–1986* (London: Routledge 1989); Kenneth E. Collins, *Second City Jewry: The Jews of Glasgow in the Age of Expansion, 1790–1919*, 1st edn (Glasgow: Scottish Jewish Archives 1990); Cecil Bloom, 'The politics of immigration, 1881–1905', *Jewish Historical Studies – Transactions of the Jewish Historical Society of England* vol. xxxiii (1992–1994), 187–214; David Feldman, *Englishmen and Jews: Social Relations and Political Culture 1840–1914* (New Haven: Yale University Press 1994); John A. Garrard, *The English and Immigration 1880–1910* (London: Oxford University Press 1971); Lloyd P. Gartner, *The Jewish Immigrant in England 1870–1914* (London: George

Allen & Unwin 1960); Colin Holmes, *John Bull's Island: Immigration and British Society 1871–1971* (London: Macmillan Press Ltd 1988); Panikos Panayi, *Immigration, Ethnicity, and Racism in Britain 1815–1945* (Manchester: Manchester University Press 1994); Kenneth Lunn (ed.), *Hosts, Immigrants and Minorities: Historical Responses to Newcomers in British Society, 1870–1914* (Folkestone: Dawson 1980); Aubrey Newman (ed.), *The Jewish East End, 1840–1939* (London: Jewish Historical Society of England 1981).

6 Waltraud Ernst and Bernard Harris (eds), *Race, Science and Medicine, 1700–1960* (London: Routledge 1999); Bernard Harris, 'Anti-Alienism, health and social reform in Late Victorian and Edwardian Britain', *Patterns of Prejudice* vol. 31, 1997, 3–34; Lara Marks, 'Ethnicity, religion and health care', *Social History of Medicine* vol. 4, no. 1, 1991, 123–128; Lara Marks and Michael Worboys (eds), *Migrants, Minorities and Health – Historical and Contemporary Studies* (London: Routledge 2000); Lara Marks, *Model Mothers: Jewish Mothers and Maternity Provision in East London, 1870–1939* (Oxford: Clarendon Press 1994); Anne Hardy, *The Epidemic Streets: Infectious Diseases and the Rise of Preventive Medicine 1856–1900* (Oxford: Oxford University Press 1993).

7 Kenneth E. Collins, *Be Well! Jewish Immigrant Health and Welfare in Glasgow, 1860–1914* (East Linton, Scotland: Tuckwell Press 2001).

8 Hardy, *Epidemic Streets*, 203.

9 Marks, *Model Mothers*.

10 For example: Graham Mooney, *Intrusive Interventions: Public Health, Domestic Space, and Infectious Disease Surveillance in England, 1840–1914* (Rochester NY: Rochester University Press 2015); John Booker, *Maritime Quarantine: The British Experience, C.1650–1900* (Aldershot: Ashgate 2007); Tim Carter, *Merchant Seamen's Health, 1860–1960: Medicine, Technology, Shipowners and the State in Britain* (Woodbridge: The Boydell Press 2014).

11 Amy Fairchild, *Science at the Borders: Immigrant Medical Inspection and the Shaping of the Modern Industrial Labor Force* (Baltimore: Johns Hopkins University Press 2003); Nayan Shah, *Contagious Divides: Epidemics and Race in San Francisco's Chinatown* (Berkeley: University of California Press 2001); Alexandra Minna Stern, 'Buildings, boundaries, and blood: medicalization and nation-building on the U.S.-Mexico border, 1910–1930', *The Hispanic American Historical Review* vol. 79, no. 1, 1999, 41–81; Howard Markel and Alexandra Minna Stern, 'Which face? Whose nation? Immigration, public health, and the construction of disease at America's ports and orders, 1891–1928', *American Behavioral Scientist* vol. 42, no. 9, 1999, 1314–1331; Alan M. Kraut, *Silent Travelers: Germs, Genes, and the 'Immigrant Menace'* (Baltimore: Johns Hopkins University Press 1995); Alan Kraut, 'Plagues and prejudice: Nativism's construction of disease in nineteenth- and twentieth-century New York City', in David Rosner (ed.), *Hives of Sickness: Public Health and Epidemics in New York City* (New Brunswick: Rutgers University Press 1995), 65–90; Anne-Emanuelle Birn, 'Six seconds per eyelid: The medical inspection of immigrants at Ellis Island, 1892–1914', *Dynamis* vol. 17, 1997, 281–316; Dirk Hoerder and Horst Rössler (eds), *Distant Magnets: Expectations and Realities in the Immigration Experience 1840–1930* (New York: Holmes & Meier Publishers, Inc, 1993); Howard Markel, 'Cholera, quarantines, and immigration restriction: The view from Johns Hopkins, 1892', *Bulletin of the History of Medicine* vol. 67, 1993, 691–695; Howard Markel, '"Knocking out the cholera": Cholera, class, and quarantines in New York City, 1892', *Bulletin of the History of Medicine* vol. 69, 1995, 420–457; Howard Markel, *Quarantine! East European Jewish Immigrants and the New York City Epidemics of 1892* (Baltimore: Johns Hopkins University Press 1997); Howard Markel and Alexandra Minna Stern, 'All quiet on the Third Coast: Medical inspections of immigrants in Michigan', *Public Health Reports* vol. 114, no. 2, 1999, 178–182; John Parascandola, 'Doctors at the gate: PHS at Ellis Island', *Public Health Reports* vol. 113, no. 1, 1998, 83–86; Charles E. Rosenberg, *The Cholera Years – The United States in*

1832, 1849, and 1866, With a New Forward edn. (Chicago: University of Chicago Press 1987); R. T. Solis-Cohen, 'The exclusion of aliens from the United States for physical defects', *Bulletin of the History of Medicine* vol. 21, no. 1, 1947, 33–50.
12 Markel, *Quarantine!*, 5.
13 Fairchild, *Science at the Borders*, 16.
14 Peter Baldwin, *Contagion and the State in Europe, 1830–1930* (Cambridge: Cambridge University Press 1999).
15 *The Lancet*, 3 September 1892, 592.
16 'Complaints of the German YMCA, London', letter dated 27 April 1893, CLRO PSCP, (June–Aug., 1893).
17 Katherine Foxhall, 'Fever, immigration and quarantine in New South Wales, 1837–1840', *Social History of Medicine* vol. 24, no. 3, 2011, 624–642 (639).
18 Evidence of Dr Herbert Williams, Report of the Royal Commission on Alien Immigration (London: HMSO, 1903) Vol. II – Minutes of Evidence, [Cd.1742] 7131–7142.
19 Evidence of Dr Shirley Murphy, *RCAI Minutes*, 5007.
20 *Report of the Royal Commission on Alien Immigration* (London: HMSO, 1903) Vol. I – The Report, [Cd.1741], 'Memorandum', 49.
21 Ibid, 41, Recommendation, 4)g).

16

THE EVOLVING HISTORIOGRAPHY OF THE EXTREME RIGHT IN BRITAIN

Graham Macklin

In recent decades, historians have forged an increasingly sophisticated set of analytical tools through which to understand and interpret Fascism. Whether by design or default Colin Holmes', *Searching for Lord Haw-Haw: The Political Lives of William Joyce* (2016), the culmination of a lifetime's research on conspiratorial antisemitism and British fascism, alights upon many of these prevailing developments. Focusing on the tawdry and brutish life of William Joyce, the former Director of Propaganda for Sir Oswald Mosley's British Union of Fascists (BUF), who earned notoriety as one of Britain's most notorious renegades; hanged for treachery in 1946 after broadcasting for the Nazis during the Second World War, Holmes' study provides a prism through which many of these historiographical developments refract. Indeed, it is emblematic of developments such as the 'cultural' turn in the study of Fascism; the increased attention to its transnationalism and 'universal' appeal; the importance of understanding its *groupuscular* organisation; its extreme misogyny; and, as Holmes has shown repeatedly during his career, the centrality of antisemitism to its racial nationalist worldview. The subject of Holmes' biography reinforces another historiographical trend, the increased willingness of scholars to move beyond a mono-dimensional focus on the figure of Sir Oswald Mosley, erstwhile Leader of the BUF, the organisation he founded in 1932 as a vehicle for his frustrated authoritarian ambitions.

Traditionally, and with the exception perhaps of dystopian fiction, there is one overarching historiographical argument: British fascism was not just a 'failure' but an 'inevitable failure' because it was 'alien' to British political and cultural traditions, nourishing a comfortable and comforting national myth of Britain as a 'tolerant country'.[1] In keeping with this argument, there was something irrevocably 'foreign' about 'Fascism' politically, culturally and aesthetically. The historian Sir Charles Petrie was perhaps only half joking when he suggested that had Mosley decked his followers out in blue pullovers, instead of aping Mussolini's Blackshirts, 'much would have been forgiven him'. There is also tendency within the literature, which bends towards personification, which harnesses the history of broader movement to the biography of a single individual. For historians like Robert Paxton the BUF represents 'one of the most interesting failures' precisely because it was the vehicle upon which Mosley squandered his supposedly considerable political talents: fascism as personal tragedy. This narrative, of wasted intellect squandered on gutter politics, has continued to endure.

Within this narrative exists a second strain of interpretation predicated upon a basic incredulity as to why one would bother studying such an 'unsuccessful' phenomenon in the first place. Stanley Payne once imperiously dismissed British fascism as a 'political oxymoron' that had generated a voluminous literature 'inversely proportionate to its significance'. Seeing no need to add further to such self-evidently superfluous scholarship, Payne devoted a mere three pages, one of which was photos, to the British case in *A History of Fascism, 1914–1945* (1996), out of a total of 613. Other verdicts are equally withering: 'Seldom indeed, has so much ever been written about so little,' opines W. D. Rubinstein, whilst Anthony Julius scorns British fascism as both dreary and derivative. Such arguments have been internalised by historians of British fascism themselves. Richard Thurlow, author of the seminal *Fascism in Britain*, which first appeared in 1987 and was updated in 1998, felt compelled to agree with Payne that 'rarely can such an apparently insignificant topic have been responsible for such an outpouring of ink'. Such reservations did not preclude him from adding a further 298 pages to the topic, however.[2] Other historians, writing later but no less apologetically, have continued in the same vein, lamenting that British fascism's historiographical cannon was now so 'vast' that 'it even surpasses the attention conferred on the Blackshirts during the 1930s'.[3]

This relatively brief historiographical survey aims to examine some of the main trends in the evolving historiography of British fascism and extreme right-wing politics before moving on to note a few examples from the present author's own approach to the subject which has wilfully added to this supposedly unnecessary 'outpouring of ink'. The first serious attempts to historicise British fascism took place in the immediate aftermath of the Second World War when many understandably assumed that it was safe to speak of the phenomenon in the past tense. Two of the earliest studies were particularly notable. *Fascism Inside England* (1946) by Frederick Mullally, an assistant editor at *Tribune*, provided perhaps the first historical overview of the movement and was written amidst the first rumblings of a 'neo-fascist movement'. Mullally was one of the first to publicly employ the term 'neo-fascist' in a British context as such groups began to re-emerge on East London's streets. The second had a rather different focus. *Racketeers of Hatred* (1946) by Louis Bondy, a London-based antiquarian bookseller, provided a well-researched account of the role British fascist activists played in the international antisemitic machinations of the Nazi propaganda machine. It remains useful to this day.

Thereafter there was a fifteen-year hiatus before British fascism received a substantive treatment. First out of the gate was *The Fascists in Britain* (1961), penned by Colin Cross, a political journalist and lobby correspondent, which provided a breezy overview of interwar British fascism, sketching out its main parameters. It was another eight years, however, before Robert Benewick provided the first historical treatment with *Political Violence and Public Order: A Study of British Fascism* (1969), subsequently revised in 1972. Viewing British fascism through a public order lens led Benewick to conclude that its legacy as a political tradition was located not so much in its obvious racialism, 'but the principle established that it is just and proper to legislate for the protection of a particular segment of the community'.[4] Regardless of whether one agrees with this interpretation or not, its verdict, that British fascism was principally important insofar as it provided insight into the state management of public order, was influential for historians including Thurlow.

The next development driving forward scholarship came from within the fascist movement itself. The publication of Mosley's self-exculpatory memoir, *My Life* (1968), piqued scholastic and public interest, which gathered further momentum with the publication of *Oswald Mosley* (1975), a widely acclaimed though deeply flawed biography by Robert Skidelsky, a young Oxford graduate friendly with Mosley's son at university. Thereafter two less than flattering volumes of memoirs by Mosley's eldest son, Nicholas, *Rules of the Game* (1982) and *Beyond the Pale* (1983), offered historians new insights into the internal dynamics of British fascism, whilst simultaneously angering and appalling Mosley's wife and children who perceived their revelations as a betrayal.

Thereafter, another external factor propelled research and interpretation forward. Growing agitation for the release of Home Office files relating to British fascism which ironically united left-wing MPs with right-wingers and fascist sympathisers bore fruit with the release of the 'Mosley papers' – four tranches of files released between 1981 and 1986. Though the state retained a vast swathe of records, this partial disclosure gifted historians a wealth of new primary material relating to British fascism and State management of political extremism. This new documentary trove provided the basis for several future studies including Thurlow's *Fascism in Britain* (1987). A decade later historical scholarship received a further boost following the release of a further wave of primary material, this time from the Security Services (MI5), who from 1997 onwards, have bi-annually deposited large tranches of material that significantly augment our knowledge, both of interwar and early post-war periods, particularly in relation to its transnational dimensions and internal dynamics.

If the interpretive drivers of change were principally archival during this period, the focus of study remained largely unchanged. Mosley continues to dominate the historiography, which also automatically skewed scholarly attention towards the interwar years. Stephen Dorril's monumental biography, *Blackshirt* (2006), for all the wealth of new information it provided, was largely centred upon the 1930s though also provided some illuminating insights into Mosley's post-war activities too. Two subsequent studies tracked further backwards rather than forwards. David Howell's *Mosley and British Politics, 1918–1932* (2014) charting 'Oswald's odyssey' from socialism to fascism, whilst Matthew Worley's more narrowly focused *Oswald*

Mosley and the New Party (2010) assessed Mosley's failed and frustrated attempts to realign British politics in 1931 following his departure from the Labour Party. Both focused on Mosley's pre-fascist career. My own monograph, *'Very Deeply Dyed in Black': Sir Oswald Mosley and the Resurrection of British Fascism after 1945* (2007), was one of the first works giving sustained attention to Mosley's post-war politics and his efforts to reanimate fascism around a 'Europe-a-Nation' – a creed at odds with the 'Britain First' fascism of the 1930s.[5]

The historiographical focus has, however, broadened out to encompass Mosley's leading lieutenants. This is not an altogether novel development. W. F. Mandle originally surveyed the upper echelons of the BUF in 1966[6] though it was another thirty years before the first detailed historical treatments of individual ideologues began to surface – the exception being William Joyce, on whom more below. Key ideologues and propagandists like A. K. Chesterton, John Beckett, Wilfred Risdon and Jorian Jenks have all received their biographical due though, ironically, Alexander Raven Thomson, the leading BUF ideologue, still awaits a published biography.[7] The lower tiers of BUF membership have not benefitted from the same level of scholarly attention, however. Despite G. C. Webber's pathbreaking study of the BUF membership in 1984[8] it was nearly another two decades before the East End epicentre of BUF support received the attention it deserved with Tom Linehan's *East End for Mosley* (1996). Julie Gottlieb (2003) has provided a notable survey of the female membership, complemented by individual biographies,[9] whilst Tom Villis (2013) has since brought the notable Catholic component of its membership into relief. The historiography has continued to expand beyond biographies and memberships to explore a range of 'regional' variants too, though much of this research currently remains buried in unpublished PhD theses.[10] Likewise, a burgeoning interest in 'sub-national' fascisms has yielded case studies of Wales,[11] Scotland[12] and Northern Ireland,[13] enhancing our understanding of the wider dimensions of 'British' fascism, oft treated as a synonym for 'English'.

Holmes' biography of Joyce highlights and indeed reinforces another thematic trend that emerges from the historiography, a 'patriotism perverted' by a pathological antisemitism that drove numerous fascists and their fellow travellers into the National Socialist camp and thereafter into treachery. The overarching trajectory of this pro-Nazi tendency (which moved politically, socially and indeed psychologically from a position of ardent appeasement during the 1930s to shame, guilt and denial after 1945) sits at the heart of a triptych of works published over four decades by Richard Griffiths: *Fellow Travellers of the Right* (1980); *Patriotism Perverted: Captain Ramsay, the Right Club and British Anti-Semitism, 1939–40* (1998); and *What Did You Do During the war? The Last Throes of the Pro-Nazi Right, 1940–1945* (2016). This fascinating trilogy has since been complemented by Paul Willetts, *Rendezvous and the Russia Tea Rooms* (2016) which shines further light on the hardcore subversive antisemitic milieu grouped around Captain Maule Ramsay and Anna Wolkoff.

The release of MI5 files has also enabled several enlightening studies which deepen our knowledge of the government response to British fascism, namely the role of the Security Services in demolishing the movement in May 1940. *The Secret*

War Between the Wars: MI5 in the 1920s and 1930s (2014) by Kevin Quinlan made judicious use of these files as does *M: Maxwell Knight, MI5's Greatest Spymaster* (2017), an illuminating new biography of the famed MI5 agent-runner Charles Maxwell Knight who oversaw the covert operation that persuaded the British government to ban the BUF and to intern its leading luminaries. The activities of the 'fifth column' during the 'Phoney War' period has also generated considerable interest. A. W. Brian Simpson's magnum opus, *In the Highest Degree Odious: Detention Without Trial in Wartime Britain* (1992), remains, and probably will remain for the time being, the standard work on the internment of British fascists during the summer of 1940. That said, the continued release of MI5 files to The National Archives has greatly enhanced our knowledge of this 'watershed moment' in British fascism's history.[14]

May 1940 did indeed constitute a historical caesura. Internment brought British fascism to a grinding halt a full five years before Nazism's own *Götterdämmerung* in 1945. Thereafter the historical reputation of British fascism was irreparably tarnished by the disgrace of its past glorification of Nazism, to which it had eagerly hitched its wagon. This placed its adherents and exponents firmly on the wrong side of the national narrative as victors in an 'anti-fascist' war – the cornerstone of post-1945 British history. It is perhaps for this reason that Joyce's treachery continues to fascinate, amplifying this stigma. Indeed, as Holmes shows in his discussion of the lengths British fascists went to manipulate history in a bid to exonerate him and *ergo* themselves, they were only too aware of the lasting damage his actions inflicted upon the movement.

Joyce's life spawned numerous biographies prior to Holmes' own definitive study, the first published only two years after his execution: *The Meaning of Treason* (1949) by Rebecca West. This interest shows no sign of abating. Indeed, Holmes' biography has not been the last. Joyce is central to Josh Ireland's *The Traitors* (2017), which explores his life alongside several other notorious British collaborators. Whilst Joyce was emblematic of treachery, numerous others chose the same path, many profiled in Sean Murphy's *Letting the Side Down: British Traitors of the Second World War* (2003) whilst the activities of those who joined the British Free Corps, a shambolic assemblage of deserters, dreamers, adventurers and brigands whom the Nazis sought to mould into a British Waffen-SS unit, are detailed in Adrian Weale's *Renegades: Hitler's Englishmen* (2002) which remains the best overarching account.

Anti-fascists mocked Mosley's symbol, the flash and circle, which depicted 'unity in action', as being no more than a 'flash in the pan'.[15] This was true in a wider historical sense. The BUF lasted only eight years – from 1932 to 1940 – highlighting a structural problem: the historiography of British fascism remains disproportionately weighted towards the study of these eight years to the detriment of the movement's subsequent post-war trajectory, which has already temporally exceeded the existence of Mosley's brief interwar interlude to the power of ten. One might speculate as to the reasons for this imbalance. The overarching one relates perhaps to the question of perceived historical importance. Historians of post-war fascism have faced a further uphill struggle to convince the doyens of 'Fascist Studies' that 'Fascism' even existed as a phenomenon after 1945. Whilst space precludes a wider examination of this debate one might briefly summarise by stating that for these scholars 'Fascism' was the product of a unique historical 'epoch' with a finite end and thus could safely be considered 'dead' after its military defeat. This conceptualisation undoubtedly stunted the temporal development of the field beyond 1945, at least initially. Insofar as the British case is concerned academic interest in post-war British fascism remained virtually non-existent, meaning that the proliferation of violent, racist *groupuscules* and their firebrand leaders active from the 1940s onwards were of quixotic interest only to journalists like George C. Thayer, author of *The British Political Fringe* (1965), himself, perhaps tellingly, an American, who was one of the few to expend any serious effort exploring the survival and perpetuation of the racial nationalist and 'Jew wise' tradition.

The political threat posed by the rise of the National Front (NF) in the aftermath of Enoch Powell's 'Rivers of Blood' speech and the ongoing politicisation of immigration reenergised journalistic and academic interest in extreme right-wing politics. Even then, however, it was not for a full decade after its foundation that the first account of the NF and its political roots appeared, penned by *The Guardian* journalist Martin Walker (1977). There followed several important psychological (Billig in 1978), sociological (Fielding in 1981) and political science (Taylor in 1982) studies. Historians by comparison were slow into the breach. Once the political threat posed by the NF subsidised, following its calamitous showing in the 1979 general election, so too did academic interest in the continued interest in the extreme right. Ironically, half a century after its foundation, the NF, which posed a greater electoral threat than Mosley's BUF ever did, still awaits a serious historical treatment.

But whilst historians have perhaps been slow to provide empirical histories of post-war, extreme right-wing groups, major developments have taken place with regards their conceptual apparatus. The 'cultural turn' in history was, for scholars of British fascism, magnified by Roger Griffin's slightly mischievous assertion that a 'new consensus' had now emerged surrounding the 'primacy of culture' within the discipline.[16] Whilst the debate arising from Griffin's claim is beyond the scope of this survey, the focus upon fascism as a 'cultural' rather than simply a 'political' movement, which it highlighted, certainly precipitated an analytical reinvigoration of the field, redirecting it away from well-trodden debates about the 'failure' of British fascism towards more nuanced understandings of the fascist 'experience' from within. This new methodological and theoretical approach begat several illuminating studies including Linehan's *British Fascism* (2000) and Gottlieb and Linehan's *The Culture of Fascism* (2004), whilst Copsey and Richardson's *Cultures of Post-War British Fascism* (2015) and Copsey and Worley's *'Tomorrow Belongs to Us': The British Far Right since 1967* (2018), extended the insights gleaned from this re-articulation of fascist history into the post-war period.

This new cultural paradigm also spoke to the corpus of Holmes' scholarship: the centrality of antisemitism and antisemitic conspiracy theory to British fascism, exemplified in both *Anti-Semitism in British Society, 1876–1939* (1979) and, latterly, his biography of Joyce. Indeed, as the anti-fascist playwright David Edgar observed in 1977, 'conspiracy theory runs through contemporary British fascist ideology like Blackpool runs through rock'.[17] Holmes was not of course the first scholar to recognise this. W. F. Mandle's *Anti-Semitism and the British Union of Fascists* (1968) appeared, ironically, the same year as Mosley's autobiographical effusion sought to ventilate his reputation for antisemitic politicking for which, in the shadow of the Holocaust, had blighted efforts to resurrect his political career. However, one of Holmes' lasting contributions has been the appreciation that antisemitism was never simply a vector through which to mobilise crude racial and religious hostility in support of fascist ideologies, but rather an explanatory and interpretive ideological frame through which the nation's ills were diagnosed and its 'cure' prescribed. This focus, to which cultural renditions of British fascist ideology have added, endures. Daniel Tilles' *British Fascist Anti-Semitism and Jewish Responses, 1932–1940* (2016) recently explicitly re-centred the role of anti-Jewish prejudice within British fascist ideology, whilst providing new insights into how the Jewish community fought to countermand its influence.

My own work, which has also focused heavily upon significance of anti-Jewish prejudice for extreme right-wing groups, undoubtedly owes much to Holmes' influence, not least because as an undergraduate I sat his course on antisemitism in British society at Sheffield University. My first academic publication was a micro-study of an 'anti-alien' agitation in Hampstead, north London, highlighting how antisemitism provided the *modus operandi* for fascist *groupuscules* through which they sought to reanimate public support for their cause after 1945.[18] Many of those involved in this antisemitic protest graduated to playing a pivotal role in the formation of Mosley's Union Movement in 1948, the focus of my first monograph, *Very Deeply Dyed in Black*. Further studies have examined this persistence of prejudice through a biographical prism. The first, an excavation of the 'two lives' of the architectural historian John Hooper Harvey[19] who, over the course of a lifetime, held, articulated and refined his antisemitic prejudice, enabling his belief in the 'blood libel' to transition from visceral pro-Nazi publications to academic textbooks. The second, an exposition on Robert Gordon-Canning, one of Mosley's leading lieutenants whose long-standing personal entanglements and interests in the Middle East, including a friendship with the Mufti of Jerusalem, who shared his hatred of Jews, fused in his mind to become a call for a 'Fascist Jihad'.[20]

Much work remains to be done, however. More research is needed into the role of more minor individuals, publishing houses and grouplets for the propagation of antisemitic animus. Groups such as the British Brothers League, organised by William Henry Shaw to agitate against Jewish immigration in East London in 1902, are in dire need of a historian to lift them from obscurity and establish their importance for the subsequent evolution of extreme right-wing movements, the BUF included. Likewise much remains to be said about the plethora of 'Jew wise' groups littering Britain's antisemitic demi-monde during the 1920s and 30s, though Nick Toczek's *Haiters, Baiters and Would-Be Dictators* (2016), a non-academic study of The

Britons publishing house and its founder Henry Hamilton Beamish marks a start in this direction.[21] Historians might further enrich our understanding by providing further studies of the Chester-Belloc circle, or indeed figures like Nesta Webster, the 'grand dame' of conspiracy theory.

Addressing the temporal imbalance within British fascist ideology mentioned earlier, my own research has focused largely, though by no means exclusively, upon the post-war period, examining the role of extreme right-wing *groupuscules* as important 'carrier groups' for ideological experimentation, evolution and transmission, as a means of keeping the 'sacred flame' alive until the liberal interregnum crumbles and a 'new dawn' rises.[22] Transnational approaches to history have also impacted our perceptions of how extreme right-wing movements have evolved together rather than being isolated within hermetically sealed 'national' histories.[23] This has been the focus of my most recent research exploring various facets of horizontal exchange and interchange between extreme right-wing movements and activists in the post-war period,[24] whilst also retaining a focus upon the evolution of antisemitic conspiracy theories within a transnational context.[25]

For many years, the study of post-war British extreme right interested only a handful of historians. In recent years, however, the field has expanded exponentially, perhaps because of scholars reaching saturation point with regards the interwar period, for the time being at least. To date the bulk of attention has been lavished, unsurprisingly, upon Britain's neo-Nazi tradition. Notable studies including *White Riot: The Violent Story of Combat 18* (2001) and *Mr. Evil* (2000), a biography of the London 'nail bomber' David Copeland, both by anti-fascist journalist Nick Lowles. Historians, however, have made serious exertions to excavate the milieu, reflected in Nicholas Goodrick-Clarke's *Black Sun: Aryan Cults, Esoteric Nazism, and the Politics of Identity* (2001) and Paul Jackson's *Colin Jordan and Britain's neo-Nazi Movement* (2016), a study of Britain's 'neo-nazi godfather' – another study made possible by new archival releases.

Political events themselves, as much as archival releases, have regularly driven the focus of scholarly research too. In this regard, the limited electoral insurgency of the British National Party (BNP) between 2002 and 2010 was no different. Scholars were rather faster responding to the rise of the BNP than they had been to the NF in the 1970s. A flurry of scholarly articles followed, as did as several monographs foremost amongst which were Nigel Copsey's *Contemporary British Fascism* (2009), which focused on the party's short-lived 'quest for legitimacy' and Matthew Goodwin's *New British Fascism* (2011), which illuminated the nature of the party's membership, electoral support, and voter base.[26] Whilst historians, political scientists and sociologists have dominated the field, it has not been their sole preserve. John Richardson's *British Fascism: A Discourse-Historical Analysis* (2017) employs discourse analysis to critically interrogate fascist linguistics, providing an indispensable study in the process. Whilst slightly beyond the purvey of this historiographical survey, in the sense that it is not a racial nationalist or 'fascist' movement, the English Defence League and its accompanying anti-Muslim satellites have been the subject of superlative sociological studies by Joel Busher, *The Making of Anti-Muslim Protest*

(2016) and Hilary Pilkington, *Loud and Proud* (2016). My latest work, a forthcoming monograph, tentatively entitled *White Racial Nationalism in Britain* (2018), seeks to draw many of these strands together, through an exploration of the ideological and political evolution of the British fascist tradition from its origins in the obscure racial nationalist and pro-Nazi sects of the interwar period but with especial emphasis upon its post-war development. It is hoped that this study might provoke historians to more fully understand, and to take more seriously, the importance of studying post-war extreme right-wing politics.

One final development worthy of mention relates to the historical trajectory of British fascism itself. Extreme right-wing mobilisation rarely takes place without stimulating opposition and yet our understanding of anti-fascist and anti-racist counter-mobilisations, at both local and national levels, often lags behind, focusing on 'set-piece' skirmishes instead of unearthing how sustained resistance has shaped the subsequent trajectory of extreme right-wing and fascist politics. National studies such as Copsey's *Anti-Fascism in Britain* (2000) have, however, recently been augmented by detailed case studies of cultural resistance to the extreme right, encompassing the Anti-Nazi League and Rock Against Racism as well as political and physical resistance to the extreme right from the 'Battle of Cable Street', which inflicted a symbolic though by no means fatal defeat on the BUF in 1936, through to studies of groups like the Asian Youth Movement in the 1970s.

There are many known unknowns with regards the evolution of the post-war extreme right, and much remains to be said about local and transnational cultures and networks of mobilisation. The continued excavation of its post-war movements, ideologies and adherents will, however, enable scholars to better map the continued morphology of extreme right-wing politics in Britain. Meanwhile the development and deployment of increasingly sophisticated interpretative tools, when coupled with the ongoing dialectic between new archival releases and new possibilities for scholarship, continues to pave the way for exciting, innovative, historical research.

Notes

1 Martin Pugh, *'Hurrah for the Blackshirts': Fascism and Fascists in Britain between the Wars* (London: Pimlico 2006), 1.
2 Richard C. Thurlow, *Fascism in Britain: From Oswald Mosley's Blackshirts to the National Front* (London: I.B. Tauris 1998), x.
3 Julie V. Gottlieb, *Feminine Fascism: Women in Britain's Fascist Movement* (London: I. B. Taurus 2003), 2. For a comprehensive bibliographic survey see Philip Rees *Fascism in Britain* (Sussex: Harvester 1979). Craig Fowlie, 'The British Far Right since 1967 – A bibliographic survey', in Nigel Copsey and Matthew Worley (eds), *Tomorrow Belongs to Us: The British Far Right Since 1967* (Abingdon: Routledge 2018) provides a more up-to-date overview.
4 Robert Benewick, *The Fascist Movement in Britain* (London: Allen Lane 1973), 305.
5 David Renton, *Fascism, Anti-Fascism and Britain in the 1940s* (Basingstoke: Palgrave McMillan 200) also explores this era.
6 W. F. Mandle, 'The leadership of the British Union of Fascists', *Australian Journal of Politics and History* vol. 12, no. 3, December 1966, 360–383.

7 There is, however, Peter Pugh 'A Critical Biography of Alexander Raven Thomson', PhD thesis, University of Sheffield, 2003 and Matthew McMurray, 'Alexander Raven Thomson, philosopher of the British Union of Fascists', *The European Legacy* vol. 17, no. 1, 2012, 33–59.
8 G. C. Webber, 'Patterns of membership and support for the British Union of Fascists', *Journal of Contemporary History* vol. 19, no. 4, 1984, 575–606.
9 See for instance Susan and Angela McPherson, *Mosley's Old Suffragette: A Biography of Norah Dacre Fox* (Raleigh, NC: Lulu Enterprises Inc. 2011); Nina Boyd, *From Suffragette to Fascist: The Many Lives of Mary Sophia Allen* (Stroud: History Press 2013); Stephen M. Cullen, *Fanatical Fay Taylour: Her Sporting and Political Life at Speed, 1904–1983* (Warwick: Allotment Hut 2015).
10 Craig Morgan, 'The British Union of Fascists in the Midlands, 1932–1940' (PhD thesis, Wolverhampton University 2003) and Andrew Mitchell 'Fascism in East Anglia: the British Union of Fascists in Norfolk, Suffolk and Essex, 1933–1940', PhD thesis, University of Sheffield. 1999 for instance.
11 Richard Wynn Jones, *The Fascist Party in Wales?* (Cardiff: University of Wales Press 2014).
12 Gavin Bowd, *Fascist Scotland: Caledonia and the Far Right* (Edinburgh: Birlinn 2013).
13 James Loughlin, 'Rotha Lintorn-Orman, Ulster and the British Fascists movement', *Immigrants & Minorities* vol. 32, no. 1, 2014, 62–89 and James Loughlin, 'Hailing Hitler with the Red Hand: The Link in Northern Ireland 1937–40', *Patterns of Prejudice* vol. 50, no. 3, 2016, 276–301.
14 Jennifer Grant, 'The Role of MI5 in the internment of British Fascists during the Second World War', *Intelligence and National Security* vol. 24, no. 4, 2009, 499–528 highlights what can be learned from these new releases.
15 Nigel Jones, *Mosley* (London: Haus 2004), 113.
16 Roger Griffin, 'The primacy of culture: The current growth (or manufacture) of consensus within Fascist Studies', *Journal of Contemporary History* vol. 37, no. 1 (2002), 21–43.
17 David Edgar, 'Racism, Fascism and the politics of the National Front', *Race and Class* vol. 19, no. 2, 1977, 111–131 (116).
18 Graham Macklin, '"A quite natural and moderate defensive feeling"? The 1945 Hampstead "anti-alien" petition', *Patterns of Prejudice* vol. 37, no. 3, 2003, 277–300.
19 Graham Macklin, 'The two lives of John Hooper Harvey', *Patterns of Prejudice* vol. 42, no. 2, 2008, 167–190.
20 Graham Macklin, 'A Fascist "Jihad": Captain Robert Gordon-Canning, British Fascist Antisemitism and Islam', *Holocaust Studies* vol. 15, nos. 1–2, 2009, 78–100.
21 Nick Tozcek, *Haters, Baiters and Would-Be Dictators: Anti-Semitism and the UK Far Right* (Abingdon: Routledge 2016).
22 For instance, Graham Macklin 'Co-opting the counter culture: Troy Southgate and the National Revolutionary Faction', *Patterns of Prejudice* vol. 39, no. 3, 2005, 301–326 and Graham Macklin 'The "cultic milieu" of Britain's "New Right": Meta-political "fascism" in contemporary Britain', in Nigel Copsey and John E. Richardson (eds), *Cultures of Post-War British Fascism* (Abingdon: Routledge 2015) 177–201.
23 For two notable exceptions see Andrea Mammone, *Transnational Neofascism in France and Italy* (Cambridge: Cambridge University Press 2015) and Matteo Albanese and Pietro del Hierro, *Transnational Fascism in the Twentieth Century: Spain, Italy and the Global Neo-Fascist Network* (2016).
24 Graham Macklin, 'The British far right's South African connection: A. K. Chesterton, Hendrik van den Bergh and the South African intelligence services', *Intelligence and National Security* vol. 25, no. 6, 2010, 823–842; 'Transnational activism on the far right: The case of the BNP and the NPD', *West European Politics* vol. 36, no. 1, 2013, 176–198; and

'"There's a vital lesson here. Let's make sure we learn it": Transnational mobilization and the impact of Greece's Golden Dawn upon extreme right-wing activism in Britain', in Nigel Copsey and Matthew Worley (eds), *Tomorrow Belongs to Me* (Abingdon: Routledge 2017) 185–207.
25 Graham Macklin, 'Transatlantic connections and conspiracies: A. K. Chesterton and *The New Unhappy Lords*', *Journal of Contemporary History* vol. 47, no. 2, 2012, 240–269.
26 Matthew J. Goodwin, *New British Fascism: Rise of the British National Party* (Abingdon: Routledge 2011).

SECTION 5
Marginal, neglected and reimagined histories

Jennifer Craig-Norton

Introduction

Numerous contributors to this volume have demonstrated the impact of the Sheffield School on the development of immigrant and minority historiography, both within the UK and in broader, transnational contexts. Nearly three decades ago, Colin Holmes' *John Bull's Island* greatly widened the field by exploring the migration of over fifty national/ethnic/religious groups to Great Britain, inviting both further investigation of those immigrant groups and the expansion of the discipline by later scholars. The maturation of migration and minority studies in the intervening period has produced a substantial body of scholarship that encompasses detailed examinations of the movement, reception, adaptation, integration and identity of specific migrant/minority groups as well as meta-analysis of migration and transmigratory patterns. These developments have also highlighted the fact that some migrant groups whose histories were once neglected or marginalised are now far less so, while others whose histories were once well known later fell out of mainstream discourse. The welcome and sustained growth of the field has indicated new directions for research, or the need for re-evaluation and re-examination of prior studies, both through new insights – such as Gemma Romain's contribution to the conference focusing on LGBT themes – and new archival discoveries, which herald the emergence of untapped subjects meriting inquiry and analysis. Twenty-first century scholars approaching these neglected and marginalised histories, whether from British, pan-European or global perspectives, draw upon the earlier work of pioneers in the field who challenged existing paradigms and narratives, bringing fresh perspectives and new voices to migrant and minority studies.

Contemporary historical investigations have revealed that in some cases, these neglected histories, while ignored in current historiography, have actually been well documented in other contexts. Thus, Milosz Cybowski, in his study of Britain's early nineteenth-century Polish refugees, has contrasted the contemporaneous visibility of the émigrés in 1830s and 1840s and their extensive coverage in later Polish scholarship with their near invisibility in modern British migration historiography. Cybowski demonstrates a confluence a factors: an emphasis on the political activities of Polish migrants, a relative lack of interest in early nineteenth-century migration by British historians and a subsuming of Polish-British immigration within larger contexts of Polish-European exile contributed to their having been pushed to the margins of British migration studies, despite having been the largest minority refugee group in Britain at the time. Though widely recognised, discussed and even financially supported by the British government, Cybowski argues that a waning interest in the Poles' fates, especially after 1850, contributed to their having been pushed to the margins of modern narratives of British migration.

Asians are another migrant group whose complete story had been neglected in contemporary British historiography. Prior to Rozina Visram's pioneering studies in the 1980s, the predominant narrative examined Asian migration as a post-Second World War, postcolonial phenomenon, but as Visram conclusively demonstrates here, emigrants from Asia have made contributions to and impacts upon British society and culture from as far back as 1600. Imperialism provided the context for early Asian immigration as colonial officials brought their Asian domestics into Great Britain, and 'lascars' and other Asian employees of the East India Company journeyed back and forth between India and the United Kingdom. By the early nineteenth century, a small but robust community of Asians had settled in Britain, many remaining in domestic and labouring positions, but some branching out in entrepreneurial and professional ventures. Though their numbers remained modest, this long-established immigrant community contributed to British society in myriad ways throughout the nineteenth and early twentieth centuries and provided an infrastructure for the much larger wave of Asian migration to Britain in the post-Second World War period. Visram's study exemplifies the ways in which migrant histories can be, and indeed must be, continually re-evaluated, questioned and challenged.

The history of Asian migration, though only partially told, was nevertheless represented in the work of the early migration historians. Not so the Gypsies (or Romani), who remained, even in the late 1970s, in David Mayall's words 'one of the most neglected, invisible and forgotten' minority groups in British and European scholarship. Although folklore groups of the late nineteenth century had studied the Romani, these examinations, like those of many minority groups, tended to either romanticise or pathologise the subject. Mayall and those who followed provided critical approaches to the historiography of Gypsies and Romani including re-evaluations of early literature. Early in his academic career Mayall was inspired to examine the historical marginalisation of a people who themselves lived on the margins of society, bringing him into the orbit of Colin Holmes, and leading to his long-standing involvement with the journal *Immigrants and Minorities*. When Mayall set out on his research, there was no such thing as Gypsy or Romani studies, no existing body of scholarship and little enthusiasm for the subject. But, as he thoroughly details, the ensuing four decades have seen the development of a robust canon of literature signalling the establishment of an increasingly cohesive discipline, though controversies and epistemological clashes remain. The many positive Europe-wide developments – publications, conferences and the establishment of an official Network on Romani Studies – have been tempered by ongoing, sometimes acrimonious and largely unresolved controversies regarding labels, origins, ethnicity and identity as well as fundamental questions about research and its political and social policy impacts. The historiography has been enriched by the emergence of scholarship from historians of Gypsy and Romani origin, though this development also highlights issues of ownership within ethnic and minority studies, which has also been referenced in the Community chapter of this volume. In tracing his involvement with this neglected history back to Colin Holmes and the Sheffield School, Mayall underscores the impact of the those early practitioners in the development of the field of migration and minority studies.

Another elusive topic within migration scholarship has been the study of transmigration – a richly multi-faceted field that has come into focus within the academy over the past few decades. While the historiography of global/transnational processes and patterns of migration has been addressed by Tobias Brinkman in an earlier section of this volume, Nick Evans, the final contributor to this section, explores transmigration within Britain – a topic that has been neglected until fairly recently in British migration studies. Evans traces the beginnings of transmigration studies to the work of Swedish and American scholars in the 1970s who were interested in the movement of immigrants from Europe to the United States, but whose work all but ignored the routes that thousands of such migrants made across Britain, leaving in abeyance an analysis of the impact these mass migrations had upon Britain itself. Indeed, as Evans points out, even the early work of the Sheffield School included little acknowledgement of transmigration and it was not until the 1990s that historians both within and outside the Sheffield School, along with maritime scholars, museologists and others focusing on ports and local histories, began to quantify and fully explore a number of facets of transmigration within Britain. It was not until the digital age, when the resources of local archives and the interdisciplinary energies of a disparate number of scholars could be fully exploited to provide a wider lens on transmigration and its impacts on the British economy, society, culture, history and politics. Together, the contributors to this section demonstrate the breadth of possibilities within the field of British migration studies pioneered by Colin Holmes and the Sheffield School and highlight the number of histories that have been neglected, rediscovered and reimagined within its widening scope.

17

GYPSY/ROMANI STUDIES

A few reflections

David Mayall

In 1978, having completed an MA in Labour History and while working as an archivist and considering the direction I wanted to take with my research interests, I chanced upon an article by Raphael Samuel.[1] The focus of his study and approach chimed with the principles and objectives of the influential and inspirational History Workshop movement, the work of E. P. Thompson and other co-travellers and with the hidden histories of unprivileged and marginal groups, including immigrants and ethnic minorities. Gypsies were one of the most neglected, invisible and forgotten of all such groups. At that time there was nothing which might be called Gypsy or Romani studies. There were a small number of books written by scholars in other disciplines but there was no substantive study of the history of Gypsies in the UK, or indeed in Europe or the Americas. The one exception to this historical vacuum was the work of Raphael Samuel. If we were to see acknowledgement of the unseen underclass anywhere then it would be from the History Workshop group. But it was a solitary article, it was called comers and goers, and interest in this group by Samuel also came and went. If any group was ever marginalised and hidden from historical sight then it was the Gypsies. But my interest had been sparked in a group of people living on the margins of society, economically, socially and ideologically, and I decided to take this to the next stage, not sure if it was a viable project or whether I would find an institution and supervisor willing to take this on. Various paths eventually led me to Colin Holmes at the University of Sheffield.

Colin's recent edited collection on immigrants and minorities was well known to me and it seemed that research on Gypsies would fit comfortably into his general area of investigation and expertise.[2] When I started to develop this project and when I told friends and colleagues about what I was doing, it was usually met with incredulity if not outright ridicule. If I had said I was looking at any other group this would not have been the reaction. Colin was of course different. He himself had swum against the mainstream in his fight to establish immigrant and minority studies as an area for serious scholarly and historical study. His area of work stood out against the more traditional histories in his department at the University, but Colin was dogged in his establishment of this as a legitimate sub-discipline. In the early 1980s, he persuaded Frank Cass to start a journal, *Immigrants and Minorities*, with which I have been proud to be associated for many years, until fairly recently working alongside Colin in an editorial capacity, and now to have taken over as Editor-in-Chief to continue the work that Colin started in promoting, publicising and publishing in this field of study since its founding in 1981. Colin took me on as his PhD student and my work and interest in Gypsies has continued to the present.

For the term Gypsy or Romani Studies to have any meaning then it must refer to studies which have academic and scholarly credentials and credibility, range across disciplines and national boundaries, have an institutional base or bases, and have produced a substantial body of works which extend the boundaries of knowledge about the group. When I started, it would have been a major stretch of the imagination to say this existed. Now, more than thirty years later, there have been significant developments and it is possible to identify a canon of wide-ranging and influential studies which can be grouped under the encompassing heading of Gypsy or Romani Studies. It will be the purpose of this piece to reflect on some of these developments and to assess the place this has now reached.

My first reflections on the state of Gypsy Studies can be found in a short review piece published in *Immigrants and Minorities* in 1998.[3] In this I provided an account of the origins of Gypsy Studies, dating back to the highly influential work of Heinrich Grellmann, a German scholar (1753–1804). His 1783 treatise on the Gypsies was translated into English in 1787 and this became the main reference point and source for an extensive literature on the group in the nineteenth century.[4] The next phase in the study of Gypsies came with the emergence of folklore studies from the middle of the nineteenth century and the emergence of Gypsiologists or Gypsy lorists who were largely grouped in and around the Gypsy Lore Society, founded in 1888.[5] The works that emerged from this source became the bedrock of what has been described as an 'ill-defined mish mash of folklorism (often amateur) and linguistics', and which seemed to gridlock the development of Gypsy Studies beyond this for a long period.[6] It is really only in the post-war years, and with works emerging from such authors as Thomas Acton, Judith Okely, David Sibley, Yaron Matras, and in France by Jean-Pierre Liégeois, that the study of Gypsies moved beyond these confines. The title of the review article carried the question 'Gypsy studies: a new era?' I concluded my article by pointing to the growing diversity in the field of Gypsy Studies and noted: '… this very diversity, the growing willingness to address such complex issues as identity, inter-group relations and to engage with various multi- and inter-disciplinary perspectives, shows that Gypsy Studies is at last increasingly breaking free from its traditional academic marginalisation and confronting issues of historical and contemporary relevance'.[7] In answer to my own question, I pointed to the inclusion in mainstream academic publishers' catalogues of books on Gypsies, Blackwell's 'The Peoples of Europe' series having a volume on Gypsies, and the appointment of a Professor of Romani Studies at the

University of Greenwich as indicators of change.[8] To this can now be added, for example, the Romani project at the University of Manchester, the relaunch of the *Journal of the Gypsy Lore Society* as *Romani Studies* in 2000, the launch of the *Journal of Gypsy Studies* in 2016, and the Romani Studies series published by the University of Hertfordshire Press. The MigRom project at the University of Manchester, set up in 1999, states on its website that its aim is 'to investigate and promote awareness of the Romani language in its cultural and historical context'.[9] Further, it claims to have '… become one of the main international centres for academic research, networking and public engagement on Roma culture and identity'.[10] This consortium, coordinated by Professor Yaron Matras, is said to include more specialists in Romani Studies and more research staff of Romani background than any other single-funded research project currently operating. The Roma experience has been considered at the 2017 Convention of the Association for the Study of Nationalities and at an International Historical and Anthropological Conference on categories and boundaries held at the Free University of Bolzano in Italy in June 2017. It therefore seems timely, almost twenty years after my short reflections in 1998, to reflect further on these and other developments in Gypsy/Romani Studies.

As indicated above, there have been pockets of activities and publishing developments over a number of years, yet to a large extent these remained the work of individuals or small groups, largely uncoordinated and unconnected. The first major initiative to attempt to bring together all those working in the field of Gypsy/Romani Studies across Europe came in March 2010 when I attended in Brussels what was then described as 'an extraordinary seminar of experts on Roma culture and history' organised by the European Commission's Directorate General for Education and Culture. The purpose of the meeting was to develop an international network of experts in this field. I was one of four representatives from the UK, and the only UK-based historian, and one of only four historians in total. The eventual outcome was the establishment of the European Academic Network on Romani Studies (A European Union/Council of Europe joint programme), whose aim was to raise 'the visibility of existing research outside the academic community in order to foster cooperation with policymakers and other stakeholders. By creating an interface between academic researchers and political decision makers, while promoting and improving the existing resources on the European Roma communities, the project shall ultimately allow for the implementation of better conceived policy initiatives based on reliable evidence'.[11]

The coincidence of scholarship with political purpose was therefore evident at the outset, and this is a theme to which I will return later as the ramifications of this became clear. 2011–2012 was spent creating the Network and recruiting researchers which, by 2016, had grown to 420 individuals. Yaron Matras, writing in a blog on the Network's website states that its members are based at seventy different universities and research institutions in more than twenty countries.[12] These figures alone are testimony to the expansion of Gypsy Studies to a level barely conceivable when I was first writing on this in 1998. Inevitably, this has led to a concomitant expansion in conferences, research papers, articles and books.

Initially, then, this all seems very encouraging and a sign of significant advances being made. While this remains the case there is, though, another side which is revealed in the email correspondence between members of the Network over a number of years. I will deal with the themes and the nature of the debates in terms of general issues being raised and will not include specifics relating to individuals. My aim is to identify the nature and content of the debates within Gypsy/Romani Studies as revealed by a source which is not publically available and so which cannot be independently verified.

One interesting and recurrent theme, of direct relevance to this paper, is around labels and the use of the terms Roma, Gypsy and Traveller, and so by extension of Gypsy Studies and Romani Studies. The concerns raised are essentially around how the terms are used, why they are used, who uses them, their purpose and their impact. This extended to the term Gypsiologist and whether this is a derogatory term or simply a label for authors who are specialists in the study of Gypsies. This has been an ever-present theme for anyone working in the area and while it is no surprise that it is continually appearing, there is also a weariness that the same approaches and questions are being repeated endlessly. These, and indeed any, labels are there to form boundaries around a group, and create insiders and outsiders, whether by origin, nationhood or ethnicity. So these debates continue to rage with as much as fire as ever, being kept alive with tales of personal experiences, field work stories, anecdotal meetings and personal opinions. But this has not led to any kind of resolution and the same arguments, the same issues and the same entrenched opinions continue unabated.

If labels are a constant theme, then inevitably it is but a short step to that of origins. With a degree of regularity the issue of origins intrudes into many of the exchanges between the Network members, whether in relation to the historical roots of the group and its Indian ancestry or, indeed, the origins of individual contributors and their own Gypsy heritage. The main contributors to these debates remain Yaron Matras, Ian Hancock and Thomas Acton and, for a time, Judith Okely, though with additional contributions from others including Sam Beck, Ethel Brooks and Sarah Carmona. Indian origins was a theme at the International Roma Conference and Cultural Festival held in New Delhi in February in 2016. From origins it is an even shorter step to identity and ethnicity.

Identity, identity politics and ethnicity are a constant explicit or implicit element of almost every exchange between members, with notions of ethnicity tested and expounded at length. One observable development has been a slow but progressive shift away from the idea that ethnicity is bounded, fixed and mutually exclusive towards a perspective which sees ethnicity as fluid, changing and flexible. A special issue of *Roma Rights, Journal of the European Roma Rights Centre* in 2015, in memoriam of Nicolae Gheorghe, a long-time activist for Roma rights, is one example of how this alternative approach to Gypsy/Roma identity and ethnicity is gaining in standing and credibility. The surprise is that it has taken so long to reach this position. As far back as 1987 Jean-Pierre Liégeois, among others, was questioning the value of labelling and borders by seeing Gypsies or Travellers as a shifting mosaic, '… a kaleidoscope in which each element retains its distinctive features'.[13] The challenge this presented, in all its complexity, appears to now be taking shape in the form of questioning the very concept of ethnicity itself. But there remains no consensus. Some contributors now see ethnicity as irrelevant and of no value or meaning, while others still see it as a political reality and to not recognise it would be to undermine campaigns to recognise anti-Gypsy prejudice, the demand for political rights and the debates around social inclusion.[14]

Discussions around ethnicity took an interesting direction with the publicity given to the case of Rachel Dolezal, an American who was born 'white' but described herself as 'black' and of Andrea Smith, Associate Professor at the University of California, who was accused of faking a Cherokee identity. These triggered extensive correspondence around trans-ethnicity, or bi-ethnicity or bi-raciality, but these exchanges remained at the level of personal opinion and did not extend into the more sophisticated and subtle meanings of mosaic or kaleidoscope identities. Professor Ian Hancock, a Gypsy and Professor of Linguistics at the University of Texas, has also regularly had to step forward and defend his self-identification as a Gypsy. However, what the debates revealed was the porousness of any identity or boundary, whether self-ascribed or otherwise.

While each of the above themes are controversial and generate debate, and while we all welcome informed debate and the lively exchange of views, too often the correspondence between members lapsed into accusations of bitchiness, dogfights, low-level discussion and defamation. The increasingly acrimonious exchanges were often between the established players in the field, with others watching on from the ringside with occasional contributions. The correspondence between members included accusations of distorted half-truths and of comments being vengeful, triumphalist and sensationalist. What is evident is that disagreements and perfectly legitimate but competing academic positions around analysis, methodology, purpose and impact lapsed into personal insults and accusation and counter-accusation. The academic challenges and potential for reasoned exchange fell back into the trading of insults and while this is not new to Gypsy/Romani Studies, and is not unique in an academic environment, the use of email and social media give it a currency which it would not formerly have had. One eminent member of the Network even withdrew as a result of the venomous personal attacks that were received and the distorted reading of their publications.

One instance of this acrimony can be seen with the publication in October 2013 of a report by a team based at the University of Salford and led by Professor Philip Brown, Director of the Sustainable Housing and Urban Studies Unit. This report was based on a survey of all UK local authorities and interviews with professionals in selected study areas. This was then followed by an article in *People, Place and Policy* in 2014.[15] Their report was described a sensationalist (for framing the Roma as a problem because of numbers) and this was followed by challenges and criticisms about whether their 'speculations' were justifiable, whether they unwisely publicised their findings, knowing or anticipating the impact they would have, the conduct of the research leader, and whether the Salford team were competitive rather than cooperative with fellow academics. The opposed positions came to be presented as, on the one hand, anti-Gypsy racism and on the other as being motivated by a pro-Gypsy political purpose which argued for the need of affirmative action backed by affirmative research.

These debates came under the subject heading 'clash of epistemologies'. While this is certainly true, it also goes beyond this as the issue is not just about methodology and is as much, if not more, about the very nature and purpose of research, especially relating to Gypsies and Roma, and the need to give consideration to the impact of making public research findings which can impact negatively on the group. This brought to the surface whether research into the group can and should be neutral, objective and non-political and whether the findings of such research should reach the public domain without due consideration to their interpretation, use and impact. Key ethical issues were being raised around whether numbers should be endorsed if they support the need for policy interventions, and whether academics should be strictly guided by scientific principles and objectivity or whether political loyalties and political purpose and objectives should override these principles. This heated and personalised debate went to the very heart of academic enquiry and method.

Concluding thoughts

The Network had the potential to become a genuinely exciting and challenging forum for the development of research and knowledge about Gypsies. The exit and resignation of some key members, including one of the co-founders, Jean-Pierre Liégeois, and other established experts, were the first signs that this potential may not be realised. Members commented on the 'internal fractures' within the Network which were seen as wholly counter-productive. One contributor even described the Network as being dominated by a small number of individuals who attempted to de-legitimate the right of others to engage in work in this field. The observation about this field being dominated by a few is indeed accurate as the correspondence between members bears testimony, with contributions from a very small proportion of the total membership and exchanges dominated by the same set of names. The second statement, about delegitimation, is of course more controversial. The attitudes of some members have been described as counter-productive and the Network as not being academic in its behaviour because of its warlike and combative style. The implication is that the political purpose has come to dominate the scholarly. The exchanges illustrated above show that the Network has stagnated, stilled in the waters of old paradigms, seemingly reluctant and unable to move on. Contributors to the forum may still be content to row their own boats but there is a sense of going round in circles. The number of members of the Network is indicative of the volume and range of work being undertaken in Gypsy/Romani Studies across Europe but the exchanges between the members also reveal the splits and the schisms, the personal rivalries, the contrasting perspectives and the continuing presence of a relationship between

Gypsy Studies and Gypsy activism not welcomed or acceptable to all. It is perhaps less a community of scholars, which was the original intention, than a forum for personal and scholarly rivalries.

A conference held in St Andrews in November 2015, entitled 'Challenging issues in Roma/Gypsy Studies today' announced in its pre-publicity that 'the field of Gypsy Studies has become increasingly useful not only in highlighting the specific worldviews held by diverse Roma groups across the world, but also in emphasising the embeddedness of Roma communities within their respective national societies'. The text continues with an 'And yet …', pointing out that the field of Gypsy Studies 'continues to be a contested terrain …'.[16] My reflections on the more recent history of Gypsy Studies confirm that this is the case, though of itself this is not a problem as out of contest and challenge come new paradigms and new ways of thinking and understanding. My own concern is that this has not entirely been the case. The European Academic Network does have to be seen as a major enterprise to coordinate and join the work being done in the field of Gypsy/Romani Studies, but this short review has shown that the terrain has not shifted and the themes of identity, origins, ethnicity, discrimination and numbers remain the same, with only marginal changes in how these are seen and understood. But the challenges are now coming from a different direction, from those who see Gypsy/Romani Studies, and the continued emphasis on marginalisation and 'othering', as reproducing 'whiteness'. This is now being seen as the dominant academic and policy discourse which needs challenging, and that a process of decolonisation of Romani Studies (i.e. by removing the non-Roma scholars) has to take place so that there can be a 'paradigm shift'. The recent emergence of the European Roma Institute, approved by the Council of Europe member states in September 2015, has brought this challenge into the open. The ERI is a joint initiative between the Council of Europe and the Open Society Foundation, a charity led by the wealthy philanthropist, George Soros. Its purpose is to promote Roma arts, culture, history and talent, and to disseminate positive images and knowledge about Romani people. The clash with the European Network was immediate, with concerns that the ERI would seek to discredit scholarly publications, especially those produced by non-Romani scholars. In addition to this initiative, other alternatives are emerging. A Prague Forum for Romani Histories was created as an academic initiative to promote interdisciplinary and transnational scholarship, based at the Institute of Contemporary History at the Czech Academy of Sciences in partnership with the Romani Studies Seminar at Charles University.[17] Similarly, another attempt to promote interdisciplinary research and foster cooperation was the new Network of Academic Institutions in Romani Studies, established in Stockholm in 2016 and based at Södertörn University.[18] The picture then is that despite these attempts at cooperation, Gypsy Studies remains a bitterly divided arena with competing perspectives about the aims and purpose of research, the value of the scholarship by non-Romani scholars and the need for Roma themselves to engage in knowledge production, and, importantly, the political purpose of any such enterprise. The depth of the disputes led one academic to refer to the poisoned scholarly atmosphere and others to fear that standards and academic rigour risk being undermined by research that has to have a political purpose.

However, I do not want to end on a completely negative note. There are issues with how the Network has operated and the initial potential has not been fulfilled in the way that might have been hoped, but one of the extremely positive aspects of the Network is that it provides a steady stream of references to work that is published and being undertaken in the very broad field of Gypsy/Romani Studies. Certainly, the expansion of research and literature in this area is impressive and to be welcomed. Each publication can stimulate others and a momentum gathers and it is noticeable how the situation of the Roma has found its way into a multiplicity of disciplines and studies. This year alone, and this is just a very small and indicative sample, there have been studies published in the *Scandinavian Journal of History*, the *European Journal of Criminology*, *Journalism and Mass Communication Quarterly*, and *Ethnicities*. Countries covered include Sweden, Canada, America, Finland, Norway, Italy and Slovakia. This growth in academic study has taken place alongside the expansion of Roma political activity and organisation, perhaps most visible in the bodies created under the umbrella of the Council of Europe. This perhaps explains why a large number of the new studies are in the areas of education and social policy. Of the 420 members of the Network, which of course does not encompass all those working in this area, only twenty-seven were historians, indicating that while historical studies have expanded and while there are a growing number of historians of Gypsies/Roma, there is still the opportunity for further enquiry.

The tensions and difficulties in Gypsy/Romani studies reveal the highly sensitised and politicised dimension of research activity and writing which focuses on a group which continues to experience some of the longest lasting and most virulent forms of discrimination and antipathy. The growth of Gypsy/Romani studies is partly because of the snowball effect of any published work in a field of study – one work begets another. But it is more than this. It is also about the wider context of political agendas around minority rights and ethnicity, the democratising effects of the internet on spreading information, and the role played by the European Commission and Council of Europe taking Roma matters to the heart of the European political institutions and agendas.

Notes

1 Raphael Samuel, 'Comers and goers', in Harold James Dyos and Michael Wolff (eds), *The Victorian City, Images and Realities*, Vol. 1 (London: Routledge and Kegan Paul 1976), 123–160.
2 See appendix for a full list of publications.
3 David Mayall, 'Gypsy studies: a new era?', *Immigrants and Minorities* vol. 17, no. 2, 1998, 57–67.
4 Heinrich Moritz Grellmann, *Dissertation on the Gypsies, being an Historical Enquiry, concerning the Manner of Life, Economy, Customs and Conditions of these people in Europe, and their origin*, translated into English by Matthew Raper (London 1787). See also Wim

Willems, *In Search of the True Gypsy: From Enlightenment to Final Solution*, translated by Don Bloch (London: Frank Cass 1997).
5 See David Mayall, *Gypsy Identities 1500–2000: From Egipcyans and Moon-men to the Ethnic Romany* (London: Routledge 2004), chapter 6.
6 Thomas Acton, Susan Caffrey, Sylvia Dunn and Penny Vinson, 'Gender issues in accounts of Gypsy health and hygiene as discourses of social control', in Thomas Acton and Gary Mundy, *Romani Culture and Gypsy Identity* (Hatfield: University of Hertfordshire Press 1997) 164–170 (165).
7 Ibid., 66.
8 Angus Fraser, *The Gypsies* (Malden MA: Blackwell Publishing 1992).
9 MigRom. 'The immigration of Romanian Roma to Western Europe: Causes, effects and future engagement strategies'. www.migrom.humanities.manchester.ac.uk.
10 Ibid.
11 www.coe.int/t/dg4/cultureheritage/culture/romastudies/Default_en.asp. See also http://romanistudies/eu (webpage no longer available).
12 Yaran Matras, 'Do Roma need protection from themselves?', blog posting 21 March 2016: *European Academic Network on Romani Studies*: romanistudies.eu.
13 Jean-Pierre Liégeois. *Gypsies and Travellers: Socio-cultural data* (Council of Europe 1987), 7. See also Mayall, *Gypsy Identities*, ch. 8.
14 'Roma': a misnomer? On the essence of the 'cultural identity of Roma', edited by Judit Durst available at romanistudies.eu.documents/email-list-archive.
15 Philip Brown, Philip Martin and Lisa Scullion, 'Migrant Roma in the United Kingdom and the need to estimate population size', *People, Place and Policy*, an online journal, vol. 8, no. 1, 2014.
16 www.st-andrews.ac.uk/globalcinema/conference-challenging-issues-in-romagypsy-studies (webpage no longer available).
17 Prague Forum for Romani Histories: www.romanihistories.usd.cas.cz.
18 CBEES. Network of Academic Institutes in Romani Studiers: www.sh.se/nairs.

18

'THE POOREST, THE MOST INTRACTABLE, AND THE MOST PERMANENT' – THE INVISIBLE NINETEENTH-CENTURY POLE IN BRITAIN

Milosz K. Cybowski

Introduction

Although it was not until the interwar period when the post-1830 Polish exile to Western Europe became known as the Great Emigration, the contemporary refugees themselves were fully aware of the unique character of their exile. As the editors of a short-lived *Pismo wzajemnego oświecania się* [*A paper of mutual enlightenment*] put it in 1833, 'Polish emigration is one of the rarest and the strangest events of our age; thus collecting and preserving materials that one day will serve to write its history is the most important of our duties.'[1] That awareness makes research on the subject of the Great Emigration much easier for all historians and, not surprisingly, the subject has received a lot of attention from Polish scholars.

At the same time, however, the topic of Polish exiles remains marginal to many studies of nineteenth-century immigration to Britain. The first part of this chapter takes a closer look at historiography of the Polish exile, trying to establish the reasons behind the limited interest in the Polish refugees expressed by British historians and contrasting it with a wide range of scholarly works published in Polish. The second part of this work serves as a brief introduction to the subject of the Polish exiles in Britain and popularity they attracted in the 1830s and 1840s.

The invisible nineteenth-century Pole: historiography of the Polish exile

It should not be surprising that the history of Polish emigration to Britain has attracted much more attention from Polish than from British scholars. One of the earliest publications on the subject was Lubomir Gadon's three volume study published in the early twentieth century.[2] It was followed by a whole range of articles and monographs that came into being before and after the First World

War.[3] The most influential was the work of Adam Lewak, who coined the term 'Great Emigration' (*Wielka Emigracja*), which became the name used by later historians to describe both the Polish post-1830 exile and the whole period between 1831 and 1863.[4] One of the major problems with many of these studies is the fact that they tended to concentrate on the political activities of the Polish exiles, either in Britain or France, rather than on the history of migration to those countries.

Post-1945 years brought more detailed studies of liberal, democratic and socialist wings of Polish politics in exile. Because it was Britain rather than France which remained the central place of refuge for the majority of Polish radicals, there was a visible increase of works devoted to the subject of refugees' political activities in that country.[5] At the same time, very few studies dealt with the issue of exiles themselves.[6] It was Krzysztof Marchlewicz's detailed monograph which became the first major work devoted entirely to the fate of Polish exiles in Britain, their social structure, everyday life and many other subjects which had attracted very little attention in the previous years.[7] Thanks to his meticulous research conducted in British and Polish archives (particularly the British National Archives in Kew), Marchlewicz's research became the major contribution to this subject in recent decades.[8] It is also worth mentioning Radosław Żurawski vel Grajewski. Although the majority of his books and articles concentrate on the political side of the problem (with particular attention given to politics of Prince Adam Jerzy Czartoryski), on several occasions he also looked at the subject of emigration itself.[9]

Significantly, however, neither Marchlewicz's, nor Żurawski vel Grajewski's works (with the exception of one article by the former)[10] has been published in English, contributing to the 'invisibility' of the subject of Polish refugees in non-Polish historiography. There remains precious little material devoted to this issue available in English, partially because of the lack of interest from British historians, and partially because of the alleged limited significance of the Great Emigration in British and European politics of the period. Among the key works on this subject there are two scholarly, but rather outdated collections,[11] as well as several books and articles by Peter Brock (to this day one of a few non-Polish historians who has devoted his energies to researching the subject of the Great Emigration).[12] Although Brock's studies are still of some value (particularly thanks to his use of a number of local archives), when reading them we have to take into consideration his strongly Marxist approach and determination to discuss only radical groups among the Polish exiles. Brock's influence is particularly visible in Henry Weisser's analyses of contacts between British and Polish radicals.[13]

In the majority of the more popular studies of the history of Poland available in English, the history of Polish exile and history of the whole nineteenth century is usually treated with far less attention than other periods.[14] Norman Davies' *Heart of Europe* is perhaps the only exception.[15] In all these cases, however, the authors do not concentrate on Britain, and offer insights only into a more general history of the Polish Exile in Western Europe.

Bernard Porter's classic study is the only one that touches, though very briefly, on the significance and position of the Polish refugees among other national groups of exiles.[16] Interestingly, even Porter does not look at the developments which took place in the 1830s, when the Poles were at the centre of British political and public interest, but concentrates on their fate in the 1850s. A similar approach was presented in Marchlewicz's article published in English.[17] As a result, despite the fact that the Poles were 'the most numerous, the poorest, the most intractable, and the most permanent' of all émigrés who arrived in Britain in the early and mid-nineteenth century, they remain on the margins of British historiography of migration in the nineteenth century.[18] As Colin Holmes pointed out in the introduction to *Immigrants and Minorities in Britain*, 'historians have often shown a preference for ploughing well-worn furrows' and the case of the Polish refugees is only one of many examples of that tendency.[19]

The 'Eternal Poles': a short history of Polish emigration to Britain in the 1830s and 1840s

The first Poles started arriving in Britain individually and in small groups in the wake of the unsuccessful anti-Russian November Uprising (1830–31). However, the position of Britain as 'the asylum of nations' was yet to be established, and the majority of Poles preferred France to Britain as the place of their refuge. As a result, between 1831 and 1833 no more than one hundred Poles arrived in Britain and no more than a half that number decided to remain.[20] With time, however, the French government (after accepting over 3,000 Polish exiles and agreeing to support them financially) became more reluctant to accept further refugees. Although it did not lead to any significant change in the structure of the Polish Great Emigration, and France remained the centre of Polish exile, it led to an increase of the number of Poles in Britain.[21]

In 1834 212 Polish soldiers landed in Portsmouth, determined to stay in Britain rather than accept a French proposal to join the Foreign Legion in Algiers. They were followed later that year by over a hundred Poles who had taken part in the unsuccessful Savoy expedition. Two years later the occupation of the Free State of Cracow by Russia, Prussia and Austria led to a further increase of Polish exiles arriving in Britain and by the end of 1837 there were over 600 of them in Britain. The following years saw a gradual decline of total numbers of Polish refugees, partly because of the government's policy to encourage the exiles to leave the country, partly because the Poles did not have as many reasons to seek refuge in Britain as in the early 1830s. Effectively, by 1847 the numbers of Polish exiles fell to fewer than 500. Interestingly, although the Poles remained the most numerous refugees in Britain in the discussed period, British attitudes to them varied significantly from enthusiasm in the early 1830s, through a somewhat mixed reception in the later part of that decade, to a very critical approach of the 1840s.

The most significant element of pro-Polish sentiment in the early 1830s was the creation of the Literary Association of the Friends of Poland (LAFP) in February 1832. The society's aim was 'collecting, publishing and diffusing all such information respecting Poland, as may tend to interest the public mind, and keep alive in it a strong interest with respect to the condition of that brave but ill-used nation'.[22] From its inception until 1924, the organisation remained at the very centre of all pro-Polish activities taking place in Britain. Even though the numbers of Polish exiles before 1834 were relatively low, they nevertheless made a serious impact on the LAFP. Consequently, the literary activities of the Association became overshadowed by its charitable actions for the benefit of the Polish refugees in Britain. These included balls, concerts, dinners and special meetings organised on a number of various occasions. The majority of funds obtained by the LAFP during these events was devoted to the direct support of Polish exiles.[23]

The year 1834 can be considered a turning point in British interest in the Polish exiles. Although the LAFP continued to promote their cause for the rest of the decade, and to much lesser extent in the 1840s, after two years, British public opinion became tired of the subject of Polish refugees. Public response to the LAFP's initiative to provide the Poles with official government support was rather limited and the reasons behind the government's decision to offer the refugees a subsidy of £10,000 remain unclear.[24] The key element of the grant was its restricted and temporary character, but already in 1835 it became clear that the government's money was the main source of income for many Poles. Consequently, the grant was annually renewed for many years to come. The initial sum increased to £15,000 in 1839, but gradually declined in the 1840s, reaching £9,100 in 1847.[25]

The existence of the grant did not stop the LAFP from further charitable events, but in the changing political and social climate of early Victorian Britain obtaining support for the foreigners was becoming more difficult. Regardless of several successful events (such as the Polish Ball which took part in June 1844, around the time of Tsar Nicholas I's visit to Britain),[26] in the 1840s the first serious voices of criticism began to appear, indicating the diminishing sympathy for Polish refugees. Many correspondents of metropolitan newspapers indicated that at the time of the economic crisis, which characterised the first half of the decade, British philanthropy should support British workers rather than the foreigners.[27]

The last chapter of British interest in the subject of Polish refugees took place during a three-night-long parliamentary debate on the question of the annexation of Cracow in March 1847. Although it was only loosely linked to the issue of the Polish exiles and had much more in common with the early 1830s discussions on Polish-Russian relations, for the British press it was an ideal opportunity to illustrate the diminishing sympathy for Poles and Poland. As the *Morning Post* commented, 'We have heard Lord Morpeth admit in public that, when the question [of Poland] is now mentioned, it is received with the muttered observation – "Oh! This is Dudley Stuart again, with his eternal Poles"'.[28] Even though Lord Morpeth was neither a member of the LAFP, nor a particularly known supporter of the Polish cause, this voice of annoyance expressed by a member of British upper classes was the best expression of the changing attitudes towards Polish exiles.

Conclusion

Poles were the most numerous refugee group in Britain in the 1830s and 1840s and, thanks to their numbers and the significant support they received from the British public and the government, they were far from being invisible. Parliamentary debates, newspapers and various pamphlets published in that period show clearly that they were a recognised and visible element of those two decades. As this work has argued, their invisibility in modern British historiography should be linked to the lack of significant research devoted to their fate rather than to their insignificance in British nineteenth-century public and political life. Despite the wide range of research made by Polish scholars over the course of the last century, history of the invisible nineteenth-century Pole, both in the period discussed above and in the years that followed, remains a subject which awaits its incorporation in the wider narrative of nineteenth-century migrations to Britain.

Notes

1 *Pismo wzajemnego oświecania się*, vol. 10 (Besançon: [publisher unknown] 1833), 11.
2 L. Gadon, *Emigracya polska: pierwsze lata po upadku powstania listopadowego*, 3 vols. (Kraków: Spółka Wydawnicza Polska 1901).
3 See for example S. Szpotański, 'Emigracja polska w Anglii (1831–1848)', *Biblioteka Warszawska* vol. 274, 1909, 259–287, 541–562; J. Feldman, 'U podstaw stosunków polsko-angielskich, 1788–1863', *Polityka Narodów*, 1933, 7–47; T. Grzebieniowski, 'Anglia wobec sprawy polskiej', *Przegląd Współczesny*, (1938); Grzebieniowski, 'Ćwierćwiecze sprawy polskiej w Anglji', *Droga* (1931), 707–722, 818–832; O. Halecki, 'Anglo-Polish Relations in the Past', *Slavonic and East European Review* vol. 12, 1934, 659–669; M. Handelsman, *Anglia-Polska, 1814–1864* (Warszawa: Wende 1917).
4 A. Lewak, 'Czasy Wielkiej Emigracji', in *Polska, jej dzieje i kultura od czasów najdawniejszych aż do chwili obecnej*, vol III (Warszawa: Trzaska, Evert i Michalski 1930), 193–233.
5 H. Temkinowa, *Lud Polski. Wybór dokumentów* (Warszawa: Książka i Wiedza 1957); H. Temkinowa, *Gromady Ludu Polskiego (zarys ideologii)* (Warszawa: Książka i Wiedza 1962). S. Kalembka, *Wielka Emigracja. Polskie wychodźstwo politycznie w latach 1831–1862* (Warszawa: Wiedza Powszechna 1971); S. Mikos, *Gromady Ludu Polskiego w Anglii 1835–1846* (Gdańsk: Wyższa Szkoła Pedagogiczna 1962); M. Tyrowicz, *Towarzystwo Demokratyczne Polskie. 1832–1863. Przewodnik bibliograficzny* (Warszawa: Książka i Wiedza 1964); J. Żmigrodzki, *Towarzystwo Demokratyczne Polskie (1832–1862)*, 2 vols. (London: Księgarnia Stowarzyszenia Polskich Kombatantów 1983); B. Cygler, *Zjednoczenie emigracji polskiej* (Gdańsk: Wyższa Szkoła Pedagogiczna 1963).
6 We can find more complex analyses of the fate of the Poles in L. Zieliński, *Emigracja polska w Anglii w latach 1831–1846* (Gdańsk: Wyższa Szkoła Pedagogiczna 1964) and Mikos, 'Warunki bytowe emigracji polskiej w Anglii po powstaniu listopadowym', *Gdańskie Zeszyty Humanistyczne. Historia*, vol. 8, 1965, 79–98.

7 K. Marchlewicz, *Wielka Emigracja na Wyspach Brytyjskich 1830–1863* (Poznań: Instytut Historii UAM 2008).
8 Marchlewicz, 'Brytyjskie środowiska polonofilskie w dobie wczesnowiktoriańskiej', *Mazowieckie Studia Humanistyczne* vol. 2, 2002, 89–102; Marchlewicz, 'Nadzór administracyjny i policyjny nad polskimi emigrantami politycznymi w Wielkiej Brytanii w latach 1831–1863', *Kwartalnik Historyczny* vol. 61, 2004, 61–77; Marchlewicz, 'Propolski lobbing w Izbach Gmin i Lordów w latach trzydziestych i czterdziestych XIX wieku', *Przegląd Historyczny* vol. 145, no. 1, 2005, 61–76.
9 See particularly R. Żurawski vel Grajewski, 'Ucieczka Polaków z rosyjskiego okrętu "Irtysz" w brytyjskim porcie Portsmouth w roku 1844', *Acta Universitatis Lodziensis. Folia Historica* vol. 69, 2000, 59–71. See also Żurawski vel Grajewski, 'Polskie emigracje 1831–1918', in *Historie Polski w XIX wieku* (Warszawa: Wydawnictwo DiG 2015), vol. IV, 115–276.
10 Marchlewicz, 'Continuities and Innovations: Polish Emigration after 1849', in *Exiles from European Revolutions. Refugees in Mid-Victorian England* (New York: Oxford Berghahn Books 2003), 103–120.
11 W. F. Reddaway (ed.), *The Cambridge History of Poland*, 2 vols. (Cambridge: Cambridge University Press 1951). S. Kieniewicz, *History of Poland* (Warszawa: PWN 1979).
12 P. Brock, *Nationalism and Populism in Partitioned Poland* (London: Orbis Books 1973); Brock, *Polish Revolutionary Populism: A Study in Agrarian Socialist Thought from the 1830s to the 1850s* (Toronto: University of Toronto Press 1977); Brock, 'Polish Democrats and English Radicals', *The Journal of Modern History* vol. 25, no. 2, 1953, 139–156.
13 H. Weisser, 'Polonophilism and the British Working Class 1830–1845', *The Polish Review* vol. 12, 1967, 78–96; Weisser, 'The British Working Class and the Cracow Uprising of 1846', *The Polish Review* vol. 13, 1968, 3–19.
14 N. Davies, *God's Playground. A History of Poland* (Oxford: Oxford University Press 1981); A. Zamoyski, *Poland: A History* (London: William Collins 2009). See also A. J. Prażmowska, *A History of Poland* (Basingstoke: Palgrave Macmillan 2004).
15 N. Davies, *Heart of Europe* (Oxford: Oxford University Press 2001), 138–244.
16 B. Porter, *The Refugee Question in Mid-Victorian Politics* (Cambridge: Cambridge University Press 1979).
17 K. Marchlewicz, 'Continuities and Innovations: Polish Emigration after 1849', in *Exiles from European Revolutions. Refugees in Mid-Victorian England*, 103–120.
18 Porter, *The Refugee Question*, 13.
19 C. Holmes, 'Introduction: Immigrants and Minorities in Britain', *Immigrants and Minorities in British Society* (London and New York: Routledge 2016), 14.
20 For a more detailed information about the dynamics of Polish emigration to and from Britain see K. Szulczewski, *O Towarzystwie Literackim Przyjaciół Polski w Londynie. Odezwa do rodaków* (Paryż: [publisher unknown] 1857), Appendix 6.
21 See M. Cybowski, 'First and Last Refuge: France and Britain as Centres of the Polish Great Emigration', *John Bull and the Continent* (Frankfurt am Main: Peter Lang Edition 2015), 59–74.
22 Thomas Campbell to Mr. Gray, 7 March 1832. W. Beattie (ed.), *Life and Letters of Thomas Campbell*, vol. III (London: Edward Moxon 1849), 110–111. See also *Rules and Regulations of the London Association of the Friends of Poland* (London: T. Brettell 1833), 3.
23 See Szulczewski, *O Towarzystwie*, Appendix 3.
24 Marchlewicz, *Polonofil doskonały*, 95–96.
25 'Appendix 8', *Report from the Select Committee on Miscellaneous Expenditure; together with the minutes of evidence taken before them* (London: [publisher unknown] 1848), 274. See also Szulczewski, *O Towarzystwie*, Appendix 3.

26 See particularly Żurawski vel Grajewski R. P., 'Hotel Lambert wobec wizyty Cara Mikołaja I w Londynie w 1844 r.', *Acta Universitatis Lodziensis. Folia Historica* vol. 70, 2001, 133–147.
27 See for example *The Times*, 8, 11 and 15 November 1843; 6 June 1844.
28 *Morning Post*, 18 March 1847.

19

HISTORY OF ASIANS IN BRITAIN 1600–1950

Rozina Visram

Many people in Britain have assumed that British society became culturally diverse only after the Second World War with the arrival of migrants from the Caribbean and Indian subcontinent. Scholars of the Asian presence, largely social anthropologists interested in understanding the lives of post-war Asian migrants, published ethnographic studies based on their field research undertaken both in Britain and in India or Pakistan.[1] Their research suggested that there was a discernible pattern of migration and community formation starting with the arrival of single young men planning to stay a few years only, living in overcrowded housing and sending their remittances back home, and only later, in response to the tightening of immigration laws in the 1960s, being joined by wives and children.

According to Roger and Catherine Ballard, Asian communities in Britain from rural backgrounds despite their religious and regional diversity passed through similar phases of development. Based on their own research among the Sikhs in Leeds undertaken between 1971 and 1974 and from evidence in available ethnographic literature they asserted that it was possible to identify four chronological phases in the development of South Asian settlements.[2] The first phase, from around the middle of the nineteenth century through to the post-war period to 1960, saw the arrival of early individual pioneers who came for a variety of reasons, including as students or visitors. Others were employed as seamen. In time, small settlements of ex-seamen were formed in port cities such as London's East End. Then there were the pedlars hawking their wares of clothing door to door. By the 1930s small colonies of pedlars were dotted around some British cities. For the Ballards, the significance of these early pioneers, other than as courageous individuals, lay only as a bridgehead for the arrival of significant numbers in the second half of the twentieth century.

The 1950s began the mass migration of single young men from rural backgrounds in India, Pakistan and later Bangladesh who came to fill the labour gap in British factories and foundries. They did not intend to settle permanently. According to the Ballards, they regarded their villages as home while Britain remained 'a social vacuum, a cultural no man's land'.[3] Faced with a hostile environment they set up networks of mutual support. To circumvent discrimination and lack of promotion, some started their own small-scale businesses such as market stalls.

The 1960s began the third phase as families were united in Britain and the original intention of returning home after five years was abandoned when British immigration laws changed. For the Sikhs, the 1960s was very much a period of consolidation. All-male households disappeared as traditional family life became possible. It was only at this stage that the infrastructure usually associated with community life was established. Asian business enterprises, serving both ethnic and English clientele, expanded; places of religious worship, cinemas, travel agencies, as well as social and cultural organisations were set up. Some joined political parties.

The 1970s saw the emergence of the second generation born and educated in Britain. The Ballards suggest that although this was not necessarily an entirely new phase, the Sikh community in Leeds showed discernible subtle changes. Families moved away from inner city ghettos to the suburbs. These educated Sikhs exposed to both British and Punjabi cultural heritages lived lives of what came to be termed 'between two cultures'.[4] But according to the Ballards, in time these immigrants learned to negotiate their multiple identities. Later, they became more politicised and formed organisations against racism and racial violence. Obviously, the timing and duration of each phase varied from group to group. But in the Ballards' view, theirs was a useful model for comparative analysis and it came to be followed in later ethnographic publications to a greater or smaller degree.[5]

However, the history of Asian settlement in Britain did not begin in the post-war period as my own research based on extensive archival sources shows. It goes back to the 1600s, as a result of the long history of contact through trade, conquest and colonisation between Britain and India beginning with the founding of the East India Company. By 1945 a small but enterprising community of both professional and working-class Asians already lived in Britain, and community infrastructure, ethnic shops, restaurants, places of religious worship and social, cultural and political organisations already existed. The post-war migration was a continuation of the process. This challenges the accepted settlement pattern as suggested by the early anthropologists.

What led me to research and write about the history of Asian migration to Britain? The prevailing Anglo-centric bias and interpretations in the history curriculum of the London schools where I began teaching in 1972 seemed to me to provide a parochial view of Britain's history and a limited worldview. However, while teaching about the First World War to a group of fourth year examination pupils, and browsing through A. J. P. Taylor's, *History*, I came across one particular photograph. Among a group of European soldiers were three wounded Indians, one on a stretcher. It was the caption that arrested me. It read, 'Wounded Indians far from home'.[6] This was a defining moment that would lead me on to the path to my pioneering study of Asian settlement in Britain, *Ayahs, Lascars and Princes* and the revised and expanded edition, *Asians in Britain*.[7]

I knew about Indian soldiers being deployed beyond India's borders as an imperial fire brigade in colonial wars of conquest. But Indian soldiers on the Western Front fighting in a white man's war in Europe? That made nonsense of the ideology of the Raj. The photograph remained in my memory. Much later, I came across photograph albums of Indian soldiers in the trenches of the Western Front in the Imperial War Museum archive and extracts of their letters – the Censored Mails – in the India Office Library and Records, now at the British Library.

Racism experienced by black and Asian communities in the 1970s and 1980s provides another backdrop to my research.[8] Perceived as recent arrivals and economic migrants, they were viewed as intruders into British society who had contributed nothing and as such had no place in Britain. Seen as scroungers, their lives were disfigured by discrimination, marginalisation and even racial violence. Margaret Thatcher, in 1978, raising the spectre of hostility to immigrants and calling for a 'clear end to immigration', argued that 'people are really rather afraid that this country might be swamped by people of a different culture'.[9] Meanwhile, *Time*, citing Gallup polls, alleged that forty six percent of Britons interviewed claimed 'race relations were getting worse, while forty nine percent wanted the government to offer immigrants financial help to leave the country'.[10] Schools reflected similar attitudes. For black and Asian students, racist taunts and abuse in the playground were not uncommon experiences. White teachers, too, could have low expectations of their pupils.

Black and Asian parents and educationalists increasingly concerned at the treatment of their children by the British school system and the effect on their children's achievement began to campaign for change. The impact of a Euro-centric curriculum on their children was another issue of concern. And the history curriculum became one arena for change. To reflect the 'multicultural' nature of British society and to counter a total absence of blacks and Asians from the 'island story' version of British history, some of us believed that the history of black and Asian people should be integrated as part of British history given the long interconnectedness of Britain with Africa, the Caribbean and the Indian subcontinent.

By this time, following its initial Multi-Ethnic Policy Statement issued in 1977, the Inner London Education Authority (ILEA), after a period of consultation with various community groups, parents, teachers and educationalists, issued an Anti-Racist Statement and Guidelines for all ILEA schools to eradicate racial discrimination. Then, in 1979, as part of a joint collaboration between ILEA and the University of London Institute of Education, a Teacher Fellowship scheme was set up at the Centre for Multicultural Education (now the Centre for intercultural Education) as a cross-departmental and Institute-wide Centre with Dr Jagdish Gundara as its head to allow practicing teachers to research and produce materials in their chosen field for use in the classroom. It was this Teacher Fellowship Scheme that allowed me the opportunity, space and time to research and reflect on the process of migration, British history and the school curriculum. I was awarded a

Fellowship for the academic year 1983–84 and chose Asians in Britain from the eighteenth to the mid-twentieth century for my research.

But before that, in 1981, the first International Conference on the history of black peoples in Britain was held at the University of London's Institute of Education. There were no papers on Asians at the Conference despite the fact that at the time the term 'black' was used politically to denote African, Caribbean and peoples from the Indian subcontinent. In many ways, the 1981 Conference and the follow-up 1984 Conference heralded a breakthrough for the serious study of the history of blacks and Asians in Britain.

I must admit I knew precious little when I began my research in 1983. There were some intriguing references to Asian domestics in British households in the novels of Dickens and Thackeray. In *David Copperfield*, for example, we find Julia Mills returning from India 'steeped in money' and 'with a black man to carry cards and letters on a golden salver', and a 'copper-coloured woman in linen, with a bright handkerchief round her head, to serve her Tiffin in her dressing-room'.[11] I knew of sailors as part of the imperial maritime labour force, of one Indian MP and of course Indian soldiers in the First World War. In fact, there were several thousand Asians in Victorian and Edwardian Britain. Some were born here, others lived permanently or stayed for varying periods of time. There were students, doctors, businessmen and other professionals active in politics. Further, in response to the labour market thousands of sailors and hundreds of ayahs continued to be brought over every year, all contributing to British life.

How and where was I to begin? We now forget how much easier the task of a researcher is made by the very many electronic search engines and by having such resources as newspapers, census material or the Old Bailey Records available online. When I began, even Martin Moir's excellent *Guide* was not available.[12] As for academic studies, these focused on the arrival of Indians and Pakistanis in the post-war period as already described. As far as historical studies are concerned, Michael Banton's *The Coloured Quarter* about the East End of London has no mention of Indians, despite lascar settlers. Peter Fryer's *Staying Power*, published in 1984, does include some references to Indians from the eighteenth century. Colin Holmes, too, refers to Indians in his study, *John Bull's Island*, which came out in 1988. His information, however, comes from Fryer. There is no mention of *Ayahs, Lascars and Princes* even though it had been published two years previously, in 1986. Antoinette Burton, Michael Fisher and Shompa Lahiri have further added to our knowledge of South Asian settlements in Britain.[13] Jagdish Gundara was encouraging and gave me much valuable advice, while people I consulted were generous with their suggestions.[14] For instance, Jatinder Verma of Tara Arts Theatre and Chris Power, joint author with Nigel File of their school book, readily shared their pioneering research and pointed me to the eighteenth-century newspapers.[15] Searching for Indian servants through reels of microfilms of Burney Papers was akin to looking for a needle in a haystack. Locating the elite, for instance the Liberal MP Dadabhai Naoroji, proved relatively easy as I could find entries under his name in the British Library catalogue and with help from the archivists seek out official records at the

India Office Library and Records or in local archives. But finding the working class who not only leave no records of their own behind but also easily slip through official records proved a much harder task. The ever-helpful archivists at the India Office suggested consulting the Public and Judicial files as they might yield entries on the working class. I unearthed some by searching through the catalogue hand lists, but under categories such as 'natives of India abroad', 'the poor', 'destitute' and even 'lunatics'.

But there were unexpected finds and lucky breaks. Thumbing through George Sims' *Living London*, I chanced across a photograph of the Ayahs' Home in Hackney, East London, which opened up a further line of research in Hackney archives and the London City Mission as the Mission had assumed control of the Home and relocated it to Hackney in 1900.[16] All this helped me to build up a picture of ayahs' lives in Britain, their treatment at the hands of some callous employers, the role of the Home and the resourcefulness of the ayahs themselves.

Thanks to its huge record-keeping bureaucracy, both the East India Company and the Raj generated mountains of records, revealing, with patient research, the interaction of Asians in British life as well as the varied lives and experiences of a range of Asians, high and low, who lived in Britain. Newspapers, paintings and photographs, contemporary writings both by Indians and whites, memorials around us as well as records in the local and other archives and museums all yielded valuable material enabling me to piece together the history of Asians in Britain. What did I find?

Post-war Asian migration was not a new phenomenon, but a continuation of the process begun as a result of the exchange between colonisers and the colonised from the seventeenth century. It was not confined to England – Asians settled in Scotland, Wales and Ireland. Some of the earliest known settlers were Indian domestics, brought over by the English nabobs as their servants, ayahs or nannies. They occasionally appear in parish registers, and eighteenth-century paintings depict them as exotics, symbolic of the exalted status of their wealth acquired in India.

Then there were the many travelling ayahs who were employed by families to look after their children during the long voyage on their seasonal visits to Britain and played an important role in the comfortable living of these families. Discharged on arrival, at times without arrangements for their return to India, some advertised for a return passage. A few found employment with families in Britain. Christian charities concerned for the welfare of the abandoned ayahs established the Ayahs' Home in 1891 in Aldgate. In 1900, the London City Mission relocated it to Hackney. The only such institution with a named building, it became an important landmark, but it remained a symbol of empire, replicating many colonial attitudes and images.

Lascars or Indian sailors formed a mainstay of the British merchant marine. Originally recruited in small numbers by the East India Company from the seventeenth century to fill the manpower gap, they were employed as able seamen and cooks. With the opening of the Suez Canal in 1869 and the introduction of steam-powered liners, lascars became indispensable as firemen and trimmers in the engine rooms to stoke the furnaces, work shunned by white sailors. By 1914, lascars formed 17.5 percent of the total number of sailors on British registered ships, and their number was rising. During the two World Wars they helped to keep British supply lines open, enabling Britain to win the war. Employment on 'Asiatic Articles' (which meant less pay than European sailors and large savings for the shipping industry), coupled with their harsh treatment, led some lascars to jump ship in Britain. In time, a small population of lascars grew up in port cities like London, Glasgow, Liverpool and Cardiff.

Few surviving records provide detailed information of the day-to-day lives of these early working-class Asian communities, but what emerges is their resourcefulness and the variety of jobs they took in order to preserve their self-esteem. Some servants who stayed on in Britain could even find possibilities of advancement with the support of their employers. For instance, Munnoo, the servant of the Anglo-Irish lawyer, William Hickey, arrived in 1808 and lived with Hickey's family in Beaconsfield. He was anglicised, married an English woman, Anne, and finally moved with his own family together with Hickey to Richmond and later became a licensed victualler. Others continued to work as servants or sailors. Some sold Christian tracts, others earned a few pence as crossing-sweepers or even as purveyors of Asian culture, working as singers and musicians and vendors of Indian spices. Some even managed to set up lodging-houses and cafes for their compatriots, helped by their English wives. Contemporaries disapproved of their relations with white women owing to racist anxiety of miscegenation. Inhabiting the same places and sharing a similar subculture, in time they merged into the working-class populace of their localities.

A more visible personality, Dean Mahomed (1759–1851), emigrated to Ireland in 1782 with Godfrey Baker in whose battalion he had served as a *subedar*. In Cork, he worked as a major-domo for Baker's family, converted to Christianity and eloped with Jane Daly, whom he married. Mahomed was the first Indian author in English. His autobiography, *The Travels of Dean Mahomet*, published in 1794, remains the only description written in English by an Indian, although European sources for the transitional period from Mughal Empire to East India Company administration survive. In England, he reinvented himself as a cultural entrepreneur cashing in on his Indian identity, first setting up the Hindoostanee Coffee-House in 1810 at 34 George Street, Portman Square, offering distinctive Indian cuisine. Though favourably received, it did not last long. In Brighton, he reinvented himself again as a 'shampooing surgeon', setting up the Indian Vapour Baths and Shampooing Establishment with his second wife, Jane Jeffreys. A shrewd businessman, he used marketing and publicity to build up a clientele. And success followed. He was appointed Shampooing Surgeon to both George IV and William IV, installing an Indian vapour bath at the Pavilion. Mahomed was on the voters' register from 1841. After he retired, his son Arthur ran the Baths, but since he was not seen as Indian enough, he could not compete with rivals. Another son, Frederick, successfully ran a fencing academy with his wife, Sarah.

Frederick Akbar Mahomed (1849–84), the Brighton-born son of Frederick, was a doctor at Guy's Hospital in London. His most significant contribution to British medical science is his pioneering research on the cause and progression of hypertension. It was generally accepted that kidney damage caused high blood pressure. Mahomed's pathbreaking discovery proved that high blood pressure was a primary condition, changing our understanding of hypertension. Little, if any, significance has been added to his conclusions since his death in 1884. But Mahomed remains unacknowledged.

Since qualifications from British universities were essential for jobs in India, an increasing number of students came to Britain to study. As students, several made important academic and cultural contributions. Cornelia Sorabji, a Christian Parsi, was the first woman to study law at a British university, joining Somerville Hall in 1889. Her university career illustrates the very many hurdles women had to overcome to win educational equality. Sorabji was barred from taking her BCL examination in the schools with men. Undaunted, she put up a fight and won a special decree permitting her to sit the examination with the men, thus opening up the Bar to women. Ranjtsinhji, affectionately known as Ranji, at Cambridge from 1889 had a large fan base as a cricketer, reminiscent to footballers today, attracting column inches for his artistry, skill, innovativeness and high scoring. He played for and captained Sussex County Club and played fifteen Tests for England from 1896 to 1902. Between 1897 and 1898 he was allowed to enter Australia as part of the England team (the usual entry tax imposed on non-whites was waived). Arriving in 1924, another student, Krishna Menon (1896–1974), is significant for his publishing legacy, editing the Penguin-Pelican series with its concept of good, worthwhile books at affordable prices in paperback. His first twenty authors and titles still remain intellectually thrilling. The Pelicans are today back in print. Indra Lal Roy (1898–1918), a foundation scholar at St Paul's, managed to obtain a temporary commission in 1917 in the Royal Flying Corps despite being a British Indian citizen. Roy distinguished himself as a fighter pilot. In the history of British aviation his record of ten victories in only 170 hours and fifteen minutes of flying time at the very outset of his career is a unique achievement. He was awarded a DFC posthumously.

Asian activists campaigning with their allies against colonialism and for Indian self-government also supported wider national and international concerns. Sophia Duleep Singh was prominent in the Women's Social and Political Union and the Tax Resistance League and actively campaigned for votes for women. Taking her stand on the principle of 'no taxation without representation', she registered her defiance on several occasions. Dadabhai Naoroji successfully contested Finsbury as a Liberal in 1892, winning by a narrow majority of five votes. But standing for Parliament was no easy matter and he faced racist attacks. A model MP, Naoroji supported Gladstone's Irish Home Rule Bill, housing and women's suffrage organisations. He lost his seat in 1895 when the Liberals were swept from power. Mancherjee Bhownaggree, adopted by the Conservatives despite their earlier reservation against Indians in Parliament, won Bethnal Green in 1895, remaining an

MP till 1906. A loyal Conservative, he fully supported the 1905 Aliens Act, the first immigration bill in Britain. The last Asian to become an MP before the 1980s was Shapurji Saklatvala, Communist MP for Battersea from 1922 to 1929. His experience of labour conditions both in Britain and India drew him into radical politics. A powerful orator, he campaigned to improve conditions of labour for workers in Britain and India, seeing their lives as interdependent.

Several Asians were active in local government. Jainti Saggar, who studied medicine at St Andrews University was for eighteen years Labour councillor for Dundee. As chairman of the education committee, Saggar made persistent attempts to lower the threshold for admission into academies to secure a full education for all. Doctor Chuni Lal Katial, Labour member for Finsbury, was elected Indian mayor in 1938–9. As chairman of the public health committee, he was instrumental in setting up the Finsbury Health Centre, a radical concept of integrated health service, anticipating the National Health Service reforms by ten years. Krishna Menon, prominent in the anti-colonial movement as secretary of the India League, was for fourteen years a Labour Councillor for St Pancras, voluntarily stepping down in 1947. He is best remembered for extending the public library service, and establishing a Book Week at the Town Hall and for his cultural legacy, the St Pancras Festival.

In the interwar years several acts tightening lascars' contracts to deter their settlement were passed, making employment conditions even harsher, and eroding their rights as British citizens. The most blatantly racially discriminatory was the 1925 Coloured Alien Seamen Order, effectively de-nationalising them. Union hostility excluded many from the labour market as seen in the Lanarkshire collieries after the war. Racial discrimination, however, was not confined to the working class. Even Ranji was not immune. The 'Colour Bar' affected all: students, professionals and visitors as illustrated by the case of Sir Hari Singh Gour who was refused accommodation by a West End hotel. Equality for Asian Imperial British citizens remained illusory. As in the First World War, Indians also served in the Second World War. Here I mention Noor Inayat Khan, who played a crucial role as a wireless operator in the resistance movement as the Secret Operations Executive in occupied France. Eventually betrayed and imprisoned in 1944 she was shot. She was awarded the George Cross in 1949.

By the early years of the twentieth century, several thousand Asians had been living in Britain for generations and their numbers increased despite attempts at restriction. No statistics are available but total numbers remained small compared to post-1945 numbers. Given the depression years, racial hostility, exclusion and the increased surveillance, how did the working class and the professionals earn their living? For the ex-seamen, starting new lives was made somewhat easier by the existence of a complex but familiar set of institutions, cafes and lodging-houses in the docks, run by their compatriots who helped them negotiate their way around the complex bureaucracy of documentation and secure sea-faring jobs on European articles. Ayub Ali, for instance, who ran the Shah Jolal Restaurant in Commercial Road, provided shelter and food as long as necessary and helped them find employment. Kinship ties and village bonds also provided another network.

Others resorted to self-employment as petty traders and hawkers. There are stories of ex-sailors selling cheap perfume concocted in their own lodging-houses or Indian toffee (spun sugar). Still others worked as casual labourers in catering and the clothing trade, working as porters for Jewish tailoring firms. Some were even hired by film companies as extras for crowd scenes. For their protection, Surat Alley, the trade unionist campaigning for lascar rights, and Akbar Ali Khan set up the Oriental Film Artists' Union. Organisations like the Hindustani Social Club or the Indian Workers' Association begun in 1937 in Coventry catered for the welfare of the working-class Indians. Mixed marriages raised anxiety and their mixed race children were deemed to be a social problem. With increasing demand for sailors during the Second World War, some managed to continue as sailors.

For many working-class Indians, ex-seamen or agriculturists from the Punjab, self-employment as pedlars hawking ready-made clothes door to door became their main profession. Peddling was easily accessible, requiring little capital as three pounds could buy enough to fill a suitcase. Indian pedlars, both Sikhs and Muslims, became familiar in many towns and villages from Stornoway on the Island of Lewis to Kent in the south east of England and also Ireland during this period. Boarding with white landladies, life would have been lonely for those without the company of fellow Indians in a communal household. In time, they succeeded in establishing a clientele among the poorer working classes who lacked their own transport and were unable to afford cash purchases at regular shops. Bringing goods door to door on interest-free credit, pedlars provided a valuable service for those who could only pay in small weekly instalments. A form of trust developed, irrespective of race, culture and language. Trading in such different locations and deemed not creditworthy by white merchants, the early itinerant traders replenished their stock by obtaining supplies by post or rail from Indian silk merchants in London. Some who prospered even opened their own draperies.

Several Indian merchant firms operated in Britain by the 1930s. A 1933 survey of London and Manchester classified forty-eight businesses as 'Indian'. The Indian Chamber of Commerce was founded in 1927. There were Indian draperies, grocery stores, an Egyptian Perfumery in Romford, a Boot Store in Londonderry and in 1935 Dr Sasadhar Sinha, an economist, writer and member of the Progressive Writers Association, established the Bibliophile book shop near the British Museum. In 1932, the first Indian grocery store opened in Glasgow. An Indian estate agency, set up by Nitra and Company, arranged accommodation for students and visitors to London. The Arya Bhavan, billed as the only vegetarian guesthouse, was located in Belsize Park. Then there was the Bombay Emporium set up in 1931 in London, specialising in a range of 'ethnic' foods and condiments.

Indian cafes serving 'rice and curry' to sailors metamorphosed into a different class of restaurants in the interwar years. Veeraswamis, opened in 1926 by Edward Palmer, a descendant of General William Palmer and his wife Faiz Bux, and Shafis were well known. Palmer also founded the Veeraswamy Company marketing Indian products under the brand name, Nizam. By 1946, there were twenty Indian restaurants in London alone. There were restaurants in Glasgow and Cambridge too.

Indian doctors are considered the mainstay of the NHS today. But by 1945 there were already about 1,000 Indian doctors throughout Britain, 200 of them in London. Popular with their patients who came largely from working-class backgrounds, several are remembered for their contributions to British life. For instance, Harbans Gulati (1896–1967) pioneered the 'meals-on-wheels' service, while Chowdhary County Primary School in Laindon, Essex, was named in memory of Dharm Sheel Chowdhary (1902–59). There were academics, journalists, writers like J. M. Tambimutu, founder-editor of *Poetry London*, Mulk Raj Anand, Cedric Dover, contributor to the BBC Indian Programme and Aubrey Menen (1912–89), London-born son of an Irish mother and Indian father; and musicians, the most well known being Kaikhosru Sorabji, whose most celebrated work is *Opus Clavicembalisticum*, the longest piece of piano music.

Places of religious worship were evident from the nineteenth century: the Woking Mosque founded in 1889 and the Zoroastrian Association as early as 1861. The first Sikh Gurdwara, the Bhupindra Dharamsala, was set up in 1911, the Hindu Association was established in 1935, while the East London Mosque and Islamic Centre was opened in 1941. There were social organisations like the Indian Social Club where both the middle- and working-class Asians came together.

This article has thus shown that long before the arrival of post-1950s migrants a small but enterprising community of Asians lived in Britain and community infrastructure already existed. They were not individuals living solitary lives but part of communities, their own and the wider community.

Notes

1 Badr Dahya, 'Pakistanis in Britain: transients or settlers?', *Race* vol. 16, no. 6, 1973, 241–77; Rashmi Desai, *Indian Immigrants in Britain* (Oxford: Oxford University Press 1963); Gurdip Singh Aurora, *New Frontiersmen* (Bombay: Popular Prakashan 1967); Muhammad Anwar, *The Myth of Return Pakistanis in Britain* (London: Heinemann 1979).
2 Roger and Catherine Ballard, 'The Sikhs: the development of South Asian settlements in Britain', in James L. Watson (ed.), *Between Two Cultures Migrants and Minorities in Britain* (Oxford: Basil Blackwell 1973), 21–56.
3 Ballard and Ballard, 'The Sikhs: the development of Asian settlements in Britain', 30.
4 J. L. Watson, 'Introduction: Immigration, ethnicity and class', in Watson, (ed.), *Between Two Cultures Migrants and Minorities in Britain*, 3.
5 See for instance, Verity Saifullah Khan, 'The Pakistanis: Mirpuri villagers at home and in Bradford', Watson, *Between Two Cultures,* 57–89; Vaughan Robinson, *Transients, Settlers, and Refugees Asians in Britain* (Oxford: Clarendon Press 1986); Roger Ballard (ed.), *Desh Pardesh The South Asian Presence in Britain* (London: Hurst and Company 1994); Colin Clarke, Ceri Peach and Steven Vertovec (eds), *South Asians Overseas Migration and Ethnicity* (Cambridge: Cambridge University Press 1990).
6 A. J. P. Taylor, *The First World War An Illustrated History* (London: Penguin 1972).
7 Rozina Visram, *Ayahs, Lascars and Princes Indians in Britain* (London: Pluto Press 1986 & Routledge Revivals 2016); *Asians in Britain 400 Years of History* (London: Pluto Press 2002).
8 Colin Brown, *Black and White Britain: The Third PSI Survey* (London: Heinemann 1984) and Colin Holmes, *A Tolerant Country? Immigrants, Refugees and Minorities in Britain.* (London: Faber and Faber 1991).

9 *Time*, 20 February 1978, 'Britain: Mrs Thatcher's bold gamble', quoted in Antoinette Burton, 'Connective tissue: South Asians and the making of postcolonial histories in Britain', in Susheila Nasta (ed.) *India in Britain South Asian Networks and Connections 1858–1950* (Basingstoke: Palgrave Macmillan 2013), 197.
10 Ibid.
11 Charles Dickens, *David Copperfield* (London: Penguin 2004), 880.
12 Martin Moir, *A General Guide to the India Office Records* (London: British Library 1988).
13 Michael Banton, *The Coloured Quarter* (London: Cape 1955); Peter Fryer, *Staying Power: The History of Black People in Britain* (London: Pluto Press 1984); Colin Holmes, *John Bull's Island Immigration and British Society, 1871–1971* (Basingstoke: Macmillan 1988); Antoinette Burton, *At the Heart of the Empire Indians and the Colonial Encounter in Late-Victorian Britain* (Berkeley: University of California Press, 1998) and *Dwelling in the Archive* (Oxford: Oxford University Press 2003); Michael Fisher, *The First Indian Author in English Dean Mahomed (1759–1851) in India, Ireland and England* (Oxford: Oxford University Press 1996) and *Counterflows to Colonialism Indian Travellers and Settlers in Britain 1600–1857* (Oxford and Delhi: Permanent Black 2004); Shompa Lahiri, *Indians in Britain Anglo-Indian Encounters, Race and Identity, 1880–1930* (London: Frank Cass 2000); Michael Fisher, Shompa Lahiri and Shinder Thandi, *A South-Asian History of Britain Four Centuries of Peoples from the Indian Sub-Continent* (Oxford: Greenwood World Publishing 2007). See also, *Making Britain Project* website: www.open.ac.uk/researchprojects/makingbritain.
14 J. S. Gundara and I. Duffield (eds), *Essays on the History of Blacks in Britain from Roman Times to the Mid-Twentieth-Century* (Aldershot UK and Brookfield VT: Avebury 1992).
15 Nigel File and Chris Power, *Black Settlers in Britain 1555–1958* (London: Heinemann 1995).
16 George Sims, *Living London: Its Work and its Play* (London: Cassell 1906), Volume III, 279.

20
THE DEVELOPMENT OF TRANSMIGRANT HISTORIOGRAPHY IN BRITAIN

Nicholas J. Evans

The growth of migrant studies since the early 1970s has filled significant lacuna in the historiography of Britain during the nineteenth and twentieth centuries. In turn, British migrant historiography has simultaneously caught up with clusters of scholarship relating to the sending (emigrant) and receiving (immigrant) nations – principally at Uppsala in Sweden and Minnesota in the United States.[1] Today, when migrant history is becoming almost mainstream in British universities, it is hard to remember a time when the field was deemed 'old-fashioned' and was seen as 'obsolete' to many in the academy. There was still progress through the Sheffield School under Colin Holmes which advanced scholarly interest in immigration studies as well as scholars at the London School of Economics, especially Charlotte Erickson and Dudley Baines, who influenced emigrant studies. Until the 1990s, however, Britain's position as a major country of transit did not receive comparable attention – despite its position as a link between clusters of scholarship in Northern Europe and North America. Essential to the recent emergence of transmigrant studies – examining those who transited Britain rather than settling here – has been the bringing together of maritime and migrant histories. These had hitherto been part of very separate disciplines of British historiographical thought. Whilst overseas scholarship on transmigration has been the purview of single academic institutions, the development of transmigrant historiography in the UK has followed a very different pattern: the scholars who have been instrumental to the emergence of this subfield of migrant studies have been scattered *across* the UK. Though their work has focused on Britain itself, the field inevitably requires understanding of other geographies, spaces and places and approaches beyond solely that of the history profession. This chapter briefly seeks to explore this new field and to situate it within broader British, European and North American migrant studies, thereby complementing discourse surrounding the Sheffield School.

This contribution emerges out of two decades of research, based at the University of Hull, exploring the totality of alien migration transiting Britain between 1830 and 1930. Earlier analysis revealed that of the circa 15.6 million migrants leaving the UK and Ireland between 1860 and 1913, one-third, or 4.8 million, were aliens.[2] This scale of migration placed Britain into the upper echelons of transit migration alongside other emigrant sending countries – including Germany, Holland, Belgium and Scandinavia. Crucially, it has been possible to estimate the scale and character of transit migration – some 5 million aliens arrived in the UK during the period in question with the purpose not of settling but instead of leaving the UK within two weeks of arrival. At the time, the government and commercial agencies defined these men, women and children as en route to other countries, or as Piore would later define contemporary migrants, 'as birds of passage'.[3] My energies have focused upon the temporary sojourn of ethnic and national outsiders to Britain in transit to new lives in the USA, Canada, Latin America and South Africa. Emulating Colin Holmes' recovery of the voices of the Roma, Frank Neal's earlier work on the Famine Irish sojourning through Liverpool, Aubrey Newman's study of the Poor Jews Temporary Shelter in London, and Tony Kushner's work on transmigrants, more scholars are now recovering the migrant history of Britain's port cities by engaging with those who were transitory. Perhaps because such transients seldom appeared on census enumerators' reports, nor in the General Register Office's files of births, marriages or deaths, or transgressed the law in any significant numbers (thereby featuring in criminal reports or newspaper columns), they represent a significant silence in the British archive. It is often forgotten that three out of the four million foreigners statistically profiled as arriving at British ports in the late Victorian and Edwardian Board of Trade reports were not intent upon settling in London or the Provinces but were in fact set on new lives overseas.

The focus of this chapter is not to debate the intricacies and vagaries of my own work but instead to explore the wider context in which the Sheffield School emerged. Collectively, schools of enquiry in Sweden, England and the United States arose during the 1960s and 1970s to explain earlier migrant patterns. At a time when advanced economies were closing their doors to unrestricted immigration, their collective energies, alongside individual scholarly efforts, have helped bridge the historiographical chasm between disparate scholars of migrant, maritime and heritage studies. Whilst transmigration was previously footnoted in annals of regional or maritime history, the study of the enormous flow of outsiders travelling through Britain fully emerged in the late 1990s due to the pioneering work of Colin Holmes, who redefined the role of the alien in British society and questioned the silences on prejudice in a supposedly tolerant Britain.

This contribution on the historiography of transmigrancy is broken down into three discernible periods. It begins by discussing the pioneers of early 'transmigrant historiography', the era when the topic was a mere adjunct not of British history but 'local' facets of ethnic history in North America. Secondly, it considers the advances made by those in the Sheffield School, as well as scholars less directly involved – including Kenneth Collins and Aubrey Newman – during the 1990s, who considered organisational or port foci in the UK and recovered the local lenses of migrant studies, including, crucially, analyses of spaces and sources *outside* of London. All of these scholars focused their energies upon maritime spaces; thus, engagement with port histories of the 1970s to 1990s is important too. It concludes by exploring how the recovery of the forgotten story of transmigration has been aided by recent advances in the digital humanities. The digital turn in the internet age has enabled many dots in these areas of fragmentary scholarship to be joined with searches of official and organisational archives deposited across the UK. Collectively, the discussion demonstrates how the cluster of scholars, who kept connected through regular conferences, publications and intellectual partnerships, invigorated the Sheffield School. Especially important has been the recent work of the University of Southampton's Parkes Institute for the Study of Jewish/non-Jewish Relations, which has championed for nearly two decades the recovering of transmigration through Britain during the nineteenth and twentieth centuries.

The historiographical forgetting of transmigration

In the aftermath of America closing her door to unrestricted immigration, first in 1921 and then in 1924, the centennial anniversaries of earlier European emigrations to the United States spawned migrant studies on both sides of the Atlantic. The Minnesota School of immigrant or ethnic historians emerged from the collective energies of historians based in mid-western America from the 1930s onwards and brought academic rigour to the histories of separate states shaped by large-scale immigration from Scandinavia. Spurred on by ethnic pride after the Second World War – epitomised by then Senator John F. Kennedy's *A Nation of Immigrants* (1958) – they advanced regional and/or ethnic histories that charted the white settlement of the quintessential nation of immigrants, the United States.[4] In the Cold War era, post-Second World War insularity fuelled nationalist histories, exemplified by the works of Theodore Blegen, who published before and during the Second World War. Blegen's reduction of Britain's importance as a staging post for most Norwegian migrants to a two-page debate on the manipulation of the migrants by British companies was not unique.[5] German migrants' indirect arrival in America was largely glossed over by Marcus Hansen, and scholars of Swedish, Norwegian, Finnish and Danish migration all footnoted, rather than analysed the reasons for this indirect migration. Where it was deemed significant, the role of Britain was explained by the country's domination of freight shipping.[6] The countries haemorrhaging millions of labourers bound for America were therefore, like the founding fathers of America, guided by the commercial might of Pax Britannica when it came to the routes they migrated along.

It was left to a British scholar to integrate the story of the Europeans transiting Britain into mainstream scholarship. The seminal studies by Philip Taylor, emerging in the aftermath of the Second World War, started with his study of Scandinavians amongst the hundred thousand Mormon emigrants who sailed between 1840 and 1890 and migrated to Utah. In 1966, his *Expectations Westward: The Mormons and the Emigration of their British Converts in the Nineteenth Century*, followed in 1971 by *The Distant Magnet*, revealed the kernel of later transmigrant scholarship.[7] The latter was the first monograph-length study of European migration that revealed the central role of the British transmigrant corridor to Nordic settlement in continental North America. Taylor detailed the migrant trek across the North Sea to the Humber, the rail journey to Liverpool, and then the embarkation of millions of Europeans to America's principle harbour, New York, alongside British and Irish migrants.[8] These works were not surprising, since they were inspired by Taylor's earlier work in areas of concentrated white settlement, especially that at Utah, and his later permanent appointment at the often forgotten port of Hull, in its new Department of American Studies. Taylor's work, alongside that of the Minneapolis School, raised awareness of a sizeable white mosaic in North America and Britain's agency as a migrant corridor. They built upon earlier snippets in general survey works of Atlantic migration to the United States, especially those by Marcus Hansen and Maldwyn A. Jones.[9] Collectively, they showed not only how transmigrants influenced Britain, but also how the powerful British merchant marine came to control the transportation of migrants.

While North American scholars of migrant birth or parentage explained how the pull factor of so-called 'charter generations' of migrants influenced the flow of millions of Europeans across the Atlantic, a new generation of European scholars in the 1970s focused on transmigration through Britain, exploring the reasons behind the sustained push of emigrants from an enlarged area of Northern Europe. This period included Reino Kero's evaluation of the concentrated source of Finns' emigration, Kristian Hvidt's astute analysis of Danes' destinational determinism and their purchase of pre-paid journey tickets to America from the 1870s, as well as Frederick Hale's discussion of migrants' agency revealed through their letters home.[10] The Scandinavian trailblazers in the 1970s highlighted the centrality of both the British merchant marine and ports on both sides of Britain in the transmigration journey. Yet the amnesia among American scholars with regard to Britain's role as a stepping-stone was replicated to a lesser degree by the emerging Uppsala school of Scandinavian migrant scholarship.[11] Rather than simply underplaying the transit of Danes, Finns, Swedes and Norwegians, they overplayed the direct emigration of Scandinavians from Europe to America and the perceived importance of preserving their ethnicity within the American melting pot. Key first voyages during the age of sail such as that of the *Restauration* in 1825 were central to their recovering of the Scandinavian aspects of their Scandinavian-American migrant history.[12] Some also emphasised the Edwardian-era emergence of national steamship vessels directly linking Northern Europe to America, again emphasising the bypassing of Britain.[13] However, studies of both immigration and emigration fell into abeyance during what can be described as the dark age of migrant historiography in the 1980s. Paradoxically, as the Sheffield School emerged in Britain, it failed to capitalise upon Taylor's earlier findings and integrate the story of Britain as a staging post. Immigrant and emigrant scholarship remained disparate fields of scholarship in Britain.

The broadening of the scholarly lens

The real recovery of the flesh and detail of transmigration came not from migrant scholars but instead from Liverpool-based maritime researchers – namely academics such as Francis Hyde and his student Robin Bastin, and museologists such as Gordon Read of the Merseyside Maritime Museum. Where either popular or scholarly memory of transmigration was invoked, it occurred at points of embarkation rather than arrival in the UK. It was therefore an explanatory factor used to demonstrate the importance of the port of Liverpool as *the* European emigrant gateway to the New World. Like the scholarly biases of earlier historians eager to augment national histories rather than promote transit nations, renewed interest in the post-industrial port of Liverpool provoked research by academics in the 1970s and then museologists in the 1980s. The role of Cunard, the largest shipping company in the world, in this business was central to the works of Francis Hyde and Robin Bastin.[14] In the aftermath of 1976, and the bicentenary of the loss of the American colonies, such 'house histories' (studies of particular merchant fleets) explained the centrality of the Atlantic to the income generation of shipping lines. America was studied largely at the exclusion of Canada, Latin America and South Africa, despite new scholars researching migration from Britain to those countries.[15]

The state-sponsored Merseyside Maritime Museum's 'Emigrants to a New World' gallery that opened in 1986 in response to early 1980s race riots and Liverpool's economic decay motivated Gordon Read to build upon the work British, Swedish and America schools of migrant scholarship to portray a period when Liverpool pride was bolstered, not undermined, by thousands of migrants.[16] His research, the focus of a Churchill Scholarship to American archives, provided further firsthand accounts of the experiences of people transiting the Humber to Mersey corridor and was subsequently published as a collection of colloquium proceedings.[17] These efforts were mirrored by energies further north, where Harvey Kaplan and Kenneth Collins were forming the Scottish Jewish Archives Centre (opened in 1987) and recovering transmigrant journeys through Glasgow. Collins and Kaplan added the forgotten Scottish dimension, yet denied the significance of the Scottish land border, instead promoting Leith as a Jewish Ellis Island that it was not – initially eliding the Humber whilst promoting Leith and Glasgow.[18]

Collectively, Gordon Read, aided by Philip Taylor, Charlotte Erickson, Dudley Baines, Harvey Kaplan and Kenneth Collins, began conversations with Aubrey Newman, whose earlier work on Jewish migrant history sought to recover new insights into differing parts of Britain.[19] Again, spurred on by a centenary, this time of 1881 and its aftermath as a catalyst for Jewish migration to, through and from Britain, Newman's pioneering championing of computing for historians borrowed from the Scandinavian School and the excellent use of the migrant data contained within shipping records gathered by the Poor Jews Temporary Shelter.[20] Newman's analysis revealed that it was the combined forces of philanthropy and shipping that directed migration through the south of England. Building on the work of Lloyd Gartner and Todd Endelman, they showed that faith-based organisations could shape the direction of transmigrants arriving via the Thames.[21] Rather than America being the fabled distant magnet, or *Goldene Medinah*, they revealed a forgotten alternative destination for transmigrants who traversed Britain – British South Africa. Newman's work also provided a trans-local focus – explaining how eighty percent of Latvian and Lithuanian Jews went from one gubernia (Kovno) to one destination (Johannesburg).[22] Interestingly, during the golden era of the Sheffield School, such advances were in seeming isolation to other areas of migrant scholarship, at least as far as transmigrancy was concerned. This was also the case with other non-Jewish transients travelling during the age of the Great Migration through Liverpool. Frank Neal's work on the transmigration of the Irish through Liverpool published in 1983 thereby revealed that scholars, such as Newman at Leicester and Neal at Salford, did not have to be part of a collective team to advance the scholarship.[23] Meanwhile, in Sweden, the centrality of transport rather than ports was also beginning to gain scholarly traction. Berit Brattne and Sune Åkerman discussed in depth how transport explained the migrant route of so many Swedes analysed by the Uppsala School in 1976.[24] This built upon earlier work by Kristian Hvidt and also encouraged new work by Odd S. Lovoll, who explored how the movement of Scandinavians to North America was impacted by rival transmigrant shipping companies that challenged the dominant position of British shipping.[25]

The joining of historiographical dots and projecting narratives beyond the academy

Until the mid-1990s therefore, the aforementioned schools of migrant, maritime or port scholarship remained disconnected and localised – by either port, institution or company. Crucially, they tended to celebrate rather than interrogate the phenomenon of transmigration, for which the only guestimates of the scale were apparent. Only advances in the late 1990s by the first generation of the Sheffield School, and especially Tony Kushner, completed the story and revealed transmigration was a truly British phenomenon. Kushner's exploration of Southampton broadened the spatial perspective, completing the maritime jigsaw, yet also expanding the chronological foci – moving beyond 1914, which had become a de facto 'end point' for all analyses.[26] He revealed not merely a positive story of integrated travel to, through and from Britain, but problematised the phenomenon by analysing the impact of the closing of America's doors to unrestricted European immigration in 1921 and 1924. He revealed in a series of essays and later in the seminal *Refugees in an Age of Genocide*, the protracted journey some transmigrants encountered during the interwar period. Utilising oral history and inspired by Bill Williams, Kushner revealed the local impact of transmigrants both at the time and in subsequent memory. Expanding on the terms transmigrants and transmigrancy, he explored the intersection of transit migrants and the 'paper walls' they encountered during the interwar era.

Such novel approaches inspired a new generation of scholars – including this author and James Jordan – as the millennium approached. Inspired by the grassroots work of the Sheffield School and influenced by the new possibilities opened up by the internet age, they mined local archives and digitally linked with other scholars in Britain and overseas, together completing the missing piece of the transmigrant jigsaw. Crucially, Evans and Jordan considered both the positive and negative aspects of the business of transmigrancy, yet also included the humanitarian story and human dimension. They closed the gaps between disparate areas of the scholarship, and their work informed museology and public history – laying stronger foundations for the future. They enabled quantification of the scale of transmigrancy through Britain, showing that at least five million traversed the country between 1836 and 1914.[27] Jordan also teased out the transmigrant's positive experiences even when faced with adversity.[28] Evans and Jordan demonstrated that at Southampton a new inland facility at Eastleigh both isolated and protected those stranded in Britain and that serious money was invested into the well-being of reluctant refugees. Such perspectives challenged the Sheffield School's detailing of outsiders' various negative encounters in different parts of Britain. Crucially, scholars working in different fields were drawn together by Southampton's Parkes Institute – exemplified by the multidisciplinary work of Kushner, Jordan and Evans.

The advances in the digital humanities, or a digital turn in the transmigrant scholarship, has gone full circle in recent years. Scholars of other diasporas have begun to borrow the term transmigrancy for their own areas of migrant scholarship – as was the case with David Morris whose work on Irish transmigration via Wales applies transit migration to the internal flow of migrants.[29] Frances Williams characterised *Kindertransportees* in Scotland during the Second World War as transmigrants, based upon their overseas migration once the Shoah had ended.[30] Transit as a focus for scholarship has even been the topic of a recent special edition of the *Journal of Global History*.[31] Recently, a team of scholars at the Scottish Jewish Archives Centre has mined digital archives to not only provide more accurate data concerning the number of Jews who transmigrated via Scotland, but to reveal how many arriving as immigrants into Scotland re-migrated overseas within one or two censuses between 1851 and 1911.[32] Like Kushner's adaptation of transmigration as transmigrancy, so Collins and his team have demonstrated transmigrancy could be applied to those who sojourned through Britain (particularly Scotland) over one or two decades. There was a further cementing of these differing schools after the millennium as Britain began to embrace the opportunity to celebrate the transmigrants who had bolstered the British merchant marine and not been a drain on the state as aliens are often portrayed, whether in the past or the present.

Here, the intersection of scholars working on transmigration with heritage organisations championing the BAME (Black, Asian and Minority Ethnic) voice produced not just another essay or monograph, but heritage markers using this story – Britain as a place of transit – for broader social gain. This cascading of knowledge ensured that awareness of transmigrancy secured popular as well as scholarly attention. Driven by the example of Colin Holmes, Bill Williams and Aubrey Newman, first- and second generation Sheffield Schoolers and their allies have built upon the momentum enabling communities and local histories to be told in public spaces – whether in museums, heritage trails, school curricula or heritage plaques. Through Tony Kushner's efforts, the story was performed and displayed by his students at the Eastleigh Museum – near the site of the Atlantic Park transmigrant camp. Kushner and James Jordan, after championing the cause to Southampton City Council for decades, managed to secure the topic's inclusion in the re-developed SeaCity museum as well as developing their own unique Jewish trail including the former transmigrant hotel at Albert Road. At Hull, the author, supported by Hull City Council, saw the erection of three transmigrant plaques, a statue, walking trail, a play by The History Troupe and inclusion in the 2013–2018 City Plan. One of the legacies of Hull's designation as the UK City of Culture in 2017 is the implementation of transmigrant history into state primary school education, which may also inspire research into neglected aspects of the field.[33] As part of the 2017 City of Culture programme, the position of Hull as a migrant corridor was projected to over 342,000 people during one week of January 2017 as part of the installation 'Arrivals and Departures'.[34] Moreover, Per Kristian Sebak managed, on the centenary of the sinking of the transmigrant-carrying SS *Norge* in 2004, to persuade one of the most remote councils in the UK – at Stornoway on the Island of Lewis – to erect a plaque at the ferry terminus and re-awaken memory of the nearby grave where transmigrants were buried.[35] Transmigration and transmigrancy have not only gained scholarly traction – they have had impact beyond the academy to demonstrate how important nodal points in this story have, to quote BBC News presenter Caroline Bilton, been 'the Heathrow airport of [their] day'.[36]

Conclusion

Unlike its more established academic migrant counterparts, especially in America and Sweden, the field of transmigrant historiography in Britain remains in its scholarly infancy. Like the broader Sheffield School, the next decade looks certain to expand the field yet further. Already, many necessary connections on both sides of the Atlantic, and especially the eastern and western seaboards of the UK, have been made in this field through intellectual and technical innovation. As outlined, the myriad ways in which the findings of the Sheffield School, Aubrey Newman, Bill Williams and others have cascaded beyond the academy (and years before UK Higher Education demanded impact from research) has ensured that the work has steadily gained traction. Throughout, one ubiquitous but largely unacknowledged feature is the wide geographic distribution of the scholars interested in the topic, which has enabled it to achieve a richness it would not have otherwise attained had so many of the school not been born, lived or studied outside of London. This in part explains how and why transmigration studies could challenge the London-centric scholarship that posits the capital as the only place in the UK to receive large-scale levels of migration during the nineteenth and twentieth centuries. These new scholars of transmigration have not been afraid to consult sources outside of London, nor to mention places ranging from Stalybridge to Hartlepool, or Harwich to Cardiff, that are so frequently airbrushed out of such history. When the students of transmigration studies have progressed to scholarly careers within the academy, their students will have a much more rounded view of British transmigratory historiography – and of migrant history in particular – because we can set as seminar or lecture texts the work of members of the school – whether first, second or increasingly third generation. Though some have reached the lofty heights of the ancient universities, the majority of academics are spread thinly across the length and breadth of Britain, including nearly all Britain's leading ports (covering London, Southampton, Portsmouth, Hull, Newcastle, Dundee and Ulster), towns and cities (extending to Birmingham, Manchester, Edinburgh, Chester, Leeds and, of course, Sheffield!). This unusual feature, counter to earlier clusters of migrant scholars in a single institution – such as Minneapolis in the 1930s or Uppsala in the 1970s – will, ironically, help to ensure both its longer-term development and success.

Notes

1 See the overview of the Swedish emigrant project by Harald Runbolm, 'A brief history of a research project', in Harald Runbolm & Hans Norman (eds), *From Sweden to America: A History of the Migration. A Collective Work of the Uppsala Migration Research Project* (Minneapolis: University of Minnesota Press 1976), 11–18. On the cluster of immigrant studies in the United States see: Henry Steele Commager (ed.), *Immigration and American History: Essays in Honour of Theodore C. Blegen* (Minneapolis: University of Minnesota Press, 1961). Whilst Blegen was based at the University of Minnesota, it established its Immigration History Research Center in 1965. This in turn furthered migrant study. See Rudolph J. Vecoli, 'Return to the melting pot: ethnicity in the United States in the eighties', *Journal of American Ethnic History* vol. 5, no. 1, 1985, 7–20. Vecoli was, in turn, succeeded by as director of the IHRC by Donna Gabaccia, who synthesised mid-Western ownership of immigrant history in America. See: Donna Gabaccia, 'The Minnesota School and immigration history at Midwestern Land Grant Universities, 1890–2005', *Journal of Migration History* vol. 1, 2015, 171–199.
2 Nicholas J. Evans, 'Aliens En Route: European transmigration through Britain, 1836–1914', PhD dissertation, University of Hull, 2006, 64.
3 Michael J. Piore, *Birds of Passage: Migrant Labour and Industrial Societies* (Cambridge: Cambridge University Press 1979).
4 John F. Kennedy, *A Nation of Immigrants* (London: Hamish Hamilton 1964).
5 Theodore C. Blegen, *Norwegian Migration to America: The American Transition* (Northfield MN: Norwegian-American Historical Society 1940), 455–456.
6 Marcus Hansen, *The Atlantic Migration, 1607–1860* (Cambridge MA: Harvard University Press 1945), 172–198.
7 Taylor, *Expectations Westward*, especially 162–3, 188–193, 205–207.
8 Taylor, *Expectations Westward*.
9 Hanson, *The Atlantic Migration*; Maldwyn A. Jones, *Destination America* (Glasgow: Fontana 1977), 19–41.
10 Reino Keiro, *Migration from Finland to North America in the Years Between the United States Civil War and the First World War* (Turku, Finland: Institute of Migration 1974); Kristian Hvidt, *Flight to America: The Social Background of 300,000 Danish Emigrants* (New York: Academic Press 1975), 190–194; Taylor, *Distant Magnet*, Chapters 6–8, 107–166.

11 On the amnesia, see the one paragraph to the migrant journey in Robert C. Ostergen, *A Community Transplanted: The Trans-Atlantic Experience of a Swedish Immigrant Settlement in the Upper Middle West, 1835–1915* (Madison: The University of Wisconsin Press 1988), 6.
12 See, for example, the way even leading scholars such as Ingrid Semmingsen, framed their studies of Nordic migration by devoting her entire first chapter to the primacy of the sloop *Restauration*. Ingrid Semmingsen (translated by Einar Haugen), *Norway to America: A History of the Migration* (Minneapolis: University of Minnesota Press 1978), 10–19. The work was a translation of the earlier: Ingrid Semmingsen, *Dróm og dåd* (Oslo: Aschehoug & Co. 1975).
13 See, for example, Birger Osland, *A Long Pull from Stavanger: The Reminiscences of a Norwegian Immigrant* (Northfield MN: Norwegian-American Historical Association 1945), 70–85.
14 Francis E. Hyde, *Cunard and the North Atlantic, 1840–1973: A History of Shipping and Financial Management* (London: Macmillan 1975), 58–118; and *Liverpool & the Mersey: The Development of a Port, 1700–1970* (Newton Abbot: David & Charles 1971), 160–198; Robin Bastin, 'Cunard and the Liverpool Emigrant Traffic 1860 to 1900', MA dissertation, University of Liverpool, 1971.
15 See, for example, Marjory Harper, *Emigration from North-East Scotland*, 2 Vols. (Aberdeen: Aberdeen University Press 1988); Andrew Porter, *Victorian Shipping, Business and Imperial Policy: Donald Currie, the Castle Line and Southern Africa* (Woodbridge: Boydell 1986); Sharron Schwarz, 'Cornish migration to Latin America: a global and transnational perspective', PhD dissertation: University of Exeter, 2003.
16 J. Gordon Read (comp.), *The Leaving of Liverpool: The Story of 19th Century Emigration* (Liverpool: Merseyside Maritime Museum 1986).
17 J. Gordon Read, *Through Liverpool to North America 1830–1907: A Selection of Emigrant Narratives* (Liverpool: Merseyside Maritime Museum 1998).
18 Harvey Kaplan, 'Passage to America through Scotland', *Avotaynu*, vol. V, no. 4, 1989, 7–8; Kenneth Collins, *Be Well! Jewish Immigrant Health and Welfare in Glasgow, 1860–1914* (East Linton: Tuckwell Press 2001), 16–20; Kenneth Collins, 'Scottish transmigration and settlement: records of the Glasgow experience', in Aubrey Newman & Stephen Massil (eds), *Patterns of Migration* (London: Jewish Historical Society of England, 1996), 49–58.
19 Aubrey Newman (ed.), *Migration and Settlement: Proceedings of the Anglo-American Jewish Historical Conference held in London Jointly by the Jewish Historical Society of England and the American Jewish Historical Society, July 1970* (London: Jewish Historical Society of England 1970).
20 Aubrey Newman, 'The Poor Jews' Temporary Shelter: an episode in migration studies', *Jewish Historical Studies* vol. 40, 2005, 141–155; Aubrey Newman, Nicholas J. Evans, Saul Issroff & J. Graham Smith (eds), *Jewish Migration to South Africa: The Records of the Poor Jews' Temporary Shelter 1885–1914* (Cape Town: Kaplan Centre for Jewish Studies and Research 2006).
21 Lloyd P. Gartner, *The Jewish Immigrant in England, 1870–1914* (Detroit MI: Wayne State University Press 1960); Todd M. Endelman, *The Jews of Georgian England, 1714–1830: Tradition and Change in a Liberal Society* (Philadelphia PA: Jewish Publication Society of America 1979).
22 Newman, Evans et al. (eds), *Jewish Migration to South Africa*, 12. Kovno is today known as Kaunas.
23 Frank Neal, 'Liverpool, the Irish steamship companies and the famine Irish', *Immigrants & Minorities* vol. 5, no. 1, 1986, 28–61.
24 Berit Brattne & Sune Åkerman, 'The importance of the transport sector for mass emigration', in Harald Runbolm & Hans Norman (eds), *From Sweden to America: A*

History of the Migration. A Collective Work of the Uppsala Migration Research Project (Minneapolis: University of Minnesota Press, 1976), 176–200.
25 Kristian Hvidt, 'Informationsspredning of emigration med saerligt henblik på det atlantiske transportsystem', in *Emigrationen fra Norden indtil 1. Verdenskrig. Rapporter til det Nordiske historikermode i Kobenhavn 1971* (Copenhagen, 1971); Odd S. Lovell, '"For people who are not in a hurry": The Danish Thingvalla Line and the transportation of Scandinavian emigrants', *Journal of American Ethnic History* vol. 13, no. 1, 1993, 48–67.
26 Tony Kushner and Katharine Knox, *Refugees in an Age of Genocide: Global, National and Local Perspectives during the Twentieth Century* (Abingdon: Routledge 1999), 88–102; Tony Kushner, 'A tale of two port Jewish communities: Southampton and Portsmouth compared', *Jewish Culture and History* vol. 4., no. 2, 2001, 87–110.
27 Nicholas J. Evans, 'Indirect passage from Europe transmigration via the UK, 1836–1914', *Journal for Maritime Research* vol. 3, no. 1, 2001, 70–84; Evans, 'Aliens en route: European transmigration through Britain, 1836–1914'; Evans, 'A Staging Post to America – Jewish Migration via Scotland', in Kenneth Collins, Aubrey Newman and Bernard Wasserstein (eds.), *Two Hundred Years of Scottish Jewry* (Glasgow: Scottish Jewish Archives Centre, 2018), 301–326.
28 James Jordan, presentation to the University of Hull's North and South Culture Café, April 2016.
29 David Morris, 'Peaks and troughs: Irish transmigration through South Wales, 1850–1900', *The Welsh History Review* vol. 28, no. 2, 2016, 283–306.
30 Frances Williams, *The Forgotten Kindertransportees: The Scottish Experience* (London: Bloomsbury 2015), 1–80.
31 *Journal of Global History* vol. 11, no. 2 (2016).
32 Kenneth Collins, Neville Lamdan & Michael Tobias, '200 years of Scottish Jewry: a demographic and genealogical profile', *Journal of Multidisciplinary Research* vol. 8, no. 1, 2016, 63–84.
33 www.hulldailymail.co.uk/pioneering-hull-curriculum-project-wins-national-award/story-30351080-detail/story.html (accessed 20 December 2017).
34 www.imitatingthedog.co.uk/portfolio/made-in-hull-arrivals-and-departures/ (accessed 20 December 2017); https://culturenet.co.uk/explore/made-in-hull-migrant-research-transformed-into-visual-journey (accessed 20 December 2017).
35 Per Kristian Sebak, *Titanic's Predecessor: The S/S Norge Disaster of 1904* (Lakesvaag: Seaward 2004); Scottish Jewish Archives Centre, photographs of Stornoway. [I'd like to thank Harvey Kaplan for helping with this research.]
36 www.bbc.co.uk/news/live/uk-england-humber-37085683 (accessed 20 December 2017).

SECTION 6
Identities

Tony Kushner

Introduction

The analysis of migrant identity is not an easy task. Even within the same group and individuals within it, identities are constantly shifting and contested. As the chapters in this section emphasise, definition from the outside (whether hostile, sympathetic or ambivalent) cannot be ignored in the complex processes of identity formation. But there are grave dangers in assuming that a simplistic analysis of the relationship between 'self' and 'other', or of image and reality, is enough to understand the 'true' identity of the group under study. Reflecting new approaches to cultural studies and the construct of ethnicity, in 1990 Stuart Hall noted that:

> Identity is not as transparent or unproblematic as we think. Perhaps instead of thinking of identity as an already accomplished fact, which the new cultural practices then represent, we should think, instead, of identity as a 'production', which is never complete, always in process, and always constituted within, not outside, representation.[1]

An academic generation on, scholarship is still not immune to creating crudely defined 'boxes' in which to place the migrant. And whether internally or externally imagined, the desire to show *the* 'authentic' migrant identity is fraught with problems.

Ryan Hanley's subtle exploration of the black intellectual, Olaudah Equiano, reveals how expectations of his narrative have changed from the eighteenth to the twenty-first centuries. He has moved from being 'Equiano the African' to 'Equiano *the* African' with the inevitable problems this has created in terms of whether his is a representative story – as if any autobiographical writing could be. Attempts to pin

Equiano down in terms of time, place and concept (for example Igbo culture and South Carolina) do not do justice to the fluidity they represent in terms of place and praxis. Even in the case of the few elite slave accounts that were published in the late eighteenth and early nineteenth centuries, such as Equiano's *The Interesting Narrative*, they vary in terms of the importance placed on concepts such as race, religion and gender. And as with other migrant histories, the focus on one key figure or movement has often been at the expense of others that remain obscure in intellectually lazy attempts to create a sense of typicality.

Kathy Burrell also highlights the dangers of scholars classifying migrants too neatly. Her case study of the various movement of Poles post-1945 is another marginalised story which does not meet the expectations of the *Windrush* myth of *black* migration fundamentally changing the post-war British landscape. Yet even in the limited historiography, the categories of 'soldier, wife and worker' in relation to the Poles create their own silences and marginality – for example, that of female migrants in Britain during the late 1940s. As with Hanley's study of Equiano, the importance of the individual and how they construct and reconstruct their identities is emphasised by Burrell. Categories imposed from without, especially relating to the 'legality' or 'illegality' of those who came from Eastern Europe, have been crucial in everyday life as have the economic opportunities offered (and refused) to them. State and society imposed limitations on the freedom of these Poles. But Burrell rightly insists that there is far more to migrant life than discrimination and the necessity of finding work. On the positive side she notes the importance of adventure, the excitement of new encounters and, at a very basic level, experiencing 'fun' as migrants from a restrictive and often politically dangerous life at 'home' experienced greater freedom. More negatively, as is the case with all migrants, especially those whose journeys have in any way been less than voluntary, the risks, dislocation and costs involved must equally not be ignored. What emerges from her study of at least three major movements from the same country in as little as three-quarters of a century is the *variation* that is present and, again, the historiographical dangers of imposing simplistic categories that fail to describe one individual experience over time – let alone that of mass movements.

Donald MacRaild and Kyle Hughes in their overview of the neglected but important Ribbon movement amongst Irish migrants in the nineteenth century also reveal the difficulty of restraining migrant identity into one heading. Hard to define for those both on the inside and outside, Ribbonism had certain characteristics such as an overarching anti-Orangeism and a necessary secrecy given its potentially subversive nature in the eyes of the British state authorities. To understand it fully, MacRaild and Hughes argue, Ribbonism has to be placed in wider context. First, in relation to the social crisis of the migrant receiving society. Second, with regard to the ongoing relationship between the 'homeland' and the place of settlement for the Irish migrants. As with Hanley's study of Equiano and Burrell's of the Polish migrant, MacRaild and Hughes emphasise how the Irish migrant, for all the poverty and discrimination they faced, cannot simply be regarded as passive victims. Ribbonism was a shifting movement, but it was based on Irish migrant resistance and an identity that was transnational and increasingly diasporic, fitting neatly into the individual example of Equiano and the collective experiences of the British Poles.

Stuart Hall, whilst problematising the idea of 'authenticity to which the term "cultural identity" … lays claim', acknowledged the 'importance of imaginative rediscovery', including 'Hidden histories', in a variety of socially progressive movements, including that of anti-racism.[2] Such issues are at the heart of James Jordan's contribution to this section. Whilst it could also easily slot into 'Places and Spaces' with its focus on the East End of London, Jordan's emphasis is on individuals, both real and imaginary, present or returning to this particular and peculiar part of the metropolis, what Anne Kershen has called 'a very special and unique place'.[3] On one level, the chapter is a neatly executed piece of cultural archaeology, unearthing a doubly hidden history – both within the archive and in wider memory relating to its subject matter. In itself it is an important reminder for the scholar of migration, touched upon in *John Bull's Island*, to use visual and audio sources to expose the presence of migrants in the local landscape.[4] On another, deeper level, it asks us to probe who is speaking and on behalf of whom in the archive?

Tom Harrisson's remarkable and early BBC television film was intended as an internationalist intervention against the dangerous forces, especially racism, which he rightly perceived were pushing the world into a bloody and genocidal conflict. It thus is an early example of Hall's 'Hidden histories' and way ahead of its time in celebrating, if somewhat problematically and hierarchically, the East End's migrant diversity. It, and later radio and television documentaries on the East End, constructed (and more rarely, deconstructed) concepts of authenticity, juxtaposing the 'true' East Ender, the 'Cockney', with those of migrant origin, before recognising by the 1960s that it was possible to be both.[5]

Beyond their specific focus, all four case studies in this section raise the issue of power and how both from outside and internal forces, the identities of the individual within the migrant group are negotiated with greater or lesser freedom. Such identities change over time and reflect many different factors such as gender, age, politics, religion, and so on. Attempts, including within academia, to essentialise the identity, however well meaning in wider struggles, are always fraught with danger and fix and limit the migrant and his/her agency, including in the sphere of cultural production. Inhabiting worlds that are blatantly and simultaneously local and global, these four chapters show the complexity but also the necessity of studying migrant identities not only to understand their individual and collective experiences but also for the insights gleaned about wider society. Lastly, as Hall insisted, they make clear how representations and everyday experiences are, ultimately, impossible to untangle if the many layers of what it is to be a migrant (and non-migrant) are to be fully confronted.

Notes

1 Stuart Hall, 'Cultural identity and diaspora', in Jonathan Rutherford (ed.), *Identity: Community, Culture, Difference* (London: Lawrence & Wishart 1990), 222–237 (222).
2 Ibid., 224.
3 Anne Kershen, 'From East End 1888 to East End 2016', in Colin Holmes and Anne Kershen (eds), *An East End Legacy: Essays in Memory of William J. Fishman* (London: Routledge 2017), 6–26 (23).
4 Colin Holmes, *John Bull's Island: Immigration & British Society, 1871–1971* (Basingstoke: Macmillan 1988), passim. See especially Holmes' astute commentary on the ten carefully selected photographs following page 230.
5 More generally, see Gareth Stedman Jones, 'The "cockney" and the nation, 1780–1988', in David Feldman and Gareth Stedman Jones (eds), *Metropolis London: Histories and Representations since 1800* (London: Routledge 1989), 272–324. Characteristically for even progressive historians, this overview does not mention Jews and their role in constructing the 'Cockney' or being perceived as its 'other'.

21

UNDERGROUND CATHOLIC NETWORKS IN IRELAND AND BRITAIN

The case of Ribbonism before the famine and after

Donald M. MacRaild and Kyle Hughes

Ribbonism was a tradition, not an organisation; it never was one continuous entity. Nor was there one invariable Ribbon objective (or set of objectives) consistently adhered to across time and place. Instead, Ribbonism was denoted in many underground groupings in parts of Ireland and within Irish communities in Britain, often with only tenuous (if any) links which operated variously as anti-Orange, Catholic *confrères*, bent on trade-union-type protection, racketeering, immigrant aid, and pub-based forms of conviviality.[1] Whilst the Ribbon tradition inherited some of the characteristics of the many eighteenth-century rural redresser movements (of which the Whiteboys were the most pervasive), its direct ancestors were the Defenders.

Defenderism bequeathed much to Ribbonism: personnel certainly (though the secretive nature of both movements makes identification of members difficult); anti-Orangeism (if not to say anti-Protestantism); Catholic self-protectionism in the midst of land hunger and a contracting domestic linen industry in the Ulster borderlands after the French Wars; and a tangible (if hazy) politics predicated initially on the Catholic Question, later on O'Connellism, and later still (in the guise of Hibernianism) on Home Rule. In short, the term Ribbonism can be used to describe a variety of underground Irish societies which shared certain characteristics manifested in oaths, passwords, organisational structures, terminology, and secrecy which sought to protect popular Catholic interests in a broad sense through much of the nineteenth century.

The word 'Ribbonism' was a neologism created by the press and officials to describe the totality of Irish protest and group violence. Ribbonmen rarely referred to themselves as Ribbonmen, for it was usually a name given to them by others. Nevertheless, groups of disaffected Catholics styled as Ribbonmen first came to prominence in rural Ulster from 1810 during a period of sectarian strife which mirrored earlier outbreaks of violence during the 1780s and 1790s.[2] They differed little from Defenders at this point; indeed, the names Defenders and Ribbonmen were used interchangeably in the Ulster border counties for much of the 1810s.[3] At the same time, Catholic agitators in County Down were referred to as both 'Threshers' and Ribbonmen; while in Donegal the thriving illicit poteen-making business was also said to be the work of Ribbonmen.[4] Having spread to Roscommon, Mayo and Galway, 'Ribbonmen', by 1818, resembled earlier violent agrarian redresser groups, plundering farmhouses for arms and attempting to intimidate local landowners.[5] A different, proto-trade union and labour enforcement racket, but one that expressed a sense of Irish identity and a fervent Catholic sectarianism, also called Ribbonism, emerged in Dublin in the 1820s and 1830s, as was brought to light by several show trials. Evidence heard in court claimed there was a sophisticated interconnected network, with subscription-paying members in various counties, and in Britain.[6] The spreading of Ribbonism beyond the island was repeated in the flurry of activities affecting numbers of Irish people in British towns, including Liverpool, in the early 1850s, when the Dublin police broke up what they believed was a huge Ribbon network.

The British dimension of Ribbonism was principally a function of migration. The presence of Ribbonism there corresponded to a complex interaction of migrating members, risk-spreading beyond the island of Ireland itself, and the functional value of immigrants in terms of leadership, funding and general support. In maintaining lines of movement, communication and activity between the islands, these Ribbonmen provide evidence commensurate with Delaney's clarion call for a history of Ireland beyond the island, and a focus on how the diaspora affected Ireland itself.[7]

These factors, and the way they were discovered, reported, and acted on, are the themes of this chapter. For together they represent an aspect of the Irish immigrant experience which was an important dimension of community life for some migrants in Britain. Ribbonism connected ordinary immigrants through networks of publicans, Ribbon society officials, and tramping agents. There is an embracing definition, which focuses on the concepts of Catholic self-help, emigrant aid, and proto-trade unionism. Such an approach merges our interests in labour and migration with an appreciation of the sectarian peculiarities of Irish life. As exemplars of this important, but understudied, clandestine immigrant culture, the focus here is on two discrete sets of episodes of Ribbon activity in Britain in the 1820s and 1830s, and again in the 1850s. This approach enables us to illustrate the persistence of a Ribbonite tradition and the similarities noticed across the periods in question.

Ribbonism spreads to Britain in the 1820s and 1830s

The years between Napoleon's final defeat in 1815 to the Year of Revolutions, in 1848, contain much evidence of sustained Irish participation in British radical movements. Yet, migrants also maintained their own organisations. Although Irish trade unionism and radical political movements were particularly noticeable in the textile centres of Scotland and north-west England, the two most influential Irish movements – one Catholic, the other Protestant – were Orangeism (formed in

1795) and Ribbonism. From an early point, and certainly long before the famine, the persistence and spread of Ribbonism reflected the growing Irish population. We might expect Ribbonism to be concentrated where the Irish themselves were most numerous, and certainly centres such as Liverpool, Manchester, and Glasgow witnessed peaks of activity and hardy traditions. However, small towns also had instances of Ribbon networking. Ilkeston in Derbyshire, Warrington in Cheshire, or Hanley in Staffordshire, each witnessed some activity and came to the authorities' notice at times.

Ribbonism spread to Britain in the period after the French Wars. In 1822, there was considerable activity between the islands, as revealed when an informer carried the 'goods' (Ribbon slang for passwords) to London, having received them from two men from Ireland who went to considerable lengths to avoid the authorities, travelling on to the Continent, via Hull.[8] That Irish authorities noticed these British activities is a matter of note. The investigations of the Dublin Town Major, Henry Sirr, revealed, through informers, early examples of attempts to bring Manchester and Liverpool into union with Dublin Ribbonism:

> The establishment of Irish societys [sic] in this country [i.e. Britain] are for the purpose[s] of receiving fugitives from Ireland that escapes from it. London is full lately from Cork and Limerick and there is not a county but have them in the friendship here from Scotland to the southernmost part of England.[9]

Sirr's investigations led to a major trial in Dublin where it emerged that some of the principal defendants had criss-crossed the Irish Sea on Ribbonite business, including a coal-heaver named Michael Keenan.[10] Keenan had been negotiating the union of Dublin and Liverpool Ribbon societies with the result that 'The reorganisation was [...] finally effected in February 1822 with the establishment of a national board, for which purpose Liverpool was considered an integral part of Ireland itself: itself one of the nine committees "in the North", it was entitled to send two delegates.'[11] Soon after, Keenan and others were arrested and tried for administering illegal oaths, unaware that their every move had been reported back to the authorities by a number of spies and informers.[12] The trial that followed revealed that Ribbonmen, spies, and the state moved in transnational circuits connecting the islands. The game of cat and mouse between the state and disaffected Irish Catholic conspirators continued into the 1830s and beyond, with British cities being major hubs of Ribbon activity. There was surveillance and spying, informer stipends funded by government, and eventually arrests and trials, all part of a culture where policing was every bit as conspiratorial as the conspirators themselves.

State actions against men such as Keenan, in what amounted to show trials, were not successful in thwarting Ribbonism in the short or long term. Periods of quiet may be noticed, but the basic principles of clandestine Catholic collective self-help and labour protection never went away, but morphed, shifted, took on different forms in new places. Certainly, authorities continued to name these types of activities as Ribbonism until at least the early 1870s.

Sheer numbers of migrants suggest Ribbonism was always likely to find fertile ground in Britain. The famine doubled the population of the Irish in Britain, but the 1830s also saw large rises, notably in exactly the place where secret societies were said to prosper. During this decade, the Catholic population of Liverpool increased from 11,016 to 18,900 – most of these being Irish.[13] Consequently, Ribbon society membership sharply rose as all the major towns and cities of the north and central Scotland were becoming homes to ever-larger groups of Irish. Between 1841 and 1861, the Irish-born population of Britain nearly doubled to 805,717, with between 35 per cent and nearly 50 per cent resident in just four cities: London, Liverpool, Manchester and Glasgow – three of the four hotspots of Ribbonism. The Home Office also received reports, in 1841, from the Lord Lieutenant revealing that, following investigations of Ribbonism in Ireland, he was able to report the existence of branches in Manchester, Sheffield, Whitehaven, Lancaster, 'and other places both in England and Scotland'.[14]

Ribbonism was not a Republican movement. At no point, did it resemble its more illustrious fellow secret society, the Fenians. It is true that at various points during the nineteenth century Ribbonmen aspired to some conception of a 'free Ireland' shaped loosely by popular perceptions of the principles of the French Revolution. Their politics were ill-defined, however, and much of the time Ribbonmen were engaged in factional disputes, labour struggles, and anti-Orange violence. It fought the causes of waged rural labour and regulating local labour supplies on Ireland's two main canals (the Royal and Grand), but especially in Dublin from the 1820s.[15] Where Ribbonism was prominent in Ulster as a marker of Catholic resistance to Orange sectarianism, it must be seen in the context of growing Catholic assertiveness – something made more palpable in 1829, when Daniel O'Connell's emancipation movement was successful in opening up public offices to Catholics. In Britain, too, attitudes towards Ribbonism were couched in politico-religious terms. The 'Ribbon threat', consistently kept in the mind's eye of the public by reactionary journals like the *Standard* or *John Bull*, was one by-product of the wider phenomenon of Victorian anti-Catholicism.[16]

Ribbon societies readily dispensed forms of social politics, most notably by harbouring fugitives from the authorities. On both islands, Ribbonmen overtly undermined the efforts of the police and courts to bring perpetrators to justice, and used physical force of a type approved of by militants.[17] Much endeavour in Ireland was directed as 'a recoil of [i.e. against] Orangeism', and as a counter-blast to the growth of this and other ultra-Protestant societies,[18] and this also was true in the sectarian hotspots of western Scotland and Lancashire. Here, Ulstermen imported their rancorous, sectarian traditions, and Ribbonism was but one component.

Dublin Castle, the seat of the Irish administration, knew of the importance of these expatriate networks: the Liverpool police, for example, were often called on to look out for particular characters in their city's pubs, which were hubs of Irish popular politics.[19] Indeed, Belchem sees Ribbonism as central plank of Liverpool's Catholic community, a key marker of the ethnic consciousness that came to dominate the city's Irish Catholic communities for over a century. Here, as in Dublin, the organisation acted as a waterfront trade union, with knowledge of the latest goods, signs and passwords, all of which was vital if newly arriving migrants were to obtain work. By the mid-1830s the city had thirty branches and 1,350 members. It is further suggested that clerical opposition to Ribbonism strengthened, rather than diminished, its radical appeal.[20] In all, the Liverpool variant not only looked like its Dublin equivalent, it was actually connected to it, as Keenan's trial in 1822 showed, and as the trials of Dublin Ribbon leader Richard Jones in the early 1840s and later episodes also revealed.

Activity was not, however, restricted to Ribbonism; and Ribbonism was not sealed off from other currents pressing for change. Irishmen in Britain also played important roles in parallel trade unions. In Scotland, for instance, working-class activism was strongest where the Irish were most numerous, not least in weaving districts. Lancashire cotton workers' organisations also enjoyed high Irish participation rates, and the most famous of all the early cotton union leaders, John Doherty, the founder of the General Union of Spinners (1829), was a Donegal-born immigrant himself. Doherty was one of thousands of Irish textile workers who left Ireland's waning industry for British factories or outwork. Indeed, Doherty became, in E. P. Thompson's assessment, 'the greatest of the leaders of the Lancashire cotton workers'.[21] Ribbonism was, then, one of a variety of instruments of communal protection that drew Irish interest.

Ribbon activity occurred in most urban communities associated with heavy Irish migration, thus causing consternation among the authorities who expended great energy investigating it. Put simply, the authorities feared Ribbonism's *potential* size and exaggerated its *actual* extent. Yet, the organisation has traditionally yielded little interest among the historians of the Irish in Britain.[22] Indeed, Ribbonism is traditionally glossed over, though Belchem especially, but also Ó Catháin, MacRaild and McBride, have gone some way to right the oversight by describing strong and enduring webs of Ribbonism in northern England and Scotland.[23] That said, the limited extent of the historiography is still out of kilter with longevity of Ribbonism. Within some Irish communities in Britain, the overspill of Irish culture was apparent, when Ribbonism sprang to the notice of the authorities because of internal struggles between Leinster and Ulster factions. In 'their connexion in England + Scotland', wrote one observer, these Ribbonmen 'are divided like Ireland, but the most numerous body are [sic] connected with the Ulster Delegates'.[24]

Migrating from a culture of clannish, close-knit communal ties, Irishmen passed easily from the rank and file to the centre of labour activism in Britain. Irish leadership in labour movements and social protests extended from the heights of John Doherty, down deep into the mass of the workforce – to the level of, what we would today call, the shop stewards.[25] It has been suggested that, during the 1820s and 1830s, the Irish were major players in the union activities of northern textile workers, and were involved in 'every major trial of strength between cotton hand-loom weavers and their employers' and were prominent among the linen and stuff weavers of Barnsley and Leeds; on the Liverpool waterfront; and among Manchester's building operatives.[26] In 1834, during his tour of Britain as part of the Royal Commission into the Irish Poor Law, Cornewall Lewis was told that the Irish are 'more prone to take part in trades unions, combinations and secret societies than the English' and 'are the talkers and ringleaders on all occasions'.[27] Where the Irish were numerous, for example in textile districts of the north of England, trade combinations were, according to Daniel O'Connell, *deeply tinged with Ribbonism*'.[28]

In the 1830s, with migration from Ireland expanding markedly, the Irish presence in wider working-class organisations also grew. What complicated matters was the combination of trade unionism – itself far from fully accepted by the establishment and employers – and Ribbon-type characteristics. The Irish facility with clandestine modes of operation granted unionism a certain strength while undermining its position with the classes above. The opponents of these ethnic and class formations were naturally local elites, such as magistrates, employers, and the police. These opponents also enjoyed strong support from the Catholic Church and Daniel O'Connell and both presented huge obstacles to potential trade union success by proscribing membership of oath-bound organisations. From the early 1830s the Catholic clergy pressed hard against the oaths associated with labour combinations – both in Ireland and northern England – which were what Bishops Briggs of the Northern Union described as threats to the 'working man's eternal welfare'. The church's response was to forge a layer of social welfare provision of its own.[29]

Part of Ribbonism's notoriety derived from a belief that it was a political conspiracy. Tory newspapers in the 1830s blamed the occurrence of clandestine groups like these on Daniel O'Connell's Repeal Movement. The showman, O'Connell, did not always dampen enthusiasm for such claims.[30] Equally, his son, W. H. O'Connell, boasted that '... when he visited Manchester there was a fellow there dressed as a pedlar, who tried to introduce Ribbonism into that town. The next time he came there they laid hold of him, carried him out and ducked him in the pond, and from that day to this no Ribbonman had made his appearance in Manchester.'[31] Another son, Maurice O'Connell, told a Repeal meeting about two repeal wardens in Airdrie, Bernard Kane and Robert Short, who had declared themselves in favour of Ribbonism before recanting when threatened with expulsion.[32]

Armagh to Stafford via Liverpool: Ribbonism in the early 1850s

During the late 1840s and early 1850s, notwithstanding the terrible conditions that brought about hunger and disease, there was a large and persistent outbreak of popular unrest on the borders of Down, Armagh, Monaghan, and Louth. These activities were severe enough to prompt a parliamentary enquiry and demands for new legislation to punish violent redressers.[33] It was in evidence given to this enquiry that the long-serving Resident Magistrate, Captain Bartholomew Warburton, echoed widespread attitudes when he reckoned that, in the early 1850s, the Ribbon 'confederacy' remained 'very considerable' in Manchester and Liverpool. Evidence garnered from the Ribbonmen tried in Dublin suggested the organisation extended far beyond the limits of Lancashire and Scotland, which the select committee had characterised as its British extent.[34] Captain George

Fitzmaurice, stipendiary magistrate, latterly posted in turbulent Crossmaglen, at the heart of the inter-county aggravation of the early 1850s, had undertaken an extensive investigation of Ribbonism in the north at the behest of the Viceroy of Ireland, Lord Clarendon.

Fitzmaurice was asked where the 'central authority' of Ribbonism was based. He responded rather vaguely: 'I believe it is at Belfast, so it is said; some say it is at Liverpool; others at Glasgow'.[35] When quizzed about the amounts of money Ribbonmen could generate, Fitzmaurice reckoned £250 had been raised to defend a Ribbonman against a murder charge by sending collectors out to the main centres: Belfast, Liverpool, Glasgow, and Dublin.[36] Senior policeman, John Henry Brownrigg, demonstrated to the committee clear knowledge of the webs and networks of post-famine Ribbonism:

> This unlawful and pernicious society is in a complete state of organisation; its members are divided into districts, parishes and committees, or lodges, with their respective officers. It has branches in Liverpool, Glasgow and Manchester, while delegates from these towns, and from several districts in Ireland, meet periodically at their head-quarters to transact the business of the body, to agree upon and disseminate the new pass-words, signs &c. [...] The headquarters of this society is moveable; sometimes it is held in Dublin, at other times at Glasgow, Liverpool or Belfast [...] who are the actual leaders [...] is only known to a few of the principal delegates [...].[37]

Brownrigg was a seasoned, professional, public servant. Warburton was another experienced man who stated 'the Ribbon Society exists to a great extent in Manchester and Liverpool'. Warburton explained how he had communicated with police in the two British cities whilst trying to intercept letters sent between the organisations in Ireland and England. He recognised post-marks from the cities on communications to Ribbonmen in Ireland, but denied knowledge of Ribbonism being any more widespread than these two centres.[38] Warburton was asked whether Ribbonmen based in England had different objectives than local trade unions; he thought they did, arguing their aims remained Irish, bound up with grievances about landownership. When asked how men in England could affect matters in Ireland, he responded by saying that 'if a man makes his escape, and there is a warrant against him in Ireland, and he goes to Liverpool or Manchester, he is sure to find protection there, and be put in the way that authorities cannot possibly lay hold of him'.[39] Irish magistrates, then, were not able to confirm such extensive penetration of British towns and cities by Ribbonmen; Warburton, for example, spoke only of his direct knowledge of Manchester and Liverpool associations, evinced by evidence brought before him.[40]

The early 1850s, therefore, saw a significant amount of concern about the extent of Ribbonism in Britain. Early in 1853, there was a flurry of communication between Dublin Castle and various police officials in England, especially in the classic hotspot of Liverpool, but also in lesser places, such as Hanley in Staffordshire.

The arrest in Liverpool, in 1853, of publican and emigrant 'man-catcher', William Robinson,[41] shows that his prosecution was supported by evidence which the Crown Solicitor of Ireland, William Kemmis, acquired in relation to the arrest of eight Ribbonmen in a pub, the Elephant and Castle, in Hanley.[42] The Hanley swoop was the work of Wicklow-born professional policeman, J. H. Hatton.[43] Hatton had worked closely with Under-Secretary Thomas Drummond, in the 1830s, and was well aware of the Ribbon threat.[44] News of the seizure of the Ribbonmen's goods from Robinson and his connections led the *Morning Chronicle* to firm conclusions as to the existence of Ribbonism in Britain. Noting how Ribbonism was already a well-known feature of Lancashire life, 'yet their extent was unknown, and their power under-estimated'. It continued, saying that 'within the last few days [...] some very startling discoveries have been made, which show that Ribbonism is no longer confined to Ireland, but is in full force and operation in every considerable town in England and Scotland'.[45]

Robinson's arrest was not an isolated example. Nor was Hatton's evidence the only testimony against him. Various claims were made about men communicating to him in Liverpool, with lodges of Ribbonmen across north-west England and Ireland in cahoots.[46] In the end, Robinson was tried with three other men in Dublin.[47] At the same time Dublin police broke up a Ribbon ring based on an Irishman named Hugh Masterson, who was arrested in his house in Warrington.[48] During his interrogation Masterson described Ribbonism as a Catholic self-defence association. He also knew Robinson, who wrote to him.[49] The British/Irish connection was once again exemplified by the arrest and conviction of a small-trader called James Hagan,[50] who worked in Belfast's Smithfield Market. In March 1854, his trial asserted that he was the county delegate for Antrim. Attorney General, Abraham Brewster, suggested that Belfast – with its transport and trade links with Liverpool and Glasgow – was well placed to be a centre of Ribbon activity. Hagan's trial also heard of Ribbonmen in counties Dublin, Meath, Derry, Monaghan, and Louth, of letters from Hagan found in the house of a Ribbonman in Randalstown, county Antrim, and of Ribbon meetings held in Downpatrick, County Down.[51]

Conclusions

In the period under discussion, the Irish-born in Britain doubled in number, before peaking in the 1870s. Such numbers would not be achieved again till 1971. Mass Irish immigration into Victorian Britain also was a moment of social crisis in the receiving communities, or least in many of them. Out-migration of Britons was growing, industrial transformation was rendering many handicrafts obsolete, or at least drove down wages and labour opportunities. The Irish years of famine also were dubbed the 'Hungry Forties' in Britain. The combination of social and economic difficulties, sectarian antipathy, and national difference, each contributed to the distinctive character of Irish immigrants. It is small wonder that the Irish retained instruments of communal cohesion and self-defence.

The brief examples of Ribbon activity in Britain discussed here illustrate the importance of retaining homeland connections for the Irish in Britain. Indeed, they rather suggest that successive generations did so. At the most general level, the Ribbon associations of Irishmen at home and in Britain suggests the efficacy of following Delaney's exhortation to place Ireland in a broader frame, and to explore how homeland was influenced by new lands.[52] Plainly, the police in Ireland and the administration in Dublin were of the view that the Irish in Britain were key agents in the endless swirl of social and political turbulence that affected Ireland. Agents, paid spies, and countering networks were all part of a web of containment which stretched across both sides of the Irish Seas. Voluminous official reports, transcripts, and correspondences, indicate that this was so. Perhaps the principal observation should, however, be that the authorities in Ireland were very clearly of the mind, not only that the Irish in Britain were involved in conspiracies and disorder at home, but also were ringleaders. From this flows a further comment: that the Irish were not passive recipients of hostility or economic difficulty. They fought for their place in a sometimes hostile world. Ribbonism was one functional tool for doing so.

Notes

1 Tom Garvin, 'Defenders, Ribbonmen and others: underground political networks in pre-famine Ireland', *Past and Present*, vol. 96, no. 1, 1982, 133–55; M. R. Beames, 'The ribbon societies: lower-class nationalism in pre-famine Ireland', *Past and Present* vol. 97, no. 1, 1982, 128–43; and John Belchem, '"Freedom and friendship to Ireland": Ribbonism in early nineteenth-century Liverpool', *International Review of Social History* vol. 39, no. 1, 1994, 33–56; Jennifer Kelly, *'The Downfall of Hagan': Sligo Ribbonism in 1842* (Dublin: Four Courts Press 2008); idem, 'An outward looking community? Ribbonism and popular mobilization in Co. Leitrim, 1836–1846', PhD thesis, Mary Immaculate College, University of Limerick, 2005. Also see a recent essay by Michael Huggins, 'Whiteboys and Ribbonmen: what's in a name?', in Kyle Hughes and Donald M. MacRaild, *Crime, Violence and the Irish in the Nineteenth Century* (Liverpool: Liverpool University Press 2017), 21–37.
2 Letter from General George Vaughan Hart to Marquess of Abercorn, 12 August 1810: Public Record Office of Northern Ireland [PRONI], Abercorn Papers, D623/A/166/8. Although George Cornewall Lewis detailed Ribbon-type activities five or so years earlier. George Cornewall Lewis, *On Local Disturbances in Ireland and on the Irish Church Question* (London: R. Fellowes 1836). David W. Miller, *Peep O'Day Boys and Defenders: Selected Documents on the County Armagh Disturbances, 1784–1796* (Belfast: PRONI 1990); Jim Smyth, *The Men of No Property: Irish Radicals and Popular Politics in the Late Eighteenth Century* (Basingstoke: Macmillan 1992 repr. 1998).
3 Letter from John Slacke to William Gregory, 17 January 1817: National Archives of Ireland, State of the Country Papers, 1831/35.
4 Desmond Murphy, *Derry, Donegal and Modern Ulster, 1790–1921* (Derry: Aileach Press 1981), 61–65. On Thresher violence see *The Times*, 30 July 1814; Sean Farrell, *Sectarian Violence and Political Culture in Ulster, 1784–1886* (Lexington: Kentucky University Press 2000), 60–61; Allan Blackstock, *Loyalism in Ireland, 1789–1829* (Woodbridge: Boydell & Brewer 2007), 159–160.

5 Abstract of reports which have been received from General Officers and Brigade Majors of Yeomanry in Ireland on the state of their respective districts during the month of November 1818: PRONI, MIC224/106, Letters, 1818. [Copied from National Archives [TNA], London, Home Office Papers, Ireland: Correspondence and Papers, 1782–1851, Home Office [HO] 100/194,195.]
6 *A Report of the Trial of Michael Keenan for Administering an Unlawful Oath* (Dublin: J. Exshaw 1822); M. J. Martyn, *An Authentic Report of the Trial of Richard Jones for Ribbonism* (Dublin: Grant & Bolton 1840).
7 Enda Delaney, 'Our island story? Towards a transnational history of late modern Ireland', *Irish Historical Studies* vol. 37, no. 148, 2011, 83–105.
8 Letter from 'A' to Major Sirr, 7 May 1822: Trinity College Dublin, Major Henry Charles Sirr Papers, Letters, 869/1.
9 Ibid.
10 *Trial of Michael Keenan*; also, see *A Report on the Trial of Edward Browne and others for Administering and of Laurence Woods for Taking an Illegal Oath* (Dublin: J. Exshaw 1822).
11 John Belchem, *Irish, Catholic and Scouse: The History of the Liverpool-Irish, 1800–1939* (Liverpool: Liverpool University Press 2007), 97–98.
12 *Trial of Michael Keenan*.
13 1836 (40) *Royal Commission on the Condition of the Poorer Classes in Ireland*, Appendix G: *Report into the State of the Irish Poor in Great Britain*, 1834, 9.
14 'Ribbonism in England and Scotland', 22 November 1841: TNA, HO Papers, HO45/184.
15 Labour historians have tended to see the Irish and their activities as contra-class, with ethnicity viewed as a form of collective consciousness beyond the indigenous mainstream. An exception being Steve Fielding, *Class and Ethnicity: Irish Catholics in England, 1880–1939* (Buckingham: Open University Press 1993), 1–18.
16 See as examples, *The Standard*, 29 September 1837; *John Bull*, 16 August 1840.
17 According to his biographer, Mitchel 'championed the Ribbon societies and "their killing of odious landlords, agents, tithe proctors, bailiffs"'. B. McGovern, *John Mitchel: Irish Nationalism, Southern Secessionist* (Knoxville: University of Tennessee Press 2009), 101.
18 *Standard*, 28 October 1837. Though this organ reckoned the data for 1831, which saw Ribbon offences in Leinster running at five times the Ulster rate, as a contradiction to the claim that Ribbonism was inspired solely or mostly by Orangeism.
19 Belchem, '"Freedom and Friendship to Ireland"', passim.
20 Ibid., 34–50.
21 E. P. Thompson, *The Making of the English Working Class* (London: Penguin 1968 edition), 471. More generally, see R. G. Kirby and A. E. Musson, *The Voice of the People: John Doherty, 1798–1854: Trade Unionist, Radical and Factory Reformer* (Manchester: Manchester University Press 1975).
22 There is a short but informed description of Ribbonism in England in Lynn Lees, *Exiles of Erin: Irish Emigrants in Victorian London* (Manchester: Manchester University Press 1979), 223. For other brief mentions, see Rachel O'Higgins, 'Irish influence in the Chartist movement', *Past and Present* vol. 20, 1961, 83–96; J. H. Treble, 'The attitude of the Roman Catholic church towards trade unionism in the north of England', *Northern History* vol. 5, 1970, 93–113; G. P. Connolly, 'The Catholic Church and the first Manchester and Salford trade unions in the age of the Industrial Revolution', *Transactions of the Lancashire and Cheshire Antiquarian Society* vol. 135, 1985, 125–39; R. Swift, *The Irish in Britain, 1815–1914: A Documentary History* (Cork: Cork University Press 2002), 149. J. Treble, 'Irish Navvies in the North of England, 1830–50', *Transport History*, vol. 6, 1973, 243, mistakes Ribbonism for a rural organisation

irrelevant in the British urban scene. Similarly, W. J. Lowe, *The Irish in Mid-Victorian Lancashire: The Shaping of a Working-Class Community* (New York: Peter Lang 1990), 180 includes brief contextualisation of Ribbonism in England which aligns it with the Whiteboys as a group 'formed to enable the poor and vulnerable in rural Ireland to resist the demands of landlords'.
23 Belchem, '"Freedom and Friendship to Ireland"', 33–56; 'Sectarianism, ethnicity and welfare: collective mutuality among the Liverpool Irish', in A. Knotter et al. (eds), *Labour, Social Policy and the Welfare State* (Amsterdam: Stichting Beheer IISG 1997), 35–44; 'Ribbonism, nationalism and the Irish pub', in idem, *Merseypride: Essays in Liverpool Exceptionalism* (Liverpool: Liverpool University Press 2000), 67–100. Donald M. MacRaild, '"Abandon Hibernicisation": Priests, Ribbonmen and an Irish street fight in the North East of England', *Historical Research* vol. 76, no. 194, 2003, 557–573; Máirtín Ó Catháin, 'Bullet moulders and Blackthorn men: a comparative study of Irish nationalist secret society culture in Mid-Nineteenth-Century Scotland and Ulster', in R. J. Morris and Liam Kennedy (eds), *Ireland and Scotland: Order and Disorder, 1600–2000* (Edinburgh: John Donald 2005), 153–162. Terence McBride, 'Ribbonmen and radicals: the cultivation of Irishness and the promotion of active citizenship in mid-Victorian Glasgow', *Irish Studies Review* vol. 23, no. 1, 2015, 15–32.
24 'Ribbonism in England and Scotland, copies of papers relating to Ribbonism transmitted to the Irish Government by Wm Fausset, Esq, Co. Sligo'. Undated letter from Fausset to the Irish government, Dublin; TNA, HO/45/184.
25 Donald M. MacRaild, *The Irish Diaspora in Britain, 1750–1939* (Basingstoke: Palgrave Macmillan 2010), chapter 5 for more on Irish immigrants' relations with, and within, British labour.
26 Treble, 'Attitude of the Roman Catholic church', 96–99.
27 *Royal Commission on the Condition of the Poorer Classes in Ireland*, xxiii.
28 *The Standard*, 16 January 1838 on Irish trade union activity in Glasgow and Manchester.
29 Treble, 'Attitude of the Roman Catholic church', 100–102; G. P. Connolly, '"Little brother be at peace": the priest as holy man in the nineteenth-century ghetto', in W. J. Shiels (ed.), *Studies in Church History: The Churches and Healing* (Oxford: Basil Blackwell 1982), 191–205 (204).
30 *Freeman's Journal*, 14 July 1838.
31 *Nation*, 5 October 1844.
32 *Nation*, 9 November 1844.
33 *Report from the Select Committee on Outrages (Ireland); together with the proceedings of the committee, minutes of evidence and index* HC, 1852 (438).
34 1852 Select Committee on Outrages, 12, 16.
35 Ibid., 58.
36 Ibid., 67.
37 *Select Committee on Outrages* (1852), testimony of John Henry Brownrigg, Deputy-Inspector of Police, Ireland, 119.
38 *Select Committee on Outrages,* 1, 17, 19, 126–128, 158–164, 661.
39 Ibid., 19, 158–164. A view supported by Belchem, '"Freedom and Friendship to Ireland"', 44.
40 *Select Committee on Outrages*, 19.
41 *Morning Chronicle*, 21, 27 January 1853. *Freeman's Journal*, 28 January 1853; 'Ribbonism in England, expediency of extending to England and Scotland the laws in force against secret societies', testimony of J. H. Brownrigg, 2 January 1862: TNA, Treasury Solicitor and HM Procurator General: Law Officers' and Counsel's Opinions, TS25/1227); *Morning Chronicle*, reported in *Nation*, 29 January 1853.

42 'Ribbonism in Britain'. A series of letters between Dublin, Stafford and London concerning Hatton's apprehension of the Hanley Ribbonmen. TNA, HO 45/5128s, ff 442–452.
43 John Herson, *Divergent Paths: Family Histories of Irish Emigrants in Britain, 1820–1920* (Manchester: Manchester University Press 2014), 192–195.
44 A seasoned officer, he had established the Sussex police force in 1840 and the Staffordshire force in 1842. Unlike Drummond, Hatton seemed convinced by the dangers presented by an organisation such as this. He certainly reported the presence of Ribbonmen in the police force of Ireland, in 1839, when he was questioned by the Select Committee of that year. For Hatton's evidence, see 1839 (486) *Report from the Select Committee of the House of Lords appointed to enquire into the State of Ireland in respect to crime*, three parts, III: 2946, 7 May 1839. For the Staffordshire evidence, see NA 45/5128 f.1–8, correspondence between Kemmis and Hatton.
45 *Morning Chronicle*, 27 January 1853.
46 *The Standard*, 27 January 1853.
47 *Nenagh Guardian*, 5 March 1853; *Nation*, 16 April 1853.
48 *Glasgow Herald*, 11 February 1853; *Lancaster Gazette*, 19 February 1853; *Freeman's Journal*, 5 February 1853. A detailed description of Masterson's background and testimony can be found in *The Standard*, 9 March 1853; *Morning Post*, 7 February 1853.
49 *Nation*, 16 April 1853.
50 Not to be confused with James Hagan, of Sligo, who turned Queen's evidence and underpinned a trial of Ribbonmen in the early 1840s. See, Kelly, 'The Downfall of Hagan'.
51 *Belfast Newsletter*, 21–24 March 1854.
52 Delaney, 'Our island story?'

22

'THE MOST VARIED, COLOURFUL, CONFUSING HUBUB IN THE WORLD'

The East End, television and the documentary imagination, July 1939[1]

James Jordan

On the evening of Wednesday 12 July 1939, less than three years after the start of regular broadcasting, and only seven weeks before the closure necessitated by the Second World War, BBC television presented *East End*, a 45-minute documentary in which social anthropologist and co-founder of Mass Observation Tom Harrisson 'explore[d] London's East End, introducing Cockney and Jew, Lascar and Chinaman, and others of its inhabitants'.[2] This programme combined pre-recorded telecine (film) sequences, 'live' studio-based interviews, artisan demonstrations and design effects, all bound together by Harrisson's presentation and commentary. Unfortunately, as with so much early television, there is no surviving copy of the programme, but with the help of press reviews, personal papers and production files held in the archives of the BBC and Mass Observation it is possible to reconstruct it and a sense of how 'the most varied, colourful, confusing hubub in the world' was depicted in the black and white world of television.[3]

***

In *John Bull's Island* (1988), a book which thirty years after its first publication remains essential reading for anyone interested in migration studies, 'race' and the construction of British identity, Colin Holmes examined the long history of Britain as a country of immigration.[4] Many of Holmes' interests and concerns subsequently featured in the work of Tony Kushner, a not unsurprising fact given that the former was, to quote the latter, 'an inspiring undergraduate teacher and excellent PhD supervisor'.[5] That acknowledgement appears in Kushner's *We Europeans?* (2004), the first monograph to examine the original Mass Observation project co-founded by Harrisson in the 1930s. As part of his study Kushner includes a brief discussion of *East End* against the context of Mass Observation's interim report into anti-semitism of the same year, concluding that while the programme was undoubtedly 'progressive and anti-racist', it suggested a 'sense of hierarchy' between groups and could be 'crude and reductionist' in its use of 'race'.[6] The following builds on that assessment by considering *East End* in terms of television praxis, exploring – a verb which feels particularly germane here – how it created an image of the East End for an audience that was probably more used to seeing West End productions than schlepping round the East.

The BBC and the East End

In *Exploring the East End* (BBC Home Service, 5 November 1948) art historian Millicent Rose took BBC radio listeners on one of the first visits to the London that lay east of the Aldgate Pump, describing the architecture, the people and their history. Although the East End could appear to the uninitiated as 'a dreary waste of bricks and mortar', Rose argued, 'thanks to the vitality and character of its inhabitants' it was in fact vibrant and alive.[7] She returned to the area one year on with *The East End in Fiction* (Third Programme, 15 October 1949), discussing how authors including Jack London, Walter Besant and Charles Dickens had represented and shaped popular perceptions of the area. This was not necessarily a full or accurate picture. In her analysis of *Dombey and Son*, for example, Rose demonstrated Dickens' tendency to avoid the 'densely populated core of the East End' in favour of the outlying regions. Instead for Rose it was the writing of Arthur Morrison that first and better captured 'the atmosphere of the locality', not just because of the focus but because he wrote 'as a worker and not merely a sightseer'. Her most fulsome praise, however, was reserved for Israel Zangwill, the first author 'to portray [the East End] from within', looking not 'for the melodramatic or the picturesque, but for the ordinary life of everyday in Whitechapel':

> Because he came as an intimate and not as an alien, he can see the tall tenements and the courts of low cottages, not as 'stables' – Morrison's word for them – but as places that individual families know as home. It's the individuality of every detail, the pressing personality of every figure, that make Zangwill's *Children of the Ghetto* [1892] such a wonderful picture of city life.

Zangwill's work chronicled the Jewish East End, a subject to which BBC radio and television would return regularly in the 1950s and 60s, featuring works and interviews with a new wave of authors that included Lionel Bart, Bernard Kops, Wolf Mankowitz and Arnold Wesker. There were also numerous documentaries and adaptations of personal memoirs that revealed how the East End was changing in appearance and appeal. For example, a number of stars of stage and screen, including Bud Flanagan, David Kossoff and Alfie Bass, reminisced about the area in Jo Joseph's *Our East End* (BBC Home Service, 16 January 1962), with their Jewishness, a marker of difference for Harrisson in 1939, assimilated into the narrative rather than explicitly foregrounded. There was also *50 Years in Stepney* (BBC Home Service, 17–21 January 1966), in which Rose Henriques read extracts from her biography of her late husband, the social worker and magistrate Basil Henriques. In the first of five fifteen-minute episodes Henriques, recalling the words of Millicent Rose, described 'the appallingly overcrowded slums of Stepney' as a place she 'grew to love because of its beauties of people and place, and in spite of its hardships, its evils and smells'.[8] And yet she also spoke of Stepney in romanticised terms, remembering it as a predominantly Jewish area which offered refuge for those who were 'the descendants of early refugees or were themselves newly established in this benevolent country of asylum'.

In the final episode of *50 Years* Henriques described how post-war Stepney had 'greatly changed', with the '[n]ewcomers from all the Commonwealth countries' taking the place of the Jews who had moved to the suburbs:

> Our Hessel Street market was formerly almost an enclave of Eastern Europe, with its stalls and shops owned by venerable old Jewish men and women. Today it's more like Marseilles or Port Said. Very few Jewish shopkeepers remain, but every kind of Asian, African, Indian and West Indian spices, vegetables and pulses are on sale by their Commonwealth owners. Add a great proportion of Maltese and Cypriots, and our cosmopolitan population is complete.[9]

It is a description of a cosmopolitan East End, one that engenders a strong sense of belonging while highlighting transience and internal difference, that would not have been out of place in Harrisson's documentary of 1939, even if her Hessel Street would have felt like Port Said to him.

Documentary television and *East End*, 1939

In July 1939 Grace Wyndham Goldie reviewed Harrisson's *East End* for *The Listener* magazine. It was, she wrote succinctly, 'another experiment in television documentary. Progress, brothers, progress.'[10] There was certainly a paucity of documentaries at the time, with one observer identifying the lack of 'something approximating to documentary cinema films' as 'the most serious gap in television programmes'.[11] In fact Steve Bryant suggests in *Visions of Change* that while '[i]t is arguable that the first television programme was a documentary ... the bulk of the television service before the war was live programming and, though factual material was featured, whether it could be called "documentary" is debatable'.[12] Even so, it is something of a surprise to discover that the word 'documentary' appears only three times in the pre-war television programme titles and descriptions in the *Radio Times*.[13] The first, *The World of Women: The Making of Documentary and 'Secrets of Nature' Films* (BBCtv, tx. 25 January 1937), demonstrated 'the special methods' by which such films were made, 'the apparatus used, and also some examples of the finished product'. Two years later *Salute to America* (BBCtv, 8 May 1939), described 'the contemporary American scene' combining film and 'personal reactions to the New Deal, American literature and language, the mixture of races, and the varied scene which is America'.[14]

The final of the three was a programme entitled simply *Soho* (BBCtv, 19 April 1939) in which producers Mary Adams and Andrew Miller-Jones '[brought] to the studio the people who gather at Cafe Cosella', a restaurant and 'meeting-place for artists, musicians, buskers, show people, and exiles from the Continent'.[15] There had been 'just five producers for the entire television output' at the start of British television broadcasting in November 1936, and while their duties were defined by categories such as talks, variety, drama and music, '[i]n practice these were only nominal responsibilities, and producers would work on variety, talks, or opera as production contingencies required'.[16] By 1939, the number of producers had grown to 24, including Adams and Miller-Jones. Adams had joined the BBC in 1930 after taking an undergraduate degree in Natural Science at Cardiff and an MSc from Cambridge in 1925. Initially a Talks Assistant in the Adult Education Department, she transferred to television as a producer in January 1937. Miller-Jones had graduated from Oxford University in 1932 before spending five years working as a writer, director and editor for Steuart Films, Gaumont British Instructional Limited, Paul Rotha and Strand Films. He joined the BBC as a producer in television in May 1937 and by 1951 was regarded as the 'mainstay of the Talks Department' where he and Adams were 'responsible for the whole of the television talks output'.[17]

On the 25 May 1939 Adams sent Miller-Jones a list of 'one or two programme ideas' she thought he 'might like to talk over with [fellow producer Spencer] Reynolds', including 'East End from Tom Harrison', scheduled for the 12 July, adding, 'Please discover whether Tom is free for it'.[18] Shortly afterwards Reynolds began collecting material, sending a memo to Bill Barbrook, responsible for the BBC's fledgling film unit, in which he enquired about 'any general shots illustrating life and conditions in the East End ... I believe you have a considerable amount of river stuff which would be of use'.[19] Barbrook's reply confirmed that while he had 'nothing representing the life and conditions in the East End', he had 'some cuts of St Katherine and West India Docks – passing traffic on the river from the Pool downwards to Woolwich'. In light of this, Miller-Jones and Reynolds decided to undertake new filming on Sunday 9 July:

> I suggest that shots be taken of Middlesex Street from the various places surveyed, with particular emphasis on individuals, crowd scenes round barrows and, of course, [market seller] Mike Sterne (sic) – a shot from the side if possible, so that the fact that his lips are moving and no sound coming from them does not seem too awkward.
>
> For the Jewish sequence I suggest big close-ups of Commercial Road and Mile End Road, and long shots of the exterior of St. Mary's, Whitechapel. Shots of foreign-sounding shop names taken from angles, and one of two medium shots of tailors' windows.[20]

While this was only three days before transmission, the script and structure was already in place, albeit still being refined. Harrison had sent his outline to Miller-Jones in June, writing, 'Here are my ideas as I have been able to think them so far, and after smooching [sic] about the East End a bit', with his covering note adding, 'Data unchecked ... Directly this script is copied, revised or removed by you, I will get on to the FACTS + PEOPLE.'[21]

Although only a first draft, the content of Harrisson's script is instructive as to how he conceived of the programme, the area and its inhabitants. In respect of the latter it presented the East End in universal terms, as a working 'League of Nations', full of people of 'every colour and tongue':

When I first went to live there, I thought it would be necessary to wear special clothes and speak a special accent, as I have had to do elsewhere when studying human beings. It wasn't necessary at all. […] People come and go, people of all nations and sorts, so quickly and so easily through this vast basin of bubbling mass existence, that no person, however strange, is a stranger in the East End.[22]

The synopsis also made clear, however, that Harrisson was interested in the cultural and racial diversity of the area, representing its inhabitants through a series of interviews that would emphasise difference between the minority groups and be linked together by music, sound effects and pre-recorded film sequences.[23]

Those interviews were to begin with a lascar sailor, 'someone who shows the colour of East End', who Harrisson suggested should first appear in-vision 'maybe playing a mouth organ, singing a nostalgic song'. Next there would be 'a Chinaman … or perhaps three Chinamen … doing a definite thing, such as trading or smoking or playing Fan-Tan' to the sound of 'Chinese music, exotic, rapid, elaborate'. They would, Harrisson wrote, 'speak for themselves, but NOT to put across information, simply doing their own things'. It would be left to Harrisson to 'give facts about them PERSONALLY, who each is and their story'.

Next the programme would turn to Spitalfields, home to the Huguenot weavers, 'a community as old as our sort of civilisation'.[24] Harrisson wanted to interview the Olympic gold medallist Jack Beresford, whose father Julius, born Julius Wiszniewski, was a partner in the furniture making business of Beresford & Hicks that was based in Curtain Road, the local centre of the industry. Harrisson, conscious of the need for narrative, hoped that Beresford would know nothing of the Huguenot weavers, allowing the conversation to develop into 'some chat on the variety of E[ast] E[nd] life, races, etc, to colour up the programme that way again'. In emphasising the variety he also emphasised difference, and in the next section difference meant division, separating Cockney from Jew as if the two were incompatible:

> The greatest race of the East End, after the Cockney, and in numbers, is the Jewish. Whole areas of Stepney and Bethnal Green are almost predominantly Jewish, with synagogues, Jewish libraries, their own newspapers printed in Yiddish, their own dance places, kosher butchers, eating places, social clubs. They live, all the time, side by side, on top or underneath Cockney families. Though the fascists make a great noise, there is little enough sign of anti-semitism … Most cockneys have learned to like and respect their Jewish neighbours.[25]

To an accompaniment of 'loud and difficult' Jewish music, the programme would transition to a film sequence of a Jewish marriage and then an interview with an as yet unknown 'Rabbi X', who would be asked 'about East End Jews' in general as well as the experience of refugees.

The closing scenes were to involve two high-profile mainstream figures who represented the East End in other ways. The first was Father John Groser, the radical East End priest, with Harrisson's commentary again drawing attention to internal tensions that existed. It did so through Groser's campaigning for cheaper, better housing and more equitable rents:

> In the East End the rent situation is appalling … and many of the landlords … are Jews, wealthy ones who live in other parts of London. … It was an Anglican clergyman who really made the East End see what they could do about it. And he took great care that it was done so that there was no taint of anti-semitism or racial feud in it.

The final film sequence would go to the market stalls of Petticoat Lane, before finally George Lansbury, the social reformer and Labour MP for Bow and Bromley, would conclude by offering his view of 'the giant cauldron' that was the East End.

Harrisson's script would go through several revisions before transmission and while the final version was similarly structured to the original outline, there were significant differences. In part these were prompted by the demands of the medium:

> One thing I should like to impress on you … is the necessity for covering the commentary with adequate vision and I think the only way of doing this is to divide the paper into two columns, with vision on one side and sound on the other. As it stands at the moment the sound is definitely predominant and you show grave signs of having been infected with sound technique! The sound transitions … are useless unless they are accompanied by an equally effective vision mix.[26]

But the changes were also imposed by the unavailability of Beresford, Groser and Lansbury, the identity of the other guests, and by the replacement of 'Rabbi X' with Basil Henriques, the social reformer whose life would be the subject of *50 Years in Stepney* nearly thirty years later.

Broadcast live from Studio A, Alexandra Palace, at 9.20pm on 12 July 1939, *East End* required the use of four cameras (two tracking and two fixed) and two microphones (a boom and a stand microphone). It began with an in-vision caption that read simply 'East End', superimposed over a telecine sequence of 'the river, smoking chimneys, ships unloading, dray horse, feet walking along pavement'. The first voice heard, coming through the monitor mike, was that of Harry Haynes, a docker for twenty years: 'They say its streets are paved with gold'. A switch to Camera 2 revealed the other side of the studio, a wallpaper set constructed to resemble a 'room in [the] East End' with a real kitchen range. In-vision was Mrs Green, an East End housewife described by Harrisson as the 'motherly type' and at the heart of what was to follow. She would lead Harrisson's exploration, being the catalyst for discussion and presenting an insider's voice to complement Harrisson's outsider. Kushner has noted that '[i]n contrast to the other minority characters introduced, she was portrayed as being integral to the area and an organic part of it'. And yet while integral and organic, she was played by actor Dora Gregory, dressed in a costume of blouse, skirt and apron provided for her by the BBC.

In the setting of the kitchen Mrs Green made a pot of tea for Harrisson before sitting down to discuss the East End, an area Harrisson found 'just as interesting' as 'the Arctic or Pacific Islands were when I was an explorer'. Mrs Green gave him a scripted answer, lines that were performed, in which she told him about her streets and neighbours. Harrisson wanted to know more, not just about her immediate neighbours, but 'the whole of the East End'.

Following the structure of the synopsis, Harrisson began by defining the East End in geographical terms, with the use of a pointer and map. A second telecine sequence followed, showing the docks ('the clearing house of Europe'), where ships came from 'every nation' although 'the people who unload the ships are all one nation … the Cockney'. Back in the studio Harrisson interviewed Harry Haynes, who was sitting astride a bollard in front of a penumbrascope screen onto which were projected shapes and shadows of the dockside's derricks and cranes.[27] Against this backdrop Haynes, representing the dockers and the Cockney 'nation', gave scripted answers to Harrison's questions on the life of the casual docker, including the pleasures of an outdoor life and the daily struggle for work, while an in-vision map and pointer would highlight locations when mentioned.

Haynes also spoke of meeting 'all kinds of sailors' as part of his job, adding that 'plenty of them are Lascars', providing a cue to the next telecine film sequence, depicting simply 'Lascars', and commentary from Harrisson: 'Most of the dirty work on ships coming into London from the East is done by Lascars. They are Indians.' While they are in most cases employed under the condition that they 'have to make the return journey', some would be 'native seamen' who 'like the look of the East End and so settle here'. They are, he concluded, 'presenting a new racial problem for the East End'.

This 'new racial problem' was represented by San Wan Singh, a Lascar seaman turned pedlar who lived off Commercial road having arrived in London three years before. Back in the studio Singh was to be sitting on a packing case in front of a penumbrascope screen that continued to show the derricks and cranes, but with the image reversed to suggest a different perspective. Singh and Harrisson spent several minutes discussing his journey to London and life as a pedlar, with his answers given 'live' on the evening, meaning they are not recorded in the camera script. But there are directions for some answers, such as Singh 'describes Albany Passage and talks about the way Indians live all over the place, without any club or centre'.

Such directions suggest that Harrisson wanted to control the programme's structure and, with it, meaning. To conclude the interview with Singh, for example, he deliberately asked about his dealings with the Chinese community, dealings which were non-existent because he had 'never been in that part of London. They all live in one place, they're not like the Indians, living all over the East End'. That one place was Pennyfields, 'one shabby street' commonly known as Chinatown, an area 'everyone has read about … in their mystery stories'.

These words accompanied another telecine sequence during which Harrisson would also describe how, while the population had 'dwindled' in recent years, 'the Chinese still feel that this bit of London is China for them. They care more for China than for England.'

When the camera returned to the studio there were to be 'two Chinese', Chung and Heng, sitting in front of the penumbrascope's 'pagoda and washing background'. Again Harrisson would ask general and specific questions about their lives, the Chinese community and their interaction with other groups. Once again, as with San War Singh, their answers were 'live' and not recorded in the camera script. Harrisson's questions once more guided the answers and the direction, allowing him to conclude, in a markedly different way to the warning of racial problems that preceded the Lascar story, that 'the Chinese are a self-contained community in the East End, and one that lives on good terms with its neighbours, as one race that makes East End life so varied and colourful'.

These first three interviews took the programme to its midpoint and a return to Mrs Green, whose discussion with Harrisson would make clear that the East End was not home solely to Lascars and Chinese. Indeed, 'you scarcely ever see them unless you go round the parts where they live'. This discussion of the cosmopolitan nature of the East End drew on the original introductory sequence outlined in Harrisson's first draft, referring once more to the area as a 'League of Nations' and recounting in brief Harrisson's initial experiences of the area.

While the first half of the programme considered what might today be called economic migrants, the next considered those who had fled from persecution, a topic that was of contemporary interest but largely absent from the programme. Alexandra Palace had been used as a camp for Belgian and other refugees during the Great War, and the preceding months had seen Studio A broadcast a number of programmes which considered the modern refugee problem, but the majority of the references here were rooted in the past. 'For hundreds of years refugees have been coming to England and the first place they drop off is the East End', Harrisson began, before interviewing Harry Lucking, one of 'the few who remain of the silk weavers descended from the French Huguenots' who provided the programme with a quill winder, and Kate Rolfe, a young weaver, who demonstrated the weaving process. It was the weaving rather than the flight from persecution which made the link to the next telecine sequence section:

> But not all garments made in the East End are made of silk, as anyone who knows the area around Whitechapel Church will tell you. St Mary's Whitechapel stands in the centre of a district predominantly people by those of Jewish faith. The roads to right and left of it show how much the Jews have made this part of London home. They have their own newspapers which are printed in their own language. Nearly every shop bears a Jewish name and many sell clothes which are made by Jews working long hours in their own home.

Back in the studio Jewish seamstress Rene Seghall was working at her sewing machine, with the penumbrascope now casting a background shadow of a Star of David, a marker of identity that contrasted with the professional images of derrick and cranes for Haynes and Singh, or the mixture of pagoda and laundry for Chung and Heng. Harrisson spent a few moments asking about her work before moving on to his next guests, Basil Henriques and Wolf Michaels, an 18-year-old upholsterer in Curtain Road and member of the Bernhard Baron Settlement Boys Club run by Henriques.

Henriques was a regular broadcaster for the BBC and high-profile member of assimilated and anglicised Anglo-Jewry.[28] He had come to St George in the East in October 1913 where he and his wife established a boys' club with the aim of enabling 'the British-born or British-educated children of foreign-born parents to become good Englishmen and to remain good Jews, and also to be of service to their non-Jewish neighbours'.[29] Nine months before the broadcast he had spoken at a meeting of the July Society about the East End. He referenced how 'the walls of the ghetto still remained' even if they were not physical, citing four reasons for this: the dietary and sabbatical laws, Jewish trades and standards of living. 'The Jews in the East End do not come into contact with the right kind of Anglicising influence', he concluded. 'As a result, they feel superior to the Christians and apathetic towards the country to which they owe so much.'[30]

It was a message of integration and allegiance that would also be found in the programme. On the day of the broadcast Henriques had 'rushed to Alexandra Palace' in the evening after a day full of meetings, taking Michaels with him. It was, Henriques noted in his diary, 'Very interesting and very tiring.'[31] Henriques had drafted his contribution in advance, being sent to Miller-Jones on the 7 July with a warning that it was '*very*' rough'. The text in the surviving script is only piecemeal, a series of prompts for the full version and it may not reflect accurately what was broadcast that evening, but it does create a sense of how he presented a 'broader picture of the Jewish community in the East End'. Moreover, being able to prepare in advance would give him a more erudite appearance:

> There has been practically no Jewish immigration into East London since the war … Unwalled Ghetto … Most Jews in East London today want to assimilate in every way, except in religion … The average Cockney had respect for another man's religion. A new completely un-English spirit of intolerance has grown up … East London is notorious for its slums and its fine social work …

After Henriques had spoken, Harrisson asked Michaels about his work before interviewing Beresford's replacement Walter C. Potter, who worked for timber merchants William Mallinson and Sons. Potter answered questions about the furniture trade using photographs and furniture provided by Beresford and Hicks, and in some cases answering to a script that was Beresford's not his. This discussion then led directly into the final section, a piece on the markets of Petticoat Lane, 'the Mecca of the East End on Sunday'. The film sequence which followed would presumably have been that recorded on the previous Sunday, silent footage of crowds and trading, including, one assumes, the side-on shots of trader Mike Stern. This would cue to the studio where Mike Stern would perform selling a garment while standing in front of the penumbrascope's image of a tailor's dummy.[32] As with the other interviews its focus was about the diversity of the area, relationships between groups and what had changed over the years.

A handwritten addition to the camera script suggests that instead of an intended quote from Byron's *Don Juan*, the programme's final word went to Harrisson: 'Though there is racial prejudice, poverty, pain,' he said, 'the EastEnders do lead a whole life. They face facts ... side by side all sorts of job, the constraints of housing, malnutrition and congestions. Yet they get more out of it on the whole than any other people I've come across. The hallmark of the East End is its civility, its vitality, its tremendous interest in being alive.'

As a television documentary, *East End* was as varied, colourful and confusing as the East End it depicted. As a summary of attitudes to 'race' and Britishness in Britain, it was similarly complicated, demonstrating how identities were being constructed from both within and without, simultaneously emphasising difference and a sense of belonging to the area. That is, in its production, construction and narrative sweep, while celebrating the cosmopolitan, it also highlighted that there were tensions and prejudices. At times, like the later documentaries of Millicent Rose and Rose Henriques, it offered a view from above, and in this instance one that could control the meaning via still relatively new techniques as well as 'casting', but it also offered for the first time on television the chance to hear authentic voices of minority groups from within, at a point before the war changed attitudes and sensitivities. It was a programme not without its flaws and contradictions, but it was with hindsight a remarkable achievement for pre-war television and one that demonstrated the technical innovations of the emerging medium. More generally this article shows the potential for the historiography of migration to be further enhanced through the study of television and radio as exemplified by the resources of the BBC archives.

Notes

1 My thanks to the Alexandra Palace Television Society, the BBC's Written Archives, Mass Observation and the University of Southampton, with particular thanks to Katie Ankers, El Boonen and Louise North at the BBC.
2 *Radio Times*, 7 July 1939, 17.
3 Draft synopsis, *East End*, BBC Written Archives Centre, Caversham (hereafter BBC WAC), T5/160 TV Drama: East End.
4 Colin Holmes, *John Bull's Island: Immigration and British Society, 1871–1971* (Basingstoke: Macmillan 1988).
5 Tony Kushner, *We Europeans?* (Aldershot: Ashgate 2004), 3.
6 Kushner, *We Europeans?*, 3, 91 and 91–97 *passim*.

7 *Exploring the East End*, BBC WAC Talks Scripts. Unless otherwise stated all subsequent quotes are taken from the scripts held at WAC.
8 *Fifty Years in Stepney*, BBC Home Service, 17 January 1966.
9 *Fifty Years in Stepney*, BBC Home Service, 21 January 1966.
10 Grace Wyndham Goldie, 'Television: Justice and Grace Darling,' *The Listener*, 20 July 1939, 151.
11 'Hollywood Writer No. 2', *Radio Times*, 21 October 1938, 17.
12 Visions of Change: The Evolution of the British TV Documentary: Volume 1: BBC 1951–1967, BFIV2068, 3.
13 This is based upon an analysis of the *Radio Times* 30 October 1936-1 September 1939.
14 *Radio Times*, 22 January 1937, 5–6, and 5 May 1939, 14.
15 *Radio Times*, 7 and 14 April 1939, 15.
16 Jason Jacobs, *The Intimate Screen: Early British Television Drama* (Oxford: Oxford University Press 2000), 36–37.
17 Administrative Office (Television) to HSA, 16 October 1947, BBC WAC L1/1547/1 Left Staff File Andrew Miller-Jones.
18 Mary Adams to Andrew Miller-Jones, 25 May 1939, BBC WAC T32/330 TV Talks Memos 1937–50. Adams and Miller-Jones had already worked with Harrisson on a number of projects.
19 Reynolds to Barbrook, 21 June 193 with handwritten reply 22 June 1939, BBC WAC T5/160 East End.
20 Miller-Jones to Reynolds, 7 July 1939, BBC WAC T5/160 East End.
21 BBC WAC T5/160 East End.
22 Draft synopsis, BBC WAC T5/160 East End.
23 *Radio Times*, 7 July 1939, 17.
24 See Kushner, *We Europeans?*, 96–97.
25 For a critique of this description see Kushner, *We Europeans?*, 95.
26 Miller-Jones to Harrisson, 23 June 1939, *Mass Observation Archives: East End* TopicCollection-62_648-693.
27 The penumbrascope projected shadows onto a background screen, meaning that a set could be changed at 'the touch of a switch'. 'Enter the Penumbrascope!', *Radio Times*, 24 June 1938, 15.
28 Kushner, *We Europeans?*, 96.
29 UoS Archives, MS 132 AJ 195/4/1 Folder 2.
30 In November and December 1938 he also spoke to the Princes Road Synagogue Society, Liverpool, on the 'Causes of Anti-Semitism in East London' and to the Liberal Jewish Men's Society in London on 'Jewish Problems in the East End'. UoS Archives, MS 132 AJ 195/3/28 and MS132 AJ220/3/2 The Papers of Basil Henriques.
31 UoS Archives, MS132 AJ220/1/10/3.
32 For more on Mike Stern see http://spitalfieldslife.com/2011/09/25/dennis-anthonys-petticoat-lane/ and www.soundsurvey.org.uk/index.php/survey/radio_recordings/1930s/1425/.

23

THE EQUIANO EFFECT

Representativeness and early black British migrant testimony

Ryan Hanley

In 2006, slavery historian James Walvin declared that 'Equiano has gone from obscurity to international celebrity in a single generation'.[1] In the decade since Walvin's pronouncement, the extent of Olaudah Equiano's modern-day renown as the greatest black intellectual of the eighteenth-century Atlantic world seems to have become unassailable. Looking back, what is most surprising about Equiano's inclusion in a 2004 publicly voted list of '100 Great Black Britons' is not that an eighteenth-century anti-slavery polemicist made the top five, but that he was only ranked fourth.[2] Ever since the turn of the millennium, Equiano has become, like so many historical celebrities, something of a brand, and having his name in the title of an academic article or book has become rather a selling point. Looking through the titles of some recent publications about him, one might be forgiven for assuming him to be the hero of a series of adventure novels: 'Equiano's Refusal'; 'Equiano's Trifles'; *Equiano and the Igbo World*; and *Equiano's Daughter* are just a handful of examples.[3] The catalogue of the British Library lists 113 articles for which 'Equiano' is listed as a key word, and 110 printed books. This is of course a crude measure of scholarly interest, but comparing these figures with other writers from the period certainly implies that Equiano is by far the biggest star in the constellation of black authors who produced autobiographies during the era of the transatlantic slave trade.

Equiano's autobiography, *The Interesting Narrative*, has similarly come to dominate how eighteenth-century black Atlantic writing – and indeed the slave trade – is taught at universities and schools in Britain. Students can now choose between several unabridged modern editions of the text, or from one of many more edited selections, either in slim, standalone volumes or as part of anthologies.[4] Paring down Equiano's work for students in this way is not without its risks however, as demonstrated by Srinivas Aravamudan's stinging 2001 dismissal of Adam Potkay and Sandra Burr's selections as 'Equiano Lite'.[5] These debates resurfaced in 2012 with the publication of a collection, edited by Eric D. Lamore, dedicated solely to teaching Equiano.[6] After successive cohorts have placed Equiano at the centre of teaching about slavery, abolition, migration and black history, students now fully expect to see him on their reading lists.

This is, of course, excellent news for both black British historiography and the study of black migration to Britain. Equiano, alongside perhaps Mary Seacole, has long represented the 'advance guard' of the ongoing march to 'decolonise' British university and school curricula, which have historically underplayed black perspectives. However, Equiano's comparatively privileged position within the mainstream of teaching and research begs a number of questions, especially when considered in a wider context in which many of his black contemporaries remain signally under-researched. What is it about him and his work in particular that continues to attract such a disproportionate amount of attention from historians and literary scholars? *How*, precisely, has his work been used in historiography and literary criticism? And finally, how has his domination of the study of black Atlantic migrant testimony affected the field as a whole? To begin to answer these questions, this chapter examines how Equiano came to dominate historiography on both black British writing and eighteenth-century black Atlantic migration. It explores the much celebrated (and contested) notion that the *Interesting Narrative* represented an authentic first-hand account of enslavement, the middle passage, slavery, emancipation, and global migration. This enables us to unpick the historiographical status of *The Interesting Narrative* as a *representative* story of enslavement and migration, and what this has meant for the fields of black British and black Atlantic historiography.

Beginning in the late 1960s with Paul Edwards' landmark edited reproductions of *The Interesting Narrative*, Equiano's has been the most widely available example of early published black migrant and slave testimony.[7] However, it was not until the early 1970s that the historiography of the black presence in Britain emerged as a distinct subfield, with major contributions by Walvin and Folarin Shyllon, among others.[8] Partially because of the availability of his work, Equiano was hailed in these studies as 'the first national leader of black people in Britain', and 'the most famous African in late eighteenth-century England'.[9]

While such celebratory accounts were intimately bound up with contemporaneous concerns over race relations (Shyllon's two books were published by Oxford University Press for the Institute of Race Relations), the historiography of black migration to Britain took on a more overtly political impetus – and indeed a more straightforwardly Marxist perspective – in the years after the 1981 'race riots'. In some cases, this resulted in less of a focus on individual intellectual 'elite' figures in favour of emphasising collective forms of resistance, cultural hybridity and social survival.[10] In others – most notably Peter Fryer's seminal *Staying Power* – discrete prosopographical sections situated by now familiar figures like Equiano ('the first political leader of Britain's black community') in a much broader historical perspective.[11] Meanwhile, following the lead of their American and African counterparts, literary scholars in Britain began to take serious notice of eighteenth-century black British writing.[12] The ascendancy of New Historicism, especially, invigorated literary studies into early black British migrant testimony from about the late 1980s onwards.[13] While historians and literary critics occasionally collaborated very fruitfully during this period (Henry Louis Gates Jr. and Charles T. Davis' edited collection *The Slave's Narrative* is one important early example), historians slowly began to cede the dedicated study of eighteenth-century black British writing to their colleagues in Literary Studies departments from around the early 1990s.[14]

Perhaps ironically, New Historicist readings of *The Interesting Narrative* demanded a far more wide-ranging contextual basis than had traditional historiographical accounts. By placing the text itself at the centre of analysis, rather than deploying it as evidence to support a broader hypothesis, literary scholars such as Geraldine Murphy and Potkay extended its relevance beyond the traditional realms of colonialism, slavery and abolition, and into other areas such as transnational history, religious history and the history of capitalism.[15] Postcolonial theorists including Aravamudan simultaneously developed new reading methodologies that situated Equiano's life and work in the historical and cultural contexts of endemic (textual) black resistance to racism and slavery.[16] As we will see, such contributions became especially pertinent when Equiano's precise status as a postcolonial subject came under scrutiny during the first decade of the twenty-first century.

During these early years of the new millennium, productive dialogue between New Historicist and postcolonial literary criticism gave rise to a historically grounded, cultural materialist perspective that has dominated western scholarship on early black writing almost ever since. Influential readings by Roxann Wheeler, Helen Thomas, Felicity Nussbaum and Brycchan Carey carefully situated writing by Equiano and others in their generic, political and socio-cultural contexts by examining their symbiotic relationships with discourses of race, formal Romanticism, eighteenth-century masculinity and sentimental abolitionist rhetoric, respectively.[17] This has yielded a new appreciation for Equiano as not only a political leader and innovative writer, but a culturally significant figure in British and Atlantic world history in the broadest possible sense. (The same process has affected, though to a much lesser extent, the black epistolerian and businessman Ignatius Sancho, whose *Letters* were first published posthumously in 1782.) At roughly the same time as this scholarly reappraisal was taking place, Equiano's primacy among black British intellectuals was consolidated in the public imaginary through an excellent, though controversial, biography by Vincent Carretta.[18]

During this period, historians seem to have struggled to decide what to do with early black writing as a source on migration. On one hand, the advent of the 'New Imperial History', which sees mainland Britain as a major site of imperial contact, has intensified the demand for historiography that takes proper account of the central contribution and agency of black and minority ethnic groups in Britain.[19] On the other, the welcome move away from 'elite' histories has meant increasing value is attached to the category of 'ordinariness' in subjects of historical research. This has led to speculation as to how representative figures like Equiano can really have been, and thus, how useful their testimony can be to historians. The exceptional detail and clarity with which Equiano was able to recount his experiences has become, for some historians, evidence of his unrepresentative status. As Kathleen

Chater puts it, 'it is always more interesting and representative to look at what is so ordinary that it is not considered worth reporting'.[20]

This focus on representativeness, in Equiano's case in particular, is significant because it prizes open the fault lines between literary and historiographical notions of source value. Never were these distinctions more evident than during a sometimes-acrimonious debate over Equiano's place of birth. Carretta's publication in 1999 of naval and baptismal records suggesting that Equiano was in fact born in South Carolina, and not in West Africa as claimed in *The Interesting Narrative*, has loomed large over almost all subsequent work on this most famous of formerly enslaved writers.[21] As anyone familiar with Equiano's life and work knows, he had been accused of lying about his origins in 1792 by proslavery advocates keen to peddle a racist depiction of Africans as untrustworthy and devious. As Carey has pointed out, in this context Carretta's suggestion could therefore not be made without 'considerable moral and ideological risk'.[22] Moreover, by far the most widely read and widely taught passages from *The Interesting Narrative* have been the powerful first-person accounts of kidnap, enslavement and the horrors of the middle passage. Some historians of pre-colonial West Africa had considered Equiano's descriptions of his childhood as the earliest printed first-hand account of Igbo culture.[23] Given the centrality of *The Interesting Narrative* to the field, the suggestion that these accounts might have been fabricated has forced a re-evaluation of not only this text, but all early black autobiography, at the most fundamental level. Moreover, it has placed the issues of authenticity and representativeness, first raised by S. E. Ogude in the early 1980s, squarely back at the centre of the modern study of early black British writing.[24] Indeed, the most vituperative exchanges in what has proved an occasionally ill-tempered and exceptionally lengthy debate have centred upon the very nature of historical investigation, the question of what constitutes a 'real' historical source, and the appropriate uses – and limits – of first-person testimony in the study of historical migrations.

It is not within the remit of this chapter to rehearse the two opposing positions in this debate in their entirety.[25] It might suffice for current purposes merely to say that criticisms of Carretta's use of naval and baptismal records are usually based on his perceived failure to properly value ethnographic research into African cultures, oral histories and the depiction of West African traditions in *The Interesting Narrative*. It bears noting that the self-defined 'literary solution' to this problem, apparently favoured by Carretta himself, is that the historical accuracy of Equiano's account is less important than its impact on the British abolitionist movements. Therefore, as Potkay puts it, 'whether or not Equiano is from Africa is beside the point because *The Interesting Narrative* is far less significant as a factual account of one man's life than as a rhetorical performance of considerable skill'.[26] Historians, meanwhile, have begged to differ with this assessment of what is important about Equiano's work, and which of its characteristics qualify it as a legitimate object for scholarly inquiry. Paul Lovejoy, among the most outspoken critics of Carretta's methodology, draws attention to the disciplinary divide in approaching early printed black autobiography: 'Carretta's interpretation is not historical reconstruction but a nod towards "it doesn't matter", when it does. Vassa was born somewhere, and the historian has to make an assessment while some literary critics may not think this is essential.'[27] Similarly, Trevor Burnard maintains that Equiano's significance had proceeded almost entirely from the veracity of his account:

> The authenticity of his account is [...] crucial to its lasting significance. We don't read the *Interesting Narrative* because it is well-written [...] we read it because it is *true*; because it is an eyewitness account [...] of the cruelties of the Middle Passage, in particular, and Atlantic slavery in general.[28]

A more pressing issue, especially for postcolonial scholars and historians of pre-colonial Africa, is the hierarchy of source value supposedly implied by Carretta's methodology. Are documents produced by British and colonial institutions, such as naval registers and baptismal records, necessarily more reliable than first-hand testimony? John Bugg, for example, raises the very reasonable point that an emancipated slave voyaging on the eighteenth-century Atlantic might well invent a free-born American identity as protection from enslavement by privateers or impressment by the Royal Navy.[29] Similarly, both historians and anthropologists have noted that *The Interesting Narrative* contains information about eighteenth-century Igbo culture that predates any other published account by decades. Ethnographers Catherine Acholonu and Dorothy Ukaegbu have verified aspects of Equiano's description of Igbo life using oral histories and material culture.[30] Lovejoy, supporting and reinforcing Acholonu's claims, sums up the problem in methodological terms: 'written documentation confronts oral sources and traditions, as related through the memories of an individual and filtered with acquired information from a variety of sources'.[31] Nevertheless, these historians argue, *trusting* in early black autobiographical accounts of West Africa, even in the face of conflicting evidence, continues to yield important new insights and anthropological discoveries. As Lovejoy has pointed out, 'the text itself points to authenticity, not fraud'.[32]

All this debate over the factual authenticity of *The Interesting Narrative* raises important methodological questions around what migrant and slave testimony is actually *for*. It seems that all sides of the argument agree upon the significance of 'representativeness' in Equiano's autobiography. When Mary Wollstonecraft reviewed *The Interesting Narrative*, shortly after the release of the first edition in 1789, she complained that 'he is entangled in many, comparatively speaking, insignificant cares, which almost efface the lively impression made by the miseries of the slave'.[33] Her concern that the individual tribulations encountered by Equiano pale into insignificance beside his representative story of slavery continues to be shared among modern readers. Writing in 2013, for example, Jon Sensbach declared Equiano 'the quintessential survivor of the Middle Passage'.[34] Similarly, Carretta has always worked hard to ensure his subject's continuing relevance to scholars in the wake of his own discoveries:

> Paradoxically, Equiano's voice is so representative [...] because his own life was so unrepresentative. [...] By combining his own experiences with those

of other people of African descent, Equiano refashioned himself as *the* African so that he could represent the millions of other Africans who lacked his mobility and access to education and publication.[35]

Postcolonial literary scholars, meanwhile, have been more critical of Equiano's apparent position as the sole nominated representative of over twelve million enslaved Africans. Aravamudan, writing at the height of what he calls 'the multicultural moment' in 1999, very convincingly argues against the notion of the 'ethnic representative' in the literary canon as a validation of English cultural hegemony: 'By viewing Equiano through the optic of minority literature or making him represent an African American or black British slot in an ever-expanding canon, the modern reader also edifies nation into imperium.'[36] Nevertheless, and despite Aravamudan's warnings, *The Interesting Narrative* continues to be taught, in universities and secondary schools, as the quintessential, representative account of slavery and black migration to Britain.

The shift from 'Equiano the African', to 'Equiano *the* African', is the joint work of two sets of readers occupying either side of a 200-year gulf. That Equiano was a celebrity during his own lifetime, and a fundamentally significant figure for the first wave of British abolitionism, has become an academic truism – though it is debatable just what that meant for how his work was bought, sold, borrowed and read. What *has* become increasingly clear over the past two decades, however, is that debates over authenticity and representativeness have served to consolidate, rather than undermine, his primacy in the so-called 'black literary canon'. Less clear is how this overwhelming focus has changed the way we think of early black British writing as a corpus. Certainly, if we accept Equiano's contemporaneous celebrity as both a function and product of abolitionist propaganda – that is, if we take no issue with Carretta's suggestion that Equiano wanted to 'do well by doing good' in the promotion and sale of his book – then we must be willing to apply a different type of evidentiary scrutiny in future readings of it.[37] For historians, this might mean that we should be willing to read it for what it can tell us about the cultural work of the abolition movement, rather than the lived experience of slavery. If we accept Equiano's modern form of celebrity – that is, his perceived representativeness of a whole category of historical witnesses – as part of the ongoing postcolonial intellectual project, then we must be willing to question our own assumptions about what we as historians expect from early black autobiography. Ultimately, we must come to terms with the fact that the notion of a representative, monolithic 'black perspective' on slavery and forced migration is as illusory as it is unhistorical.

In the past few years, historians and literary critics have reached a kind of silent *rapprochement* on the issue of Equiano's nativity, and most (including myself) now subscribe to a cautious 'agnosticism' on the subject. Indeed, James H. Sweet's perspective, while broadly less supportive of Carretta than his critics, promises a productive reconciliation by reframing the discussion not as one concerned with origins, but with identity:

> Recognising 'Igbo' and 'Carolina' as fluid, socially determined signifiers, rather than as fixed categories, forces a deeper critical assessment of the context in which made these documentary claims. Through Equiano's optic, perhaps he could be both 'Igbo' and 'Carolina,' depending on the circumstances.[38]

Increasingly, scholars are increasingly following Sweet's lead by turning to the cultural and religious duality informing these sources, as well as issues of national and even local identity.[39] In new ways and for new reasons, the study of eighteenth-century black migrants to Britain has returned to examining the nature and status of diasporic identity. The first revolution, it seems, is nearly complete.

How, then, might historians want to use early black British migrant testimony in the future? Clearly, interdisciplinary methodologies and collaborations present some challenges, but these are vastly outweighed by the opportunities for exciting fresh directions in scholarship and new uses for the material. Intersectional approaches, using these sources to consider issues of race and migration alongside those of gender, sexuality and class, represent one especially promising interdisciplinary avenue for further exploration. More fundamentally, though, scholars need to continue to recognise the scope, dynamism and sheer variety of early black British migrant testimony. The best-known black authors of this period, Equiano chief among them, are routinely read, near-exclusively, in the context of slavery and abolitionism. This is of course, entirely understandable and necessary – black intellectuals were critical and central actors in the campaigns to end slavery, regardless of whether they are now deemed abolitionists or not.[40] The tremendous impact made by particular authors such as Equiano on popular attitudes towards slavery may well explain their pre-eminence.

However, a broader reading of black migrant testimony from this period demonstrates that black intellectuals were also much more than abolitionists or representatives of the enslaved. As I have said elsewhere, black migrants never confined themselves to such questions; they participated in almost every facet of eighteenth-century British life.[41] For example, the first black author to be published in Britain, Ukawsaw Gronniosaw, was far more interested in promoting evangelical Calvinism than abolishing slavery.[42] The infamous Robert Wedderburn was a radical revolutionary, would-be regicide, political theorist, sometime brothel-keeper and general thorn in the side of the British establishment for the first three decades of the nineteenth century.[43] Mary Prince was at the heart of a scandal that embroiled her in two widely reported libel trials in 1833.[44] Attention to these stories yields new insights into British and Atlantic world history at the broadest level. Their implications for the historiography of national identity and migration are, potentially, profound.

All of this autobiographical material is now readily accessible to historians interested in eighteenth-century migration to Britain. The debates and discussions that have characterised the scholarship of the past fifty years indicate that the material can be, at times, controversial. Nevertheless, by breaking free of a restrictive and exclusive over-emphasis on one or two 'special' figures, by embracing new interdisciplinary methodologies, and by moving away from the illusory notion of a wholly 'representative' perspective, early published black testimony can help unearth the heart of the eighteenth-century migrant experience.

Notes

1 James Walvin, 'Celebrity slave with a credible tale to spin', *Times Higher Education Supplement*, 17 November 2006 [Online] Available from: www.timeshighereducation.com/books/celebrity-slave-with- a-credible-tale-to-spin/206818.article (accessed 01/09/2016).
2 Patrick Vernon, '100 Great Black Britons', 2004 (modified 24 June 2011), available from the *100 Great Black Britons* website at www.100greatblackbritons.com/results.htm (accessed 27/01/2017).
3 George C. Grinnel, 'Equiano's refusal: slavery, suicide bombing, and negation', *European Romantic Review* vol. 27, no. 3, 2016, 365–373; John Bugg, 'Equiano's trifles', *ELH* vol. 80, no. 4, 2013, 1045–1066; Chima J. Korieh, *Olaudah Equiano and the Igbo World: History, Society and Atlantic Diaspora Connections* (Trenton NJ: Africa World Press 2009); Angelina Osborne, *Equiano's Daughter: The Life & Times of Joanna Vassa, Daughter of Olaudah Equiano, Gustavus Vassa, the African* (London: Krik Krak 2007).
4 The major academic unabridged editions are Olaudah Equiano, *The Interesting Narrative*, ed. Brycchan Carey (Oxford: Oxford University Press forthcoming 2017); Olaudah Equiano, *The Interesting Narrative of the Life of Olaudah Equiano, or Gustavus Vassa, the African*, ed. Werner Sollors (New York: Norton 2001); Olaudah Equiano, *The Interesting Narrative and Other Writings*, ed. Vincent Carretta (London: Penguin 1995).
5 Srinivas Aravamudan, 'Equiano Lite', *Eighteenth-Century Studies* vol. 34, no. 4, 2001, 615–619; Adam Potkay and Sandra Burr (eds), *Black Atlantic Writers of the Eighteenth Century: Living the New Exodus in England and the Americas* (London: Palgrave 1995).
6 Eric D. Lamore (ed.), *Teaching Olaudah Equiano's Narrative: Pedagogical Strategies and New Perspectives* (Knoxville: University of Tennessee Press 2012).
7 Olaudah Equiano, *Equiano's Travels: His Autobiography: The Interesting Narrative of the life of Olaudah Equiano or Gustavus Vassa the African*, ed. by Paul Edwards (London: Heinemman 1967); see also Paul Edwards (ed), *Through African Eyes* (Cambridge: Cambridge University Press 1966).
8 Folarin Shyllon, *Black People in Britain, 1555–1833* (Oxford: Oxford University Press 1977); Folarin Shyllon, *Black Slaves in Britain* (London: Oxford University Press 1974); James Walvin, *Black and White: The Negro and English Society 1555–1945* (London: Allen Lane 1973).
9 Shyllon, *Black People in Britain*, 239; Walvin, *Black and White*, 52.
10 See, for example, Ron Ramdin, *The Making of the Black Working Class in Britain* (Aldershot: Wildwood House 1987).
11 Peter Fryer, *Staying Power: The History of Black People in Britain* (London: Pluto Press 1984), 102; see also Paul Edwards and James Walvin, *Black Personalities in the Era of the Slave Trade* (London: MacMillan Press 1983), 78, which described Equiano as 'the most complex and articulate, as well as the most active' black abolitionist.
12 For American and African literary criticism on Equiano, see, for example, Henry Louis Gates Jr., *The Signifying Monkey: A Theory of African-American Literary Criticism* (New York: Cambridge University Press 1988); William Andrews, *To Tell a Free Story: The*

First Century of Afro-American Autobiography, 1760–1865 (Urbana: University of Illinois Press 1986); S. E. Ogude, *Genius in Bondage: A Study of the Origins of African Literature in English* (Ile-Ife: University of Ife Press 1983).
13 Two particularly influential studies are Keith Sandiford, *Measuring the Moment: Strategies of Protest in Eighteenth-Century Afro English Writing* (London: Associated University Presses 1988); Angelo Costanzo, *Surprising Narrative: Olaudah Equiano and the Beginnings of Black Autobiography* (New York: Greenwood Press 1987).
14 Henry Louis Gates Jr and Charles T. Davis (eds), *The Slave's Narrative* (New York: Oxford University Press 1985).
15 Geraldine Murphy, 'Olaudah Equiano, accidental tourist', *Eighteenth-Century Studies* vol. 27, no. 4, 1994, 551–568; Adam Potkay, 'Olaudah Equiano and the art of spiritual autobiography', *Eighteenth-Century Studies* vol. 27, no. 4, 1994, 677–692.
16 Srinivas Aravamudan, *Tropicopolitans: Colonialism and Agency, 1688–1804* (Durham NC: Duke University Press 1999), 233–288.
17 Brycchan Carey, *British Abolitionism and the Rhetoric of Sensibility: Writing, Sentiment, and Slavery, 1760–1807* (Basingstoke: Palgrave Macmillan 2005); Felicity Nussbaum, *The Limits of the Human: Fictions of Anomaly, Race and Gender in the Long Eighteenth Century* (Cambridge: Cambridge University Press 2003); Helen Thomas, *Romanticism and Slave Narratives: Transatlantic Testimonies* (Cambridge: Cambridge University Press 2000); Roxann Wheeler, *The Complexion of Race: Categories of Difference in Eighteenth-Century British Culture* (Philadelphia: University of Pennsylvania Press 2000).
18 Vincent Carretta, *Equiano, the African: Biography of a Self-made Man* (Athens: University of Georgia Press 2005).
19 Kathleen Wilson and Catherine Hall are two highly influential proponents of the 'new imperial history'. See Kathleen Wilson, *A New Imperial History: Culture, Identity, and Modernity in Britain and the Empire, 1660–1840* (Cambridge: Cambridge University Press 2004); Catherine Hall, *Civilizing Subjects: Metropole and Colony in the English Imagination, 1830–1867* (Chicago: University of Chicago Press 2002).
20 Kathleen Chater, *Untold Histories: Black People in England and Wales during the Period of the British Slave Trade, c. 1660–1807* (Manchester: Manchester University Press 2009), 9.
21 Carretta had actually published this evidence in 1995, in a footnote to his Penguin edition of *The Interesting Narrative*, and again in an article in 1998, but the controversy did not ignite until the publication of Vincent Carretta, 'Olaudah Equiano or Gustavus Vassa? New light on an Eighteenth-century question of identity', *Slavery & Abolition* vol. 20, no. 3, 1999, 96–105. See also Vincent Carretta, 'Three West Indian writers of the 1780s revisited and revised', *Research in African Literatures* vol. 29, no. 4, 1998, 73–86.
22 Brycchan Carey, 'Olaudah Equiano: African or American?', *1650–1850: Ideas, Aesthetics, and Inquiries in the Early Modern Era* vol. 17, 229–246 (235).
23 See, for example, Catherine Aholonu, 'The home of Olaudah Equiano: a linguistic and anthropological survey', *Journal of Commonwealth Literature* vol. 22, no. 1, 1987, 5–16.
24 S. E. Ogude, 'Facts into fiction: Equiano's narrative reconsidered', *Research in African Literatures* vol. 13, no. 1, 1982, 31–43.
25 Carey gives a good overview in Carey, 'Olaudah Equiano: African or American?', 229–246. Carretta has since continued the debate with specific reference to methodology in Vincent Carretta, 'Methodology in the making and reception of *Equiano*', in Lisa Lindsay and John Woods Sweet (eds), *Biography and the Black Atlantic* (Philadelphia: University of Pennsylvania Press 2014), 172–191.
26 Adam Potkay, 'History, oratory and God in Equiano's *Interesting Narrative*', *Eighteenth-Century Studies* vol 34, no. 4, 2001, 603–604.

27 Paul Lovejoy, 'Issues of motivation – Vassa/Equiano and Carretta's critique of the evidence', *Slavery & Abolition* vol. 28, no. 1, 2007, 121–125 (121).
28 Trevor Burnard, 'Goodbye, Equiano, the African', *Historically Speaking* vol. 7, no. 3, 2006, 11.
29 John Bugg, 'The other interesting narrative: Olaudah Equiano's public book tour', *PMLA* vol. 121, no. 5, 2006, 1424–1427.
30 Catherine Obianuju Acholonu, 'The Igbo roots of Olauadah Equiano', in Chima J. Korieh, *Olaudah Equiano and the Igbo World* (Trenton NJ: Africa World Press 2009), 49–66; Dorothy Chinwe Ukaegbu, 'Status in Eighteenth-Century Igboland: perspectives from Olaudah Equiano's *Interesting Narrative*, in Korieh, *Equiano and the Igbo World*, 93–116.
31 Paul Lovejoy, 'Autobiography and memory: Gustavus Vassa, alias Olaudah Equiano, the African', *Slavery & Abolition* vol. 27, no. 3, 2006, 317–347 (325).
32 Paul Lovejoy, 'Construction of identity: Olaudah Equiano or Gustavus Vassa?', *Historically Speaking* vol. 7, no. 3, 2006, 8–9 (9).
33 Cited in Equiano, *Interesting Narrative*, ed. Carretta, xxvii.
34 Jon Sensbach, 'Black pearls: writing black Atlantic women's biography', in Lisa A. Lindsay and John Wood Sweet, *Biography and the Black Atlantic* (Philadelphia: University of Pennsylvania Press 2013), 93–107 (96).
35 Vincent Carretta, 'Methodology in the making', 191. Emphasis in original.
36 Srinivas Aravamudan, *Tropicopolitans: Colonialism and Agency, 1688–1804* (London: Duke University Press 1999), 235.
37 Vincent Carretta, 'Does Equiano still matter?', *Historically Speaking* vol. 7, no. 3, 2006, 2–7 (4).
38 James H. Sweet, 'Mistaken identities? Olaudah Equiano, Domingos Alvares, and the methodological challenges of studying the African Diaspora', *American Historical Review* vol. 114, no. 2, 2009, 279–306 (281).
39 See, for example, Brycchan Carey, 'From Guinea to Guernsey and Cornwall to the Caribbean: recovering the history of slavery in the western English Channel', in Katie Donington, Ryan Hanley and Jessica Moody (eds), *Britain's History and Memory of Transatlantic Slavery: Local Nuances of a 'National Sin'* (Liverpool: Liverpool University Press 2016) 21–38; Ryan Hanley, 'Calvinism, proslavery and James Albert Ukawsaw Gronniosaw', *Slavery & Abolition* vol. 36, no. 2, 2015, 360–381; Edward L. Robinson Jr., '"Of remarkable omens in my favour": Olaudah Equiano, two identities, and the cultivation of a literary economic exchange', in Kendahl Radcliffe, Jennifer Scott and Anja Werner (eds), *Anywhere But Here: Black Intellectuals in the Atlantic World and Beyond* (Jackson: University of Mississippi Press 2014) 187–208; Peter Jaros, 'Good names: Olaudah Equiano or Gustavus Vassa', *Eighteenth Century: Theory and Interpretation* vol. 54, no. 1, 2013, 1–23; Vincent Wimbush, *White Men's Magic: Scripturalisation as Slavery* (Oxford: Oxford University Press 2012).
40 See Manisha Sinha, *The Slave's Cause: A History of Abolition* (New Haven CT: Yale University Press 2016).
41 This is the subject of my forthcoming monograph, *Beyond Slavery and Abolition: Black British Writing, c.1770–1830* (Cambridge: Cambridge University Press, forthcoming 2018).
42 Hanley, 'Calvinism, proslavery, and James Albert Ukawsaw Gronniosaw'.
43 See Robert Wedderburn, *The Horrors of Slavery and Other Writings*, ed. Iain McCalman (Princeton NJ: Marcus Weiner 1991).
44 See Mary Prince, *The History of Mary Prince*, ed. Moira Ferguson (Ann Arbor: University of Michigan Press 2007).

24
FRAMING POLISH MIGRATION TO THE UK, FROM THE SECOND WORLD WAR TO EU EXPANSION

Kathy Burrell

This chapter is about Polish migration to the UK since the Second World War and how academic authors have framed these different movements in their publications. Polish migration has, since 2004, become integral to wider discussions about migration in the UK. How this population, possibly the largest the country has ever seen in a single movement, has fitted into the British context has been fascinating to see – the widespread geographical distribution across the country, the closer ties afforded by new mobilities, but of course also the persistence of anti-foreigner sentiment. It makes a timely intervention then, to consider Polish migration in a wider temporal perspective, to remember the post-war movement of refugees, those who came during the Socialist regime and after its collapse, to think about how these two countries have been historically linked through these migrations, and, above all, to pay attention to how all of these developments have been represented in academic writing. Taking three broad eras of migration, post-Second World War, socialist era and the post-socialist period, this chapter pays attention to the different tropes which have emerged in these representations – soldier, wife, worker – exploring what they tell us about Polish mobilities, and what they tell us about the limitations we face, and create, when writing about migration.

The Second World War and afterwards

Not surprisingly, most of the historical literature on Polish migration to the UK focuses on the Second World War and its aftermath. This migration was created initially by wartime displacement, and subsequently cemented by the resettlement of refugees in the UK through the government's European Volunteer Worker scheme, and by a specific programme which was established to resettle demobbed Polish troops, and their families, who had fought with the Allied forces during the war.[1] As Holmes tells us, just over 160,000 Poles settled in the UK via these routes.[2] Perhaps most famous in the early historiography of this migration is Zubrzycki's defining work on the Polish Resettlement Act in 1948, outlining in comprehensive detail what this act entailed, how it channelled the demobbed Polish soldiers into work across the country, and how from this a Polish community came to be established.[3] Sword continued this work, investigating the creation of this highly nationally conscious Polish community and following its development over time, paying close attention to wider political and diplomatic dimensions, demographics and community structures especially.[4] Although there is broad agreement over the facts and contexts of this migration and settlement, however, it is possible to discern different approaches in how this movement has been viewed and presented.

One of the most interesting aspects of the writing on this era of Polish migration has been how strongly the figure of the soldier has permeated the image and identity of both the population and the academic historiography. It has been the experience of the Polish soldier which has come to shape understandings of this movement and has been used to promote Polish identity in the UK subsequently. Even the infrastructure of the nascent community groups grew around demobbed troops meeting up and the emergence of 'Ex-Servicemen's Clubs', as well as, eventually, Polish churches and Saturday schools. Stachura, for example, places the experience of the soldier centre stage, focusing closely on the political dimensions of this migration movement and the sense of betrayal felt by the Polish soldiers at the Yalta peace conference, when Eastern Europe was 'lost' to the Soviet sphere of influence.[5] Having fought 'for your freedom and ours' these soldiers were left without a free homeland to return to, and this loss comes through keenly throughout all the work on this migration.[6] Since the war caused this migration, and shifting geopolitics shaped people's settlement, there is a strong thread weaved throughout most of the literature on generals, soldiers, military battles and high level diplomacy – General Anders, The Battle of Monte Cassino, The Battle of Britain, Yalta. Arguably, this literature simply mirrors the outward-facing identity of the Polish community. As Garapich argues, political exile carries a revered status within Polish national identity, and this specific memory of the valiant Polish soldier is regularly and purposefully revitalised within the UK through an 'émigré culture of representation … based on reminding British people about the sacrifice made by Polish soldiers'.[7] If in the USA Polish migrants were essentialised as 'dumb Polaks', in the UK the brave but betrayed soldier became the more pervasive and cultivated trope.

Such a dominant focus in both writing and practice, however, brings with it a danger of eclipsing other experiences of being Polish in the UK beyond being a soldier. It is important to remember that a great number of resettled Poles had not been in the forces at all and that many had endured different paths as refugees and deportees. While there are no figures to enumerate how many of the Polish population who settled in the UK who had experienced such trauma, it is well documented that a large proportion of those who left Poland during the war had been living in the eastern part of the country and were forced out through Soviet deportation to Siberia.[8] A number of academics have focused directly on these 'alternative', more difficult and less publicly shared narratives and the ongoing work that has had to be done to preserve and honour them. Temple has investigated the way these journeys are recounted in oral history interviews, Winslow has explored the long-lasting psychological trauma endured by these refugees and exiles, and in my work I wrote about the salience of these memories at different scales – individual and embodied biography, inherited history and 'postmemory', and wider community identity – highlighting the emotional significance attached to the vast array of exile literature which had been produced.[9] It is also important to note that such heavy focus on military bravery could also have had the effect of sidelining the depth of trauma that the soldiers themselves endured during and after the war – a trauma that could not fit into this performance of valiant masculinity.[10]

Gender then is another key limitation of this soldier focus. It is worth reasserting first here that women also served in the armed forces, a fact that can get lost in some of this imagery but is underlined by Kushner and Knox with their inclusion of a quote from a woman who fought with the Air Force in their chapter about Polish refugees.[11] This issue of inclusion in the armed forces also has an important age dimension, because many of those who ended up in the UK came as children or teenagers and so were not old enough to fight; again, such a focus can occlude their experiences. For Temple, moreover, this highly gendered reading of the Polish community more fundamentally neglects the role of women, often left 'behind the scenes' but undertaking crucial, though less glamorous and acknowledged, work to sustain national traditions and social networks – cooking Polish food, making national costumes, organising events, teaching the next generation about their Polish roots.[12] If in many accounts of Polish migration everyday life is considered, in less detail, towards the end of the volume, her history puts this centre stage, teasing out the day-to-day workings, tensions and struggles of life in the UK rather than writing about famous generals and key battles. The limits of the soldier trope are clear – it has been a useful and needed tool, harnessed to promote the population externally and strengthen internal bonds, but it could never account for all of the nuances of the experience of being Polish in the UK.

The last theme to consider here is one which has great contemporary resonance, and that is how the Polish population, as 'foreign' but white newcomers, were received in those early years, and how this migration fits into the broader picture of Britain as both an evolving multicultural and postcolonial society. In some of the wider discussions about the racialization of immigration policy in the post-war years European migration has tended to be overlooked, with the focus instead being on new Commonwealth movements.[13] The most arresting and critical work on whiteness and immigration, furthermore, can be found in the array of discussions of race and migration policy rather than in those studies which focus on Poles directly.[14] There is a recognition of the relevance of this issue scattered throughout the Polish migration literature of course – while Lane discusses the hopes that the British government had for the Poles to 'assimilate', and its related misunderstanding in assuming race to be the most relevant factor for 'fitting in' and underestimation of the strength of national identity held by an exiled population,

Nocon investigates the limits of the UK's 'welcome', showing the discrimination faced by Polish immigrants.[15] Along with the legacy of post-war trauma, the pain of not being able to return home, the struggle to build new homes, the difficulties adjusting to the labour market and often working below qualifications, and suspicion, lack of understanding and hostility from local populations, Polish migrants did not have an easy early settlement. There is scope yet, however, for academic writers to take a more critical view on what whiteness meant for Polish migrants in post-war Britain, and on how othering and orientalism worked in this context, and to update understandings and steer the focus away from the now rather dated and limiting interest in assimilation and acculturation, something which runs through many of the texts.

Socialist era

It is more difficult to write about Polish migration during the era of the Socialist regime; not only is there far less material out there investigating this, but in reality migrations during this period do not fit easily into an organising narrative. In my own research I interviewed people who left Poland to come to the UK throughout the duration of the regime, and I ended up talking to people who left at different times, in different circumstances, for different reasons. It is still possible to discern some underpinning themes in how movements from this time are discussed however.

The first point to think about here is again the significance of gender to discussions of Polish migration, because, as Sword asserts, about three-quarters of those who came after 1956 (when there was a thaw on prohibitions on moving out of the country) and before the 'Solidarity era' of the early 1980s, were women coming to marry either Poles already settled in the UK, or second generation British-Polish men.[16] According to Patterson, *Dziennik Polski*, the Polish daily newspaper, even carried numerous matrimonial adverts from Polish women keen to come to the UK to marry.[17] This has meant that these women migrants have tended to be defined, by others, by their marriage prospects and choices, rather than by any deeper individual migratory agency. If the Polish immigrant of the war era was the soldier, by the late 1950s this had changed to the wife. In my interviews with women who came during this time, however, I was able to flesh out the experiences women had in moving from Poland to the UK. I did not interview anyone who had migrated purely to marry, and I found instead that marrying was sometimes a bi-product of migrating – meeting someone once here, or marrying sooner in a relationship in order to be able to stay. The most interesting material which emerged, rather, was about the differences in day-to-day life between the two countries, and for those women who migrated with husbands and families, the stark differences in household provisioning they found here – going from a situation where, due to the shortage economy, you had to be an active expert in managing, networking and the art of getting by, to having to learn a new and sometimes bewildering consumer landscape, and inhabiting a new, more passive, relationship with public space in the process.[18] My interviews from this era also shed light on the emotional experience of migrating across the Iron Curtain – from anxious border crossings to sustaining family ties in the face of geopolitical barriers. The experience of mobility during the socialist period is an important one to assert because even though it was difficult to move, and most people were not able to keep their own passports at home and had to apply to be able to leave Poland, it emphasises the porosity of this Iron Curtain and the strength of the links that reached out across it.[19]

The other theme which does emerge in some of the historiography is the salience of the political nature of some of this later migration as thousands of people left due to their activities or links with the Solidarity movement. This brings an interesting juxtaposition, because this migration, which unfolded on a much smaller scale to the UK than to the US, could easily be framed in terms of political integrity, resistance, activism and exile, and could be read as a moral successor to wartime movements.[20] In that respect, it might be expected that they would be welcomed as new generation 'soldiers'. What some research has suggested, however, is that 'on the ground', newcomers from Socialist Poland were more likely to be treated with suspicion for being from a Socialist regime than heralded as heroes.[21] Social interactions between these new migrants and the existing population seemed to amplify the differences between the lived experiences and socializations of the two countries, rather than offer a renewed community narrative.

Post-socialist period

The collapse of the Socialist regime in 1989 gave new impetus to Polish emigration (to the UK, but also to southern Europe especially), and with this change the site of mobility tensions relocated from the difficulties of leaving Poland to the complications of being in the UK and grappling with visa and border arrangements.[22] This post-socialist period has an obvious dividing point in the form of the 2004 expansion of the European Union which enshrined the legal right to live and work in the UK for people from Poland and the other accession countries. Taking the 1990s and early 2000s era first, the research that has been done does emphasise the uncertainty and precarity of being a Polish immigrant in this context. Rogaly's work, for example, investigates the difficult working conditions and wider vulnerability of Eastern Europeans in the agricultural sector, many of whom came over through the Seasonal Agricultural Workers' Scheme.[23] Düvell researched Polish migrants' experiences of being both documented and undocumented in the UK at this time, underlining the extent those without the right papers were open to exploitation.[24] My interviews from this era also explored the problem of a sense of perceived illegitimacy, because even though the people I interviewed had all the appropriate documents to live and work here they still faced hostility and suspicion at the UK border when travelling to and fro, being made to feel like second-class, or non-citizens.[25]

With this context in mind, it is easy to see why 2004 has been identified as a watershed moment in Polish-UK mobility.[26] There has been such phenomenal, and multidisciplinary, academic interest in Polish migration to the UK since EU enlargement that it is impossible to cover all the main arguments here, but there are some themes once again which seem to have had particular traction. Sticking with this concept of mobility first, there has been considerable attention paid to the type of migration movement this might turn out to be – temporary, permanent, circular – and the extent to which this new mobility regime might fundamentally change the nature of intra-continental migration.[27] A lot of studies have focused on migration strategies and intentions, finding fluidity in these over time.[28] For some commentators too, this new mobility did seem to signal a new and qualitatively easier type of east-west migration, and a more widely symbolic dismantling of internal European borders.[29] The timing of Internet, Skype and smart phone developments have also been key for the experiences of these migrants who can keep in touch with home much more readily now.[30] In my work I looked at other new infrastructures which have supported this increased mobility, such as the low-cost airlines and courier services sending parcels back and forth, but, as with most studies, I found that this freedom and movement does come with monetary, physical and emotional costs, and has its own frictions.[31] This focus on mobility issues is likely to persist with the unfolding of 'Brexit', as travelling itself becomes a different experience for Polish-UK migrants once again.

Another discernible trope to emerge from research on post-accession migration has been the consistent framing of Polish migrants as 'workers' – many of the early accession migration reports focused predominantly on the impact of this migration on the UK labour market and on the encouraging occupational mobility of Polish migrants over time.[32] Other studies, however, have pointed to the 'brain drain' that the young, highly skilled migrants experienced in the UK, taking jobs well below their qualification levels.[33] The high levels of precarity many Polish and other accession migrants face here has also emerged as an important theme; Anderson, for example, highlights the high numbers of migrants in agency and temporary work and the low wage levels, uncertainty and anti-social hours that much of this kind of work entails.[34] Work place identities and interactions have also been investigated, such as Datta's work on the lives of Polish builders in London and their 'cosmopolitan' encounters.[35] Taken together, these kinds of studies illustrate the diversity of work experiences, the stratification of skills and qualifications among the migrant population, and by revealing vulnerabilities, hint at more continuities with the pre-2004 period, and particularly the experiences of Polish agricultural workers, than previously assumed.

There is a danger, however, that too much focus on work – on the labour market, and occupational changes – can define Polish migrants too narrowly. For many of the young people who came, adventure was a stronger allure than the prospect of work itself. Some of the most interesting discussions on motivations also take a longer-term view, exploring ideas about 'normalcy' and the desire to find a 'normal life' in the context of post-socialist transition in Poland.[36] The focus on jobs, therefore, cannot account for the whole experience of being Polish in the UK. It also misses the rest of the lives that people have been living here – family life, transnational connections, local home making, social life, networks and encounters, leisure and fun, discrimination and fear – as well as their histories beforehand.[37] There have been many rich projects which have teased out these different aspects of the migration experience: Gill on place-making, White on families, Ryan et al. on social networks, McGhee et al. on housing, to name just a few.[38] Different aspects of gender, race and ethnicity have also been reflected on, drawing out the impact of migrating on the performance of gendered norms, and on the particular position that Poles hold, once again, as a white but 'foreign' presence.[39] It would be difficult to find another group as closely researched as post-accession Polish migrants now, but it is clear, in light of the 2016 'Brexit' result and its aftermath, where research will need to go next; if anything has been missing in the historiography it has been a sufficiently nuanced appreciation of the depth of anti-Polish sentiment in the UK. There is still more work to do.

Conclusion

Appraising the historiography of Polish migration has necessitated taking a long temporal perspective, considering work which has appeared over the past sixty years. It has been possible to not only chart the different movements from Poland in these texts, but also academic trends and priorities as they have shifted over time. The initial interests in assimilation and acculturation have given way to more varied readings of migration experiences, for example, as the wider research field has matured. Taking a long view also makes it possible to see how these different waves of migration piece together, what is common and what is different. What is interesting is that although the circumstances of the different eras change, there are continuities which pull them together, not least the vulnerability Polish migrants have perennially faced, albeit in different manifestations. This raises an important point because it reminds us, as academics, of the responsibility we bear when writing about migration. We choose how to frame these people's lives – whether through statistics, archives or interview quotes – and we choose which questions to ask, which facets to play up and which aspects to sideline. Do we celebrate the freedom and hope of migration, or do we illustrate the risks and costs to the migrants? Do we run the risk of disempowering whole populations when we foreground difficult experiences? There is an embedded power in academic writing here which bears more scrutiny. There is also an inherent limitation, as this chapter has shown, because the human experience can never be easily categorised into boxes or typologies. When we enforce order onto these histories we risk eclipsing important parts of them. So, for Polish migration, we can understand why the key tropes of soldier, wife and worker have been so salient, but we can also see their limitations, and, ultimately, grasp what these categories themselves tell us about the wider production of academic knowledge.

Notes

1 See John Allan Tannahill, *European Volunteer Workers in Britain* (Manchester: Manchester University Press 1958).
2 Colin Holmes, *John Bull's Island: Immigration and British Society, 1871–1971* (Basingstoke: Macmillan 1988), 212.
3 Jerzy Zubrzycki, *Polish Immigrants in Britain* (The Hague: Martinus Nijhoff 1956).
4 Keith Sword, *Identity in Flux: The Polish Community in Britain* (London: SSEES, University of London 1996); Keith Sword with Norman Davies and Jan Ciechanowski, *The Formation of the Polish Community in Great Britain: the M. B. Grabowski Polish Migration Project Report* (London: SSEES, University of London 1989). On community see also Kathy Burrell, *Moving Lives: Narratives of Nation and Migration among Europeans in Post-war Britain* (Aldershot: Ashgate 2006), 141–179; Thomas Lane, 'Victims of Stalin and Hitler: the Polish community of Bradford', *Immigrants and Minorities* vol. 20, no. 3, 2001, 43–58; Sheila Patterson, 'The Polish exile community in Britain', *The Polish Review* vol. 6, no. 3, 1961, 69–97. More generally see Tony Kushner and Katharine Knox, *Refugees in an Age of Genocide* (London: Frank Cass 1999), 217–240.
5 Peter D. Stachura (ed.), *The Poles in Britain 1940–2000: From Betrayal to Assimilation* (London: Frank Cass 2004).
6 See also Burrell, *Moving Lives*, 50–51, 82; Kathy Burrell, 'Male and female Polishness in post-war Leicester: gender and its intersections in a refugee community', in Louise Ryan and Wendy Webster (eds), *Gendering Migration: Masculinity, Femininity and Ethnicity in Post-war Britain* (Aldershot: Ashgate 2008), 71–88.
7 Michał P Garapich, 'Odyssean refugees, migrants and power: construction of "other" and civic participation within the Polish "community" in the United Kingdom', in Deborah Reed-Danahay and Caroline B. Brettell (eds), *Citizenship, Political Engagement, and Belonging: Immigrants in Europe and the United States* (New Brunswick NJ: Rutgers University Press 2008), 124–143 (131–132).
8 Thomas Lane, *Victims of Stalin and Hitler: The Exodus of Poles and Balts to Britain* (Basingstoke: Palgrave Macmillan 2004); Burrell, *Moving Lives*, 42–48; Keith Sword, *Deportation and Exile: Poles in the Soviet Union, 1939–48* (Basingstoke: Palgrave 1996); Natalia S. Lebedeva, 'The deportation of the Polish population to the USSR, 1939–41', *Journal of Communist Studies and Transition Politics* vol. 16, no. 1–2, 2000, 28–45.
9 Bogusia Temple, 'Time travels: time, oral history and British-Polish identities', *Time and Society* vol. 5, no. 1, 1996, 85–96; Michelle Winslow, 'Polish migration to Britain: war, exile and mental Health', *Oral History* vol. 27, no. 1, 1999, 57–64; Kathy Burrell, 'Personal, inherited, collective: communicating and layering memories of forced Polish migration', *Immigrants and Minorities* vol. 24, no. 2, 2006, 144–163.
10 See Burrell, 'Male and female Polishness'.
11 Kushner and Knox, *Refugees in an Age of Genocide*, 224.
12 Bogusia Temple, 'Constructing Polishness: researching Polish women's lives', *Women's Studies International Forum* vol. 17, no. 1, 1994, 47–55; Bogusia Temple, '"Gatherers of pig-swill and thinkers": gender and community amongst British Poles', *Journal of Gender Studies* vol. 4, no. 1, 1995, 63–72; Bogusia Temple, 'Diaspora, diaspora space and Polish women', *Women's Studies International Forum* vol. 22, no. 1, 1999, 17–24.
13 There is very little discussion of this in Ian R. G. Spencer *British Immigration Policy since 1939: The Making of Multi-Racial Britain* (London: Routledge 1997) for example.
14 See Kathleen Paul, *Whitewashing Britain: Race and Citizenship in the Postwar Era* (New York: Cornell University Press 1997) and Wendy Webster, *Englishness and Empire, 1939–1965* (Oxford: Oxford University Press 2005), along with Linda McDowell

on Latvian women, Europeans and whiteness: Linda McDowell, *Hard Labour: The Forgotten Voices of Latvian Migrant Volunteer Workers* (London: University College London Press 2005). 98–99, 195–196; Linda McDowell, 'Old and new European economic migrants: whiteness and managed migration policies', *Journal of Ethnic and Migration Studies* vol. 35, no. 1, 2009, 19–36.
15 Lane, 'Victims'; Andrew Nocon, 'A reluctant welcome? Poles in Britain in the 1940s', *Oral History* vol. 24, no. 1, 1996, 79–87.
16 Sword, *Identity in Flux*, 204.
17 Sheila Patterson, 'Polish London', in Ruth Glass (ed.), *London: Aspects of Change* (London: MacGibbon & Kee 1964), 309–342 (338).
18 Kathy Burrell, 'Managing, learning and sending: the material lives and journeys of Polish women in Britain', *Journal of Material Culture* vol. 13, no. 1, 2008, 63–83.
19 See also Becky Taylor and Martyna Śliwa, 'Polish migration: moving beyond the Iron Curtain', *History Workshop Journal* vol. 71, no. 1, 2011, 128–146; Kathy Burrell, 'The enchantment of western things: children's material encounters in late socialist Poland', *Transactions of the Institute of British Geographers* vol. 36, no. 1, 2011, 143–156.
20 See Garapich, 'Odyssean refugees'.
21 On this see Aleksandra Galasińska, 'Gossiping in the Polish club: an emotional coexistence of "old" and "new" migrants', *Journal of Ethnic and Migration Studies* vol. 36, no. 6, 2010, 939–951; Sword, *Identity in Flux*, 207–213; Garapich, 'Odyssean refugees'.
22 See Kathy Burrell, 'Materialising the border: spaces of mobility and material culture in migration from post-socialist Poland', *Mobilities* vol. 3, no. 3, 2008, 353–373.
23 Ben Rogaly, 'Intensification of workplace regimes in British horticulture: the role of migrant workers', *Population, Space and Place* vol. 14, no. 6, 2008, 497–510.
24 Frank Düvell, *Polish Undocumented Immigrants, Regular High-skilled Workers and Entrepreneurs in the UK* (Warsaw: Institute for Social Studies, Warsaw University 2004).
25 Burrell, 'Materialising the border', 358.
26 See Kathy Burrell, 'Introduction: migration to the UK from Poland: continuity and change in East-West European mobility', in Kathy Burrell (ed.), *Polish Migration to the UK in the 'New' European Union: After 2004* (Farnham: Ashgate 2009), 1–19.
27 For example John Eade, Stephen Drinkwater and Michał P. Garapich, *Class and Ethnicity: Polish Migrant Workers in London: Full Research Report. ESRC End of Award Report, RES-000-22-1294* (Swindon: ESRC 2007); Naomi Pollard, Maria Latorre and Dhananjayan Sriskandarajah, *Floodgates or Turnstiles? Post-EU Enlargement Migration Flows to (and from) the UK* (London: Institute for Public Policy Research 2008).
28 See Stephen Drinkwater and Michał P. Garapich, 'Migration strategies of Polish migrants: do they have any at all?', *Journal of Ethnic and Migration Studies* vol. 41, no. 12, 2015, 1909–1931.
29 For example Adrian Favell, 'The new face of east west migration in Europe', *Journal of Ethnic and Migration Studies* vol. 34, no. 5, 2008, 701–716.
30 Kathy Burrell, 'Time matters: temporal contexts of Polish transnationalism', in Michael Peter Smith and John Eade (eds), *Transnational Ties: Cities, Migrations, And Identities* (New Brunswick NJ: Transaction Publishers 2008), 15–38 (29–33).
31 See Kathy Burrell, 'Going steerage on Ryanair: cultures of air travel for migration from Poland to the UK', *Journal of Transport Geography* vol. 19, no. 5, 2011, 1023–1030; Kathy Burrell, 'The recalcitrance of distance: exploring the infrastructures of sending in migrants' lives', *Mobilities*, 2016 on-line first.
32 Martin Ruhs, *Greasing the Wheels of the Flexible Labour Market: East European Labour Immigration in the UK. Centre on Migration, Policy and Society Working Paper no. 38* (Oxford: University of Oxford 2006); Stephen Drinkwater, John Eade and Michał

P. Garapich, *Poles Apart? EU Enlargement and the Labour Market Outcomes of Immigrants in the UK. IZA Discussion Paper no. 2410* (Bonn: Institute for the Study of Labor 2006); Bridget Anderson, Martin Ruhs, Ben Rogaly and Sarah Spencer, *Fair Enough? Central and East European Migrants in Low-wage Employment in the UK* (London: Joseph Rowntree Foundation 2006).

33 Agnieszka Fihel and Pawel Kaczmarczyk, 'Migration – a threat or a chance? Recent migration of Poles and its impact on the Polish labour market', in Burrell (ed.), *Polish Migration*, 23–48.

34 Bridget Anderson, 'Migration, immigration controls and the fashioning of precarious workers', *Work, Employment and Society* vol. 24, no. 2, 2010, 300–317 (304–305).

35 Ayona Datta, 'Places of everyday cosmopolitanisms: East European construction workers in London', *Environment and Planning A* vol. 41 no. 2, 2009, 353–370.

36 Aleksandra Galasińska and Olga Kozłowska, 'Discourses on a 'normal life' among post-accession migrants from Poland to Britain', in Burrell (ed.), *Polish Migration*, 87–105.

37 See Sarah Spencer, Martin Ruhs, Bridget Anderson and Ben Rogaly, *Migrants' Lives Beyond the Workplace: The Experiences of Central and East Europeans in the UK* (York: Joseph Rowntree Foundation 2007).

38 Nick Gill, 'Pathologies of migrant place-making: the case of Polish migrants to the UK', *Environment and Planning A* vol. 4, no. 5, 2010, 1157–1173; Anne White, *Polish Families and Migration Since EU Accession* (Bristol: Polity Press 2011); Louise, Ryan, Rosemary Sales, Mary Tilki and Bernadetta Siara, 'Social networks, social support and social capital: the experiences of recent Polish migrants in London', *Sociology*, vol. 42, no. 4, 2008, 672–690; Derek McGhee, Sue Heath and Paulina Trevena, 'Post-accession Polish migrants – their experiences of living in "low-demand" social housing areas in Glasgow', *Environment and Planning A* vol. 45, no. 2, 2013, 329–343.

39 Bernadetta Siara, 'UK Poles and the negotiation of gender and ethnic identity in cyberspace', in Burrell (ed.), *Polish Migration,* 167–187; McDowell, 'Old and new'; Violetta Parutis, 'White, European, and hardworking: East European migrants' relationships with other communities in London', *Journal of Baltic Studies* vol. 42, no. 2, 2011, 263–288.

AFTERWORD

Tony Kushner

In discussions over this volume, Colin Holmes was keen that it should be a *festschrift* and not a memorial volume. Colin continues to research and write and to do so powerfully as his masterful study of William Joyce and co-edited volume commemorating the life and achievements of Bill Fishman amply illustrate. In short, his work is *ongoing*!

But a final word is needed in relation to his legacy. The twenty-four essays here are testament to the stimulation of his work, including his inspiration as a teacher and supervisor. The authors here have taken his work further (including and quite rightly, providing new perspectives). But what emerges most strongly from each of these contributions is that however much progress has been made in unearthing new histories, new sources and new approaches is that we are still in our infancy in studying the inner lives of migrant groups in a British context (and all the global histories they represent) *and* the wider significance these have in defining that elusive concept of national identity.

This new work in the field and that which needs to be carried out does not reflect a failure of Colin Holmes' behalf in opening it up. On the contrary, it reveals the remarkable vision he had in showing by example that it mattered. It is to be hoped that in generations to follow, the history profession in Britain will see such work as 'mainstream' and fully worthy of being researched and taught. In his fierce determination to continue regardless of the dominant tendencies of his profession and his success in doing so, a huge debt of gratitude is thus owed to Colin Holmes. This volume is but a small tribute to the (to repeat, ongoing) work of a brave and determined scholar. The challenge now is for future generations to continue his outstanding example. In the meantime, Colin, as his old Yiddish *fraynd* Bill Fishman, would have put it, *Biz Hundert un Tsvantsig*.

APPENDICES

COLIN HOLMES – A LIFE AND CAREER

1. Colin Holmes: publications

Current work

Editor of an unpublished memoir, 'Chapters of Accidents,' by the novelist Alexander Baron

Publications

Books:

Searching for Lord Haw-Haw: The Political Lives of William Joyce (London: Routledge 2016)
A Tolerant Country? Immigrants, Refugees and Minorities in Britain (London: Faber 1991). Reissued by Routledge 2015
John Bull's Island: Immigration and British Society 1871–1971 (London: Macmillan 1988 Reprinted 1992, 1994, 1998). Reissued by Routledge 2015
Anti-Semitism in British Society 1876–1939 (London: Arnold 1979). Reissued by Routledge 2015

Edited books

An East End Legacy: Essays in Memory of William J. Fishman edited with Anne J. Kershen (London, Routledge 2017)
S. Pollard, *Essays on the Industrial Revolution in Britain* (Aldershot: Ashgate 2000)
Migration in European History Vols. 1&2 The International Library of Studies on Migration (Cheltenham: Elgar 1996)
Outsiders & Outcasts: Essays in honour of William J. Fishman edited with Geoffrey Alderman (London: Duckworth 1993)

Economy and Society: European Industrialisation and its Social Consequences edited with Alan Booth (Leicester: Leicester University Press 1991)

Essays in the Economic and Social History of South Yorkshire edited with Sidney Pollard (Barnsley: SYCC 1977 Reprinted 1979)

Immigrants and Minorities in British Society (London: Allen & Unwin 1978). Reissued by Routledge 2015

The End of the Old Europe edited with Sidney Pollard (London: Arnold 1973)

Industrial Power and National Rivalry edited with Sidney Pollard (London: Arnold 1972)

The Process of Industrialisation edited with Sidney Pollard (London: Arnold 1968)

Contributions to books

'The Reubens Brothers: Jews, Crime and the East London Connection 1887–1911' in: C. Holmes and A.J. Kershen (eds.) *An East End Legacy: Essays in Memory of William J. Fishman* (London: Routledge 2017), 93–116

'William Joyce and the German Connection' in: I. Wallace (ed.) *Voices from Exile: Essays in Memory of Hamish Ritchie* (Leiden, Boston: Brill, Rodolpi 2015), 259–275

Entries on The Boer War; the British Brothers' League; *The Cause of World Unrest*; H.A. Gwynne; J.A. Hobson (Vol. 1) and Beatrice Webb (Vol. 2): in R.S. Levy (ed.) *Antisemitism: A Historical Encyclopaedia of Prejudice and Persecution* (Santa Barbara: ABC-CLIO 2006)

Entries on Richard Bell; British National Party; British Union of Fascists; Cable Street; Barbara Castle; Walter Crane; Hugh Dalton; Tom Driberg; Robert Forgan; John Gollan; Victor Gollancz; Colin Jordan; James Klugmann; Oswald Mosley; National Front; New Party; Olympia rally; D. N. Pritt; Public Order Act (1936); Red Lion Square Riots; William Rust; Shapurji Saklatvala; Richards Stokes; R.H. Tawney; John Tyndall; Union Movement; Martin Webster; Tom Wintringham; Konni Zilliacus: in J. Ramsden (ed.) *Oxford Companion to 20th Century British Politics* (Oxford: Oxford University Press 2002)

'Die Einwanderung nach Grossbritannien in Vergangenheit und Gegenwart': in K. Schönwälder & I. Strum-Martin (eds.) *Die Britische Gesellschaft zwischen Offenheit und Abgrenzung Einwanderung und Integration vom 18. bis zum 20. Jahrhundert* (Berlin: Philo Press 2001), 17–33

'British Government Policy towards Wartime Refugees': in M. Conway & J. Gotovich (eds.) *Europe in Exile: European Exile Communities in Britain 1940–45* (Oxford: Berg 2001), 11–34

'On the Damascus Road: The first steps in my conversion to Economic and Social History': in P. Hudson (ed.) *Living Economic and Social History* (Glasgow: Economic History Society 2001), 145–149

'Introduction': in K. Taylor (ed.) *Holocaust Denial* (London: Searchlight Educational Trust 2000), 4–6

'Foreword': in R. Kershaw & M. Pearsall *Immigrants and Aliens: Sources on UK Immigration and Citizenship* (London: Public Record Office 2000),ix–xiiii

'Sidney Pollard 1925–1988': in S. Pollard, *Labour History and the Labour Movement in Britain* (Aldershot: Ashgate 1998), xix–xx

'Cosmopolitan London': in A.J. Kershen (ed.) *London: The Promised Land?* (Aldershot: Avebury Press 1997), 10–37 [see *Times Higher Educational Supplement* 19 September 1997]

'Hostile Images: Immigrants and Refugees in Nineteenth and Twentieth-Century Britain': in J. & L. Lucassen (eds.) *Migration, Migration History, History: Old Paradigms and New Perspectives* (Bern: Land 1997), 317–334

'Introduction' and 'The German Gypsy Question in Britain 1904–06': in C. Holmes (ed.) *Migration in European History* Vol. 2 (Cheltenham: Elgar 1996), 481–500

'Jewish Economic and Refugee Migrations, 1880–1950': in R. Cohen (ed.) *The Cambridge Survey of World Migration* (Cambridge: Cambridge University Press 1995), 148–153

Entries on: Diane Abbott; J.R. Archer; John Beckett; Reginald Bridgeman; G.D.H. Cole; Walter Crane; Hugh Dalton; Maurice Dobb; Tom Driberg; R. Palme Dutt; Robert Forgan; Victor Gollancz; J.B.S. Haldane; H.M. Hyndman; Hewlett Johnson; James Klugmann; Harold Laski; C. L'Estrange Malone; Robert Maxwell; Ivor Montagu; Oswald Mosley; George Orwell; Reginald Paget; Raymond Postgate; D. N. Pritt; William Rust; S. Saklatvala; Hartley Shawcross; Sydney Silverman; Reginald Sorensen; Richard Stokes; John Strachey; R.H. Tawney; Keith Vaz; J.H. Wilson; Tom Wintringham; Konni Zilliacus: in T. Lane (ed.) *Biographical Dictionary of European Labour Leaders* (London & New York: Greenwood Press, 1995)

Entries on: Anti-Semitism; Fascism; Immigration; Refugees; Sir Oswald Mosley: in F. Leventhal (ed.), *Encyclopaedia of Twentieth Century Britain* (New York: Garland Publishing 1995)

'London: the World's Metropolis': in F. Dijkstra & J. Peck (eds.) *European Studies* (Leeuwarden: Noordelijke Hogeschool 1994), 43–51

'Historians and Immigration': in M. Drake (ed.) *Time, Family and Community* (Oxford: Open University with Blackwell, 1994), 165–180

Entries on: 'Anti-Semitism in British Society 1876–1939'; 'Attack and Counter-Attack'; 'The Balance Sheet: Summary and Evaluation': in H.A. Strauss (ed.) *Hostages of Modernization. Studies on Modern Antisemitism 1870–1933/39* (Berlin, New York: de Gruyter 1993), 326–349, 425–434, 435–451

'Introduction': in N. Merriman (ed.) *The Peopling of London* (London: HMSO 1993), viii–ix

(with G. Mitchell) '*When it was Dark*: Jews in the Literature of Guy Thorne': in J.A. Morris (ed.) *Exploring Stereotyped Images* (Lampeter: Edwin Mellen Press 1993), 231–245

'"British Justice at Work": Internment in the Second World War': in P. Panayi (ed.) *Minorities in Wartime* (Oxford: Berg 1993), 150–165

'The Chinese Connection': in G. Alderman & C. Holmes (eds.) *Outsiders & Outcasts: Essays in honour of William J. Fishman* (London: Duckworth 1993), 71–93

'The Ritual Murder Accusation in Britain': in A. Dundes (ed.) *The Blood Libel Legend. A Casebook of Anti-Semitic Folklore* (Madison: University of Wisconsin Press 1991), 99–134

'The Webbs and Japan': in H. Cortazzi & G. Daniels (eds.) *Japan and Britain 1859–1991* (London: Routledge 1991), 166–176

'Immigration': in T. Gourvish & A. O'Day (eds) *Britain since 1945* (London: Macmillan 1991), 209–232

(with Alan Booth) 'Sidney Pollard: His Life and Work': in C. Holmes & A. Booth (eds.) *Economy and Society: European Industrialisation and its Social Consequences* (Leicester: Leicester University Press 1991), ix–xxvii

'Immigrants and Refugees in Britain': in W.E. Mosse (ed.) *Second Chance: Two Centuries of German-Speaking Jews in the United Kingdom* (J.C.G. Mohr, Tübingen 1991), 11–30

'Historians and Immigration': in C. Pooley & I. Whyte (eds.) *Migrants, Emigrants and Immigrants* (London: Routledge 1991), 191–207

'Great Britain: Fascism' and 'Oswald Mosley': in I. Gutman (ed.) *Encyclopaedia of the Holocaust* (New York: Maxwell Macmillan International 1989), vol. 2 605–607 and vol. 3 995–996 respectively

'Alexander Ratcliffe, Militant Protestant and Antisemite': in T. Kushner & K. Lunn (eds.) *Traditions of Intolerance, Historical Perspectives on Fascism and Race Discourse in Britain* (Manchester: Manchester University Press 1989), 196–217

'The Social Origins of D.H. Lawrence': in C. Heywood (ed.) *D.H. Lawrence: New Studies* (London: Macmillan 1987), 1–15

'Public Opinion in England and the Jews 1914–1918': in R.A. Rockaway and S. Simonsohn (eds.) *Michael: On the History of the Jews of Diaspora* Vol. X (Tel-Aviv: Diaspora Research Institute 1986), 97–115

'Bibliographical and Historical Introduction' to V.F. Gilbert & D. Tatla (eds.) *Immigrants, Minorities and Race Relations: A Bibliography of Theses and Dissertations presented at British and Irish Universities 1900–1981* (London: Mansell Press 1984), xv–xxiii

(with Barbara Hill) 'Robert Forgan': in W.W. Knox (ed.) *Scottish Labour Leaders 1918–1939*, (Edinburgh: Mainstream Publications 1984), 110–113

'The Promised Land? Immigration in Britain 1870–1980': in D.A. Coleman (ed.) *The Demography of Immigrants and Minority Groups in the United Kingdom* (London: Academic Press 1982), 1–21

'Immigration': in M. Drake & T.C. Barker (eds.) *Population and Society* (London: Batsford 1982), 172–202

'Index of Hatred 1871–1981' – Introduction to R. Singerman, *Anti-Semitism: An Annotated Bibliography and Research Guide* (New York: Garland Press 1982), ix–xxv

(with Barbara Hill) 'Robert Forgan': in J. Saville & J.M. Bellamy (eds.) *Dictionary of Labour Biography* Vol. 6 (London: Macmillan 1982), 111–114

'John Beckett': in J. Saville & J.M. Bellamy (eds.) *Dictionary of Labour Biography* Vol. 6 (London: Macmillan 1982), 24–29

'East End Crime and the Jewish Community 1887–1911': in A. Newman (ed.) *The Jewish East End 1840–1939* (London: Jewish Historical Society of England 1981), 109–123

'The German Gypsy Question 1904–6': in K.J. Lunn (ed.) *Hosts, Immigrants and Minorities: Historical Responses to Newcomers in British Society 1870–1914* (Folkestone: Dawson 1980), 134–159

(with K.J. Lunn) 'Introduction' to K.J. Lunn (ed.) *Hosts, Immigrants and Minorities. Historical Responses to Newcomers in British Society 1870–1914* (Folkestone: Dawson 1980), 1–21

'Anti-Semitism and the BUF': in K.J. Lunn & R.C. Thurlow (eds) *Essays in British Fascism* (London: Croom Helm 1980), 114–134

'Germans in Britain 1870–1914': in J. Schneider et al., *Wirtschaftskrafte und Wirtschaftswege: Festschrift für Hermann Kellenbenz* (Nuremberg: Klett-Cotta 1978), vol. 3, 581–593

'J.A. Hobson and the Jews': in C. Holmes (ed.) *Immigrants and Minorities in British Society* (London: Allen and Unwin 1978), 125–157

'Immigrants and Minorities in British Society': in C. Holmes (ed.) *Immigrants and Minorities in British Society* (London: Allen and Unwin 1978), 13–22

'Samuel Roberts and the Gypsies': in S. Pollard & C. Holmes (eds) *Essays in the Economic and Social History of South Yorkshire* (Barnsley: South Yorkshire County Council 1977), 233–246

Documentary contributions to J. Salt & B.J. Elliott, *British Society 1870–1970* (London: Hulton Educational Publications 1975), 96–109, 150–167, 183–185, 230–245

Pamphlets

'Historical Revisionism in Britain: The Politics of History': in *Trends in Historical Revisionism* (London: Centre for Contemporary Studies 1985), 4–8

The Vitality of Anti-Semitism: The British Experience since 1945 (London: Centre for Contemporary Studies 1981)

Bibliographical studies

Theses and Dissertations on the History of Education presented at British and Irish Universities between 1900 and 1976 (Lancaster: History of Education Society 1979)

Theses and Dissertations in Economic and Social History in Yorkshire Universities 1920–74 (Sheffield: University Library 1975)

Sheffield University Theses, Dissertations and Special Studies in Economic and Social History 1920–74 (Sheffield: University Library 1974)

Journal articles

'Frank Cass (1930–2007)', *Immigrants and Minorities*, vol. 27, 2009, 118–122

(with G. Alderman) 'The Burton Book', *Journal of the Royal Asiatic Society*, vol. 18, 2008, 1–13

'C. C. Aronsfeld [1910–2002]', *Patterns of Prejudice*, vol. 37, 2003, 83–85

'Sidney Pollard 1925–1998', *Proceedings of the British Academy*, vol. 105, 2000, 513–534

'Sidney Pollard', *History Workshop Journal*, Issue 49, 2000, 277–278

'Traitors: Fascism in World War Two', *Searchlight*, no. 293, 1999, 14–15

Review Essay: L. Dinnerstein, *Anti-Semitism in America* and F. C. Jaher, *A Scapegoat in the New Wilderness. The Origins and Rise of Anti-Semitism in America*, in *American Jewish Archives*, vol. XLV11, 1996, 75–81

'Invisible People', *Renaissance and Modern Studies*, vol. 38, 1995, 1–20

Contribution to 'The Battle of Cable Street', *Contemporary Record*, vol. 8, 1994, 110–111

'Private World of Public Records', *Parliamentary Brief* (May–June 1994), 62

'"Germany Calling": Lord Haw-Haw's Treason', *Twentieth Century British History*, vol. 5, 1994, 118–121

'The Irish in Britain', *Modern History Review*, vol. 5, 1994, 9–12

Review article: 'Death's Shadow: Reflections on the Holocaust', *Jewish Journal of Sociology*, vol. XXXIV, 1992, 43–50

(with Kenneth Lunn) 'Editorial', *Immigrants and Minorities*, vol. 10, 1991, 1–2

'Kings of the Ring', *International Journal of the History of Sport*, vol. 8, 1991, 429–432

'Building the Nation: The Contributions of Immigrants and Refugees to British Society', *Journal of the Royal Society of Arts*, 1991, 725–734

'Enemy Aliens?' *History Today*, 1990, 25–31

'The British Government and Brendan Behan, 1941–1954: The Persistence of the Prevention of Violence Act', *Saothar: Journal of the Irish Labour History Society*, vol. 14, 1989, 125–128

'Internment, Fascism and the Public Records', *Society for the Study of Labour History Bulletin*, vol. 52, 1987, 17–23

'Immigration into Britain: The Myth of Fairness. Racial Violence in Britain 1911–19', *History Today*, vol. 35, 1985, 41–45

'Immigration into Britain: Introduction', *History Today*, vol. 35, 1985, 16–17

'Immigrants, Refugees and Revolutionaries', *Immigrants and Minorities*, vol. 2, 1983, 7–22

'Introductory Editorial', *Immigrants and Minorities*, vol. 1, 1982, 1–15

'The Tredegar Riots of 1911: Anti-Jewish Disturbances in South Wales', *Welsh History Review*, vol. 11, 1982, 214–225

'Government Files and Privileged Access', *Social History*, vol. 6, 1981, 333–350

'The Ritual Murder Accusation in Britain', *Ethnic and Racial Studies*, vol. 4, 1981, 265–288

Review article: 'The Secret that Wasn't', *Jewish Quarterly*, vol. 28, 1980–81, 54–56

Review article: 'B.M. Wasserstein, *Britain and the Jews of Europe 19039-1945*', *Jewish Journal of Sociology*, vol. XXII, 1980, 59–72

H.O. 144/6719/485074 'The Raid on the Headquarters of the CPGB', *Society for the Study of Labour History Bulletin*, no. 40, 1980, 23–28 (with A.H. Ion) 'Bushidō and the Samurai: Images of Japan in British Public Opinion 1893–1914', *Modern Asian Studies*, vol. 14, 1980, 309–329

'The Social Origins of D.H. Lawrence', *Literature and History*, vol. 6, 1980, 82–93, 142

'The German Gypsy Question 1904–06', *Journal of the Gypsy Lore Society*, vol. 1, 1980, 248–267

'Trotsky in Britain: The Closed File', *Society for the Study of Labour History Bulletin*, no. 39, 1979, 31–39

'New Light on the "Protocols of Zion,"' *Patterns of Prejudice*, vol. 11, 1978, 13–18

'New Light on the 'Protocols of the Elders of Zion'', *Patterns of Prejudice*, vol. 11, 1977, 13–21. [See *The Times*, 17 February 1978, 1–2]

'Strangers in the Land', *Patterns of Prejudice*, vol. 10, 1976, 1–6

'East End Anti-Semitism, 1936', *Society for the Study of Labour History Bulletin*, no. 32, 1976, 26–33

'Violence and Race Relations in Britain 1953–1968', *Phylon*, vol. XXVI, 1975, 113–124

(with Gina Mitchell) '"In his Image": Jews in the Literature of Guy Thorne', *Patterns of Prejudice*, vol. 9, 1975, 18–24

'In Search of Sidney Street', *Society for the Study of Labour History Bulletin*, no. 29, 1974, 70–77

'The 1885 and 1888 Jewish Tailors' Strikes in Leeds', *Journal of the Yorkshire Archaeological Society*, vol. 45, 1973, 158–166

'Bukharin in England', *Soviet Studies*, vol. XXIV, 1972, 86–90

'Goldwin Smith, a Liberal Anti-Semite', *Patterns of Prejudice*, vol. 6, 1972, 25–30

'The Hyndman-Blumenfeld Correspondence in 1913', *Society for the Study of Labour History Bulletin*, no. 24, 1972, 27–29

'History, Social History and the Social Sciences: Problems General and Particular', *Sociological Analysis*, vol. 1, 1971, 121–134

'Nativism and Violence', *Race Today*, vol. 3, 1971, 99–100

'Joseph Banister's Anti-Semitism', *Patterns of Prejudice*, vol. 4, 1970, 29–31

'Houston Stewart Chamberlain in Great Britain', *Wiener Library Bulletin* vol. XXIV, 1970, 31–36

'Economic and Social History in the School Curriculum', *Higher Education Journal* 1968, 24–28

Newspaper articles

'Lives Remembered: Emmanuel Cooper', *The Times*, 10 February 2012

'Victor George Kiernan', *The Times*, 14 May 2009

'Frank Cass', *The Times* online, 13 November 2007

'Professor Sidney Pollard', *The Times*, 18 December 1998

'Professor Sidney Pollard', *The Independent*, 10 December 1998

'Immigration: the issue that could take centre stage', *The Times*, 5 April 1990

(with A. R. J. Kushner) 'The Charge is Ritual Murder', *Jewish Chronicle*, 29 March 1985
'Anti-Semitism in Britain 1939–1979', *Jewish Chronicle*, 14 September 1979

Academic blog

'Searching for Lord Haw-Haw. The Political Lives of William Joyce', History Matters, Department of History, University of Sheffield. December 2016

2. The Sheffield School – Colin Holmes postgraduate supervision

At Northumbria

H. Carter   PhD   2003

At Sheffield

S. M. Kelly   PhD 2002
M. Winslow   PhD 2001
J. Heppell   PhD 2000
E. Gilbert   PhD 2000
A. Mitchell   PhD 1999 (with R. C. Thurlow)
Y. Sellek   PhD 1999
D. K. Renton   PhD 1998
T. P. Edmunds   PhD 1998
J. Hanson   PhD 1995
I. Kellerman   MPhil 1995
D. MacRaild   PhD 1993 (with D. Martin)
S. Harris   PhD 1993
D. Lodge   MPhil 1992
E. Frankel   MPhil 1990
G. M. Mitchell   PhD 1990
P. Panayi   PhD 1988 (with M. Bentley)
A. R. Kushner   PhD 1986
B. Cheyette   PhD 1986 (with K. Graham)
M. Thomas   MPhil 1985
D. Mayall   PhD 1982
R. J. Harrison   PhD 1979
B. J. Bush   MPhil 1979
J. J. Bennett   MPhil 1979
K. J. Lunn   PhD 1978
F. K. Donnelly   PhD 1976 (with S. Pollard)
G. W. Dimmock   MA 1975
T. C. Allen   MA 1974
J. E. Morell   MA 1974
L. Waldenberg   MA 1973

3. Colin Holmes interview with Alan Dein
21 February 2017

THE INTERVIEWER: Colin, to begin, may I ask your date and place of birth?

PROFESSOR HOLMES: My date of birth has three 8s in it, 8/8/38, which in Jewish culture means I am thrice blessed. I was born at South Normanton in Derbyshire. When I was growing up there, the pit was the main show. The Holmes family were miners, basically. But my mother's family was slightly different. She was born into a farming background.

My mother was quite an intelligent woman but, like people of her age – she was born in 1902 – was never really allowed to fulfil her potential, so she went out and worked in service, in other words she was employed by people who wanted maids to look after their homes for them. As a result, my mother had a genteel aspect to her. I am not suggesting my father was a direct opposite. He was obviously quite ambitious at one stage of his life because he was a group scoutmaster and in the Church of England choir. But my mother was the dominant force in my life. She was determined that I would get on, as they say. Not that she had any idea about university or university education but I was certainly going to have a white-collar job. That would have satisfied her. She was the driving force behind me, basically, in those early days.

THE INTERVIEWER: What did your father want you to do? Did he explore the possibility of continuing the mining stock?

PROFESSOR HOLMES: My father didn't want me to continue that tradition. You must remember from '39 my father wasn't at home. He was drafted into munitions work and I have one very vivid memory when I said to my mother, "There's a man who's come to the door." She replied, "Let him in," and I went to the door and opened it and I didn't recognise this man, and I ran back to my mother and said, "But I don't know who this man is," and she said, "It's your Dad."

I suspect that by the time I was born my parents' marriage wasn't as good as it should have been and in a sense my mother poured her love into me: "*He's* going to fulfil my hopes, *he's* going to fulfil my aims, *he's* going to fulfil my ambitions, *he's* going to be different: *he's* not going to go into the pits, *he's* not going to go along the traditional route,' so it was very important for *her* that I did well. I felt I was under an obligation to do well.

My father was never hostile to me. I was just never particularly close to him. But I do owe a lot to him, in a way, because he once bought an eight-volume set of encyclopaedias. My mother was really annoyed at the money that had been spent. But in fact that purchase fired my academic interests. I read and re-read these volumes, particularly every Sunday morning, in front of a big fire in the front room: I'd lie on the floor, I'd read and I'd be enthralled by it all. Those eight volumes were very significant in my intellectual development, I think, and I owe that to my father.

One of my most vivid early memories is my mother holding me up against the window. My sister was there too and the skies to me seemed like blood red. When I asked my mother years later, "When you held me up against the window in the small bedroom, what was going on?" She said, "Oh, that was the bombing of Sheffield, that was the blitz of Sheffield." I remember a great deal about the War. Every week my Aunt bought me the *War Illustrated* so in a sense I could plot all the battles and know all that was going on and I knew everything that was happening, at a very early age. I think individuals influence one's life but also social circumstances do, and I was a war child, basically. If you ask, "Why did you become a historian?" I think that's one of the reasons, that I was a war child and I have these images from the War and that drew me towards history, contemporary history particularly.

When I was at school, it was straightforward traditional political history, the Civil War, Tudors, basically, but nothing beyond that, but I quite liked it then and I was very good at it. I always used to get high marks. When I went to secondary school other influences entered my life. The person who really affected me at Tupton was called Bond, Ulysses Edward Bond, known always simply as Bond. I remember my first sight of him as if it were yesterday. I was twelve, in my first year at grammar school, and he came in wearing his gown, strode across to the desk with his books in his hand, put his books down and said, "My name is Bond, B.O.N.D, and my car's a Ford, F.O.R.D."

I remember him once coming over to me in class and saying, "Come on, Holmes, you're a neat little boy. Let's get some good work out of you" – here was somebody who was taking an interest and I could respond to that. Although Bond looked old to me, he was actually only thirty-seven! He'd been in the desert with Montgomery and been awarded the Military Cross. I had him for History in the sixth form and to me he was a fantastic teacher. He would say things like, "By the way, we don't want to talk about the Thirty Years' War today. Why don't we talk instead about Archbishop Makarios in Cyprus? It's far more interesting," and I could respond to that. I thought it was teasing things out and extending one's boundaries and I liked that very much.

Nottingham was a relatively new university when I went up in '57. The university itself was very go-ahead and attracted quite a lot of public school types as well as grammar school products from London and elsewhere in the South, so that was another area of experience opening up, which I wouldn't have had if I'd gone to the village secondary modern school and ended up with a clerk's job in a neighbouring city or town, or whatever.

THE INTERVIEWER: I wonder at what point, when you were at grammar school, did you believe that that was your path, you were going to go to university?

PROFESSOR HOLMES: Up to when I was about fourteen, I thought I wanted to be a laboratory assistant. But I didn't necessarily want to become a historian. I should also tell you that although I was very good at History I did in fact nourish ambitions by the sixth form to be a lawyer. I fancied myself at the Criminal Bar, surprisingly enough. But Bond comes back into the story because he said to me at the end of one class, "What are you going to do at university, Holmes," and I said, "Well, I think I might do law, sir," and he snorted and said, "Law? You want to do law?" and then he remarked, "And become a solicitor, conveyancing property for middle class people in some provincial town?" He said, "Go and read History, it's far more interesting," so I thought right, well, alright, that's what I'll do.

I was never in the top form, until my O level years and as a result I hadn't done Latin. I was therefore told, "You are obviously university material for History but you can't go to university to read History without Latin. Well, you can, you know, but your choice is very limited." The headmaster, a classics graduate from Oxford, then said, "Don't worry, I'll take you for Latin O level and you can do that whilst taking your A levels." Then, tragically, he committed suicide: he hanged himself in the summer holidays. Consequently, that option went: and the school made no provision for Latin. Therefore, I had a very limited range of options open to me. I could go to Nottingham or Hull without Latin. The alternative was to read something like the BSc Econ (London).

I didn't feel confident enough to go to London but there was also a Politics and Modern History degree at Manchester, which was highly regarded, and I was interviewed and they wanted me, but I decided not to go. Manchester overpowered me slightly – still does, to some extent. The reason I went to Nottingham was that Bond, who had taught me History, had been to Nottingham when it was a university college and he said, "Why don't you go to Nottingham?" So, I applied to Nottingham and was interviewed. I don't think the interview went very well, because one of the lecturers interviewing me thought I was a rather jaundiced young man. But anyway, they did accept me and I went up in '57.

I remember very vividly my first official contact as a student. B.L. Hallwood was the Vice-Chancellor of Nottingham. He knew exactly what was going on in the university and when he addressed all the freshers – and here was my first formal contact with the University as an undergraduate – I still remember quite clearly his opening remarks: "This is rather a *good* university. You are rather *lucky* to be here." You see, he believed in the place and that set the tone for Nottingham, but it didn't set the tone for me because I didn't get off to a very good start in History.

Initially, I really relished the prospect of studying medieval history because I had not done that at school and I thought this was a new world, a different world, with a different culture. But it was killed for me by the people who taught it. They were the most boring and uninteresting people – lecturers who couldn't teach. That was a big disappointment and I got disenchanted with other parts of the syllabus and I thought, "This isn't working out for me." But then, as happens in life, at Nottingham a lifeline was thrown to me when Peter Payne came. He was a Nottingham graduate and had completed a PhD there. He taught European Economic History and I could identify with that. That seemed to me to be fascinating and relevant, you know, the rise of Germany, the industrial power of Germany, the decline of France, the Russian Revolution and the economic factors behind it. I thought this was great, this is something completely different from the French Revolution or the English Civil War.

Also, I went to lectures by J. D. Chambers. Chambers was a fascinating lecturer and could make things relevant – the Poor Law, the state of labour and things like that. I thought this was where I was meant to go, this was the kind of history that interested me. So, I went to see the Head of History and told him, "I'd really like to change from political history." He said, "You can't." I asked, "Why?" He countered with, "What to do you want to do with your life," and I said, "Well, I'd really like to lecture I think in university." He remarked, "You can't possibly do that." I told him: "Professor Chambers thinks I might, I've got some ability here." He said, "Well, if you feel that way, go, I'll transfer you," so I transferred to Economic and Social History, which was a sub-department.

I completed two years of Political History and then I did the final year in Economic and Social History and graduated in Economic and Social History in 1960. That was much better for me than staying with the political historians. I remember loving the dissertation that I wrote for my BA Degree. It was a study of Chartism in Nottingham and I really liked that and one of my former colleagues in the department at Sheffield once said to me, "I still think it's your best piece of work ever." [Laughter] It is actually quite widely quoted. I really enjoyed Economic and Social History … I really got into it. I loved it, you know, very much so.

My work on Chartism in Nottingham was like a trailblazer and I trawled through all the local papers in the Summer vacation and obtained various pamphlets as well and read those and it was quite a big piece of work.

I wanted to continue my work on Chartism in Nottingham because I felt there was more to do when I was awarded a Revis Scholarship to pursue post-graduate work at the University. When I said to Chambers that I really wanted to continue with that topic he replied, "Oh, no, you can't do that." He said: "I want you to write on H. S. Tremenheere." Puzzled, I asked, "Who's that?" He said, "He was the first inspector of mines and schools." I said, "Oh, right." Chambers went on: "Because if we don't do it, in Nottingham, Beales at the LSE will get a student onto it and we've got to be in there first." My response was: "Well, I'm not sure I want to do that," and he said, "Well, if you don't do that, you won't get the scholarship." Therefore I had a bad start to my post-graduate career – I was directed onto a topic that I didn't really want to do.

The research didn't go well because this was the days before modern computers and I remember presenting Chambers with the first chapter of the thesis and he lost it. He was a superb undergraduate teacher but he wasn't a good postgraduate supervisor, so I really didn't enjoy my post-graduate career at all.

I became disenchanted with the Tremenheere topic, it didn't grab my attention and I wasn't terribly involved in it. Therefore, I was in a slight quandary: what do I do in terms of a career? The other complication was that by that time I'd got married and I had to have some money. Consequently, I went teaching for a year while I was finishing off the thesis. I then remember going to see Chambers one Saturday morning – he always saw his postgraduates on Saturdays – when he said to me, "Are you happy," and I said, "Well, who is?" and he continued, "Well, quite happy?" I said, "Yes, happy-ish." Then out of the blue came his remark, "Would you like a job?" I could only say, "Well, what are you offering me?" He replied, "There are two jobs going, there's one at Liverpool, there's one at Sheffield." My reply was: "which one would you go for if you were in my position?" He said, "Well, I wouldn't go to Liverpool because the professor there, is dead from the neck up." (Chambers was always terribly discreet!) He said, "I'd go to Sheffield. Pollard is there, he's a coming man. Mind you," he said, "he's Jewish and a Marxist." That was enough for me: "Oh, right," I said, "I'll try for Sheffield then." He said, "I've got the details in my drawer." He retrieved the papers and then observed, "The closing date's gone but don't worry, I'll write to Pollard and tell him that you're interested." I said, "Okay." Then I received a letter asking me to go for an interview.

I was interviewed by three people: Pollard was there, along with J.C. (Jack) Gilbert, the Professor of Economics, and also George Potter, the Professor of Medieval History. Pollard eventually emerged and told me of Sheffield's offer. He rather frightened me because when he came out, he said, "We'll appoint you for one year," and I said, "Oh, God, one year. What security is there?" and he said, "We'll look at you and then decide whether you're worth keeping on for a second year and in the second year we'll look at you again and decide whether you're worth keeping on for a third year." I then thought, "I'll take a chance on it." Of course that was normal procedure for the appointment of assistant lecturers, but it seemed as if it was a terribly precarious venture. But anyway, I accepted the post and came here in '63.

I knew Pollard's work – I knew he was a very prominent historian. I knew less about Gilbert. I knew even less about Potter. I remember very little about the interview, except that when I entered the room Gilbert got up and locked all the filing cabinets, as if he didn't trust me. I think Chambers must have given me a very good reference and I think I must have impressed them to some extent in the interview, and Pollard obviously saw something in me which he wanted to continue with and develop, so that was it, basically, and I was in.

My remit was to teach European and American Economic History, which was a course Pollard himself had taught, and that was quite a heavy teaching load because in those days there was a general degree in Sheffield as well as an honours degree, so you would lecture to the honours degree on a certain theme and then you'd have to repeat that to the general studies students as well, so you were having to double the lectures, as it were.

I didn't particularly enjoy the American part. I liked the European because I'd actually been enthused by that when Payne had taught me at Nottingham. Pollard very quickly said he wanted us to produce some documents on European Economic History and that meant getting to the sources and turning these into a book, which could then be used by students. That led eventually to three volumes of documents on European Economic History; we were getting material from the German, from the Spanish, from the Italian, from the French, from the eighteenth century up to 1939.

THE INTERVIEWER: When you moved to Sheffield and you were working with Pollard, did you have any longer-term plans of where you wanted your research to go or what you would like to do?

PROFESSOR HOLMES: No, I didn't, actually. I didn't want to do anything on Tremenheere – I had had enough of that. That was part of the past. But I think I was already interested in the history of migration, because I remember gathering a big file of material on Belgian refugees who came to Britain in the First World War, a quarter of a million of them, in fact, and I drafted something out on that episode. But compiling the documentary histories with Pollard was very demanding in terms of time and it went on for about five years putting those documents together. That took up an awful lot of time and energy and I wasn't thinking terribly of where to go after I stepped outside that. I wasn't particularly ambitious, I mean I was in the university and in a sense I had made it and after three years, I was a lecturer. I wouldn't have to satisfy another board for another five years. I thought by then I will have shown that I can do something, as a teacher, as a researcher, or possibly both, and I just ploughed on with the documents, determined to get them out of the way. But at some point, of course, I would have to think about what to do after that.

Apart from Pollard there was another very important early influence in Sheffield. I was having lunch with Pollard in the staff club one day and this man shambled over to us, and Sidney Pollard said to me, "This is Harry Armytage, he is Professor of Education." Armytage spent about 45 minutes with me in his room after lunch and he advised, "Don't get too involved in university administration. What you must do," he went on, "is organise your time so that you produce research because if you want promotion, the people on the Promotions Committee won't care a damn about how good a teacher you are, how much administration you've done. They want to see what publications you've written." He also told me: "Remember this, if you write a book, it remains forever, it doesn't go away; books survive and are your legacy." He then urged me: "Push on with your research."

After that point, whenever I saw Harry Armytage, he would say, "How are things? What are you doing now?" He was just terribly effervescent, enthusiastic, and again he must have seen something in me and wanted to nourish me and develop me and I was very grateful for that.

THE INTERVIEWER: In the sixties and early seventies, in the canon of British historians, or maybe even global historians, were there any particular people that you were particularly interested in or following?

PROFESSOR HOLMES: I was actually reading Tawney. I mean Tawney is one of my great heroes. I was also starting to read American immigration history and John Higham's, *Strangers in the Land* is a book that I very much enjoyed and which influenced me. Then, of course, by that time I was developing my own interest in immigration. There wasn't very much by way of historical literature on immigration at that time. Most of the work was being done by sociologists. Kenneth Little had written *Negroes in Britain* and Michael Banton *The Coloured Quarter*, but they were sociologists, social anthropologists. There was very little, in terms of historical material, for me to draw on and I think that's one of the reasons I was attracted to Higham because, he was a historian, he'd considered recent migration into the US, and I now believed something similar was needed for Britain and that awareness gradually developed.

The 1960s were what I call the decisive decade on immigration. You see first the Race Relations Act, the National Front at the end of that period, and the first immigration controls, Powellism, and the deportation of undesirable aliens. This is dramatic stuff and I think there is room for a book on immigration called "The Decisive Decade", looking at all this, probing it further than it's been examined so far. I was surrounded by all these issues, you know. And I was aware the face of Britain was changing. We were experiencing the continued immigration from the Caribbean and then later particularly from the Indian sub-Continent.

Even so, I remember, years later, when I was once introduced to the intending First Year History students, the person said, "And over here we have Professor Colin Holmes. I don't really know what he's interested in, minorities of all sorts, really, East and West and that kind of thing, you know." My work was still regarded by some as quite peripheral. There was a certain stigma to it.

I think the Pollard link is also important in taking me towards migration history Pollard was Jewish. He was in the Kindertransport. He came out when he was thirteen, from Vienna. He had one relative here in this country and that relative didn't really want to take him in, because Pollard's parents insisted that he was brought up as an orthodox boy and the family in London weren't orthodox, so Pollard was sent up to Whittingehame in Scotland to work on the land. The idea was he would then transfer to Palestine.

He didn't have any English when he left Vienna. He wanted to be a scientist but he couldn't because he didn't have access to laboratories and therefore had to change his direction entirely. He used to get up at half-past four in the morning and study by candlelight to get on. During the War, he was called into the Army and served as an interpreter because he had German, obviously. After the War he went to the LSE, took a First in two years, then was awarded a PhD and by '53 was appointed at Sheffield as a Knoop Fellow. From '38 to '53, that's some journey. That was a remarkable story. It intrigued me and fuelled my interest in thinking well, people are looking now at New Commonwealth and Pakistani immigration, as it was called then, but there was this earlier immigration, of Jews, so why don't I consider Jewish immigration?

I put a proposal together and I sent it to Edward Arnold because they'd published the three volumes of documents on European Economic History. John Davey, then the Commissioning Editor there, said, "It's interesting but I don't think it's something we want to publish." He was quite right, in a way. My proposal did contain some new information but in 1960 Lloyd Gartner had written on the Jewish immigrant and ten or so years later John Garrard had published *The English and Immigration*, which is a comparative of the Jewish immigration and the post-War New Commonwealth immigration. And soon afterwards Bernard Gainer's *The Alien Invasion* had travelled over some of the terrain of Jewish migration. So, Davey said to me, "Why don't you consider writing on antisemitism, which is the bigger issue relating to Jews? There's need for a book on that," and I said, "Well, okay, I could do that between 1870 and 1905," but he suggested I push it forward to 1939. *Anti-Semitism in British Society 1876 to 1939* grew out of that context and I was grateful that Davey put me onto that.

When I started work on this research I came into contact with C.C. Aronsfeld at the Institute of Jewish Affairs, and Aronsfeld said to me, "I think it's good that you're working in this area because many Anglo-Jews don't want to know about anti-Semitism, they like to sweep it under the carpet, they don't want it to be discussed, emphasised, or talked about." He was the exception in wanting the topic covered. Aronsfeld, another refugee from the Nazis, was a very early supporter of my research.

The sources were in the PRO, the British Library, the LSE. I was scouring everywhere for source material, anything I could put my hands on, basically. I was looking at the whole sweep, looking at overt antisemitism and also the more discreet forms of antisemitism because Aronsfeld used to say that the most influential and powerful and dangerous antisemitism is the discreet one, rather than the overt variety. When Lewis Namier applied for a Fellowship at All Souls, one of the people who interviewed him left an interesting diary where he wrote that by far the most interesting person the panel interviewed was Namier but he couldn't be appointed because he was Jewish. Now that wouldn't be apparent to Namier. That was a sort of remark, put into a private diary that is actually more revealing than hearing somebody who is overtly hostile to Jews, say, in the East End, fulminating about "the Jewish bastards are coming in and taking our jobs". You know where one is coming from; the other one is more subtle, more dangerous.

I was reading a good deal of Tawney at this time and he talks of *histoire intégrale*. You have to look everywhere; consider matters social, cultural, economic and political. It's the whole sweep of society you have to embrace. You cannot just focus on diplomatic documents or something like that. That argument rang a bell with me. That was the kind of history which had excited me at Nottingham, getting beyond the Popes and Kings, and entering into other worlds. When researching the histories of immigration and antisemitism, I could undertake that kind of journey. I could look at literature that was antisemitic, I could examine public documents that were available; I could trace the life of British Brothers' League in the newspapers, you know. There was a whole cache of material there, and the book is heavily documented. That's been one of my styles. People say, "There's always a book in your footnotes." That's not ostentation, it's because I think it's very important to bring this information to light and to have it represented.

THE INTERVIEWER: As you were identifying the kind of material that is out there and kind of pulling it together, what was the reaction of your contemporaries, the historians of the seventies?

PROFESSOR HOLMES: I've already suggested I think people thought it was something of a fringe area, basically. Not everybody. There were people like James Walvin at York who by now were working in this area as well. But I wasn't surrounded by colleagues who were focussing on similar themes. They were concentrating on more conventional areas. But one has to draw strength and sustenance from wherever it comes and when my book on antisemitism was published it received an early review in the *Jewish Chronicle* from Bill Fishman who wrote – I remember the quote very well – "This book is a splendid consummation of a scholarly research." That's a nice compliment, and I thought, "Well, there's another scholar who recognises what I'm doing," and so from that point onwards Bill and I kept in touch. Bill was always a very helpful influence. He would say things like, "How old are you boychik?" and I'd say – I don't know, "55", and he would say, "55? I hadn't even *started* at your age. You've got *years* in front of you – *years*." Bill believed in what I was doing and he was always supportive and helpful.

THE INTERVIEWER: How about those people within the Jewish community who were concerned about the research into antisemitism?

PROFESSOR HOLMES: I don't think Aronsfeld liked my book on antisemitism too much but he didn't break the contact. Overall, I think the Jewish community was quite intrigued that somebody who wasn't Jewish was writing on a Jewish problem.

I think my research, especially, my big work, is not public history but it does have a public policy dimension, it has a message, a lesson, a theme, which is relevant to what's going on and I think that is also important for me. I find it very difficult – I find it very difficult – to take a scene, say, in Tudor England and relate it to what's going on around us. Now Tawney could do that but I think that's incredibly difficult, whereas material on antisemitism, material on immigration, material on fascism, you can see there's a public dimension to it; it has a resonance to what is going on around us and that's the kind of history I need to write to function properly.

THE INTERVIEWER: I wonder whether this is the point, Colin, where you felt, "This is where you wanted to dedicate your career, your particular interest and research skills?"

PROFESSOR HOLMES: I did feel that way about the book on antisemitism, actually. I felt quite euphoric. I really enjoyed writing it and I felt this is an area where I can make an impression, and I think I have made an impression. "Path breaking", Anthony Julius called it recently, and I thought, yes, this is the area I want to work in, this is my métier, I have found where I want to be. I don't want to go off elsewhere. This is my home, my academic home, as it were. This is where I can make a contribution, where I can get that long-term legacy Harry Armytage was talking about when he first met me in the early 1960s in Sheffield.

THE INTERVIEWER: When it comes to antisemitic related material, I just wonder whether you felt you were also going into areas of society that most probably some would argue are not particularly pleasant?

PROFESSOR HOLMES: I have spent most of my academic life in the company of crooks, psychopaths and fanatics. This is the world that I have moved in, but you need to understand these people, you need to be aware of them, because as Norman Cohn says, they sometimes come up from the underworld and they usurp the dignity of the traditionalists, as he puts it, they do have an impact on mainstream society. It is very important to recognise where these people are, who they are, what motivates them. Again it is that public policy dimension; you have to understand it to make a difference.

THE INTERVIEWER: What kind of people are we talking about? At what point did you start to rub shoulders or find you needed to find documents that related to, for example, the British Brothers or the BUF. How do you access that kind of world?

PROFESSOR HOLMES: Accessing the British Brothers' League is not difficult because they didn't really leave anything by way of published papers. You go to the East End Press for the history of the BBL. On Mosley, of course, there's a massive newspaper archive, there is also a wedge of documentary material, there are pamphlets and books that are published by his organisation, there are oral sources. The same is true of William Joyce. We can listen to his radio broadcasts, he wrote a couple of books and he left newspaper articles. In that sense it isn't difficult. The major difficulty I experienced with accessing materials came with official records, because when I first started my researches much of the material simply wasn't available. I would contact the Home Office and sometimes they would grant me what in those days was called privileged access, to material which wasn't normally available. The whole area has opened up more recently. But even now, there are areas, there are certain matters, which are not in the public domain.

THE INTERVIEWER: I suppose that must have been quite an experience when you are in the PRO National Archives, as it is now, and finding documentation that has not been seen or looked at for years and you are the first academic eyes on these letters and correspondence?

PROFESSOR HOLMES: Yes, like the file on the anti-Jewish riots in South Wales in 1911. I was given privileged access to that, so no researcher had seen that file before and, as I say, there was a sense of exhilaration and excitement, *to me anyway*, in actually seeing that material and being able to use it and being able to quote from it. The only condition the Home Office made regarding that particular file was that I submitted my article to them before it appeared in print. I think all they altered was little more than one comma, which is fine, I can live with that. [Laughter]

THE INTERVIEWER: Could we talk a bit about the idea for a journal as well, because obviously I know the journal *Immigrants and Minorities* comes out a couple of years later. Can you just tell me a little bit about how that came about?

PROFESSOR HOLMES: This question links to something I developed in Sheffield. There was a view in History – but not in Economic and Social History – that we didn't keep people here to do research we sent them on elsewhere, possibly to Oxbridge to properly finish their education. I never went along with that belief because to Chambers Nottingham was always a worthwhile place for students to engage in research. And I thought similarly about Sheffield. And one of my people, part of the so-called "Sheffield

School", was Ken Lunn. He wrote a thesis under me on the Marconi scandal, which has never been published but it's a fine piece of work. Ken came to me one day and said he had been reading *The Times Higher Ed.* when he saw an advertisement from Frank Cass for new journals. Ken suggested to me that we put a proposal to him for a journal on immigrants and minorities. I said "okay". He responded: "Will you write the proposal then?" Which I did and sent it off to Cass. We subsequently received a call inviting us down to London to see FC. When we saw him he was in ebullient mood and I warmed to him straight away. We talked about the proposal and he suddenly said: "I'm a forty second man me, I'll take it, take the journal." And that was it, we were in business.

THE INTERVIEWER: How did you pitch the journal? What was it?

PROFESSOR HOLMES: We believed issues relating to immigrants and minorities had been present throughout history and there was a considerable cache of historical material which had never been fully recovered, not only in Britain but also overseas. Our task was to recover it. We also thought it was very important to publish an annual bibliography of the material that was being produced so that scholars could keep up to speed. We also settled on carrying book reviews. That's the way we structured the journal. And it went like a dream with Frank Cass. I got on with him very well. I admired him really. I thought he'd done very well for himself and he was always very open, very straightforward with me.

THE INTERVIEWER: And, any particular individual articles or people that wrote for the journal that confirmed your reasons for creating the journal?

PROFESSOR HOLMES: Yes, I think that Murdoch Rodgers wrote an interesting piece in the early days of the journal on Lithuanians in Scotland, a migration contemporaneous with the Jewish immigration but which had been overlooked. I think his essay grew out of a piece of work done in Edinburgh University, as an undergraduate there. I do remember that article quite vividly.

THE INTERVIEWER: Was this interest in migration something that you could see that was kind of happening in other parts of academia, in other parts of the country?

PROFESSOR HOLMES: Yes, it was happening in Sussex for example. Sussex was focused largely on recent migration. Nicholas Deakin was there. So was Sheila Patterson. Their work had a heavy social policy dimension.

THE INTERVIEWER: Also was Al Thompson doing stuff later on more oral history?

PROFESSOR HOLMES: Yes that's right. So, there was a growing interest. And among the pioneers Jim Walvin and Michael Banton remained busy. The whole thing was starting to shift and change. In Southampton in September last year, I explained how difficult life could be in the early stages. But obviously the younger people who are working now don't really find that so much. For example, Tony Kushner has built a very flourishing school in Southampton working on Jewish themes and the history of Jews is widely represented in that department. Opinion has shifted. The area has become more integrated into academia. But it's taken some time for that to happen.

Many of the people who taught history in the 1960's were Oxbridge orientated, Oxbridge educated, and immigration wasn't particularly high on the agenda there. In those days, they were still thinking in terms of conventional history and that fed into the atmosphere. You did get the odd text people from that background produced, but Popes and Kings and the movers and shakers of high politics remained important in the curriculum.

I think my career would have been much easier if I'd stuck to the conventional path, taken Pollard's advice and gone for straightforward European history and I'd written something like an economic history of France, or something on the Panama scandal. Bob Coats, who taught at Nottingham, told me that his career was held back by the fact that he worked on academic economics which wasn't a fashionable area. He said if you work in an area that isn't mainstream it's much harder to make progress in your career. Which is absolutely true, I think. But on the other hand, you see, you live only once, there's no replay in life and I would have regretted not taking the path that I followed. I might have written on, say, the secondary banking crisis of the early 1970s- I could do that- and it would have been interesting, but wouldn't really have gripped my attention. It's not something I really wanted to do.

There's been a tremendous revolution in historical writing since I started out. Remember I set out fresh on my journey in the last century, a long time ago, a long time ago. And, the world does change, it does shift.

THE INTERVIEWER: And *John Bull's Island* – what was the focus of that book?

PROFESSOR HOLMES: That book concentrated on 1871 to 1971 because I thought this was a key period. By 1971 you've got a set of comprehensive immigration controls. The '71 act really draws together legislation of the 60s and so you've really got the barriers coming down with a vengeance then. Go back to the earlier years from the 18th century to 1905 and there's freedom of movement – the fence starts to be erected in 1905, and by 1971 the controls are really firmly in place. There's no problem in the 1960's in deporting people. It's very difficult now to deport people who are regarded as undesirable, not in the public interest, but in those days for example we sent people like Colonel Amekrane back to Morocco to face a firing squad, and that's the 1960's. It's a different world, you know.

The book is about three themes. First of all, who is coming and why, what sort of lives they have when they are here, and thirdly what are the reactions to them, and the interactions between those three themes. The opening section takes the discussion to about 1914, the next concentrates on the First World War, and its immediate aftermath, the next on the interwar period, moving on then to the Second World War and then the years from 1945 to 1971. The books ends when I go back through these periods and attempt to draw it all together. Trying to identify similarities and differences and their implications.

I was discussing Jews, I was considering Blacks, I was investigating the Italians, I was incorporating Gypsies as well, I was focussing on people from the Caribbean and on migrants from the Indian subcontinent, and the Hungarian refugees in '56. It's very wide-ranging, you know, because I think you've got to draw the net very wide, or otherwise people slip away, become forgotten. What do we know about people who came from Egypt, for example, after Suez, the Jews who came out then? Next to nothing. And no-one has produced a comprehensive book on the Hungarian refugees who came to Britain, not even at the time of the fiftieth anniversary of the uprising in 2006. It's been virtually washed away. So, I was considering all sorts of groups in an attempt to be comprehensive, including Arab seamen in the North-Eastern ports, and also those refugees who came from Nazi Germany in the late 30s.

THE INTERVIEWER: It's such a big subject. I suppose you were researching areas you hadn't looked at before?

PROFESSOR HOLMES: It was absolutely pioneering work. There was some secondary material, but much of my book is based on the archives. It was an enormous task, you know.

THE INTERVIEWER: Where did you want to go after that, did it take you into a particular area?

PROFESSOR HOLMES: Well, I had in mind to write a book called "Dark Shadow", a study of racism in Europe and America between about 1870 and 1945 or something like that. That was actually in the back of my mind, but in the course of writing *John Bull's Island* I came across fascist hostility towards refugees of the 30s, and that brought me again into contact with William Joyce. I began to keep a file on Joyce, and slot things into it, and then I thought well, I think I'd rather like to write on that.

THE INTERVIEWER: At that point, what did you know about Joyce? What did Joyce mean to you?

PROFESSOR HOLMES: Not very much. There was only one biography at the time, written by Jack Cole in 1964, and I knew that Cole wasn't a historian. He was in fact a writer, and also worked on radio. There are no footnotes, nothing like that, and I thought I could probably do a better job than this. Here was a challenge, and of course it's not completely unrelated to what I'd done before. It does link in to the antisemitism book, it does link to the migration. It links particularly to antisemitism because Joyce's life was dominated by hatred of Jews, and so trying to understand him, developed my interest in antisemitism. My argument is that he was an exterminatory antisemite. He thought that the Second World War might have been avoided, if rich Jews had been strung up from a lampposts of Westminster, which is frightening stuff. As for Jewish communists, he had no problems about recommending they should be shot in the streets in the 30s.

One of my other arguments is that Joyce was a narcissist. It's difficult to say why he was a narcissist but he certainly had an overbearing sense of self-importance. He knew that he was right. He wouldn't brook argument, he wouldn't tolerate difference. Life was not made up of greys, life was made up of black and white. If you're on my side it's fine, but if you're on the other side it's dangerous for you. Although we can't psycho-analyse him, I think there is narcissism here. You might say, well, I'm not absolutely convinced by that claim. But read the diary he kept towards the end of the war. He wrote here: if he'd been at Hitler's right hand "the war would have been over 4 years ago" and Germany would have been victorious. Joyce would have guided Germany to victory. Now, that staggering sense of self-importance *is* narcissism. *I* know and *I* should have been listened to. There's other evidence like that as well and I think it comes basically from his mother really. Their suffocating relationship where she made him the centre of the universe had consequences for him. He found it almost impossible to maintain personal relationships. He always knew best about everything. He was insufferable.

THE INTERVIEWER: At this point when you started working on it, had you sort of officially retired at that point?

PROFESSOR HOLMES: No. I was coming towards the end of my career and I was still collecting material, so I wasn't retired. But the Joyce book really took off after I'd actually retired from Sheffield. It was then I started to pursue it vigorously and push it as far as I could. And as I read into the literature I became increasingly disenchanted by the existing material on Joyce and I thought it needs to be re-interpreted. It's not right. That was a big task in itself.

It was a difficult book to write because Joyce is a complex character and I didn't want to write just a simple biography because Pollard used to say to me, "biographies aren't really worth very much because they focus entirely on the individual". But my book sets Joyce in his context of his day and what's going on around him and I think that biography should do that.

I had a problem with it as a lot of the files were not available and when they started to be released in the 80s they came not in an avalanche but in dribs and drabs. I thought, "Well if you give the book in now, something's going to come out soon that could alter the argument." People said to me, get it to print, but I'm glad that I didn't because I think the book benefits tremendously from waiting for that material to come out. I dare say that there may be something else out there that we don't know about, but after a long time I had reached a stage where I thought, "Yes I think

I understand him. I think I can explain him. I can't really do much more with it, there's enough material anyway, so that's it – give it a chance, give it a go."

My career has three legs to it if you like. Immigration, antisemitism, and Fascism and all these are often interrelated. I've opened up new areas in those three themes in three definitive books, people say. But they're not completely separate. There are these linkages. "Only connect," E.M. Forster said. It's something of which Tawney's emphasis on "histoire intégrale" also reminded me.

THE INTERVIEWER: It's so important to research the area of anti-semitism/racism but it's also in some senses it's quite bleak, isn't it?

PROFESSOR HOLMES: It is bleak and I remember one year when I was teaching the course on racism in Sheffield a mature student, came to me and said he really want to take the course but just wondered whether it might make him constantly depressed. I said "It's up to you to make that decision, I can't make that decision for you." But I think it's very important to understand such matters.

THE INTERVIEWER: And how about yourself, did you at times, you know find it a little depressing?

PROFESSOR HOLMES: It is depressing because you know it's startling to consider human nature in the sense of where people might go in a particular journey. In that sense it's particularly frightening. But as I say I think you've got to understand it and come to terms with it. That's what history's all about, isn't it, at the end of the day? It's not just about recreating something between 1545 and 1546, it's what is the significance of this and how does it speak to our world today? That's always been important for me. And I think that also links with the fact I've tried to write in a very readable kind of way, make books accessible to the general public as well as to an academic readership. Some people in academia to be quite honest with you "can't write for toffee", as my mother would say. I remember Bob Coats saying to me at Nottingham, when I was a student, that he'd read this article in the *Bulletin of the Institute of Historical Research* and although he knew all the words he couldn't make sense of the sentences. Some people write in a language which is totally impenetrable and there's no point in that. When students used to try that with me, I used to say go away and rewrite this, read Orwell, and learn how to write. Because communication is very important, you know, I've never been interested in writing just for the cognoscenti. There's a bigger audience out there and I think that needs to be recognised. And I think that awareness has come out in my postgraduates as well. I think Tony Kushner's books speak as it were to big issues which are at present or have been part of British society and which we need to understand.

THE INTERVIEWER: I don't know how many students you've had over the years, how many students you've kept in touch with, I presume there must be a lot?

PROFESSOR HOLMES: There are, there are quite a number and some have gone on to have chairs in other universities. For example, Panikos Panayi has a chair at de Montfort now, Tony Kushner has a chair at Southampton, Don MacRaild has a chair at Roehampton, Bryan Cheyette has a chair at Reading, David Mayall has a chair at Derby, Barbara Bush is emeritus professor at Sheffield Hallam. There was, you see, a Sheffield School, so called, that worked with me in the areas of race, immigration and related issues. I think that phrase Sheffield School is actually from a book review. And quite a number of those people were at the Southampton conference in September last year, which Tony Kushner arranged in my honour and which led to this *festschrift*. It was also very of humbling in a way that the people there from other universities whom I'd not seen, or been in direct contact with, talked about the importance of my work, and its influence on their own research. It was an expression of respect I suppose and I think it's very important to have respect. People may not agree with what I write, but at least they can respect the research and the writing.

THE INTERVIEWER: And at the time in Sheffield I wonder did you feel you had the support of the University at that time?

PROFESSOR HOLMES: That's a difficult question. I was very happy in Sheffield. When I left I said that I'd been really blessed because, if I can use Marxist terminology, I hadn't been alienated at all because my life and my work had run together. I'd been very happy in what I did and not a lot of people can say that. If I'd been outside digging a hole in the road from 6 or 7 o'clock on a wet morning, would that have been pleasure for me? No it wouldn't, it would have been a form of hell! Would it have been pleasurable to be a brickie carrying humps of bricks here there and everywhere? No, but I didn't have that – I did what I wanted to do. I enjoyed doing it and in that sense I was very fortunate in my life. But having said that, because I was very happy here, I wasn't particularly ambitious to move. And I think after a while people think, "he's a permanent fixture here". I think that recognition of my work really came from outside. I was very fortunate late on in having a dean, Andrew Gamble – he later went to a chair and fellowship at Cambridge – who believed in me and initiated the process which resulted in my promotion to a personal chair. But I think it's fair to say generally some people in Sheffield at that time didn't quite recognise what they'd got here. It was only in 1994 to support and promote my research and that of colleagues from Geography and Sociology, that the University established the Migration and Ethnicity Research Centre. Four years later I had retired.

THE INTERVIEWER: And it may have been different somewhere else? You never know …

PROFESSOR HOLMES: You never know, and of course I did it my way, and that's the best way to do it. I'm very surprised that you haven't asked me one question: why are you interested in Jews, you're not a Jew? Answering that, there is an interesting article by Walter Laqueur in *Commentary* where he writes that the history of antisemitism needs more studies by non-Jews because they have insights into the problem that Jews don't have, Jews are too close to it. I took some confidence from Laqueur's comment. You can have a different perspective, you can see nuances that aren't immediately apparent if you're the victim. I think I also see myself as an outsider. Pollard was an outsider because he was Jewish, he was from Vienna. There's a link there, there's a bond there. I thought if I ever published my collected essays I'd call the book *On the Outside Track*. That's where I'm most comfortable. I don't particularly want to be part of an establishment. I'm quite happy where I am, you know.

I do get support, because a lot of my close friends are Jewish. My oldest – no, my second longest friendship – is with Geoffrey Alderman and he's always been very supportive of my work. He thinks that I am *the* historian of antisemitism in Britain. He will tell anybody that, and that's reassuring coming from somebody like him who is a very rigorous historian and an Orthodox Jew. And I heard from one of my former postgraduates – herself Jewish – after the Joyce book was out – and she said, "Mazel tov, keep writing." And one of her friends had said, "keep writing for us". Now that's important, that's important to me.

My home background didn't spark my interest in antisemitism. I never heard any whisper of it, and I wasn't particularly aware of Jews at university. Some people there were Jewish. But it didn't really register with me. I wasn't taught by anybody who was Jewish, I think Pollard is the big factor in raising my awareness. He died in '98, the year that I retired. He came to Britain in the year I was born and he died in the year that I retired. I had invited him to my leaving "do" in the Department but he'd died just before it took place.

THE INTERVIEWER: What did he say to you about your work?

PROFESSOR HOLMES: Sidney was somebody who wasn't terribly effusive but I know that he said to people: "Colin's a real academic, because he checks, and he checks again, He's obsessive about his sources, and that's a real academic." And he encouraged me, he gave me advice like Harry Armytage did. Sidney once said to me, "You must always take a big topic and break it down into small segments and focus on a segment at a time and in that way you'll stay on top of it. Don't try to gather everything together before you write."

THE INTERVIEWER: I just wonder what kind of antisemitism he may have experienced at Sheffield?

PROFESSOR HOLMES: It created a lot of antipathy towards him in certain circles, people could be very sniffy about him. It's that amorphous antisemitism, you see. There's been a very strong current of it in British society and I think it probably remains. Why did Chambers have to say to me at Nottingham, that Pollard was Jewish? A coming man but a Marxist and a Jew? I mean the two things are gratuitous. Why not say simply he's a coming man?

It's not gone away by any means, no. You hear people in Sheffield talking about four by twos, people have probably never met a Jew. [Laughter] It's there, in the culture.

THE INTERVIEWER: Suppose now if you were to embark on research studying the Polish people who arrived here in such big numbers in the 2000s?

PROFESSOR HOLMES: I do have an interest in Eastern Europe, I taught a course at Sheffield on Eastern Europe between 1918 and 1968. There is more work to be done in that area. The Poles need greater attention. The Hungarians are still neglected. One of my former students wrote a thesis on the Balts who came to Britain after 1945 from Latvia, Lithuania and Estonia. Emily Gilbert has not gone into an academic career but she self-published her work which has now been taken up by a publisher. There is far more work to be done on the European Volunteer Workers who came into Britain after 1945 at a time of national labour shortage. The best book on that is still Tannahill's, which is years old, 1954 I think. There are these areas which I would have been tempted to develop and expand if I had the time.

THE INTERVIEWER: What's your next project?

PROFESSOR HOLMES: Well, it requires very careful thought after the Joyce book. That involved a lot of heavy-lifting as they say in the trade. I do have a manuscript by Alexander Baron, "Chapters of Accidents", the novelist's memoir of his life up to 1948. There is an interest in getting this published. I would edit that for publication. I doesn't need to be rewritten because Baron himself wrote it. But just one of two things need explanatory footnotes and one or two paragraphs are ambiguous. Also, I do have an unpublished novel called "Into the Vortex" – a study of a woman who went to Germany and broadcast for the Nazis, a woman from Brighton. There is a PRO file on her. She married a Russian in Berlin and then we lose trace of her and so from that point onwards I can fantasise about her life. But to finish that novel I need to be more familiar with the streets of Berlin in the war. Because as Christhard Hoffmann said to me it's no good saying she was walking down this street if it had bomb damage and it was impassable. Someone would be bound to pick that up. You have to be very careful. Whether the novel ever gets published I don't know. I am happy with the opening couple of chapters but I'll send it out to people when I feel ready and see if it ought to see the light of day.

I've also thought about a book of essays on fascists, antisemites and nativists. Pen pictures of leading fascist figures, significant antisemites, important anti-immigration campaigners. There are other people apart from Powell in the 60s. You've got Cyril Osborne, MP for Louth, who was really continuing in the kind of tradition of the Tories who supported the

British Brothers' League. He has disappeared off the historical map. There is a lot of material there, parliamentary debates, press releases. Bringing some of those people to life again could be interesting. Just a sample. But I haven't thought that one through,

THE INTERVIEWER: A big final question. With the depth of your research into antisemitism in this country, is there a personality trait or a background that will create people that will end up in your pen pictures. Is there a particular breed?

PROFESSOR HOLMES: You can in some cases. Joyce is an example. To understand Joyce you have to understand his psychology. But with other people you just don't. They get carried along with social circumstances. And to find the personality issues that might drive some figures is almost impossible. I can't psychoanalyse Cyril Osborne. He was dead long ago. But why was he so active against migration from the 50s? Why could he say things like: "it isn't the Irish that are the problem. I was always happy to have an Irishman at my side in the trenches, but blacks are different"? Where does that come from? Because blacks were in the First World War as well. They were fighting and dying, Indians were dying and being cremated near Brighton. Even so, except in certain cases – such as Joyce – I would generally be wary of talking about a personality type among nativists and fascists.

THE INTERVIEWER Some of these people might not have had a great amount of contact with these people.

PROFESSOR HOLMES You don't have to. Quite often people are hostile towards migrants and they have never met them. People say it is all a question of numbers. It isn't. Numbers can be very small but you can still get hostility. One of the fiercest examples of hostility in the early twentieth century was towards German Gypsies, yet there were only a handful of these. They meet more antipathy than the Jews or the Irish or the Italians. In Kettering, for example, overnight they keep them in the pigpens. Now that's symbolic and then we deport them back to Europe. These people and their children would end up in Hitler's camps. You've only got a small number of them but the tension they create is unbelievable. I've written on this and it is the kind of thing that should not be ignored. People say have smaller numbers and the question will be solved but it won't. Hostility doesn't obviously turn in numbers.

THE INTERVIEWER: If someone came to you because of knowledge of your career and said, "Should I be going down this road. Should I be looking at some element of immigration studies?"

PROFESSOR HOLMES: I would say you do what you want to do because if there is no ego involvement then you won't do a good job. You have to be involved and committed to what you are going to do. There is no point in being half-hearted about it. If you want to work on this area go ahead and do it. You may not have an easy path but at the end of the day you have to live with yourself. And I can live with myself and what I have written, so far.

One of the influences on *my* academic life has been Victor Kiernan. Victor was, like Harry Armytage, a polymath. He could read in Latin and Greek, French and Spanish, Urdu. He had a Chair in Edinburgh. Began at Edinburgh in 1947 and finished with a personal Chair there. He wrote a big chapter for my first edited book *Immigrants and Minorities in British Society*. Far too long. We had to cut it down but I've retained the unedited edition essay at home and I thought he's looked at public house signs, he's looked at literature, he's looked at music, he's looked at dance, he's drawing all this into a coherent whole, an approach reflected in my later work. Kiernan is another influence upon me, along with Higham and Tawney. His historical approach is one that I like. He moved out of Edinburgh when he married and went to Stow on the borders and towards the end of his life he said he had looked out over the city – Edinburgh – and seen a sunset and would chase it to its very end. That's what I'll do. I'll keep chasing it and keep chasing. It isn't over yet.

NAME INDEX

Acholonu, Catherine 266
Acton, Thomas 198, 200
Adams, Caroline 66
Adams, Mary 253–254
Adi, Hakim 97
Adler, Hermann 113
Adler, Nathan Marcus 113
Aguilar, Grace 108–109
Akbar, Arifa 11
Åkerman, Sune 229
Alba, Richard 36–37
Alderman, Geoffrey 60, 104, 107–108, 110, 112–115, 130, 308
Ali Khan, Akbar 221
Ali, Ayub 220
Ali, Monica 62
Alley, Surat 221
Amekrane, Mohamed 303
Amin, Idi 138
Anand, Mulk Raj 222
Anders, Władysław 273
Anderson, Bridget 277
Aravamudan, Srinivas 262, 264, 267
Arendt, Hannah 139, 143–145
Armytage, Harry 296–297, 300, 308, 311
Arnesen, Eric 159
Arnold, Edward 298
Arnold, Elaine 167
Aronsfeld, C. C. 298–300
Ashwood Garvey, Amy 97
Auerbach, Sascha 75

Bade, Klaus Jürgen 44
Bailkin, Jordanna 142, 156

Baines, Dudley 224, 228
Baker, Godfrey 218
Baker, Phil 77
Baldoli, Claudia 122
Baldwin, Peter 176
Ballard, Catherine 213–214
Ballard, Roger 213–214
Ballinger, Pamela 123
Banton, Michael 60, 216, 297, 302
Barbrook, Bill 254
Baron, Alexander 62, 309
Baron, Salo 110
Bart, Lionel 252
Bass, Alfie 252
Bastin, Robin 228
Baumel-Schwartz, Judith 131
Beamish, Henry Hamilton 13, 189
Bean, Richard 62
Beck, Sam 200
Beckett, John 185
Belchem, John 243
Belle, Dido Elizabeth 93
Bellos, Linda 98
Benewick, Robert 13, 184
Benton, Gregor 76
Bentwich, Norman 110, 129, 132
Beresford, Jack 255–256, 259
Berghahn, Marion 129
Besant, Walter 61, 252
Bhachu, Parminder 142
Bhownaggree, Mancherjee 219
Bickers, Robert 74–75
Billig, Michael 187
Bilton, Caroline 231

Blegen, Theodore 226
Blumenfeld, Simon 62
Bolchover, Richard 129
Bond, Ulysses Edward 292–293
Bondy, Louis 183
Booth, Charles 65
Bottignolo, Bruno 119
Bourne, Stephen 97
Brattne, Berit 229
Brearley, Mike 4
Bressey, Caroline 29, 56–57
Briggs, Bishops 244
Brinkmann, Tobias 8–9, 29, 195
Brock, Peter 207
Brodie, Israel 113
Brodkin, Karen 155, 159
Brooks, Ethel 200
Brown, Philip 201
Brownrigg, John Henry 245
Buckman, Joseph 49, 104, 110
Bugg, John 266
Burke, Thomas 62, 74–75, 77
Burnard, Trevor 266
Burr, Sandra 262
Burrell, Kathy 236, 274–277
Burton, Antoinette 216
Bush, Barbara 17–18, 150, 307
Busher, Joel 189
Bux, Faiz 221

Caesar, John 92
Caffay, William 96–97
Caretta, Vincent 94, 264–267
Carey, Brycchan 264–265
Carey, Sean 65
Carleton, Billie 73
Carmona, Sarah 200
Carr, E. H. 60
Cass, Frank 17, 198, 302
Castles, Stephen 45
Cesarani, David 15, 112, 120
Chadwick, Trevor 133
Chambers, J. D. 294–296, 301, 308
Chang, Elizabeth 77
Chater, Kathleen 93, 265
Chaucer, Geoffrey 61
Chesterton, A. K. 185
Cheyette, Bryan 28, 307
Chezzi, Bruna 123
Chimni, B. S. 28
Chistolini, Sandra 118
Choo, Ng Kwee 72
Chowdhary, Dharm Sheel 222
Clarendon, Lord 245
Claydon, Charlotte 97

Clayton, Antony 77
Coard, Bernard 91
Coats, Bob 303, 306
Cohen, Stuart 112
Cohen, Susan 132
Cohn, Norman 300
Cole, Jack 304
Coleridge-Taylor, Samuel 97
Colley, Linda 26
Collins, Kenneth 175, 225, 228
Colls, Robert 26
Colpi, Terri 117–121
Cook, Thomas 75
Copeland, David 189
Copsey, Nigel 187, 189–190
Cornwall Lewis, George 244
Craig-Norton, Jennifer 104, 132
Cross, Colin 13, 183
Cugoano, Ottobah 94, 98
Cunningham, William 23
Curio, Claudia 131
Cybowski, Milosz 193–194
Czatoryski, Adam Jerzy 207

Dabydeen, David 93–94
Daly, Jane 218
Daniels, Roger 35–36
Dare, Richard 93
Datta, Ayona 277
Davey, John 298
Davies, Norman 207
Davis, Charles T. 264
Davis, Morry 109, 115
Davis, Myer 108–109
Deakin, Nicholas 302
Dein, Alan 2, 4–5, 291
Delaney, Enda 156, 240, 247
Dickens, Charles 62, 96, 108, 216, 252
Digby, Kenelm 178
Doherty, John 243
Dolby, William 75
Dolezal, Rachel 201
Dorril, Stephen 184
Douglas, Mary 55
Dover, Cedrik 222
Driver, Nelly 16
Duffield, Ian 96
Duleep Singh, Sophia 219
Dummett, Ann 139
Dummett, Michael 154
Durham, Martin 16
Düvell, Frank 276

Eade, John 60, 66
Eatwell, Roger 15

Edwards, Paul 93–94, 263
Eisenstadt, Shmuel N. 47
Ekarte, Daniels 98
Elton, Geoffrey 16
Endelman, Todd 49, 60, 114, 228
Equiano, Olaudah 94, 98, 236–237, 262–268
Erickson, Charlotte 224, 228
Evans, Neil 12, 14
Evans, Nick 29, 195, 225, 229–231
Evans, Richard 22
Evaristo, Bernadine 94

Fairchild, Amy 175
Fassin, Didier 141
Fast, Vera 131
Feingold, Henry 129
Feldman, David 50, 110
Ferguson, Niall 22
Fielding, Nigel 187
Fielding, Stephen 51
File, Nigel 216
Firth, Raymond 118
Fisher, Michael 216
Fishman, Bill 22–23, 65, 70, 110, 282, 299–300
Fitzmaurice, George 245
Flanagan, Bud 252
Foner, Nancy 163
Forman, Ross 77
Forna, Aminatta 168
Forster, E. M. 306
Fortier, Anne-Marie 118–120, 122
Foxhall, Katherine 178
Frayling, Christopher 77
Friedman, Saul 129
Fryer, Peter 12, 27, 55, 81, 93–97, 153, 216, 263

Gadon, Lubomir 206
Gainer, Bernard 298
Gamble, Andrew 307
Gan, Wendy 77
Ganga, Deianira 122
Garapich, Michał P. 273
Garigue, Philip 118
Garrard, John 298
Gartner, Lloyd P. 1, 49, 65, 108, 110, 114, 228, 298
Gaster, Moses 109
Gates, Henry Louis Jr. 264
Gatrell, Peter 27
George IV. 218
George, M. Dorothy 92–94
Gheorghe, Nicolae 200

Gilbert, Emily 309
Gilbert, J. C. 295–296
Gilbert, Vic 18
Gill, Nick 278
Gilroy, Paul 28
Giudici, Marco 117, 123
Glazer, Nathan 45
Glover, David 29
Goldberg, David Theo 28
Gomez, E. T. 76
Goodhart, David 24
Goodrick-Clarke, Nicholas 189
Goodwin, Matthew 189
Gottlieb, Amy Zahl 130
Gottlieb, Julie 185, 187
Goulbourne, Harry 28
Grant, Colin 12
Green, Jeffrey 97
Gregory, Dora 257
Grellmann, Heinrich 198
Griffin, Roger 187
Griffiths, Richard 185
Gronniosaw, Ukawsaw 268
Groser, John 256
Gulati, Harbans 222
Gundara, Jagdish 215–216
Guske, Iris 131
Gwynn, Robin 63

Hale, Frederick 227
Hall, Stuart 236–237
Hallwood, B. L. 293
Hancock, Ian 200–201
Hanley, Ryan 235–236, 267–268
Hansen, Marcus 226–227
Hardy, Anne 175
Hardy, Thomas 94, 116
Harris, Bernard 175
Harrisson, Tom 237, 251, 253–260
Hartley, L. P. 3
Haynes, Harry 256–257
Henriques, Basil 252, 256, 259
Henriques, Rose 252–253, 260
Herbert, Ulrich 47
Hertz, Joseph 113, 116
Herzl, Theodor 109
Hickey, William 218
Hickman, Mary 155
Higham, John 2, 3, 297, 311
Hill, Paula 112
Hillyard, Paddy 156
Hirschell, Solomon 108
Hirschfeld, Gerhard 129
Hoerder, Dirk 37
Hoffmann, Christhard 8–9, 29, 309

Hogarth, William 93
Høgsbjerg, Christian 97
Holmes, Colin 1–5, 7, 12–18, 22–30, 36, 40, 44, 52, 56, 59–60, 70, 72–73, 75, 81, 103, 105, 112, 117, 123, 129, 135, 138, 149, 151, 153–154, 159, 182, 185–187, 193–198, 208, 216, 224–225, 251, 272, 282–311
Howell, David 184
Hughes, Colin 119
Hughes, Kyle 236
Huntington, Samuel 36
Huntley, Eric 91
Huntley, Jessica 91
Hvidt, Kristian 227, 229
Hyamson, Albert 109
Hyde, Francis 228

Ignatiev, Karen 159
Inayat Khan, Noor 220
Ireland, Josh 186

Jackson, Paul 189
Jacobovits, Immanuel 113
James, C. L. R. 97
James, Leslie 97
Jarrett-Mavauley, Delia 97
Jeffreys, Jane 218
Jenkinson, Jacqueline 14
Jenks, Jorian 185
Johnson, Linton Kwesi 91, 97
Jones, Claudia 98
Jones, Maldwyn A. 227
Jones, Richard 243
Jonson, Ben 61
Jordan, James 4, 229–231, 237
Joseph, Jo 252
Joseph, Zoe 133
Joyce, William 23, 182, 185–186, 282, 301, 304–305, 310
Julius, Anthony 183, 300

Kane, Bernard 244
Kaplan, Harvey 228
Katz, David 107
Kaufmann, Miranda 93
Keenan, Michael 241–242
Kennedy, John F. 226
Kero, Reino 227
Kershen, Anne J. 50, 57, 64, 81, 83, 237
Kiernan, Victor 311
Killingray, David, 98
Kleßmann, Christoph 47
Knox, Katharine 27, 274
Kohn, Marek 74

Kopelowitz, Lionel 115
Kops, Bernard 62, 252
Kosack, Godula 45
Kosmin, Barry 113
Kossoff, David 252
Kraut, Alan, 175
Kulczycki, John J. 48, 51
Kushner, Tony 3, 5, 7–8, 14–15, 18, 27, 103, 105, 112, 122, 129, 131, 134–135, 149, 153, 225, 229–231, 251, 256, 274, 303, 306–307

La Rose, John 91
Lahiri, Shompa 216
Lal Katial, Chuni 220
Lal Roy, Indra 219
Lamore, Eric D. 262
Lane, Thomas 274
Lansbury, George 256
Laqueur, Walter 60, 308
Lawrence, Patricia 77
Lee, Gregory B. 74
Leigh, Michael 157
Lewak, Adam 207
Lewis, Harry 64–65
Liégeois, Jean-Pierre 198, 200, 202
Linehan, Thomas 112, 185, 187
Lipman, Vivian 64, 109–110
Litsenberg, Sol 108
Little, Kenneth 93, 96, 297
Lock, John 93
London, Jack 61–62, 252
London, Louise 105, 112, 130–132
Lovejoy, Paul 265–266
Lovoll, Odd S. 229
Lowles, Nick 189
Lucassen, Jan 37, 44
Lucassen, Leo 37
Lucking, Harry 258
Lunn, Ken 4, 7, 12, 15, 130, 149, 302

Macklin, Graham 150–151, 185, 189
MacRaild, Donald 17, 156, 236, 243, 307
Maglen, Krista 29, 150, 175
Magnus, Katie, Lady 109
Mahomed, Dean 218
Mahomed, Frederick Akbar 219
Mallinson, William 259
Mandle, W. F. 13, 185
Mankowitz, Wolf 62, 252
Manning, Patrick 1
Marchlewicz, Krzysztof 207–208
Margoliouth, Moses 81
Marin, Umberto 117–118
Markel, Howard 175

Marks, Lara 64, 175
Marrus, Michael 38
Marson, Una 97
Marx, Karl 3, 83
Massey, Doreen 29, 56, 61, 66
Matera, Marc 97–98
Matras, Yaron 198–200
Maxwell Knight, Charles 186
May, J. P. 70–72
Mayall, David 16–18, 194, 198, 203, 307
McBride, Terence 243
McGimpsey, Christopher 17
Medwell, Ann 93
Menen, Aubrey 222
Menon, Krishna 219–220
Merriman, Nick 81–82
Merriman-Labor, A. B. C. 97
Michaels, Wolf 259
Mignard, Pierre 94
Miller-Jones, Andrew 253–254, 259
Moir, Martin 216
Morpeth, Lord 209
Morris, David 230
Morrison, Arthur 252
Mosley, Nicholas 184
Mosley, Oswald 13, 64, 182–187, 301
Mosse, Werner 130, 134
Moynihan, Daniel 45
Mullally, Frederick 183
Murphy, Geraldine 264
Murphy, Richard C. 47–48
Murphy, Sean 186
Murphy, Shirley 178
Murray, Elizabeth Lady 93
Myers, Kevin 103
Myers, Norma 93

Namier, Lewis 299
Naoroji, Dadabhai 216, 219
Nasar, Saima 29, 105
Neal, Frank 225, 229
Nee, Victor 36–37
Newman, Aubrey 65, 110, 225, 228–231
Nicholas I. 209
Nicol, Andrew 139
Nocon, Andrew 275
Noiriel, Gérard 36, 44
Nora, Pierre 143
Nussbaum, Felicity 264

Ó Catháin, Máirtín 243
O'Conell, Maurice 244
O'Conell, W. H. 244
O'Connell, Daniel 244
O'Neill, Mark 76

Ogude, S. E. 265
Okely, Judith 198, 200
Olusoga, David 11–12
Orwell, George 306
Osborne, Cyril 309–310

Padmore, George 97
Palmer, Edward 221
Palmer, Robin 118
Palmer, William 221
Panayi, Panikos 18, 26, 51, 55–56, 81, 130, 153, 307
Patterson, Sheila 164, 302
Paxton, Robert 183
Payne, Peter 294, 296
Payne, Stanley 183
Peel, Robert 111
Pepys, Samuel 63
Perry, Kennetta Hammond 169
Petrie, Charles 182
Phillips, Mike 24, 153
Phillips, Trevor 24, 153
Piciotto, James 108
Pilkington, Hilary 190
Piore, Michael 225
Pollard, Sidney 2, 22, 295–296, 298, 303, 305, 308
Porter, Bernard 208
Potkay, Adam 262, 264–265
Potter, George 295
Potter, Walter C. 259
Powell, Enoch 12–13, 72, 187, 297, 309
Power, Chris 216
Prince, Mary 268

Quinlan, Kevin 186

Ramji, Hasmita 142
Ramsay, Maule 185
Ranjtsinhji, Kumar Shri ("Ranji") 219
Rathbone, Eleanor 132
Raven Thomson, Alexander 185
Raynor, John 157
Read, Gordon 228
Reynolds, Spencer 254
Richardson, John 187, 189
Risdon, Wilfred 185
Roche, Barbara 24
Rodgers, Murdoch 17, 118, 302
Rogaly, Ben 276
Rogers, John 94
Rohmer, Sax 62, 73, 77
Rolfe, Kate 258
Romain, Gemma 29, 193
Rose, Millicent 252, 260

Name index

Roth, Cecil 64, 84, 107–109, 111
Rotha, Paul 254
Rothberg, Michael 28
Rothschild, Nathaniel Lord 178
Rubinstein, William D. 130, 183
Runblom, Harald 44
Russell, Charles 64–65
Ryan, Louise 278

Sacks, Jonathan 113
Saggar, Jainti 220
Saklatvala, Shapurji 220
Sala, George 71
Samuel, Herbert 128
Samuel, Raphael 29, 197
Sancho, Ignatius 94, 98, 264
Schaffer, Gavin 149–150
Schiff, Otto 110
Schonfeld, Solomon 133
Seabrook, Jeremy 132
Seacole, Mary 96, 98–9, 263
Sebak, Per Kristian 231
Seed, John 75
Seghall, Rene 259
Sensbach, Jon 266
Sexton, James 74, 76
Shah, Nyan 175
Shatzkes, Pamela 130
She, Lao 57
Shepard, Naomi 128
Sherman, A. J. 128
Sherwood, Marika 14, 98
Short, Robert 244
Shukur, Abdus 65
Shyllon, Folarin 263
Sibley, David 55, 198
Sim, George 216
Simpson, A. W. Brian 186
Singh Gour, Hari 220
Singh, San Wan 257–258
Sinha, Sasadhar 221
Sirr, Henry 241
Skidelsky, Robert 13, 184
Small, Stephen 28
Smith, Andrea 201
Smith, Edward 94
Snowman, Daniel 132
Solomons, Ikey 108
Solomos, John 28
Sorabji, Cornelia 219
Soros, George 203
Soskice, Frank 157
Sponza, Lucio 118–119, 121
Stachura, Peter D. 273
Statt, Daniel 63

Steidl, Annemarie 34
Stern, Mike 254, 260
Stuart, Lord Dudley 209
Sweet, James H. 267–268
Sword, Keith 273, 275

Tannahill, John Allan 309
Tawney, R. H. 5, 297, 299–300, 306, 311
Taylor, A. J. P. 214
Taylor, Philip 226–227
Taylor, Stan 187
Temple, Bogusia 274
Tenfelde, Klaus 48
Thackeray, William Makepeace 216
Thatcher, Margaret 13, 215
Thayer, George C. 187
Thomas, Helen 264
Thompson, Al 302
Thompson, E. P. 3, 197, 243
Thompson, Paul 29
Thurlow, Richard 12–15, 18, 22, 183–184
Tolia-Kelly, Divya 142
Tothchild, Donald 141
Tremenheere, H. S. 294–296

Ugolini, Wendy 104, 117, 121–122
Ukaegbu, Dorothy 266

Verma, Jatinder 216
Vertovec, Steven 85–86
Villis, Tom 185
Visram, Rozina 27, 81, 194, 213–217

Walker, Martin 187
Walter, Bronwen 64, 155
Walvin, James 23, 27, 81, 262–263, 299, 302
Warburton, Bartholomew 244–245
Ward, Arthur 62
Warriner, Doreen 133
Warsi, Sayeeda, Baroness 142
Wasserstein, Bernard 129
Weale, Adrian 186
Webber, G. C. 185
Webster, Nesta 189
Webster, Wendy 169
Wedderburn, Robert 268
Weisser, Henry 207
Weller, Sam 62
Wesker, Arnold 62, 252
West, Rebecca 186
Wheeler, Roxann 264
White, Anne 278
White, Jerry 50
White, Rachel 91
Whiteman, Doris 131

Wilkin, Andre 118
Willetts, Paul 185
William IV. 218
Williams, Bill 22, 50, 104, 120, 133, 229–231
Williams, Frances 131, 230
Williams, Henry Sylvester 98
Williams, Herbert 178
Wills, Clair 56
Wilson, Harold 157
Winder, Robert 25, 81
Winslow, Michelle 274
Wintin, Nicholas 133
Wiszniewski, Julius 255
Witchard, Anne 55, 57, 74–75, 77

Wolf, Lucien 108–109
Wolkoff, Anna 185
Wollstonecraft, Mary 266
Wood, Benjamin 92
Wood, John 92
Worley, Matthew 184, 187
Wright, Thomas 71
Wyman, David 129
Wyndham Goldie, Grace 253

Zangwill, Israel 62, 252
Zubrzycki, Jerzy 273
Żurawski vel Grajewski, Radosław 207
Zuroski Jenkins, Eugenia 77

PLACE INDEX

Aldgate 217
Armagh 244

Barnsley 243
Beaconsfield 218
Belfast 245
Berlin 38
Birmingham 85, 133, 232
Bradford 84, 86
Brighton 218, 310
Bristol 84
Brixton 85, 164

Cambridge 84, 221
Cardiff 71–72, 218
Chester 232

Dublin 243, 245
Dundee 232

East End (of London) 22–23, 29, 50, 57, 59–67, 84–86, 175, 188, 213, 217; television documentary 237, 251–260
Edinburgh 84, 232
Exeter 84

Germany 39, 46–48
Glasgow 84, 123, 175, 218, 221, 228, 241–242, 245
Gloucester 84

Hackney 217
Hamburg 177

Hampstead 188
Hanley (Staffordshire) 241
Hull 84, 227, 232

Ilkeston (Derbyshire) 241
India 213
Ipswich 84
Ireland 217–218, 239–247

Johannesburg 229

Kenya 138
Kovno 229

Lanarkshire 14
Lancaster 242
Leeds 14, 49, 84, 104, 110, 213–214, 232, 243
Leicester 85, 143–144, 229
Leith 228
Limehouse 55, 72, 75–77
Lincoln 84
Liverpool 29, 84, 98, 218, 225, 227–229, 240–246; Chinese in 55, 57, 70–72, 76
London 38, 56–57, 71, 81–87, 99, 118–119, 143, 164, 177–178, 218, 221, 225, 232, 242; exhibition *The Peopling of London* 24, 81–82; Migration Museum project 24–25; 'super-diversity' 85–86 *see also* Aldgate, Brixton, East End, Hackney, Hampstead, Limehouse, Notting Hill, Southall, Tooting, Wembley

Place index

Manchester 14, 22, 50, 56, 81, 84–85, 104, 133, 221, 232, 241–245

New York 227
Newcastle-upon-Tyne 84, 232
Northern Ireland 185
Norwich 84
Notting Hill 73, 85, 165
Nottingham 86, 122, 143, 165

Oxford 84

Pakistan 213
Portsmouth 15, 208, 232

Salford 229
Scotland 118, 120, 123, 185, 217, 230, 240, 242, 302
Sheffield 232, 242, 292
South Wales 84, 119, 301

Southall 85
Southampton 15, 229–230, 232
Stafford 244

Tanzania 138
Tiger Bay (Cardiff) 29
Tooting 85

Uganda 138, 141
Ulster 232
Uppsala 227
Utah 227

Wales 123, 185, 217, 230
Warrington (Cheshire) 241
Wembley 85
Whitehaven 242

Yarmouth 84
York 84

SUBJECT INDEX

Algerians in France 37
Aliens Act (1905) 29, 175, 178–179, 220, 303
anti-Catholicism 3, 242
anti-fascism 190
anti-migrant hostility 2–3, 26, 36, 51, 72, 76, 120–122, 140, 188, 204, 272, 278, 310 *see also* antisemitism, nativism, sinophobia
anti-racism 96, 190, 237
antisemitism 12–14, 16, 24, 149, 151, 182–183, 187–188, 251, 255, 298–302, 304–306, 308
anti-slavery activism 94, 98
archives 24, 91, 95, 99, 228, 230
art 28, 91, 93–94
Asians in Britain *see* South Asians in Britain
assimilation 51, 111, 118, 167, 169, 259, 274–275, 278
authenticity 237, 260, 263, 265–267
autobiography 119, 262, 265, 267
ayahs 217

Baltic people in Britain 309
Belgian refugees in Britain 296
Bengalis in London 60, 62, 65–66
black and Asian history 11, 91–99, 153, 215–216
black and Asian people in Britain 11, 28, 57, 83, 91–99, 149, 153, 155–159, 162–169, 174, 215–216, 262–269, 304, 310
British Brothers League 188, 299, 301, 309
British National Party (BNP) 189

British Union of Fascists (BUF) 13, 182–189, 190, 301
Britishness/Englishness 26–27

Catholic Church 33, 244
celebratory narratives of migrant experience 103–105, 110, 117, 123, 128–134, 143 *see also* 'model minority'
Chinese in Britain 57, 70–77; 255, 257–258 *see also* sinophobia
cholera epidemic (1892) 176–178
class 8, 37, 45–52, 104, 121, 243, 268
Cockney 255, 257
colonialism 28, 144, 162, 217
colour 149, 153–159, 220
Commonwealth Immigrants Act (1962) 65, 140, 154
community history 48–49, 51, 103–105, 119–120, 138–139, 143–144

diaspora 268; Irish 240; Italian 119–122
digital humanities 230
disease control 39, 174–179
domestics 97, 134–135

East African Asians in Britain 29, 105, 138–145
education 15–16, 24, 91–92, 99, 169, 215–216, 262–263
English Defence League 189
ethnic history 14, 16, 35, 80, 114
ethnicity 8, 12, 37, 45–52, 200–201, 203–204, 227, 278

Subject index

European Volunteer Workers 272, 309
exhibitions 24, 81–82, 91, 120, 143, 228
exile 206–210

family 163–169, 278
fascism 13, 15–16, 23, 150–151, 182–190, 255, 305, 309 *see also* Italian Fascism
film 28
food 86, 220–221

gender 8, 16, 24, 29, 37, 52, 121, 134, 162–169, 236–237, 268, 274–275, 278
Germans in Britain 14, 83–84
Greek Cypriots in Britain 85, 155–156
Gujaratis in Britain 85
Gypsies/Romani in Britain 72, 194–195, 197–204, 304, 310
Gypsy/Romani studies 198–204

Hanseatic League 82–84
heritage projects 24, 105, 144, 225, 230
higher education 219
History Workshop movement 22, 197
'home' 29, 122, 142, 247
Huguenots in Britain 27, 60–63, 83, 105, 255, 258
Hungarian refugees (1956) 304, 309

identities 26–27, 51, 123, 139, 142–145, 200, 203, 235–237, 260, 268
illegality of migrants 38–39, 236
Immigrants & Minorities 4, 7, 16–18, 44, 198, 301–302 *see also* Sheffield School
immigration controls 39–40, 303; in the United States 39, 175–176, 179 *see also* disease control
Indians in Britain *see* South Asians
Irish in Britain 28, 37, 51, 56, 62–64, 83–87, 175–175, 310; race relations in the post-war period 149, 154–156; Ribbonism 236, 239–245
Irish in New York 17
Italian Fascism 119–120, 122
Italians in Britain 84, 104, 117–123, 175; anti-Italian hostility 118, 120, 122, 310
Italians in France 37

Jewish immigrants to the United States 34
Jews in Britain 28, 56, 82–84, 86–87, 176, 304, 310; community history and historiography 27, 104, 107–116; in East End of London 61–65, 175, 256, 258–259; and race relations in the post-war period 149–150, 156–158; refugees from Nazism 104–105, 110, 128–135; working class 14, 48–51, 110–111 *see also* antisemitism

Kindertransport 2, 130–133, 230, 298

labels defining immigrant and minority groups 138–145, 200, 236, 277–278
labour history 14–15, 22, 37, 44, 243
lascars 92, 217–218, 220, 255, 257–258
Latin Americans in Britain 85
life histories 66 *see also* autobiography, memoirs
literature 28, 62, 74–77, 94, 216, 252
Lithuanians in Britain 14, 17, 302

maritime studies 224–225, 228
Marxism 45, 49, 263
masculinity 168
memoirs 119, 133, 252
memory 56, 122–123, 134, 143 *see also* heritage projects
migration history 80; and British historiography 1, 26, 297, 299, 303; ethnic paradigm 35–36, 80, 227; frames 278; immigration 14, 80–87, 303–304; maritime history 225–226, 228; oral history 29, 133, 163, 229, 275–276; postcolonial studies 28, 264, 266–267; social history 35, 44, 51; spatial turn 57, 98; transnational approach 9, 29, 33–34, 38, 40, 264; urban approach 81 *see also* refugees
migration studies 23; anthropology 27, 213; cultural studies 29; geography 98, 118–119; queer studies 29, 193; sociology 27–28, 36, 45
military participation 121, 215, 273–274, 310
'model minority' 123, 139, 143–144
multiculturalism 24, 86, 98, 103, 153
museums 24, 28–29, 123, 217, 228
music 99
Muslims 3, 221

National Front (NF) 13, 187, 297
nativism 2–3, 11, 309
non-state actors 40
Nottingham University 292–295, 299, 301, 306

Pakistanis in Britain *see* South Asians
Parkes Institute for the Study of Jewish/non-Jewish Relations at the University

of Southampton xiii, 4, 114, 230, 302, 307
photographs 99, 119, 217
places 55–57, 61, 98–99
Poles in Britain 83, 86, 175, 309; after Second World War 237, 272–278; nineteenth century 194, 206–210
Poles in Germany 8, 37, 46–48
port cities 29, 39, 174, 213, 218, 225–226, 229, 232
public health 173–179

race 12–13, 15, 154–155, 159, 260, 268, 278, 307
race relations 28, 150, 154, 162–164, 263
Race Relations Act (1965) 150, 157, 297
racism 15, 24, 26, 28, 73, 149, 164, 167–169, 202, 215, 220, 304
radio 118, 301
refugees 25, 27–28, 38, 40, 60, 83, 105, 110, 112, 122, 128–135, 138–141, 206–210, 253, 272–273, 296, 304
religion 52, 236
return migration 37, 39

Scandinavian transmigrants 226–228
Sephardic communities 33
sexuality 29, 164, 268
Sheffield School 4, 7, 12–18, 26, 104, 129, 149, 195, 224–227, 229–230, 290, 301, 307
Sheffield University Department of Economic and Social History 3, 22, 295–298, 301, 305, 307
shipping lines *see* transport

Sikhs in Britain 85, 142, 213–214, 221 *see also* South Asians
sinophobia 72–77
slavery 17, 93, 262–263
social history 14–16, 22, 44–52, 97
South Asians in Britain 35, 85–86, 194, 213–222, 255, 257–258, 297–298, 304, 310
spaces 55–57, 61, 98, 226

television 11, 28, 154
trade unions 48–50, 76, 111–112, 240, 243–244
transmigration 8–9, 29, 38–40, 135, 175–176, 195, 224–232
transnational identities 105, 237 *see also* diaspora
transnational migrant networks 34–35, 122, 237, 278
transport 39–40, 228–229, 277
Turks in Germany 37

welfare policies 140–141, 150, 162–169, 217, 244
West Indians in Britain 37, 85–86, 150, 162–169, 297–298, 304
whiteness 28, 155, 159, 164, 167, 203, 274–275
Windrush myth 24, 56, 73, 98, 149, 153–154, 236
women 8, 16–17, 23, 66, 92, 99, 134, 163–164, 236, 274–275

Yellow Peril *see* sinophobia

Taylor & Francis eBooks

www.taylorfrancis.com

A single destination for eBooks from Taylor & Francis with increased functionality and an improved user experience to meet the needs of our customers.

90,000+ eBooks of award-winning academic content in Humanities, Social Science, Science, Technology, Engineering, and Medical written by a global network of editors and authors.

TAYLOR & FRANCIS EBOOKS OFFERS:

- A streamlined experience for our library customers
- A single point of discovery for all of our eBook content
- Improved search and discovery of content at both book and chapter level

REQUEST A FREE TRIAL
support@taylorfrancis.com

Routledge
Taylor & Francis Group

CRC Press
Taylor & Francis Group

Printed in Great Britain
by Amazon